The following guides by Dawn Apgar are available from Springer Publishing to assist social workers with studying for and passing the ASWB® examinations necessary for licensure.

Bachelors

Social Work Licensing Bachelors Exam Guide, Fourth Edition

Test focuses on knowledge acquired while obtaining a Baccalaureate degree in Social Work (BSW). A small number of jurisdictions license social workers in the Associate category and require the ASWB Associate examination. The Associate examination is identical to the ASWB Bachelors examination, but the Associate examination requires a lower score to pass.

Masters

Social Work Licensing Masters Exam Guide, Fourth Edition

Test focuses on knowledge acquired while obtaining a Masters degree in Social Work (MSW). There is no postgraduate supervision needed.

Clinical

Social Work Licensing Clinical Exam Guide, Fourth Edition

Test focuses on knowledge acquired while obtaining a Masters degree in Social Work (MSW). It is usually taken by those with postgraduate supervised experience.

Dawn Apgar, PhD, LSW, ACSW, has helped thousands of social workers across the country pass the ASWB® examinations associated with all levels of licensure. She has consulted with many universities and professional organizations to assist with establishing licensure test preparation programs.

Dr. Apgar has done research on licensure funded by the American Foundation for Research and Consumer Education in Social Work Regulation and has served as chairperson of her state's social work licensing board. She is a past President of the New Jersey Chapter of NASW and has been on its National Board of Directors. In 2014, the Chapter presented her with a Lifetime Achievement Award. Dr. Apgar has taught in both undergraduate and graduate social work programs and has extensive direct practice, policy, and management experience in the social work field.

Social Work Licensing Masters Exam Guide

Comprehensive ASWB LMSW Exam Review

Fourth Edition

Dawn Apgar, PhD, LSW, ACSW

SPRINGER PUBLISHING

Springer Publishing Company, LLC
www.springerpub.com

Acquisitions Editor: Cynthia Kitchel
Compositor: Transforma

ISBN: 978-0-8261-9279-0
ebook ISBN: 978-0-8261-9281-3
DOI: 10.1891/9780826192813

24 25 26 27 / 9 8 7 6 5 4 3 2 1

The author and the publisher of this Work have made every effort to use sources believed to be reliable to provide information that is accurate and compatible with the standards generally accepted at the time of publication. The author and publisher shall not be liable for any special, consequential, or exemplary damages resulting, in whole or in part, from the readers' use of, or reliance on, the information contained in this book. The publisher has no responsibility for the persistence or accuracy of URLs for external or third-party Internet websites referred to in this publication and does not guarantee that any content on such websites is, or will remain, accurate or appropriate.

Library of Congress Control Number: 2023919110

Contact us to receive discount rates on bulk purchases.
For more information please contact: sales@springerpub.com

Publisher's Note: **New and used products purchased from third-party sellers are not guaranteed for quality, authenticity, or access to any included digital components.**

Printed in the United States of America.

To Bill, Ryan, and Alex

You remind me what is important, support me so I can do it all, and always inspire me to be a better person.

Contents

CONTENT AREA IV: PROFESSIONAL RELATIONSHIPS, VALUES, AND ETHICS (25%)

Preface

Congratulations on getting to this point in your social work career. The decision to become licensed is significant, and passing the licensing examination demonstrates that you have the basic knowledge necessary to safely practice. Social workers are employed in all kinds of settings including hospitals, correctional facilities, mental health and addictions agencies, government offices, and private practices. It is essential that those served have some assurance that these practitioners are competent to provide the services that they are charged with delivering.

Regulation through certification and licensure helps to assure that social workers will interact in an ethical and safe manner, and there is oversight to address actions that are not consistent with this standard.

Passing the licensing exam is only one step in becoming certified or licensed, but it is usually the most difficult challenge faced after graduating with your degree.

> What does it take to pass the licensure exam?
>
> **A.** Keeping calm when studying and taking the test
> **B.** Analyzing the questions correctly
> **C.** Knowing the social work content areas

Getting the correct answer to this question is easy as success requires them all! You have acquired skills in all these areas during your educational preparation for professional social work practice. Remember what has worked for you in the past to manage anxiety and learn new concepts. Passing the licensure examination requires critical thinking and social workers are great at problem-solving or coming up with logical solutions to problems.

Although there are other test preparation materials produced, this guide provides all these essential elements in a single, manageable, easy-to-use format.

Individuals who are studying for the social work licensing examination have a primary concern and request. They are worried that they do not know important information about the tests that will prove to be a barrier to passing, and they want a "place" to go that will have all the necessary materials in a single location. They want to focus their efforts on studying for the exam—not hunting around for what needs to be studied!

This guide was created based on this important information, and it has been gathered from thousands of social workers just like you. Although it is not produced by or affiliated with ASWB in any way, and does not guarantee a passing score on the examinations, the test-taking techniques have been developed and used successfully by others who were faced with the same challenge that you are—others who are now certified and licensed social workers! They found this information so helpful in passing because the skills that it takes to be a good social worker in practice can be very different than the skills that it takes to pass the examination.

This edition of the guide has greatly expanded content on study and test-taking strategies, including effective ways to prepare for and pass the licensing examination. Material on methods for analysing questions correctly has been added, along with examples to illustrate the strategies presented. Often social workers find this information most helpful when preparing for and taking the licensing test.

Best wishes as you study. And remember that there is never only one way to achieve a goal, so use this guide in a way that works for you as you prepare. In choosing this guide as your roadmap, you have taken an important first step on the journey of passing the examination for certification and licensure.

How to Use This Guide

This guide has been carefully constructed to provide social workers with information on the licensure examination and how to properly prepare in order to pass it; test-taking strategies and methods for analysing the questions correctly; and the content areas which comprise the test.

The first section of the guide contains essential material to understand the best way to study, the logistics associated with taking the examination, and help with identifying what is being asked in test questions so that correct answers can be selected. Understanding how the licensing exam is constructed is valuable as it helps to identify priority areas for study. Anxiety is also reduced as there are no surprises when showing up to testing centers or when taking the licensure exams.

There are no "tricks" or "secrets" to help with passing licensure tests, but there are mistakes that social workers commonly make when studying and analyzing questions that lead to difficulties in performance. This first section provides guidance that is invaluable if taking the test for the first time or again due to not passing.

The second section of the guide has summary material on all the content areas, competencies, and Knowledge, Skills, and Abilities statements (KSAs) which are used by test developers to formulate actual questions. Some test takers have referred to this section as a "MSW Program in a Box," as it contains a summary of relevant concepts learned in a graduate social work program that may be assessed on the test. The format of this section is identical to the outline or "blueprint" for the examination with all four content areas covered. Each chapter within a content area represents a competency which has been identified as essential for testing. Lastly, within each chapter is summary information on each of the KSAs that can be tested on the exam. It is important to be familiar with all the possible topics that can be assessed. Simply looking over the table of contents for this section can be a helpful orientation to the material that needs to be studied. This section ends with a full-length practice test that can be used to simulate the actual examination experience. Taking this "mock" test is a great way to culminate a study plan and so is best done just before a scheduled test date.

Pass Guarantee

If you use this resource to prepare for your exam and do not pass, you may return it for a refund of your full purchase price, excluding tax, shipping, and handling. To receive a refund, return your product along with a copy of your exam score report and original receipt showing purchase of new product (not used). Product must be returned and received within 180 days of the original purchase date. Refunds will be issued within 8 weeks from acceptance and approval. One offer per person and address. This offer is valid for U.S. residents only. Void where prohibited. To initiate a refund, please contact Customer Service at csexamprep@springerpub.com.

Section I:
About the Examination, Study Strategies, and Test-Taking Tips

The Licensure Examination

Generally, when social workers are getting ready to take the Association of Social Work Boards (ASWB®) tests, they are anxious not only about knowing the content, but also about the examinations themselves. They have many questions about the number of questions that are asked and the number of correct answers required to pass. Becoming familiar with the examination basics assists in increasing comfort with the examination conditions and structure, thereby reducing anxiety about the unknown.

TEST CONSTRUCTION

The foundation of licensure examination construction is an ASWB practice analysis. The results of the practice analysis provide the content outlines for the tests. The structure of this guide and the material contained in it are based on the most recent content outline or "blueprint" developed by ASWB for licensure tests.

While the methodology used to guide the practice analysis process is complex, it is useful to understand some of the basics. In brief, ASWB surveys licensees nationally about the extent to which they use discrete knowledge items (known as the KSAs) in their current work and the extent to which they are important in their jobs. Using these survey results, as well as subject matter experts to group and weight the items, ASWB constructs content outlines or "blueprints" for their licensure tests. Each category of examination—Bachelors, Masters, Clinical, and Advanced Generalist—has a different content outline. However, these outlines have the same basic structure:

- **Four content areas** which are broad areas assessed on the exams
- **Competencies** which are meaningful sets of knowledge, skills, and abilities that are important within each content area
- **Knowledge, Skills, and Abilities statements (KSAs)** which describes a discrete knowledge component that is the basis for individual exam questions that may be used to measure the competency

The structure of ASWB's content outlines can be conceptualized as a funnel with content areas representing the broad domains on the test, competencies consisting of more narrowly identified groupings of topics, and KSAs as specific subjects which appear on the tests. There are separate content outlines for each of the four ASWB examinations. While there is some overlap, there are also discrete KSAs. The focus of testing is to determine if social workers have the theoretical, procedural, and factual information needed to practice. Becoming familiar with the content areas, competencies, and KSAs (which are described in the second section of the guide and are listed as its table of contents) is a helpful study tip as test takers are required to remember the requisite knowledge related to these topics to guide them to the correct answers.

TYPES OF QUESTIONS

There are three types of questions—recall, application, and reasoning—on the ASWB examinations. While each exam contains a mix of these types, the composition varies depending upon the category, with the Bachelors examination having more recall and application questions and the Clinical and Advanced Generalist having more application and reasoning questions. The Masters test has an equal distribution of all three question types.

Recall questions require selection of answers based on remembering learned material. **Application questions** require using information in a straightforward, specific way, such as identifying how knowledge would be used in specific settings, with target client groups, and/or in various social work roles. **Reasoning questions** require using knowledge to make judgments using theories, ethical principles, or other social work content to drive decisions. Reasoning questions are often scenarios or vignettes, which tend to be longer and more complex. The content needed to answer each of the question types is identical, but the degree to which the topics are easily identifiable is not. Often test takers are not able to recognize that knowledge related to certain KSAs must be applied or used in their reasoning to get the correct answers as these KSAs are not explicitly mentioned.

The following illustrates how information on common psychotropic medications can be asked using all three question types.

Recall

Which medication is a mood stabilizer?

  A. Haldol
  B. Prozac
  C. Lithium

Application

A client with bipolar disorder is being hospitalized. The client is experiencing episodes of mania and depression. The client is **MOST** likely going to be prescribed?

  A. Haldol
  B. Prozac
  C. Lithium

Reasoning

A client is hospitalized due to feelings of severe hopelessness and withdrawal. Upon intake, the client cries uncontrollably throughout the interview. The family reports periods of sleeplessness, excitement, and elevated energy by the client weeks earlier. The primary intervention is the prescription of a psychotropic medication. The drug will likely aim to:

    A. Ensure that the client does not experience delusions or hallucinations
    B. Alleviate the client's depression
    C. Stabilize the client's mood swings

The answer to all three of these questions is the same—C. The recall question simply requires identifying lithium as a mood stabilizer whereas understanding that lithium, as a mood stabilizer, is used for the treatment of bipolar disorder is needed to correctly answer the application question. The reasoning question, which is the most complex of the three types, provides the symptoms of bipolar disorder, requiring first the diagnosis and then the identification of a medication that aims to stabilize the mood swings as the primary aim of the intervention.

EXAMINATION STRUCTURE AND CONDITIONS

ASWB offers valuable information about its licensure tests on its website—www.aswb.org. It may be useful to look at the *ASWB Examination Guidebook*, which is free and located there. It is not a test preparation resource, but it does contain descriptions of how to register for the exams, security protocols, monitoring of results, and other testing logistics. All the information needed by most test takers is summarized below.

All the ASWB examinations (Bachelors, Masters, Clinical, and Advanced Generalist) have the same format.

Tests in all categories consist of 170 multiple-choice questions which must be answered in 4 hours from the time that the first question is seen. The examination is computerized but requires no specialized computer knowledge. There is a brief computer tutorial that assists with orientation to the software program. Spending time getting comfortable with the device is a good idea, since it does not count toward the 4-hour time limit. Brief restroom breaks are allowed, but the clock does not stop so these activities must be included in the 4-hour limit. It is important to be judicious with the time taken for breaks.

Only 150 of the 170 questions answered are used to determine whether a passing score is achieved.

Although 170 questions are answered, 20 of these questions are not scored as they are being piloted for possible inclusion as scored questions on future ASWB examinations. Thus, only 150 questions are used to determine a passing score. The 20 pilot items are never identified (even after the test is over) and are dispersed among scored items, so it is important to treat all 170 questions as critical.

No questions should be left blank; it is important to answer all 170 questions in the 4 hours.

The licensure test is a national examination that can be used for licensure in multiple states.

It is possible to take the examination in any state/jurisdiction, even if it is not the one in which licensure is sought. In addition, a social worker does not need to live in a state/jurisdiction to be licensed there. Social workers can hold licenses in multiple states/jurisdictions and often do as they may be required when doing telehealth or providing other services to clients who live in states/jurisdictions that are different from those in which social workers live.

Licensure examinations are administered at a variety of times, but appointments are needed. Select a time when personal performance is at its peak. The exam is lengthy, so avoid taking it in the afternoon if you are a morning person or early in the morning if you are "a night owl." There are rules about scheduling and cancelling appointments which need to be closely followed. This information is available on ASWB's website (www.aswb.org).

Testing is closely monitored so it is important to be familiar with what's allowed and not allowed. Details can be found on the ASWB website.

Non-standard testing arrangements (accommodations) for the licensure test must be approved in advance.

All testing accommodations related to documented disabilities must be approved by the licensing board and arranged in advance with ASWB. Extra time is the most common accommodation granted. Some states allow for accommodations for those for whom English is not a first language; others do not. When registering for the examination with ASWB, there is a form that must be completed with appropriate supporting documentation. ASWB works with states/jurisdictions to review and grant requests as appropriate. It is important that non-standard testing arrangements be approved prior to arrival at testing centers, as there are strict rules which must be followed by site personnel who do not have the authority to change them without approved accommodations.

Examinations are scored immediately, and unofficial results are provided.

After completing the examination, there is a brief survey given about the testing experience. The computer then scores the test and the results (pass/not pass) are provided immediately. When passing, a brief report is provided with the test taker's name, test category (Bachelors, Masters, Clinical, or Advanced Generalist), test date, state/jurisdiction, and test performance (number of questions correct with the number needed to pass). A picture also appears on the passing report. These results are "unofficial" as they still must be securely transmitted electronically to the licensing board of any designated state/jurisdiction. The results do not change but must be securely transmitted to be "official."

When not passing, a brief summary is also provided. It lists the four content areas and the number of questions asked in each of the four domains. It also lists the number of questions answered correctly in each of these areas. However, which specific questions are answered correctly or incorrectly is never known. The exam is pass/fail, and a passing score can be used for certification or licensure in any state.

If there are questions about the process for sending passing exam scores to other states/jurisdictions for licensure, the ASWB website (www.aswb.org) must be consulted as it has the necessary forms and fees.

Questions to test the four content areas are in random order.

Although the KSAs are in four broad content areas which may be used to structure studying, the questions on the examination are in random order and skip across topics. There are not separate sections for human development, ethics, and so on. In fact, the specific KSA being tested by each question is not listed. Being successful requires test takers to identify the specific knowledge areas and the requisite content to get the questions correct.

It is important not to skip around and be prepared for having questions on different content areas intermixed with one another. Each question stands alone to assess knowledge related to a distinct KSA. Avoid relating questions to one another and be prepared to shift focus for each question asked. The good news is that this structure allows questions on topics which are more familiar to be intermixed with those in areas which may be more challenging. If the answer to a question is not known, be assured that the next one will likely be on a topic that is more familiar.

The number of questions needed to get correct to pass varies.

Social workers always want to know how many questions of the 150 scored items they need to answer correctly to pass the exam. Although this sounds like an easy question, it is not! Not all questions on the ASWB examinations are the same level of difficulty as determined by the pilot process, so individuals who are randomly assigned harder versions of the exams need to answer fewer questions correctly than those who were lucky enough to have easier questions. This method ensures that the examination is fair for all those who are taking it, regardless of which questions were chosen. The number of questions needed to get correct generally varies from 90 to 107 of the 150 scored items. The pass point for the version of the examination taken is only revealed after the test is finished and scored electronically. On the unofficial score report, the exam score and pass point are listed.

It is possible to use this report to gauge the difficulty of the examination taken compared with other test versions available within a category (Bachelors, Masters, Clinical, and Advanced Generalist). The version is randomly selected and cannot be requested. If the pass point needed is closer to 90, the version had harder questions, and if it is closer to 107, it had easier ones. On average, most test takers have pass points which are close to 100 questions.

Repeat test takers do not have the same questions when retaking the examination.

Many people do not pass licensure examinations the first time and need to retake them, which is allowable after 90 days. Unfortunately, test takers need to pay for the examination each time that it is taken. Often those retaking the tests go home and look up information on topics with which they struggled. While it is always good to fill in knowledge gaps, the same questions will not appear on examinations taken in the future. Other questions in the four areas are selected. As the four domains are so broad, the foci of the questions may be quite different. To be adequately prepared, it is best to go back and study all the KSAs listed in content areas associated with poor performance. Do not exclusively focus on only those which appeared previously on the tests. The 90-day wait period allows for additional studying and gives ASWB time to ensure that different versions of the examinations, with new questions, are available for repeat test takers.

Studying for the Examination

Social workers studying for the ASWB examinations always want techniques that assist them in answering questions correctly. While test-taking tips can be helpful, they are no replacements for good old-fashioned studying of content. Test-taking tips are not enough on their own to eliminate all the incorrect answers. It is knowledge of the content area that is needed to select the correct answer from those that are incorrect. Thus, a study strategy aims to ensure that the content on the examination is familiar and can be applied to the scenarios which appear on the test.

Study strategies appear before test-taking tips in this guide as knowledge of the content areas must be attained before applying certain techniques to eliminate incorrect answers. Test takers usually have their own methods for studying based upon their learning styles and the time till their test dates. There is no set number of hours that is required since some test takers are well-versed in the content areas and others need more time as they have forgotten or not learned key concepts. Regardless of the study period, it is essential to have a defined study plan which includes time set aside to review the content. This chapter provides useful information that can help guide this process, including picking a study style based on learning style and managing test anxiety.

STUDY MATERIALS AND TIME FRAME

Social workers who are studying for the ASWB tests have lots of questions about the value of study materials and the time needed to prepare. They are often overwhelmed with advertisements from exam preparation companies and do not have methods for evaluating their worth. In addition, there are pressures to take the licensing exams, but uncertainty about whether taking them too quickly will have negative outcomes. The answers to the following frequently asked questions provide critical guidance in identifying appropriate study materials and the length of time needed to pass.

Q: What material must be studied for the licensure examination?

The licensure tests assess knowledge of social work content, so it is imperative to focus on scholarly material to help fill in the gaps and make sure that there is adequate knowledge of the key concepts and terms related to the KSAs. Readiness to take the examinations can be assessed by the extent to which content on each of the KSAs can be briefly explained to someone who does not have any prior knowledge of them. The difference between passing and not passing the examinations almost always is a result of gaps in knowledge, not application of test-taking strategies, so the bulk of studying must be aimed at filling in knowledge gaps or refreshing information already learned.

The good news is that studying for the licensure examinations really begins the first day of any social work program as the KSAs represent information that it taught in any accredited institution. The topics look familiar as they are the focus of many social work courses.

As there are many KSAs that may be assessed, it is necessary to know a little bit about a lot of topics. Limiting studying to this guide or other key resources that summarize material is the best method. This is not the time to go back and read textbooks! There are so many topics assessed that it is not possible or practical to know everything related to them. This guide is geared to provide important information on these areas "under one roof." Those who pass state that they are only tested on a small portion of the content contained in this guide. Remember that not all the KSAs are on any one examination.

It is hard enough to read through all the material in this guide. Using outside resources must be done on a limited basis. If used, supplemental study materials must be *scholarly* (written by social workers with education and training—do not rely on content from websites/companies where authors' degrees are unknown), *free* (there is no need to pay for academic content as there are many scholarly resources available free online), and *brief* (quick summaries and overviews which are less than a page on a given topic are best as they highlight the most salient information). In addition, it is important not to fall prey to solicitations for "secrets" to pass the test. Study materials must reflect that which is taught in social work programs. Unfortunately, many other licensure preparation materials are not written by social workers so their content does not reflect that which is important and unique to the profession.

The content in this guide assumes that test takers have learned about these KSAs previously in their social work programs. If material is unclear or it was never learned, some supplemental information may be needed to fill in knowledge gaps. In these instances, it is best to use free resources on the internet or any other documents that have no more than a paragraph summarizing key points. Remember, it is not necessary to read a book on Freud to understand his work and its importance in explaining human development.

In addition, there is always a time lag between the generation of new social work content and when it appears on the ASWB examinations. It takes time to write and pretest questions on new material. Thus, there is no need to worry about recent innovations appearing on the licensing test. The bulk of the content focuses on theoretical underpinnings of the social work profession that do not change dramatically or quickly over time.

The exam content outlines, with the accompanying content areas, competencies, and KSAs, change very little over time. This consistency is good and bad. The good news is that there is no need to know the "latest and greatest" in all content areas. It is hard to keep completely up to date in a profession that is changing so rapidly. Now for the bad news! For many, especially if they are working in specialty areas, some of the content or answers may appear to be dated. This is often the case related to psychopharmacology because new medications are being approved and used rapidly. Remember the time lapse when studying, and do not rely on breaking news or even agency practices which may be using more current protocols.

Q: How much time must be spent studying as I want to pick a test date?

This question is impossible to answer as some test takers know the content and are ready to take examinations once they are familiar with exam format and structure, as well as the test-taking strategies. Others need to spend time studying content that was forgotten or not learned.

However, most test takers never feel "ready" to take the ASWB examinations. Not unlike other standardized examinations, such as the Scholastic Aptitude Test (SAT) or Graduate Record Examination (GRE), readiness cannot be judged by knowing everything about the content areas. The ASWB examinations are not designed for test takers to "know it all" to pass. Often, picking a test date is the hardest task; as with the SAT or GRE, a deadline for admission to college or graduate school forces individuals to select dates even when they do not feel ready. For the ASWB examination, it will be necessary to select dates in the next few weeks or months, perhaps dictated by job opportunities or promotions predicated on being licensed. It is typical that test takers walk into the ASWB examinations without feeling totally ready or satisfied with the amount of time that they had to prepare.

Often confidence is boosted by picking test dates and developing detailed study goals to be accomplished before those dates. Some fit their studying into shorter time frames in which they spend a lot of time over several days or weeks reviewing the material and others complete these reviews more slowly. Whatever strategy chosen, it is great to take the tests knowing that study plans were actually followed and time allotted for studying was actually spent.

Q: How do I get access to sample questions as I want to use them for studying?

Although individuals like to study from sample questions, this is not advisable to only rely on questions as study materials. There are many reasons for this recommendation, but here are just a few.

1. Although it makes test takers feel better when they get answers correct on sample questions, getting correct answers is not a valid indicator of really knowing all the requisite content about the KSAs. Studying information on the KSAs directly increases the ability to answer all questions on these topics, not just particular sample questions.

2. Answers to sample questions inappropriately influence decisions made on the actual examinations when asked about similar topics. For example, seeing answers that are similar to ones that were correct or incorrect for sample questions increases or decreases the likelihood of selecting or eliminating them based upon this prior experience. However, questions in the "real" examination are not exactly the same as the ones seen during studying and it is essential to evaluate all response choices independently, without any undue bias that may be caused by use of prior sample questions.

3. The sample questions studied are not going to be on actual examinations and probably are not even written by those who developed the licensure tests. Thus, the idea that many social workers have of wanting to "get into the head" of the individuals writing the exam or understand their logic is not valid—though it might make them good clinicians in real life! Unfortunately, many of the sample question apps and resources for purchase for the ASWB examinations are not even written by social workers! Thus,

trying to figure out why answers are correct which were not selected may be futile as the questions may not be actually testing social work content.

It is a good idea to take a "mock" examination which mimics the actual licensure test in length, composition, and question format. There is such an examination in the back of this guide. Additionaly, ASWB sells full-length practice tests to those who are registered to take their exams. The best way to use a full-length practice test is as follows.

1. After studying is completed and readiness to take the actual ASWB examination has been assessed, select a 4-hour period where the mock examination can be completed in a quiet environment without interruptions.

2. Answer the questions as if it were the actual examination—using the strategies and having to pick one answer—even if you are not completely sure that it is correct.

3. Keep track of the time even if short bathroom breaks are taken. Finishing the full-length practice test demonstrates the ability to get through 170 questions in the 4 hours allotted. This experience should relieve some anxiety about the timed nature of the examination. Most people complete the actual examinations in 3 to 3.5 hours so there is no need to worry about finishing as long as problem-solving is continuing and answers are selected even when there may not be complete certainty that they are correct.

4. Score the full-length practice test *after* completing it. Resist the urge to look at the answer key to see if questions are correct immediately after answering them. A "mock" examination is not to be used to determine readiness to take the actual test. Instead, it provides an idea of the length of the examination and how much focus is needed, in addition to boosting confidence that all questions can be answered in the time allotted.

CONSIDERATIONS WHEN STUDYING

Good study skills are essential when preparing for the ASWB licensure examinations. It can seem overwhelming to get ready for these high-stakes tests. Studying requires discipline and motivation. There are a few strategies that increase the likelihood of passing. Studying that builds focus and stamina, prioritizes content that is likely to be on the tests, and increases understanding results in better outcomes and leads to greater success.

Build Focus and Stamina

Most test takers have not taken standardized multiple-choice 4-hour examinations for a long time—if ever! Social workers' lives are hectic, and they rarely get a chance to really focus on a single task or have the luxury of thinking about a single topic in a deep, critical manner. Thus, many people find it helpful to study in 4-hour blocks of time rather than for a few minutes here and there. Carving out this time may be difficult, but it is beneficial because it also helps with building up concentration and focus. Remember, runners do not start with marathons; they need to build their strength and endurance over time before they can tackle 26.2 miles.

Many social workers who have passed the ASWB examinations complain about how hard it was to stay focused and how exhausting they were after finishing their tests. Preparation needs to include building up focus and stamina. The first time that test takers are engaged in critical thinking related to the content areas for 4 hours should not be during their actual examinations!

Prioritize Content

Think about the vast amount of information that is available on each of the KSAs listed in the content areas. Often social workers have trouble prioritizing the content that is important and determining how much depth of knowledge is needed in each of the topics contained in this guide. It is important to recognize that social workers who have attended social work programs at different schools, as well as courses within these programs taught by various faculty, have passed the examinations. Thus, it cannot be about specific details or stories told by one professor, but instead the "core" elements included in any overview or lecture on a topic, regardless of school or professor. These elements are the ones that must be learned and remembered because they are the basic concepts related to the knowledge being tested.

In addition, there are also "core" or essential areas seen as critical to competent practice. Can you imagine social workers leaving undergraduate or graduate programs without reviewing the signs of child abuse and neglect and the duty of mandatory reporting? Of course not! Child abuse and neglect are "core" topics that often are the basis of examination questions. The list of these areas is not fixed but includes confidentiality, assessment of danger to self and others, professional boundaries, self-determination, cultural awareness, and so on. When studying, prioritize areas that every social worker needs to know, regardless of setting or specialization. These topics are likely to be asked about on the examinations.

Concentrate on Understanding Over Memorization

When studying, it is not necessary to memorize content because terms or definitions need not be recalled from memory. ASWB examinations do not require memorization. Instead, test takers need to distinguish one answer, from several, that most directly relates to a topic or is essential based on knowledge of the content area. Thus, understanding is critical as most questions relate to application or reasoning. Test takers must be able to explain the importance of each KSA, rather than memorizing fancy terms or facts. Memorizing can lead to superficial understanding of concepts, which is not useful for the ASWB examinations.

Often, social workers are focused on using the clinical and other jargon that they learned in their social work programs; however, they may be unable to explain what these concepts mean in plain and understandable terms. For example, when asked what should happen when meeting with clients for the first time, social workers often use phrases such as, "You need to build rapport," "It is essential that you start where a client is," or "Social workers should show empathy as to what a client is going through." Though all true, these statements give little insight into any real actions that social workers must take in these first meetings. What should a social worker do to "build rapport"? How would a client know if a social worker is being "empathetic"? What would a social worker be doing or saying? Having to explain KSAs to those who know little about social work practice and ask lots of questions about the content area is far better than studying with social work colleagues who do not challenge the use of jargon or technical terms which can be confusing and do not include essential basics.

The following questions can serve as a quick assessment of whether requisite knowledge and understanding have been obtained.

1. What are the most relevant points related to this KSA that would be contained in a 5-minute "lecture" on the topic? If they cannot be easily identified, then more studying is needed!

2. What is the relevancy of this KSA to social work practice and how social workers use this information to make decisions when interacting with clients? Most questions require information to be applied in specific scenarios.

3. How does this KSA relate to the assessment and treatment of clients? Does it in any way impact problems or issues that they may be experiencing? More than half of the examination focuses on assessment, planning, and intervention (the second and third content areas), so using knowledge for reasoning in these areas is essential.

In order to get correct answers, exam questions require broad application of key concepts related to theories (e.g., the understanding that what happens to a client early in life can influence later functioning) or specific terms associated with these areas, even if the constructs are not mentioned (e.g., picking a response that best represents "family homeostasis"). For those areas in which requisite knowledge is possessed, only a quick review by reading through the content outlined in the subsequent pages of this guide is needed. If there are gaps in knowledge, more detailed studying may be needed.

Respect Learning Style

There are different learning styles that dictate methods that are most effective when having to fill in gaps in knowledge. Determining which one best fits can help ensure that studying results in learning and expedite the study process.

Visual Learners

Visual learners learn best through what they see. Although lectures can be boring for visual learners, they benefit from the use of diagrams, PowerPoint slides, and charts.

- Use colored highlighters in this guide to draw attention to key terms.
- Develop outlines or take notes on the concepts in this guide.
- Write talking points for each of the KSAs on separate white index cards.
- Create a coding schema of symbols and write them in this guide next to material and terms that require further study.
- Study in an environment that is away from visual distractions such as television, people moving around, or clutter.

Auditory Learners

Auditory learners learn best through what they hear. They may have difficulty remembering material that they read in this guide but can easily recall it if it is read to them.

- Tape-record yourself summarizing the material—listen back to reinforce what was read.
- Have a study partner explain the relevant concepts and terms related to the KSAs.
- Read the text from this guide aloud to assist with remembering content.

- Find free, short online podcasts or YouTube videos on the content areas to assist with learning.
- Talk to yourself about the content when studying—emphasizing what is important to remember related to each KSA.

Kinesthetic or Hands-On Learners

Kinesthetic learners learn through tactile approaches aimed at experiencing or doing. They need activities and physical activities as a foundation for instruction.

- Make flashcards on material because writing it down assists with remembering the content.
- Use as many different senses as possible when studying—read material when on the treadmill, use highlighters, talk aloud about content, and/or listen to a study partner.
- Develop mnemonic devices to aid in information retention (e.g., EAPIET or EAt PIE Today is a great way to remember the social work problem-solving process—Engaging, Assessing, Planning, Intervening, Evaluating, and Terminating).
- Write notes and important terms in the margins of this guide.
- Find a study partner and quiz each other on material—turn it into a game and compare the length of time that a KSA can be discussed before running out of material.

MANAGE TEST ANXIETY

Perhaps one of the biggest issues that social workers need to address when preparing for and actually taking the examinations is anxiety. Although not designed to be an exhaustive resource on how to address test anxiety, this guide would be incomplete if it did not provide some guidance to assist with anxiety during this stressful time in professional development.

It is important to acknowledge that anxiety can be useful during this process because it helps prioritize studying above other demands in everyday life. There are no methods to acquire the needed knowledge besides good old-fashioned studying. Anxiety can be a motivator to keep going over the material even when there are more interesting things to do!

Remember, everyone who is studying for the examinations is feeling the same way. Stress and anxiousness are typical so do not feel alone.

However, it is essential to manage this anxiety, and there are several strategies that can help.

1. *Make a Study Plan and Work the Plan*
   A great way to instill confidence is being able to walk into the testing center having followed a structured study plan. A study plan helps break the material into smaller manageable segments and avoid last-minute cramming.

2. *Do Not Forget the Basics*
   It is important not to neglect biological, emotional, and social needs leading up to and on the day of the examination. Get plenty of rest, build in relaxation time, and eat well to avoid exhaustion during this preparation process.

3. *Be Familiar With the Test Environment*
   Before the day of the examination, be familiar with the testing conditions. On the day of the test, be prepared early to avoid feeling rushed. Take time to carefully review

the tutorial on the computer before starting to answer questions to avoid wasting time during the exam.

4. *Use Relaxation Techniques*

   Breathe and remember to relax during the examination. Simply shutting your eyes or stretching your neck several times during the 4-hour exam can help with refocusing.

5. *Put the Examination Into Perspective*

   Rarely do people get the score they want the first time taking any standardized test. Taking the SAT or GRE more than once is the rule rather than the exception. Social workers often attach too much meaning to whether they pass the ASWB examination the first or second time. They feel their entire career rests on the results. This is not true. There are many outstanding social workers who have had to take the test multiple times. The test can be retaken so remember that this is not the only chance to pass. Do not let the test define self-worth and avoid thinking in "all or nothing" terms.

6. *Expect Setbacks*

   The road to licensure is not different than other journeys in life and not usually without unexpected delays or even disappointments. It is important to see these as typical parts of the process and not ends in themselves. Try to figure out why these setbacks in studying or passing occurred and how they can be used as feedback for making improvements. The hard work associated with getting a social work degree certainly causes some disappointments and challenges. Studying for and passing the examination is also not easy, but success is possible with keeping focused and learning from challenges encountered.

7. *Reward Yourself*

   Do not wait until passing to celebrate. Build some enjoyment into the test-taking experience by creating little incentives or rewards along the way. Go out to dinner after having studied for 4 hours on a Saturday afternoon. Get up early and study before work to enjoy a movie when arriving home. Making the study process more fun can result in studying more and improve performance on the examination.

8. *Acknowledge and Address the Anxiety*

   Ignoring the anxiety that accompanies this process does not help as it is not possible to completely eliminate it through the techniques mentioned. However, assessment is needed to determine whether it is manageable and can be addressed by some of these suggestions or it is interfering so significantly with the learning process that it results in "blanking out" or problems in other life areas. If the latter is the case, more intensive anxiety-reduction interventions are needed. Repeatedly studying the content over and over does not reduce anxiety. Although most people can develop their own strategies for anxiety management, others need outside help. Usually, individuals who need the assistance of others are those who have experienced anxiety in their lives prior to this experience. No matter what the severity—anxiety management is a critical part of every study plan!

Tips for Answering Questions Correctly

In addition to the development of a sound study plan, it is important to use strategies to help distinguish correct answers from incorrect response choices. These are not "secrets" or "tricks"—they are approaches that assist with reading the questions, understanding what is being asked, and applying critical social work content. There are common mistakes that social workers initially make when trying to answer ASWB exam questions as they test content in a standardized way. The following tips assist with using a thoughtful approach to question analysis, as well as provide important principles to remember when answering questions on the exam.

USING THE BEST OVERALL APPROACH

The KSA being assessed must be identified before looking at the answers.

It is essential that questions are thoroughly understood before looking at the answers. The most difficult part of selecting the correct answer is identifying the knowledge area and KSA that is being tested. To ensure that proper attention is given to understanding the question, a multistep process must be undertaken.

1. Read the question exactly as it is written, paying attention to key words and those in quotes. Do not look at the response choices yet!

2. Ask "What is this question about?" to determine which of the KSAs is being tested.

3. Think about the important concepts related to the KSA; they are essential in distinguishing the correct answers from the incorrect ones.

4. Examine the question again to confirm that any assumption about which KSA is being tested is correct and to determine how the important concepts related to the KSA are relevant to the question.

5. Now look at the response choices for the first time! Read each carefully.

6. Eliminate any that do not appear to be correct. If more than one response choice appears to be viable, go back and read the question again—looking only at the remaining response choices left.

It is sometimes difficult to eliminate incorrect response choices immediately, so this process may involve multiple iterations. Each time a response choice is eliminated, read the question and the response choices that are left. Going back to the question each time that a response choice is eliminated helps with keeping focused on critical content which is contained in the question.

Often test takers spend more time reading and debating between the response choices than critically analyzing questions, which is a big mistake!

When response choices are proper names, read and think about them before looking at questions.

While many questions have response choices which are long, there are others that consist of proper names, such as those of clinical terms, diagnoses, theories, or medications. When asked to select between listed terms, diagnoses, theories, or medications, it is best to read the response choices first and think about their usage, meanings, and/or applications before looking at the questions. This approach allows the use of evidence in the questions to support or help eliminate response choices based on actual knowledge about these concepts, without being biased by question wording.

If terms, diagnoses, theories, or medications listed as response choices are unknown before reading the questions, they must be eliminated and only those with which there is some textbook familiarity should be considered. There is a natural tendency to gravitate toward selecting proper names that sound good or like they "fit" without really understanding their meaning. This mistake can be avoided by making sure that only response choices which are understood with 100% certainty are considered. If those which are known can be eliminated, "mystery" terms, diagnoses, theories, or medications can then be considered.

Increasing your familiarity with key social work terms will help increase your success as it will make it easier to distinguish between the response choices provided. This study guide has an important section that defines key social work terms to assist you in your studying.

Answers must be selected for all questions—avoid skipping around or leaving answers blank.

There is plenty of time to answer the questions in the 4-hour period allotted for the test. Although the examination is timed, most people have no issue with test completion, but are very nervous about the time and feel rushed due to anxiety. Often that anxiety can fuel the desire to leave questions blank if answers are unknown or to skip around to find questions that are more familiar. Such an approach is a mistake. The questions should be answered in the order in which they are listed. Skipping around wastes time. The most time spent must be on identifying the KSA being tested or what the question is asking. Not answering a question after this analysis has occurred serves no purpose because no more information will be available later in the examination. An answer needs to be selected before moving on. Also, an answer must be selected after reading the question a few times and applying the strategies. Individuals who run out of time are "stuck" because they are waiting for the feeling of certainty in their answers that does not come in these types of standardized examinations.

Lastly, the computer can be used to "flag" questions for which correct answers are uncertain. Flagging must be avoided and only used for *a few* questions throughout the examination. There is really no reason to flag as, again, there will be no more information to help with selecting correct answers or eliminating incorrect response choices later in the examination. Flagging can cause increased unnecessary anxiety. Even when passing, test takers get a lot of questions incorrect. There is no reason to keep identifying uncertainty about whether questions are correct through flagging.

The "best" response choice is not always the correct answer.

Standardized examinations are often difficult and test takers find themselves struggling to identify the correct answer from several listed response choices. In these instances, social workers can make a common mistake such as selecting the response choice that has catchy social work phrases, such as "from a client's perspective" or "focus on a client's strengths and skills." Although these are important social work concepts, they need to relate to the KSA being tested. If response choices are judged solely based on the inclusion of important social work terms—independent of what the question is really asking—it is easy to be drawn to the "best" ones (judged solely based on the inclusion of social work jargon) even when they are not correct.

One way to avoid making this mistake is to go back and reread the question when debating between response choices. Often test takers struggle with choosing between response choices without going back to questions to reconfirm the KSAs being tested. Simply debating between response choices, without reviewing questions again, may lead to picking the "best" ones based on compelling social work content or terms—rather than their connection to the content areas.

Do not "fight" the standardized approach to testing of social work knowledge!

ASWB examinations assess knowledge of social work content in a standardized way. Often, what is learned in the classroom is very different than practice in the field. Knowledge is only one factor that drives actual behavior. Textbook knowledge also differs from practice wisdom and clinical judgments. Answers must be based upon content studied from this guide and what was learned in the classroom. Question are written to make sure that all social workers provide uniform responses. Answers cannot depend on individualized practice experiences or diverse agency protocols and policies.

When viewing questions, ask "What did I study in the guide that relates to this question?" or "Which KSA is being tested and what do I know about this content area?" Avoid inappropriately asking, "What would I do in this instance?" or "How should I handle this situation?" as these questions lead to picking response choices that draw upon practice experience, which varies across test-takers, rather than the existing knowledge base in a given area.

There is only one correct answer for each question. Since everyone has different practice experience, basing answers on what is seen or done in the field can lead to many different approaches which does not work when taking standardized tests. However, the knowledge base of the profession, as taught in social work programs, is universal, regardless of setting or practice experience. Basing responses on information that is taught in the classroom and outlined in social work textbooks ensures getting consistent answers with others—even if there are factors that make it impossible to implement them in certain work settings.

REMEMBERING IMPORTANT QUESTION FEATURES

The importance of social justice and macro practice is paramount.

The ASWB examinations assess social work knowledge, which emphasizes the importance of three practice methods—micro, mezzo (also known as meso), and macro. Even when doing clinical work, social workers differ in their intervention from others doing counseling or therapy as they recognize that many problems stem from the larger environment, including marginalization and oppression. Social workers are mandated to address the root causes of these systemic issues, rather than blaming those impacted by them. All social workers, even those specializing in clinical or micro practice methods, have these responsibilities. Thus, scenarios on the examinations that appear to be testing direct practice with individuals can actually be situations in which social workers must change policies or advocate for clients' rights in order to address issues causing distress such as discrimination and lack of adequate services.

Often test takers preparing for the examinations question whether administration/management or policy practice will be tested. Of course! Mezzo and macro social work practice are equally as important as micro practice. All ASWB exams are going to include questions aimed at ensuring social workers are change agents and fight for social justice. The profession is rooted in serving those who are poor and disenfranchised.

A strong commitment to reform can be seen in questions that involve agency policies as well. For example, supervisors are there to ensure that clients receive the most effective and efficient services possible—not to make things easier for social workers or enforce agency mandates.

It is essential to make sure the root causes of problems are addressed. There may be barriers to properly serving clients. Social workers must look at answers through the lens of what is best for clients. The self-determination of clients must only be limited in situations that could harm clients or others. The correct answers are always the ones that put clients first.

Questions often focus on conflicts between meeting clients' needs versus adhering to practices or policies created by agencies. When there is a barrier to meeting clients' needs, social workers must take responsibility for trying to remove the barriers. Social workers must fight to change rules which do not maximize client functioning. Having clients comply is blaming victims and not getting at the root causes of issues. Answers which reflect these changes are correct even when such changes seem unrealistic and lengthy. Whether or not social workers are successful does not change the mandate to challenge unjust practices. Response choices should not be dismissed just because they seem too difficult to achieve. If test takers do not challenge injustice through policy practice on their examinations, it is likely that they have answered incorrectly!

Do not get distracted by settings or scenarios.

Although there are some questions that require simple "recall" of content, many ask for the "application" of information to particular situations or scenarios. These questions come in the form of vignettes and are often the ones in which social workers make mistakes. In practice, social workers often alter their actions based on many contextual variables. However, remember that the questions on the examination are about the application of social work knowledge within the KSAs, and this knowledge does not change regardless of the setting in the vignette. In addition, any of the KSAs can be implemented in a wide variety of settings. Thus, it is important not to get "lost" in the scenario.

For example, the core components of a discharge plan are the same if it is prepared for a client leaving the hospital, a drug treatment facility, or an inpatient psychiatric treatment setting. The content (i.e., history/assessment, treatment provided, follow-up needed) may be different, but each discharge plan must contain information in these critical areas. Thus, it is essential to stay focused on the content being tested and remember that it is not necessary to have worked in the settings mentioned in the vignettes (schools, hospitals, drug treatment centers, nursing homes, etc.) to pass the examination; the KSAs or core social work content being tested is universal, regardless of venue.

Test takers often relate scenarios to the type of social work services that they have provided in the past or in their practice settings. Unless specified, social workers in scenarios could be providing a wide variety of interventions including, but not limited to, information and referral, case management, advocacy, skills training, and so on. Psychotherapeutic counseling is just one of many treatments delivered by social workers. Most scenarios are applicable to any social worker in any practice situation delivering any service as they are testing important professional content that are applied generally.

Lastly, when answering questions which involve scenarios, it is critical that response choices selected relate to the KSAs and are not just focused on "fixing" the situations. Often there are one or two response choices that may be helpful to clients in the specific circumstances described, but do not represent important social work concepts that can be applied universally to other situations or scenarios. The exam does not aim to test what social workers do in every instance, but rather knowledge that must be applied more broadly. Make sure to see the forest through the trees by not narrowly focusing on the specific client situation and missing the important broader intent of the question.

Client feelings and behaviors should not be pathologized as they may be typical reactions.

Social workers often view licensure examinations as a means to assess their clinical knowledge. They view all client behaviors through a psychotherapeutic lens and are inappropriately quick to attribute client feelings and behaviors to symptomology of disorders or dysfunction. Using this approach, social workers are apt to wrongly view clinical attributes as the focus of treatment or intervention.

For example, if clients have experienced unsuccessful infertility treatments, they are likely to feel depressed, frustrated, and hopeless. These are typical reactions which may result from not achieving desired results from medical interventions. The presence of these feelings does not mean that they must be the focus of social work treatment or clinically analyzed and diagnosed. Perhaps such clients simply need support for pursuing alternative methods for becoming parents, such as through adoption or surrogacy.

Examination questions often focus on making sure test takers do not diagnose clients with disorders unless *all* required clinical criteria are present. Feelings and emotions can be appropriate manifestations of underlying problems. Interventions or treatments must aim to address the underlying root causes of issues, not their symptoms. Anxiety, sadness, and anger are typical feelings and do not need to be addressed unless they are causing problems for clients or interfering with functioning. The mention of client emotions in questions does not mean that they are the foci of treatment or even problems.

ASWB examinations, including those focused on clinical methods, are taken by social workers employed in all types of settings and roles. Clinical work is not restricted to the provision of psychotherapy, but also includes case management and even advocacy. Most questions on the ASWB examinations are not focused on psychopathology, but instead test the broad and diverse knowledge base used by those in the profession. There are many appropriate interventions to address client problems, not just counseling. It is important not to solely focus on the treatment of client emotions as the goal of services.

There are no specific state or jurisdictional laws that should influence response selections.

The ASWB exams are used in every U.S. state, as well as the District of Columbia, the U.S. Virgin Islands, and several Canadian provinces. Correct answers are the same for all social workers taking the examinations. However, the systems of care and laws in each state/jurisdiction differ; thus, responses to situations may be varied in real-life, everyday work. This is not the case on the licensing tests, as there is only one correct answer to each question. Thus, it is essential not to consider "rules" or laws that apply or resources that may be available in only one state/jurisdiction.

A simple way to avoid unconsciously using state/jurisdiction-specific information when answering questions is to think of a different state/jurisdiction and ask, "What would a social worker living in [insert name of another state/jurisdiction here] pick as the correct answer?" If the answer is, "I don't know because I am not sure how things are done there," the response choice is mistakenly being selected based on practice systems and rules that may differ between states/jurisdictions and not universal social work content that is always applicable. If the answer chosen is the same regardless of state/jurisdiction, the selection is based on core social work content that is essential to know. Professional ethical standards apply regardless of state/jurisdiction so using them to help identify correct answers can be very helpful.

The hierarchy of clients' needs must be respected, with safety prioritized.

Questions on the examinations often require social workers to order their actions with clients or identify issues or problems that are most important in given scenarios. In practice, such decisions are often somewhat subjective and driven by practice wisdom that accounts for many clinical and contextual factors. However, on the examination, all social workers must select the same correct answers. A useful framework for prioritizing client needs and addressing them sequentially is Maslow's hierarchy of needs.

Although it is unlikely that Maslow's hierarchy of needs would ever be explicitly asked about on the examination, it is a tool that can be used repeatedly to help prioritize problems or order actions based on client need. Social workers must always address health and safety issues before moving on to those that relate to psychological functioning such as self-esteem. Thus, when questions include response choices that screen for or attend to the health and safety of clients, test takers must examine them carefully to see if there is explicit wording that indicates clients are in danger or at risk of harming others. If so, this concern must be addressed before other actions are taken.

Social workers must also provide concrete services to meet basic needs, such as housing, employment, and transportation, before moving up the hierarchy. Social workers often must drive and accompany clients to doctor's appointments or food shopping to ensure that they receive needed care and have access to fundamental resources. Maslow's framework indicates that without health, safety, and basic needs being met first, clients cannot meet their higher-level needs.

Steps in processes must not be skipped because they take too long or will not "solve" problems.

Most questions do not ask test takers to "solve" problems or even take actions that directly lead to resolving issues or situations. For example, a question may ask what a social worker should do FIRST when having an issue with a colleague. Although speaking directly to the colleague may not seem as expedient as going to a supervisor, it is appropriate to address the issue with the colleague before going up the chain of command. In addition, putting requests in writing after not getting responses to phone calls are also needed to ensure proper documentation. In practice, social workers often have deadlines and need to act quickly, requiring skipping of critical steps in processes. However, these pressures do not exist in test scenarios.

There are not long waiting lists, scarce resources, or delays in referrals that exist in scenarios unless they are explicitly stated. In actual practice, social workers encounter these realities daily and often base their decisions and actions to ensure results despite these constraints. These factors must not influence selecting a response choice unless they are explicitly stated in the question.

Often knowledge about the processes themselves are being assessed, rather than the outcomes. Unless there is a compelling reason, such as safety, which is explicitly stated in scenarios, test takers should adhere to the sequencing in established protocols, such as chains of command or documentation procedures. Actions can be taken immediately after one another so skipping any of them is not needed. Desired results will eventually be achieved, even when all steps in processes are respected.

Determining phases of the problem-solving process within scenarios is critical.

Another critical tool to assist with selecting the correct answer is the problem-solving process (i.e., engagement, assessment, planning, intervention, evaluation, and termination). Understanding the goal of each phase and the tasks to be completed therein is critical because many questions on the examination focus on making sure that things are happening in the correct order.

For example, if questions are about first meetings with clients, the activities of social workers must focus on engagement. Engagement includes finding out why clients are there and why they are seeking services now, explaining the role of social workers and what to expect in treatment, listening to clients as they explain their situations, and explaining the limits of confidentiality. Including references to specific meetings or activities completed are clues for determining what phase of the problem-solving process social workers and clients are in and what activities are appropriate next.

Actions by social workers are quite different in engagement than they are in termination. Although questions rarely explicitly state the phase, it can be identified by what has occurred, such as "when gathering information on the problem" to indicate assessment or "when developing the contract" to indicate planning. Also, it may be useful to classify answers into the phases in which they would occur in order to select what comes FIRST or NEXT.

Focusing on Question Formatting and Wording

In addition to using the best approach and remembering important question features, it is necessary to make sure to attend to question formatting and wording. Missing critical words in questions results in making avoidable mistakes. There are some basic, but essential, tips that heighten awareness and must be used to make sure that the most salient wording in questions is considered and key words are not missed. The following questions help guide critical analysis of test questions to improve performance and avoid common errors.

Q: Is there a qualifying word in the question?

Many questions contain key words that are extremely important and distinguish the correct answer from the incorrect response choices. These words are capitalized, and bolded. In addition, they can usually be seen near the end of questions. Examples of qualifying words are BEST, NEXT, MOST, and FIRST. Whenever a qualifying word is contained in a question, it is the key to selecting the correct answer from the incorrect responses and is directly related to the concept being assessed. Put the qualifying word in front of each response choice when reading it to ensure that the focus on this key word is maintained. Repeat the qualifying word before reading each response choice. By inserting the qualifying word before each response choice, you are less likely to get distracted by words that may not be salient. Qualifying words, when present, are the most important factors to consider when selecting between the response choices provided.

Q: Is demographic information about the client mentioned in the question?

If the ages of clients are included in the vignette, they must be considered as age often provides relevant information for selecting correct response choices. For example, having imaginary friends at age 4 is very different than having them at age 34. Imaginary friends in childhood are an extension of pretend play and part of Piaget's preoperational stage. However, having them in later life can be an indicator of psychosis resulting from a hallucination or delusion. Thus, in the former instance, this behavior is typical, which would require no special intervention, whereas in the latter, it is necessary to do a mental status examination or refer for psychiatric evaluation. Additionally, confidentiality and consent are handled differently for young children, as compared with adults. If questions refer to clients generally, answers are not age dependent.

When studying, social workers do not need to memorize the exact ages at which individuals leave one stage of development or reach another. However, when mentioned in questions, age can be useful to indicate where clients are in the life course and what may be expected.

Questions may also contain other important demographic information such as race/ethnicity, religious affiliation, sexual orientation, gender identity, etc. There is always a reason that this information was included in the question so it must be considered when discerning between response choices.

Q: Is this question testing the application of a specific theory, perspective, or practice model?

The ASWB examinations require basic knowledge about many theories, practice models, and perspectives related to social work practice. Whether on the undergraduate or graduate level, social workers take courses on theory and practice, learning different models of intervention. A theory is a set of interrelated concepts that are organized in a way that explains aspects of everyday life. A practice model is a way in which a theory is operationalized. And a perspective is a point of view that is usually broader and at a higher level of abstraction (i.e., strengths perspective). Having a basic understanding of various theories, practice models, and perspectives, as well as the terms that are rooted in them, is necessary.

Sometimes there are recall questions about theories, practice models, or perspectives, but knowledge in these areas is often tested through application to vignettes. For example, the last sentence before the response choices may state, "Using a systems approach, a social worker can expect this recent medical diagnosis to …" Examining the response choices through the "lens" of systems theory is essential to selecting the correct answer. Systems theory states that individuals are in continual interaction with their environment and that parts within a system are interrelated. Thus, when one subsystem is affected, they are all affected. Having this knowledge is essential as the correct answer must reflect the medical diagnosis affects others in the family or aspects of the client's life beyond health.

It is not necessary to be an expert in all theories, practice models, or perspectives. Instead, knowledge must be "an inch deep, but a mile wide" with test takers knowing multiple theories, practice models, or perspectives—not just the ones that they use in their daily work. The ones that need to be applied to scenarios may not even be best practices for the problems presented. Questions requiring application of theories, practice models, or perspectives are not asking for test takers to pick the modalities to be used, but instead which response choices represent the theories, practice models, or perspectives chosen by the question writers.

When studying, it is good to know the focus of each modality—for example, understanding the fundamental difference between structural and strategic family therapies. In addition, questions often contain terms or techniques associated with various interventions, even when the names of the treatment approaches are not mentioned. Sometimes questions do not specify paradigms but use related terms that would only be known if they were studied.

When examining questions, make sure to determine whether questions require the use of particular theories, practice models, or perspectives. If so, the answers must directly relate to these approaches, whether or not they are the best means to address the problems.

Q: Are conclusions about scenarios supported by explicit wording?

Perhaps the biggest mistake that social workers make when reading vignettes is adding material to these questions. This is done unconsciously when social workers mistakenly think of clients or situations in their own practices that are similar to those described in the question. Social workers often view scenarios through a "micro practice lens," as most social workers work directly with individuals and families. However, a client in a scenario does not need to be an individual. It can be a family, organization, group, or community so an assumption should not be made that the term "client" refers to a single individual.

Unfortunately, as social workers are in the field longer, they are more likely to make this mistake as there are more instances in which scenarios resemble their own practice experiences. For example, if clients are described as psychotic or threatening, they may be inappropriately judged as a danger to themselves or others because of social workers' past experiences with clients who were such. However, being psychotic or threatening does not necessarily imply danger. Clients can be threatening, but verbalizations could focus on not paying bills or refusing to continue with services. Threats do not necessarily involve physical harm unless it is explicitly stated in the vignettes.

To determine whether material is added to questions, ask what social workers doing macro practice might do as often the material that is added to questions involves clinical content. Social workers doing micro, mezzo, and macro social work draw from the same theoretical base and rely on the same professional knowledge. Social workers must be able to competently apply all three practice methods in their work. Often when asking whether a social worker in a scenario could be providing macro services, test takers see the situation in a new light as many vignettes do not specify the practice method used. Social workers tend to assume that micro-level or clinical services were being delivered, but these are implicit biases. It is essential to recognize that all test takers tend to read and interpret questions based upon their own practice experiences. These experiences mean that information gets unconsciously added. It is always advisable to reread questions to ensure that conclusions are supported by empirical evidence and not just assumptions which are not sustained by question wording.

Q: Are there quotation marks in the questions or answers?

Some questions include words or phrases in quotation marks that directly relate to identifying the KSAs and/or getting the correct answers. For example, a vignette may describe a client who walks into the first therapy session and states, "I don't have to tell you anything and I don't want to be here," followed by a question asking about a social worker's BEST response. Although this question does not explicitly state that it is asking how to best address resistance, it is doing so as evidenced by the client's statement. Words in quotation marks are there for a reason and usually have information that is essential for selecting correct answers.

Quotation marks can also be in response choices. Sometimes entire response choices are quoted statements, such as those which represent social workers' most appropriate reactions to clients' concerns or behaviors in scenarios. Test takers must evaluate words or phrases in answers with the same diligence that they do so in questions.

Q: Do response choices begin with verbs that can provide some assistance?

Many of the response choices to questions on the examination begin with verbs. The verbs can provide valuable assistance, especially if you are debating between multiple response choices. For example, some response choices describe social workers taking action ("tell" or "arrange") without mentioning any roles for clients. These response choices do not use an empowerment approach, which may help rule them out.

"Explore" and "engage" are verbs that usually indicate that social workers are working with clients to arrive at solutions. "Ignore" or "wait" may indicate that social workers are not helping clients address critical problems when needed.

Verbs can also be associated with phases of the problem-solving process. "Assure" is often associated with engagement, while "assess," "ask," and "determine" best describe assessment. If actions are supposed to occur at certain phases of the helping process, verbs must be examined to see if they are consistent with the requisite phase. In addition, test takers are often asked to order actions of social workers. If response choices represent different actions, examining the verbs to assist with ordering is helpful. "Acknowledge" is usually done before "explore" or "explain."

Examining verbs which begin response choices is a helpful tool to use when two or more response choices appear equally viable. As not all response choices begin with verbs, it can only be used for some question formats. However, close attention must be paid to verb choice in some instances as it provides a concise way to determine if an action by a social worker is appropriate given material in the question, as well as where it is to occur within the problem-solving process.

Q: *Does the answer explicitly or implicitly involve the client?*

Social workers view clients as experts on their own situations and they should be regarded as such. Often response choices on the examinations are not correct as they only mention social workers acting and do not involve collaboration with clients. Even when actions may seem appropriate, they may be incorrect as they do not mention roles for the client. Test takers must view response choices carefully, asking whether clients are mentioned explicitly or implicitly. Response choices based on social workers making decisions about tasks in the problem-solving process, such as appropriate interventions, are not as good as those that base these decisions on discussions with clients. Even when social workers have sound advice or can take actions to assist clients, these answers are not preferred over those which mention working *with* clients to determine the reasons for the problems or intervene. The involvement of the client is often a crucial factor in answer selection.

Q: *Is a response choice being selected solely because it contains social work jargon or buzz words?*

ASWB examinations aim to determine whether social workers really understand the concepts being tested or are just selecting response choices because they sound correct or have answers that have social work "buzz words" such as "rapport," "empathy," "support system," "joining with a client," "strengths perspective," "from a client's perspective," and so on. Often, social workers have a hard time eliminating response choices that contain jargon that is important to effective practice. These are key concepts that are the cornerstone of competent social work services. However, a word or catch phrase does not make a response choice correct. A response choice may not be correct because the other parts of it are inadequate, false, or simply do not address the problem needing attention.

When seeing social work "buzz words" in response choices, it is essential to read the response choices critically. Perhaps they will not be as appealing if synonyms for these "buzz words" are used in their place. Often incorrect response choices are made more appealing by adding social work jargon to see if test takers will be lured by their inclusion. Most of the time jargon is in the incorrect response choices, serving as distractors. Test takers should not be influenced by the inclusion of fancy social work terms in response choices and need to select response choices based on their substantive merits, ensuring that they directly relate to the assessment of the chosen KSAs.

Q: *Has the question format been examined and broken down into its requisite components?*

On the ASWB examinations, social workers often struggle with application and reasoning questions that require them to take what has been learned and use it to identify correct answers given hypothetical contexts. These items require test takers are frustrated as they do not know what is being asked in questions and how to choose between response choices which seem similar. Becoming more familiar with the construction of multiple-choice tests, as well as remembering concepts that are hallmarks within the social work profession, can greatly assist.

Many social workers do not have experience taking multiple-choice tests and are unfamiliar with the format of questions. Application and reasoning questions are like funnels with several important parts.

Background—Often a question starts with background information such as why the client is receiving services, what type of services are being received, and/or demographic information about the client (such as age, gender identity, religion, sexual orientation, or other relevant data). The background, if present, is typically the first sentence of the question. If no background information is provided then it is not relevant to addressing the presenting problem or answering the question correctly.

Presenting Problem or Issue—Most questions ask test-takers to evaluate a variety of responses or actions to appropriately address identified concerns. Presenting problems can be briefly described in a sentence or two but are sometimes lengthier, such as in reasoning questions that are assessed using vignettes or scenarios. If there is background information provided in the question, the presenting problem or issue is described in the sentence or sentences between the background and the last sentence before the response choices. If there is no background information provided, the question begins with the problem or issue which commences with the last sentence before the response choice.

Question Stem—The last sentence or portion of a sentence before the response choices helps the test-taker understand the focus or intent of the question. The question stem often includes qualifying words or the lens that needs to be considered when evaluating the response choices, such as "using a task centered approach" or "a social justice perspective." This last sentence or question stem is often very specific and points the test taker in the correct direction, establishing the criterion to be used when evaluating the response choices.

The following example identifies the key components of a question.

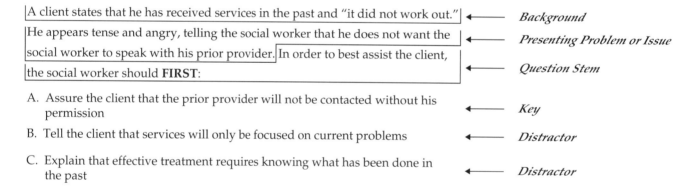

Q: Has the question been read or referred to more than once to distinguish the correct answer (known as the key) from the incorrect response choices (known as distractors)?

A key is the correct answer to the question which is based on content learned in social work educational programs. The ASWB tests assess knowledge so the key is superior to the alternatives based on conceptual information that was learned in school that is not contained in the other response choices.

Distractors are plausible, but incorrect response choices to a question. Rarely will response choices appear that can be easily eliminated. ASWB does not use "all of the above" or "none of the above" response choices. Distractors are similar in length and language to the keys or correct answer. Often distractors represent common mistakes made by social workers. Test takers often inappropriately select incorrect response choices or distractors as they feel that they incorporate or overlap correct ones. Each response choice must be assessed based on the explicit wording used and social workers must not assume redundancy between them.

Often selecting the correct answer requires rereading or referring back to the question. A good strategy is eliminating incorrect response choices in an iterative process. After eliminating the first incorrect response choice, a test taker should reread the question so its intent is clear before selecting the correct answer from the remaining alternate choice.

These are principles that must be considered when distinguishing the key from distractors. While not exhaustive, these themes are consistent across questions and can be used to assist with identifying correct answers. However, the degree to which each is relevant to a particular question varies. A question to help with test-taking is listed after each relevant concept.

- Social workers have groups, organizations, and communities as clients.
  - *Does the question specifically identify an individual or family as the client or could the level of intervention be bigger (the client is a group, an organization, and/or a community)?*
- Social workers do all types of intervention including provision of concrete services, case management, policy practice, and community organization.
  - *Does the question explicitly state the type of service being provided? If not, the KSA is universal across intervention types*
- Social workers respect client self-determination.
  - *Are any of the response choices more respectful of the client's right to make decisions?*
- Social workers are trained to identify the root causes of problems.
  - *Do any of the response choices address the underlying systematic issues rather than just those impacted?*
- Social workers engage collaboratively with clients.
  - *Do any of the response choices mention the client implicitly or explicitly as opposed to just the social worker?*
- Social workers use a systems approach to understanding functioning.
  - *Do any of the response choices consider the interplay between biopsychosocial-cultural-spiritual functioning or the micro, mezzo, and macro levels of intervention?*
- Social workers apply their knowledge in diverse settings and with many populations.
  - *Do any of the response choices reflect knowledge that can be generalized to all agencies, methods of practice, and client groups?*
- Social workers are committed to social justice and working with those who are oppressed.
  - *Do any of the response choices ensure equal rights, especially for those who are poor and/or marginalized?*

Section II:
Content and Practice Test for the ASWB Masters Examination

Self-Assessment

There is a separate content outline for each of the four ASWB examinations (Bachelors, Masters, Clinical, and Advanced Generalist). However, there is tremendous overlap in content across these tests. Sometimes a KSA is not listed in the same content area or is described slightly differently (e.g., "theories of human development" versus "developmental theories"). However, the knowledge needed to competently answer questions in this area is the same.

The good news is that doing well on one ASWB examination often means performing well on another. It is always easier to remember material that has been already learned than to learn it for the first time!

It is very helpful to review the content outline to concentrate studying in areas in which more preparation is needed. Many of these topics look familiar as they are the basis of social work educational programs. Topics in which basic content and/or key terms cannot be remembered or recalled must be foci for studying and indicated by circling "1." If some basic information and/or key terms is known about topics, there may be a need to fill in some gaps and "2" must be circled. Lastly, if all key concepts and terms of the topics, as well as their applicability to social work practice and impacts on client functioning, can be summarized, no additional preparation is needed and "3" can be circled. Adequate preparation means synthesizing material from multiple content areas and discussing all aspects of the KSAs easily and fluidly.

**Association of Social Work Boards'
Content Outline for Masters Examination**

	3 Well Prepared	2 Somewhat Prepared	1 Not Prepared

I. Human Development, Diversity, and Behavior in the Environment (27%)

Human Growth and Development

	3	2	1
Theories of human development throughout the lifespan (e.g., physical, social, emotional, cognitive, behavioral)	3	2	1
The indicators of normal and abnormal physical, cognitive, emotional, and sexual development throughout the lifespan	3	2	1
Theories of sexual development throughout the lifespan	3	2	1
Theories of spiritual development throughout the lifespan	3	2	1
Theories of racial, ethnic, and cultural development throughout the lifespan	3	2	1
The effects of physical, mental, and cognitive disabilities throughout the lifespan	3	2	1
The interplay of biological, psychological, social, and spiritual factors	3	2	1
Basic human needs	3	2	1
The principles of attachment and bonding	3	2	1
The effect of aging on biopsychosocial functioning	3	2	1
The impact of aging parents on adult children	3	2	1
Gerontology	3	2	1
Personality theories	3	2	1
Theories of conflict	3	2	1
Factors influencing self-image (e.g., culture, race, religion/spirituality, age, disability, trauma)	3	2	1
Body image and its impact (e.g., identity, self-esteem, relationships, habits)	3	2	1
Parenting skills and capacities	3	2	1
The effects of addiction and substance abuse on individuals, families, groups, organizations, and communities	3	2	1
Feminist theory	3	2	1
The impact of out-of-home placement (e.g., hospitalization, foster care, residential care, criminal justice system) on clients/client systems	3	2	1
Basic principles of human genetics	3	2	1
The family life cycle	3	2	1
Family dynamics and functioning and the effects on individuals, families, groups, organizations, and communities	3	2	1

Theories of couples development	3	2	1
The impact of physical and mental illness on family dynamics	3	2	1
Psychological defense mechanisms and their effects on behavior and relationships	3	2	1
Addiction theories and concepts	3	2	1
Systems and ecological perspectives and theories	3	2	1
Role theories	3	2	1
Theories of group development and functioning	3	2	1
Theories of social change and community development	3	2	1
The dynamics of interpersonal relationships	3	2	1
Models of family life education in social work practice	3	2	1
Strengths-based and resilience theories	3	2	1
The impact of stress, trauma, and violence	3	2	1
Crisis intervention theories	3	2	1
Theories of trauma-informed care	3	2	1
The impact of the environment (e.g., social, physical, cultural, political, and economic) on individuals, families, groups, organizations, and communities	3	2	1
The effects of life events, stressors, and crises on individuals, families, groups, organizations, and communities	3	2	1
Person-in-environment (PIE) theory	3	2	1
Communication theories and styles	3	2	1
Psychoanalytic and psychodynamic approaches	3	2	1
The impact of caregiving on families	3	2	1
The dynamics and effects of loss, separation, and grief	3	2	1

Concepts of Abuse and Neglect

Indicators and dynamics of abuse and neglect throughout the lifespan	3	2	1
The effects of physical, sexual, and psychological abuse on individuals, families, groups, organizations, and communities	3	2	1
The indicators, dynamics, and impact of exploitation across the lifespan (e.g., financial, immigration status, sexual trafficking)	3	2	1
The characteristics of perpetrators of abuse, neglect, and exploitation	3	2	1

Diversity, Social/Economic Justice, and Oppression

The effect of disability on biopsychosocial functioning throughout the lifespan	3	2	1
The effect of culture, race, and ethnicity on behaviors, attitudes, and identity	3	2	1
The effects of discrimination and stereotypes on behaviors, attitudes, and identity	3	2	1

(continued)

The influence of sexual orientation on behaviors, attitudes, and identity	3	2	1
The impact of transgender and transitioning process on behaviors, attitudes, identity, and relationships	3	2	1
Systemic (institutionalized) discrimination (e.g., racism, sexism, ageism)	3	2	1
The principles of culturally competent social work practice	3	2	1
Sexual orientation concepts	3	2	1
Gender and gender identity concepts	3	2	1
Social and economic justice	3	2	1
The effect of poverty on individuals, families, groups, organizations, and communities	3	2	1
The impact of social institutions on society	3	2	1
Criminal justice systems	3	2	1
The impact of globalization on clients/client systems (e.g., interrelatedness of systems, international integration, technology, environmental or financial crises, epidemics)	3	2	1

II. Assessment and Intervention Planning (24%)

Biopsychosocial History and Collateral Data

The components of a biopsychosocial assessment	3	2	1
The components and function of the mental status examination	3	2	1
Biopsychosocial responses to illness and disability	3	2	1
Biopsychosocial factors related to mental health	3	2	1
The indicators of psychosocial stress	3	2	1
Basic medical terminology	3	2	1
The indicators of mental and emotional illness throughout the lifespan	3	2	1
The types of information available from other sources (e.g., agency, employment, medical, psychological, legal, or school records)	3	2	1
Methods to obtain sensitive information (e.g., substance abuse, sexual abuse)	3	2	1
The indicators of addiction and substance abuse	3	2	1
The indicators of somatization	3	2	1
Co-occurring disorders and conditions	3	2	1
Symptoms of neurologic and organic disorders	3	2	1
The indicators of sexual dysfunction	3	2	1
Methods used to assess trauma	3	2	1
The indicators of traumatic stress and violence	3	2	1
Common psychotropic and non-psychotropic prescriptions and over-the-counter medications and their side effects	3	2	1

Assessment Methods and Techniques

The factors and processes used in problem formulation	3	2	1
Methods of involving clients/client systems in problem identification (e.g., gathering collateral information)	3	2	1
Techniques and instruments used to assess clients/client systems	3	2	1
Methods to incorporate the results of psychological and educational tests into assessment	3	2	1
Risk assessment methods	3	2	1
The indicators and risk factors of the client's/client system's danger to self and others	3	2	1
Methods to assess the client's/client system's strengths, resources, and challenges (e.g., individual, family, group, organization, community)	3	2	1
Methods to assess motivation, resistance, and readiness to change	3	2	1
Methods to assess the client's/client system's communication skills	3	2	1
Methods to assess the client's/client system's coping abilities	3	2	1
The indicators of the client's/client system's strengths and challenges	3	2	1
Methods to assess ego strengths	3	2	1
Placement options based on assessed level of care	3	2	1
The use of the *Diagnostic and Statistical Manual of Mental Disorders* of the American Psychiatric Association	3	2	1
The indicators of behavioral dysfunction	3	2	1
Methods to develop, review, and implement crisis plans	3	2	1
The principles and features of objective and subjective data	3	2	1
Basic and applied research design and methods	3	2	1
Data collection and analysis methods	3	2	1
Methods to assess reliability and validity in social work research	3	2	1

Intervention Planning

Methods to involve clients/client systems in intervention planning	3	2	1
The indicators of motivation, resistance, and readiness to change	3	2	1
Cultural considerations in the creation of an intervention plan	3	2	1
The criteria used in the selection of intervention/treatment modalities (e.g., client/client system abilities, culture, life stage)	3	2	1
The components of intervention, treatment, and service plans	3	2	1
Psychotherapies	3	2	1
The impact of immigration, refugee, or undocumented status on service delivery	3	2	1
Discharge, aftercare, and follow-up planning	3	2	1

(*continued*)

III.   Interventions With Clients/Client Systems (24%)

Intervention Processes and Techniques for Use Across Systems

The principles and techniques of interviewing (e.g., supporting, clarifying, focusing, confronting, validating, feedback, reflecting, language differences, use of interpreters, redirecting)	3	2	1
The phases of intervention and treatment	3	2	1
Problem-solving models and approaches (e.g., brief, solution-focused methods or techniques)	3	2	1
Methods to engage and motivate clients/client systems	3	2	1
Methods to engage and work with involuntary clients/client systems	3	2	1
Methods to obtain and provide feedback	3	2	1
The principles of active listening and observation	3	2	1
Verbal and nonverbal communication techniques	3	2	1
The concept of congruence in communication	3	2	1
Limit-setting techniques	3	2	1
The technique of role play	3	2	1
Role-modeling techniques	3	2	1
Techniques for harm reduction for self and others	3	2	1
Methods to teach coping and other self-care skills to clients/client systems	3	2	1
Client/client system self-monitoring techniques	3	2	1
Methods of conflict resolution	3	2	1
Crisis intervention and treatment approaches	3	2	1
Methods and approaches to trauma-informed care	3	2	1
Anger management techniques	3	2	1
Stress management techniques	3	2	1
Cognitive and behavioral interventions	3	2	1
Strengths-based and empowerment strategies and interventions	3	2	1
Client/client system contracting and goal-setting techniques	3	2	1
Partializing techniques	3	2	1
Assertiveness training	3	2	1
Task-centered approaches	3	2	1
Psychoeducation methods (e.g., acknowledging, supporting, normalizing)	3	2	1
Group work techniques and approaches (e.g., developing and managing group processes and cohesion)	3	2	1
Family therapy models, interventions, and approaches	3	2	1
Couples interventions and treatment approaches	3	2	1
The impact of out-of-home displacement (e.g., natural disaster, homelessness, immigration) on clients/client systems	3	2	1

Permanency planning	3	2	1
Mindfulness and complementary therapeutic approaches	3	2	1
The components of case management	3	2	1
Techniques used for follow-up	3	2	1
The elements of a case presentation	3	2	1
Methods to develop and evaluate measurable objectives for client/client system intervention, treatment, and/or service plans	3	2	1
Techniques used to evaluate a client's/client system's progress	3	2	1
Primary, secondary, and tertiary prevention strategies	3	2	1
The indicators of client/client system readiness for termination	3	2	1
Methods, techniques, and instruments used to evaluate social work practice	3	2	1
Evidence-based practice	3	2	1
Case recording for practice evaluation or supervision	3	2	1
Consultation approaches (e.g., referrals to specialists)	3	2	1
The process of interdisciplinary and intradisciplinary team collaboration	3	2	1
The basic terminology of professions other than social work (e.g., legal, educational)	3	2	1
The principles of case recording, documentation, and management of practice records	3	2	1

Intervention Processes and Techniques for Use With Larger Systems

Methods to establish program objectives and outcomes	3	2	1
Methods to assess the availability of community resources	3	2	1
Methods of service delivery	3	2	1
Theories and methods of advocacy for policies, services, and resources to meet clients'/client systems' needs	3	2	1
Methods to create, implement, and evaluate policies and procedures that minimize risk for individuals, families, groups, organizations, and communities	3	2	1
Concepts of social policy development and analysis	3	2	1
Techniques to inform and influence organizational and social policy	3	2	1
The principles and processes for developing formal documents (e.g., proposals, letters, brochures, pamphlets, reports, evaluations)	3	2	1
Methods to establish service networks or community resources	3	2	1
Community organizing and social planning methods	3	2	1
Methods of networking	3	2	1
Techniques for mobilizing community participation	3	2	1
Governance structures	3	2	1

(*continued*)

Theories of organizational development and structure	3	2	1
The effects of policies, procedures, regulations, and legislation on social work practice and service delivery	3	2	1
Quality assurance, including program reviews and audits by external sources	3	2	1
The impact of political environment on policy-making	3	2	1
Leadership and management techniques	3	2	1
Fiscal management techniques	3	2	1
Educational components, techniques, and methods of supervision	3	2	1
Methods to identify learning needs and develop learning objectives for supervisees	3	2	1
The effect of program evaluation findings on services	3	2	1
Methods to evaluate agency programs (e.g., needs assessment, formative/summative assessment, cost effectiveness, cost-benefit analysis, outcomes assessment)	3	2	1

IV.   Professional Relationships, Values, and Ethics (25%)

Professional Values and Ethical Issues

Legal and/or ethical issues related to the practice of social work, including responsibility to clients/client systems, colleagues, the profession, and society	3	2	1
Professional values and principles (e.g., competence, social justice, integrity, and dignity and worth of the person)	3	2	1
Techniques to identify and resolve ethical dilemmas	3	2	1
Client/client system competence and self-determination (e.g., financial decisions, treatment decisions, emancipation, age of consent, permanency planning)	3	2	1
Techniques for protecting and enhancing client/client system self-determination	3	2	1
The client's/client system's right to refuse services (e.g., medication, medical treatment, counseling, placement, etc.)	3	2	1
Professional boundaries in the social worker–client/client system relationship (e.g., power differences, conflicts of interest, etc.)	3	2	1
Self-disclosure principles and applications	3	2	1
Legal and/or ethical issues regarding documentation	3	2	1
Legal and/or ethical issues regarding termination	3	2	1
Legal and/or ethical issues related to death and dying	3	2	1
Research ethics (e.g., institutional review boards, use of human subjects, informed consent)	3	2	1
Models of supervision and consultation (e.g., individual, peer, group)	3	2	1

Ethical issues in supervision and management	3	2	1
Methods to create, implement, and evaluate policies and procedures for social worker safety	3	2	1
The supervisee's role in supervision (e.g., identifying learning needs, self-assessment, prioritizing, etc.)	3	2	1
Accreditation and/or licensing requirements	3	2	1
Professional development activities to improve practice and maintain current professional knowledge (e.g., in-service training, licensing requirements, reviews of literature, workshops)	3	2	1

Confidentiality

The elements of client/client system reports	3	2	1
The principles and processes of obtaining informed consent	3	2	1
The use of client/client system records	3	2	1
Legal and/or ethical issues regarding confidentiality, including electronic information security	3	2	1
Legal and/or ethical issues regarding mandatory reporting (e.g., abuse, threat of harm, impaired professionals, etc.)	3	2	1

Professional Development and Use of Self

The components of the social worker–client/client system relationship	3	2	1
The client's/client system's role in the problem-solving process	3	2	1
The social worker's role in the problem-solving process	3	2	1
Methods to clarify the roles and responsibilities of the social worker and client/client system in the intervention process	3	2	1
The principles and techniques for building and maintaining a helping relationship	3	2	1
The concept of acceptance and empathy in the social worker–client/client system relationship	3	2	1
The dynamics of power and transparency in the social worker–client/client system relationship	3	2	1
Ethical issues related to dual relationships	3	2	1
The impact of transference and countertransference in the social worker–client/client system relationship	3	2	1
The impact of domestic, intimate partner, and other violence on the helping relationship	3	2	1
The dynamics of diversity in the social worker–client/client system relationship	3	2	1
The effect of the client's developmental level on the social worker–client relationship	3	2	1
Social worker self-care principles and techniques	3	2	1
Burnout, secondary trauma, and compassion fatigue	3	2	1

(*continued*)

The components of a safe and positive work environment	3	2	1
Professional objectivity in the social worker–client/client system relationship	3	2	1
The influence of the social worker's own values and beliefs on the social worker–client/client system relationship	3	2	1
Time management approaches	3	2	1
The impact of transference and countertransference within supervisory relationships	3	2	1
The influence of the social worker's own values and beliefs on interdisciplinary collaboration	3	2	1

Key Social Work Terms

SOME IMPORTANT SOCIAL WORK TERMS

In addition to terms defined in other parts of this study guide, these 250 words or concepts are important for social workers to know as they relate to one or more of the content areas on the social work licensing exam. Studying words that may be unfamiliar will help with performance on recall or application questions. These words could also appear in reasoning questions that contain scenarios or vignettes. Sometimes the actual terms do not appear, but questions ask about key concepts that are related to these terms.

aberrant: markedly different from an accepted norm; deviant, atypical or nonconforming

abstinence: practice of not doing something; often used to describe an activity which may be enjoyable such as drinking alcohol or engaging in sexual activity

acculturation: process of individuals or groups acquiring or adopting the cultural traits, practices, and values of another culture while maintaining their own cultural identity; does not restrict need to change to those in minority

act of commission: engaging in an act of malfeasance when knowing the action or omission is illegal

act of omission: failure to perform a legal duty; social work task that is not done despite the need to do so according to established standard of care

active listening: technique that involves listening closely and asking questions as needed to fully understand latent and manifest communication, as well as feeling associated with content of message; critical to client-centered therapy

acuity: sharpness or ability, particularly of the mind, vision, or hearing

acute: short or episodic; often characterized by high intensity and unanticipated (sudden onset); not chronic

ad hoc: created or done for a particular needed purpose; occurs temporarily to fulfil a given need

advance directive: written statement of wishes regarding medical treatment to ensure those wishes are honored in the event that they cannot be communicated to doctors; types of advance directives, include, but are not limited to, living wills, medical powers of attorney and do-not-resuscitate (DNR) orders

age of consent: legal age at which a minor can legally engage in a behavior without parental consent; varies by jurisdiction and type of activity; minors are granted right to confidentiality if they are over the age of consent as they are regarded in same manner as adults

ageism: stereotyping based on age; form of discrimination

amelioration: aimed at improving or making better; lessoning of symptoms or severity of disease, illness, or disorder; eradicating a social problem

antecedents: things or events that existed before or logically precede others; often identified as causes of maladaptive behaviors

assent: agreement or approval by someone not able to give legal consent due to age or cognitive ability

assimilation: process of individuals or groups adopting the dominant cultural norms, practices, and values, often leading to the loss or suppression of their own cultural identity

atrophy: decreasing in size and function; shrinkage of muscle or nerve tissue; can be caused by aging, inactivity, malnutrition, and other injuries, illnesses, and conditions

aversion therapy: behavior therapy designed to make clients give up undesirable habits by causing them to associate these habits with unpleasant effects

bartering: acceptance of services, goods or other non-monetary payments from clients in return for services; creates the potential for conflicts of interest, exploitation, and inappropriate boundaries in social workers' relationships with clients; only permissible in very limited cultural contexts

baseline: functioning before the intervention occurs; intervention is often the service or treatment delivered by a social worker

beneficence: to act for the benefit of others; moral obligation of helping professionals to do no harm and act in the best interest of others

benign: not damaging or threatening to life; often used to describe growths that are not cancerous

boundary violation: harmful or potentially harmful deviation from established professional standards dictated by professional relationships; often involves exploitation

capacity building: intervention aimed at enhancing the abilities or resources of an individual, group, organization, or community

capitation: payment structure used with insurance companies; provider or facility is paid a fixed amount for each person; risk is taken by entity to deliver services under cost of contract; incentive to provider or facility to promote wellness

catchment area: geographic area which defines who are eligible for a service or benefit if they meet additional admission requirements (if any established)

centralization: consolidation of power or functions within an organization; associated with bureaucracy and "top down" approach to operations

chronic: long standing; persisting for a long time or reoccurring; continual

civil disobedience: nonviolent opposition or protest aimed at making government change; can include refusing to obey certain laws

client self-monitoring: form of data-gathering in which clients are asked to systematically observe and record specific targets such as their own thoughts, emotions, body feelings, and behaviors; often used in cognitive behavioral therapy

close-ended questioning: soliciting information which requires choice from a limited number of options (such as yes/no); used to structure assessment; beneficial when time is limited or specific information required

cognitive dissonance: holding two beliefs, values, or attitudes that contradict each other; can cause mental discomfort and psychological stress

cognitive distortions: inaccurate, irrational views of reality which may serve to assist with coping from adverse events; unhealthy thoughts which are often addressed in cognitive behavioral therapy

cognitive-behavioral therapy (CBT): therapeutic approach that focuses on identifying and changing negative thoughts and behaviors to improve mental health

collateral information: records or documents associated with the client that are used in the problem-solving process; may be used to corroborate information provided by the client

collective bargaining: the process by which unionized employees and their employers negotiate about working conditions, salaries, benefits, and so forth

community development: focus on enhancing social bonds between and increasing leadership skills of residents, as well as revitalizing local geographic areas

comorbidity: occurring at the same time, such as having a psychological and medical problem simultaneously; often referred to as co-occurring

compassion fatigue: stress resulting from working with those who have experienced trauma; symptoms include apathy, feeling overwhelmed, exhaustion, pessimism, and feeling powerlessness; sometimes referred to as the "cost of caring"

conflict resolution: informal or formal process that two or more parties use to find an acceptable solution to a dispute or disagreement

confrontation: therapeutic technique of calling attention to distorted thinking, behavioral patterns, or ineffective communication so that it can be addressed

congruent communication: verbal and nonverbal language and actions provide consistent messages; important for intimacy and emotional connection

conjoint therapy: partners in a relationship or members of a family are treated together in joint sessions, instead of being treated separately; also called conjoint counseling

consent: legal permission for something to happen or agreement to do something; cannot be obtained from those not legally authorized to make decisions

consultation: usually time-limited work or guidance provided due to specialized expertise; advice does not have to be followed (non-binding)

continuity of care: ensuring that there are no gaps or duplication in service; often a focus when moving from one provider to another, or being discharged from a hospital or other inpatient setting

continuum of care: range of services geared to address varying levels of need from most to least severe; needed to appropriately address problems as they get better and/or worse

contraindication: reason for a person not to receive a medication, treatment, or intervention as it not appropriate and/or could be harmful

control group: group that receives no intervention or treatment; compared to functioning of the experimental group

convalescence: time spent recovering from an illness, injury, or other medical condition; often referred to a "recuperation"

cooptation: strategy for reducing resistance by including opponents in decision making; aims to change viewpoints of those who are oppositional

cost-benefit analysis: examining the costs associated with service delivery in light of the financial benefits from program outcomes

countertransference: emotional reaction of helper which can be used to identify the reaction of others to the one being assisted; based on the helper's own psychological needs which are revealed through conscious responses; historically seen as a hinderance, but now viewed as helpful to the therapeutic process

court-ordered treatment: assessment, intervention, or service that is mandated by a judge

custodial care: assisting others to meet their basic needs and with activities of daily living; no specialized treatment provided such as health or mental health care focused on rehabilitation

DAP note: popular standardized format to write psychotherapy or progress notes (acronym for data, assessment, and plan)

decentralization: location of power and decision-making authority with those who are directly working on the frontlines instead of those in upper management positions

decompensation: loss of typical functioning; can relate to coherent thought, emotional regulation, activities of daily living, and/or cognitive functioning

deductive reasoning: "top down" approach to understanding whether or not an assumption is true; making an assumption based on widely accepted facts or premises; drawing a conclusion based on reasoning

delirium: disordered thought that can include changes in cognition (disorientation, memory impairment, or language disturbance), hallucinations, restlessness, and misinterpretation of sounds or sights; acute state which develops quickly; can fluctuate over a short period; multiple etiologies; usually temporary and treatable

delusion: false, fixed belief despite evidence to the contrary; believing something that is not true

dementia: general term for loss of memory, language, problem-solving and other thinking abilities that are severe enough to interfere with daily life; primarily impacts those over the age of 65; likelihood of developing dementia significantly increases with age

descriptive statistics: summary data that provides information about a larger sample or population; mean, median, mode, standard deviation, and so forth

desensitization: gradual reduction in adverse reaction to stimuli due to exposure or as a result of behavioral techniques aimed at reducing anxiety or fear

developmental disability: condition occurring before adulthood that results in life-long functional impairment; may be due to genetic or other disorder present at birth or an accident during childhood that causes significant difficulties with cognition, mobility, and/or other functional domains

differential diagnosis: process of distinguishing between mental, physical, or other problems that result in similar symptoms or might be causes for behavior

discharge plan: structured plan to ensure follow up, safety, and continuity of care after termination; often used when leaving inpatient and/or medical facilities; focused on sustaining any progress made and "next steps"

double bind: contradictory messages or requests in which affirmatively responding to one negates the other; situation in which any choice results in unpleasant outcome

dual relationship: having another association with a client, such as friend, family member, intimate partner, coworker, and so forth; should be avoided due to boundary violations

duty to warn: obligation of mental health professionals to inform others of dangerous client behavior; exception to confidentiality to prevent injury to others

dysphoria: general sense of dissatisfaction

ecological perspective: focuses on the interrelationship between individuals and their environment; emphasis on the interactions between people and the larger contexts in which they exist

ego dystonic: thoughts, impulses, or wishes that are repugnant or unacceptable to one's sense of self; sometimes referred to as "ego alien"

ego strength: ability to effectively cope with stressors and challenges, maintain a sense of self, and make adaptive decisions

ego syntonic: thoughts, impulses, or wishes that are acceptable to self as they are compatible with one's views and ways of thinking

encopresis: passage of feces which is involuntary; may be due to emotional or psychological problems; often treated with behavioral intervention; medical causes should be ruled out

endogenous depression: depression that cannot be linked to an external psychological stressor so it is assumed to be caused by a biological or genetic factor

enmeshed family: members have little to no autonomy or personal boundaries

entitlement: feeling that special consideration is deserved; right or benefit of a person or group; benefit program for which one has the legal right to receive

entropy: degree of chaos, randomness, disorganization, and disorder in a system or family

enuresis: urination that is involuntary; may be caused by medical problem, which should first be ruled out, or psychological distress

equilibrium: state of balance or stability

equity: approach to resource allocation in which individuals receive their fair share of the goods and services in society; distinct from equality which provides each resources to all as equity sometimes required treating people differently from others to compensate to lack of opportunities

ethical dilemma: situation in which two ethical values or standards conflict with one another

ethnocentrism: judging one's own social, cultural, or racial group as superior to others; tendency to view and/or judge others' ethnicity in light of one's own

etiology: cause of a behavior, disorder, or disease; root of the problem

exogenous depression: depression caused by a distressing event or situation; also called "reactive depression"

exploitation: taking unfair advantage of people, situations, and so forth for personal benefit

external locus of control: belief that outcomes are not under one's control, but rather due to environmental factors, luck, chance, or randomness

external validity: extent to which results are generalizable

extinction: fading and disappearance of behavior that was previously learned by association with another event; behavior eventually becomes extinct if reward no longer follows the behavior

extrinsic reward: positive consequence for behavior or action that is not natural

face validity: accepting the accuracy of a report, instrument, or document based on whether it appears to represent a construct or constructs

false negative: inaccurate test results indicating negative findings (or absence of a condition) when they are really positive (or condition is present)

false positive: inaccurate test results indicating positive findings (or presence of a condition) when they are really negative (or condition is not present)

feasibility study: assessment to determine whether goals, objectives, or plans are achievable given available resources

fee splitting: receiving compensation for referrals made to other professionals; unethical in social work practice

fee-for-service: payment method for services, in which providers set their own fees, that are paid in part or full by recipients and/or insurance companies

flooding: behavioral technique in which stimuli that cause anxiety are presented with regularity and intensity so that they no longer produce the adverse response

formative evaluation: gathering and analyzing feedback during the development or implementation of a program, project, or product; often used to help improve processes

free association: process used in psychoanalysis which encourages client to verbalize whatever thoughts come to mind, no matter how embarrassing, illogical, or irrelevant; allows unconscious ideas and feelings to be revealed so they can be interpreted

gatekeeping: people, processes, or structures that limit or obstruct access; may be tied to perpetuating systems or rationing resources

generativity: orientation towards making the world a better place for others; benevolence; most commonly occurs during middle adulthood according to Erickson

genogram: diagram illustrating a client's family members, how they are related, and their medical history; used to see hereditary patterns of behavior and medical and psychological factors that are shared or influential

gentrification: making physical improvements to housing within a neighborhood that result in attracting wealthier individuals to the area; displaces long-term residents who cannot afford to live in the gentrified area due to increased property values

globalization: growing interdependence of the world's economies, cultures, and populations, brought about by cross-border trade in goods and services, technology, and flows of investment, people, and information

grandiosity: exaggerated sense of self, importance, or ability; may be regarded as a delusion of grandeur when extreme

groupthink: when a group of individuals reaches a consensus without critical evaluation of the consequences or alternatives

hallucination: false sensory perception that is believed to be real though it is not; most common are auditory and visual; typically a symptom of a psychotic disorder, but can be caused by substance use, medical problem, or another condition

harm reduction: approach designed to reduce the negative effects of risky behaviors, rather than to eliminate the behaviors altogether

hematuria: presence of blood in a person's urine; characterized as "gross" when blood can be easily seen or "micro" when it cannot but it is visible under a microscope

histrionic behavior: manipulative behavior that is dramatic, demanding, self-indulgent, and attention seeking

human relations theory: school of organizational thought that emphasizes the importance of social and psychological factors in the workplace as a means of influencing employee productivity

hypomania: milder version of mania that lasts for a short period (usually a few days); characterized by elevated mood, enhanced irritability, higher energy level, being more talkative, and/or feeling more confident; does not cause significant distress or greatly impair functioning related to work, family or social life like mania

id: part of the personality that contains the instinctual, biological drives; most primitive component of the personality; located in the unconscious; desire for immediate gratification begins in infancy, until the ego begins to develop

ideas of reference: belief that irrelevant or benign things directly refer to oneself or have special personal significance; often referred to as "delusions of reference"

ideation: formation of ideas or beliefs; suicidal ideation requires social workers to assess for harm

impaired colleague: coworker whose functioning has deteriorated because of a physical or mental problem, including substance use, disability, death of family or friend, burnout/stress, illness, and so forth; address by bringing to the attention of the person, when feasible, so accommodations can be made to eliminate impact on service delivery

in vivo: conditions that approximate real-life; often used to describe face-to-face encounters, such as in-vivo supervision

incongruency: lack of consistency such as when a subjective assessment is at odds with reality; gap between real and ideal self

incontinence: inability to control urination or secretion of feces

inductive reasoning: making broad generalizations from specific observations; opposite of deductive reasoning

inferential statistics: used to draw conclusions about a population based on sample data

informed consent: legal permission granted with full knowledge of the possible risks and benefits

interdisciplinary: analyzes, synthesizes and harmonizes links between disciplines into a coordinated and coherent whole; distinct from multidisciplinary

intermittent reinforcement: when only some responses are rewarded; operant behavioral technique; difficult to extinguish behaviors that have been intermittently reinforced

internal locus of control: belief that things that happen are greatly influenced by own abilities, actions, or mistakes

internal validity: confidence that independent variable causes the dependent variable (cause-effect)

intersectionality: interconnected nature of social categorizations such as race, gender, and class; often refers to overlapping systems of discrimination and disadvantage

involuntary commitment: legal process that results in a person who is deemed a danger to self or others being confined to a hospital or facility without consent; length of stay varies depending on continued presence of dangerous behavior; reevaluation occurs regularly

latent content: symbolic or hidden meaning which is not overtly expressed or evident; focus of psychoanalysis as it repressed urges and desires

learned helplessness: feeling that have no control over a situation which results in behaving in a dependent or powerless manner; leads to failure to engage in opportunities to change; prevents activity or action

least restrictive environment: conditions which have the fewest controls or those which approximate the settings which would naturally occur; often with people with disabilities to ensure inclusion in greater society or avoid segregation in education

lethality: ability to cause death or serious harm

level of care: degree of assistance needed by person seeking service; determination often needed to identify appropriate reimbursement for services; related to medical necessity in health care

living will: type of advance directive in which medical treatments, procedures, and medications desired and not desired are specified in the event that patients can't communicate their wishes; may be referred to as a medical directive or an advance healthcare directive

locus of control: influence over life conditions; external locus of control regards outcomes as arising from external or situational factors that cannot be influenced while internal locus of control regards outcomes as due to one's own actions and abilities

longitudinal study: research using data that is gathered on the same subjects, cohort, or population repeatedly over time

magical thinking: belief that one's own actions influence external events in the environment; often referred to as "superstitious thinking"

maleficence: act of committing harm or evil; prevented by using evidence-based interventions and adhering to accepted standards of care

malingering: exaggerate or feign illness in order to escape duty or work; motivation to engage in behavior is intentional with external (secondary) gain

managed care: coordination of benefits by a third-party (usually payers) to reduce the cost of providing health care and ensuring continuity of treatment

mandated clients: those who receive services involuntarily as they have been ordered by courts, legal entities, or government-sanctioned organizations such as child protective services

mandatory reporting: requirement by law to inform authorities of suspected abuse or neglect; many apply to treatment of children, older adults, those with cognitive or other disabilities, and so forth; social workers serve as mandatory reporters

mania: extreme state of excitement and overactivity; often accompanied by overoptimism, grandiosity, and/or impaired judgment; preoccupation with an activity or idea when used as a suffix, such as with the impulse control disorders of kleptomania and pyromania

manifest content: material that is overtly expressed or evident; the dreams, thoughts, or fantasies that are remembered in psychoanalysis

means test: method for determining financial eligibility for a benefit, service, or program; poverty line often used as benchmark for eligibility; assessment based on income and/or assets

medical necessity: services or supplies that are deemed essential to diagnose or treat medical or behavioral conditions according to accepted standards of care

mental status exam: assessment of current mental capacity through evaluation of general appearance, behavior, beliefs, mood, and cognition (attention, orientation, memory, etc.)

microaggression: prejudiced thoughts or discriminatory actions in indirect, subtle, or unintentional forms

mindfulness: practice of cultivating present-moment awareness and non-judgmental acceptance, often used as a therapeutic technique to reduce stress and promote well-being

modeling: effective teaching technique in which learning occurs through imitating the action of others

morbidity: rate of disease in a group or population; presence of unhealthiness or psychological state marked by excessive gloom

mortality: state of being mortal (destined to die); used for death rate, or the number of deaths in a certain group of people in a certain period of time

motivational interviewing: counseling approach aimed at helping make changes; techniques focus on resolving ambivalence, eliciting change talk and behavior, and helping utilize internal motivation to make needed changes

mutual aid: reciprocal care; approach used with groups of those with same problem or condition who provide peer assistance and/or support

needs assessment: identifying resources, opportunities, and challenges to address problems or wants

negative entropy: system becoming less disordered or more ordered; growing or developing

negligence: failure to use reasonable care or caution

nonverbal communication: information which is generated from gestures, facial expressions, tone of voice, posture, and so forth; may be congruent (consistent) or incongruent (inconsistent) with verbal communication

object permanence: understanding that something exists even if it cannot be seen due to the ability to form a mental representation of the object or person

ombudsman: an official who investigate, settles, and reports on complaints which can involve violations of human rights or systemic issues; often referred to as a "public advocate" when working for a government authority

open-ended questions: inquiry that requires qualitative, more in-depth answers, not using pre-defined choices; useful in social work interview

overgeneralization: inappropriately applying conclusions based on one situation to others; falsely predicting outcomes based on past experiences which differ significantly

overrepresentation: disproportionately higher incidence or greater presence of a characteristic than expected; may be desired to ensure inclusion of minority groups; impacts generalizability of findings as proportions do not match what would be found typically or generally

palliative care: medical care that focuses on comfort rather than providing a care; goal is to reduce the severity of a disease or slow its progress

paradoxical directive: prescribing the symptoms or behaviors that are targeted for change; often referred to as "reverse psychology"

paraphrasing: therapeutic technique of using different words to re-state assertions to improve understanding and help with analyzing meaning

parity: equality between two or more constructs or policies; social workers often advocate that mental health care should be treated with same care and funding as physical care

partialization: breaking down issues or processes into incremental steps or actions

peer support: guidance by individuals with lived experiences to others facing similar challenges, often through mutual sharing and understanding

permanency planning: assessing and preparing children for long-term care when in out-of-home placements such as with family, resource families, or residential facilities

person-in-environment perspective: professional view that examines the mutual interactions and fit between clients and their social environment

pluralism: system in which two or more states, groups, principles, and so forth coexist; philosophy that society should contain those with diverse views which are promoted

positive regard: unconditional acceptance of others without judgment

power of attorney: legal authorization for a designated person to make decisions about another person's property, finances, or medical care

privileged communication: legal right to keep professional interactions private; applies to doctor-patient and lawyer-client discussions; a psychotherapist-patient privilege was established in the Federal Rules of Evidence in 1996 with the *Jaffee v. Redmond* case

pro bono: provision of services free-of-charge, typically for individuals who cannot afford them

professional development: activities aimed at advancing skills, traits and competencies that contribute to your success in the workplace

prognosis: prediction of the course, duration, severity, and outcome of a condition, disease, or disorder; helps a client weigh the benefits of different treatment options

projective test: personality test designed to let a person respond to ambiguous stimuli, presumably revealing hidden emotions and internal conflicts of the person

proxy: someone who is authorized to act on behalf of another; used to describe a decision or vote made for another

psychoeducation: providing information to those seeking or receiving mental health services and/or their families about the nature of disorders, treatment, and the skills needed to avoid relapse

psychopathology: scientific study of mental illness or disorders

psychopharmacology: use of medication to treat mental disorders; some disorders, such as those characterized by psychosis, require this approach

psychosis: incapacitating mental functioning characterized by impaired thinking, reasoning, and reality testing; distorted perceptions; inappropriate affect or emotional reactions; ideas of reference; hallucinations; and/or delusions

quality improvement: ongoing, systematic approach to identifying and addressing areas for improvement in delivery processes and outcomes

reality testing: assessing limitations in light of biological, physiological, social, or environmental actualities; distinguish between fantasy and real life

reasonable accommodation: adjustments to assure that an individual with a disability has rights and privileges equal to those without disabilities

recusal: remove from participation due to conflict or potential conflict of interest; used in law to disqualify a judge or jury by reason of prejudice or conflict of interest

referral: recommendation of a specialized service or practitioner; can involve the act of sending client

reinforcement: process in which the frequency or probability of a response is increased; used in operant conditioning

relapse: deterioration after a period of improvement

reliability: consistency in measurement or findings

respite care: temporary assistance to persons who need ongoing help to provide relief for regular caregivers; essential to avoid caregiving burnout

restorative justice: approach with emphasizes repairing harm caused by criminal behavior; emphasizes that those most affected by criminal behavior should participate in the process and resolution

restricted funds: monies or resources that can only be used for an intended purpose specified by the granter or funder

risk assessment: process of determining the danger that an individual would likely pose to self or others

role complementarity: acting in an expected manner; performing appropriately in assumed roles; opposite of "role discomplementarity"

role reversal: exchanging their duties and/or positions; can be used as a therapeutic technique in psychodrama to help increase understanding of others' feelings and experiences

rumination: regurgitating food and then swallowing it; being preoccupied with certain obsessive thoughts

safety net: programs, services, and/or benefits that assist to meet basic needs; intended to be the last resort for individuals and families

scapegoat: person blamed for the wrongdoings, mistakes, or faults of others; family role focused on creating other problems and concerns, often through misbehavior, to deflect attention away from the real family issue(s)

scientific management theory: analyzes work flows to improve economic efficiency, especially labor productivity; attempts to increase the productivity of workers through scientific study and analyzing their movements

secondary prevention: screening to identify diseases in the earliest stages, before the onset of signs and symptoms, through measures such as mammography and regular blood pressure testing

self-actualization: full realization of creative, intellectual, and social potential; results from internal drive and external reward

self-help: practice of taking personal responsibility and initiative to improve one's mental, emotional

separation anxiety: distress experienced when confronted with actual or imagined disconnection from another; typical part of child development, but may need intervention if prolonged or intense

serotonin: a neurotransmitter in the brain that is the key to mood regulation

shaping: reinforcing progressively closer approximations to the desired behaviors; behavior management technique

single-subject design: using repeated measurements before and after the introduction of intervention to see variability in thoughts, feelings, and/or actions; stable baseline required before introduction of treatment; ethical issues associated with intervention withdrawal (reversal designs)

SMART goals: objectives that are specific, measurable, achievable, relevant, and time-bound

SOAP note: format used for reporting in records of those receiving services in healthcare settings (acronym for subjective, objective, assessment, and plan)

social control: process of restricting actions of others through policy or interventions; often done to promote public safety

social desirability bias: tendency to answer questions in a manner that looks favorably; results in overreporting of good positive answers and underreporting of negative answers

social exchange theory: weighing potential benefits versus risks before taking action; change will only occur when benefits are perceived as being more salient than the risks

social role theory: considers most activity to be the acting-out of socially defined categories that have rights, duties, expectations, norms, and acceptable behaviors

social work interview: purposeful conversations between practitioners and clients, involving verbal and nonverbal communication

somatization: psychological distress that is unconsciously expressed as physical ailments; counseling can help to address; motivation is unconscious with no apparent gain for the illness or condition

specifier: extension to a formal diagnosis that specifies one or more particular features, like onset or severity

splitting: failure to recognize positive and negative qualities as a cohesive whole; symptom of borderline personality disorder; cognitive distortion characterized by "all or nothing" thinking

standard of care: level and type of service that a reasonably competent and skilled professional, with similar education and experience, would have provided under the circumstances

strategic planning: in-depth process to identify mission, vision, and goals, as well as resources needed to achieve desired outcomes; should include clients, employees, and stakeholders

stratification: arrangement or classification into different groups; often done based on power, prestige, or wealth (social stratification)

strengths perspective: focus on the resources of clients and client systems upon which to build interventions

summarizing: therapeutic technique of consolidating gains which often includes listing evidence of progress

summative evaluation: type of evaluation conducted at the end of a program or project, with the goal of assessing its overall effectiveness

superego: part of the personality that represents internalized societal rules, morals, and values

system of care: collaborative approach that involve multiple service providers, agencies, and community stakeholders to provide coordinated and comprehensive support to individuals and families

systematic discrimination: rules, practices, policies, or laws that favor one group over another due to inherent prejudice or bias; results in perpetuating a lack of opportunities and disadvantage for some within society

systems theory: examines clients within the context of their relationships, social systems, and environments, emphasizing the interconnectedness and interdependence of various factors

Tarasoff decision: landmark California court decision that stipulates that those engaged in psychotherapy have a duty to protect or warn third parties if client poses an imminent and foreseeable threats to them; established "duty to warn" mandate

tardive dyskinesia: neurological syndrome that results in repetitive, involuntary, purposeless movements; caused by the long-term use of certain drugs which are used for the treatment of psychiatric and other conditions; usually treated by stopping or minimizing use of the offending drug

task group: group formed to solve a problem, provide a service, or create a product

task-centered treatment: short-term intervention in which problems and goals/activities needed to address them are identified with clear timeframes for completion; highly structured; client responsible and highly involved in the change effort

tertiary prevention: intervention with those who are already affected; goals focused on improving quality of life by reducing limitations or delaying complications

third party payers: monetary reimbursement by insurance companies or government agencies for services provided to clients

token economy: behavior management strategy in which points to be used for a reward are awarded when desirable behavior is exhibited (positive reinforcement); points are also removed in some plans when undesirable behavior occurs (negative reinforcement)

tolerance: capacity to endure continued use or exposure without adverse reaction; can increase over time, especially with regard to drug or alcohol use

transference: emotional reactions by clients in the therapeutic process due to unresolved experiences and/or unconscious thoughts; usually focused on the helper as a result of displacement or projection

triangulation: use of exclusion or threats in a three-person relationship to maintain control; adding a third person to a two-person interaction or relationship to ease tension; often seen in dysfunctional families; use of different data sources in research to increase credibility and confidence in findings

unconditional positive regard: involves showing complete support and acceptance of a person no matter what that person says or does

uninvolved parenting: overall sense of indifference by caregivers; limited engagement with their children and rarely implement rules; not always intentional, as caregivers are often struggling with their own issues; referred to as uninvolved parenting

utilization review: process to determine the level of care needed and whether services being delivered are justified; part of quality assurance process; often conducted by third-party payers or insurers

validity: accuracy of measure or finding; extent to which survey or interview appraises what it intends to assess; differs from reliability that is necessary, but not sufficient for validity

vicarious trauma: psychological and other distress based on interactions with those who have been traumatized; usually develops over time

voucher: certificate which allows a recipient to get a designated good or service; usually prescriptive in scope (amount to be received, time frame, etc.)

withdrawal: physical and/or psychological removal from a situation, substance, or condition; symptoms may need immediate attention, including medical monitoring

xenophobia: dislike of or prejudice against people from other countries or who are different from oneself generally

Content Area I: Human Development, Diversity, and Behavior in the Environment (27%)

Human Growth and Development

THEORIES OF HUMAN DEVELOPMENT THROUGHOUT THE LIFESPAN (E.G., PHYSICAL, SOCIAL, EMOTIONAL, COGNITIVE, BEHAVIORAL)

Social work theories are general explanations that are supported by evidence obtained through the scientific method. A theory may explain human behavior by describing how humans interact with each other or react to certain stimuli. Because human behavior is so complex, numerous theories are utilized to guide practice.

Often, the name of the theory will not be used in a question, but understanding it will be essential to selecting the correct answer.

Study the theories broadly to understand their general theme or focus, and deeply enough to know the meaning of terms originating from them that may be mentioned in exam questions.

Social Development

Human beings are inherently social. Developing competencies in this domain enhances a person's mental health, success in work, and ability to achieve in life tasks.

Erik Erikson was interested in how children socialize and how this affects their sense of self. He saw personality as developing throughout the life course and looked at identity crises as the focal point for each stage of human development.

According to Erikson, there are eight distinct stages, with two possible outcomes. Successful completion of each stage results in a healthy personality and successful interactions with others. Failure to successfully complete a stage can result in a reduced ability to complete further stages and, therefore, a more unhealthy personality and sense of self. These stages, however, can be resolved successfully at a later time.

Trust Versus Mistrust

From birth to 1 year of age, children begin to learn the ability to trust others based upon the consistency of their caregiver(s). If trust develops successfully, the child gains confidence and security in the world and is able to feel secure even when threatened. Unsuccessful completion of this stage can result in an inability to trust, and therefore a sense of fear about the inconsistent world. It may result in anxiety, heightened insecurities, and feelings of mistrust in the world around them.

Autonomy Versus Shame and Doubt

Between the ages of 1 and 3, children begin to assert their independence by walking away from their mother, picking which toy to play with, and making choices about what they like to wear, to eat, and so on. If children in this stage are encouraged and supported in their increased independence, they become more confident and secure in their own ability to survive in the world. If children are criticized, overly controlled, or not given the opportunity to assert themselves, they begin to feel inadequate in their ability to survive, and may then become overly dependent upon others while lacking self-esteem and feeling a sense of shame or doubt in their own abilities.

Initiative Versus Guilt

Around age 3 and continuing to age 6, children assert themselves more frequently. They begin to plan activities, make up games, and initiate activities with others. If given this opportunity, children develop a sense of initiative, and feel secure in their ability to lead others and make decisions. Conversely, if this tendency is squelched, either through criticism or control, children develop a sense of guilt. They may feel like nuisances to others and will therefore remain followers, lacking self-initiative.

Industry Versus Inferiority

From age 6 to puberty, children begin to develop a sense of pride in their accomplishments. They initiate projects, see them through to completion, and feel good about what they have achieved. If children are encouraged and reinforced for their initiative, they begin to feel industrious and feel confident in their ability to achieve goals. If this initiative is not encouraged but instead restricted, children begin to feel inferior, doubting their abilities, and failing to reach their potential.

Identity Versus Role Confusion

During adolescence, the transition from childhood to adulthood is most important. Children are becoming more independent, and begin to look at the future in terms of career, relationships, families, housing, and so on. During this period, they explore possibilities and begin to form their own identities based upon the outcome of their explorations. This sense of who they are can be hindered, which results in a sense of confusion ("I don't know what I want to be when I grow up") about themselves and their role in the world.

Intimacy Versus Isolation

In young adulthood, individuals begin to share themselves more intimately with others and explore relationships leading toward longer term commitments with others outside the family. Successful completion can lead to comfortable relationships and a sense of commitment, safety, and care within a relationship. Avoiding intimacy and fearing commitment and relationships can lead to isolation, loneliness, and sometimes depression.

Generativity Versus Stagnation

During middle adulthood, individuals establish careers, settle down within relationships, begin families, and develop a sense of being a part of the bigger picture. They give back to society through raising children, being productive at work, and becoming involved in community activities and organizations. By failing to achieve these objectives, individuals become stagnant and feel unproductive.

Ego Integrity Versus Despair

As individuals grow older and become senior citizens, they tend to slow down and explore life as retired people. It is during this time that they contemplate accomplishments and are able to develop a sense of integrity if they are satisfied with the progression of their lives. If they see their lives as being unproductive and failing to accomplish life goals, they become dissatisfied with life and develop despair, often leading to depression and hopelessness.

On a micro level, social development is learning how to behave and interact well with others. Social development relies on emotional development or learning how to manage feelings so they are productive and not counterproductive.

On a macro level, social development is about a commitment that development processes need to benefit people, particularly, but not only, the poor. It also recognizes the way people interact in groups and society, and the norms that facilitate such interaction.

Social development implies a change in social institutions. Progress toward an inclusive society, for example, implies that individuals treat each other fairly in their daily lives, whether in the family, workplace, or public office. Social cohesion is enhanced when peaceful and safe environments within neighborhoods and communities are created. Social accountability exists to the extent that individuals' voices are expressed and heard. Reforms aimed at improving rights and more participatory governance are part of the process by which institutional change is achieved.

Emotional Development

Emotional milestones are often harder to pinpoint than signs of physical development. This area emphasizes many skills that increase self-awareness and self-regulation. Social skills and emotional development are reflected in the ability to pay attention, make transitions from one activity to another, and cooperate with others.

During childhood, there is a lot happening during playtime. Children are lifting, dropping, looking, pouring, bouncing, hiding, building, knocking down, and more. Children are busy learning when they are playing. Play is the true work of childhood.

During play, children are also learning that they are liked and fun to be around. These experiences give them the self-confidence they need to build loving and supportive relationships all their lives.

Cognitive Development

Cognitive development focuses on development in terms of information processing, conceptual resources, perceptual skill, language learning, and other aspects of brain development. It is the emergence of the ability to think and understand.

A major controversy in cognitive development has been "nature and nurture," that is, the question of whether cognitive development is mainly determined by a client's innate qualities ("nature"), or by a client's personal experiences ("nurture"). However, it is now recognized by most experts that this is a false dichotomy: There is overwhelming evidence from biological and behavioral sciences that, from the earliest points in development, gene activity interacts with events and experiences in the environment.

There are six levels of cognition:

1. *Knowledge*: rote memorization, recognition, or recall of facts

2. *Comprehension*: understanding what the facts mean

3. *Application*: correct use of the facts, rules, or ideas

4. *Analysis*: breaking down information into component parts

5. *Synthesis*: combination of facts, ideas, or information to make a new whole

6. *Evaluation*: judging or forming an opinion about the information or situation

Ideally, in order for a client to learn, there should be objectives at each of these levels. Clients may have goals to learn in any of three domains of development:

1. *Cognitive*: mental skills (knowledge)

2. *Affective*: growth in feelings or emotional areas (attitude or self)

3. *Psychomotor*: manual or physical skills (skills)

Jean Piaget was a developmental psychologist best known for his theory of cognitive development. His stages address the acquisition of knowledge and how humans come to gradually acquire it. Piaget's theory holds that children learn through interaction with the environment and others.

Piaget also developed a theory of moral development, but the work by Lawrence Kohlberg is best known in this area. He agreed with Piaget's theory of moral development in principle, but wanted to develop the ideas further.

Stage	Age	Characteristics
1. Sensorimotor	0–2 years	a. Retains image of objects b. Develops primitive logic in manipulating objects c. Begins intentional actions d. Play is imitative e. Signals meaning—infant invests meaning in event (i.e., babysitter arriving means mother is leaving) f. Symbol meaning (language) begins in last part of stage

Stage	Age	Characteristics
2. Preoperational	2–7 years	a. Progress from concrete to abstract thinking b. Can comprehend past, present, future c. Night terrors d. Acquires words and symbols e. Magical thinking f. Thinking is not generalized g. Thinking is concrete, irreversible, egocentric h. Cannot see another point of view i. Thinking is centered on one detail or event Imaginary friends often emerge during this stage and may last into elementary school. Although children do interact with them, most know that their friends are not real and only pretend they are real. Thus, having an imaginary friend in childhood does not indicate the presence of a disorder. It is a normal part of development and social workers should normalize behavior with parents who are distressed about this activity during this developmental stage.
3. Concrete Operations	7–11 years	a. Beginnings of abstract thought b. Plays games with rules c. Cause and effect relationship understood d. Logical implications are understood e. Thinking is independent of experience f. Thinking is reversible g. Rules of logic are developed
4. Formal Operations	11 through maturity	a. Higher level of abstraction b. Planning for future c. Thinks hypothetically d. Assumes adult roles and responsibilities

Kohlberg believed that moral development parallels cognitive development. Kohlberg's theory holds that moral reasoning, which is the basis for ethical behavior, has six identifiable developmental constructive stages—each more adequate at responding to moral dilemmas than the last. Kohlberg suggested that the higher stages of moral development provide the person with greater capacities or abilities in terms of decision making and that these stages allow people to handle increasingly complex dilemmas. He grouped his six stages of moral reasoning into three major levels. A person must pass through each successive stage of moral development without skipping a stage.

Level	Age	Stage	Orientation
Preconventional	Elementary school level (before age 9)	1	Child obeys an authority figure out of fear of punishment. Obedience/punishment.
		2	Child acts acceptably as it is in her or his best interests. Conforms to rules to receive rewards.
Conventional (follow stereotypic norms of morality)	Early adolescence	3	Person acts to gain approval from others. "Good boy/good girl" orientation.
		4	Obeys laws and fulfills obligations and duties to maintain social system. Rules are rules. Avoids censure and guilt.
Postconventional (this level is not reached by most adults)	Adult	5	Genuine interest in welfare of others; concerned with individual rights and being morally right.
		6	Guided by individual principles based on broad, universal ethical principles. Concern for larger universal issues of morality.

Learning theory is a conceptual framework describing how information is absorbed, processed, and retained during learning. Cognitive, emotional, and environmental influences, as well as prior experience, all play a part in how understanding, or a worldview, is acquired or changed, as well as how knowledge and skills are retained.

There are many learning theories but all can be conceptualized as fitting into four distinct orientations:

1. Behaviorist (Pavlov, Skinner)—learning is viewed through change in behavior and the stimuli in the external environment are the focus of learning. Social workers aim to change the external environment in order to bring about desired change.

2. Cognitive (Piaget)—learning is viewed through internal mental processes (including insight, information processing, memory, and perception) and the focus of learning is internal cognitive structures. Social workers aim to develop opportunities to foster capacity and skills to improve learning.

3. Humanistic (Maslow)—learning is viewed as a person's activities aimed at reaching the person's full potential, and the focus of learning is in meeting cognitive and other needs. Social workers aim to develop the whole person.

4. Social/Situational (Bandura)—learning is obtained between people and their environments, and their interactions and observations in social contexts. Social workers establish opportunities for conversation and participation to occur.

Behavioral Development

Behavioral theories suggest that personality is a result of interaction between the individual and the environment. Behavioral theorists study observable and measurable behaviors, rejecting theories that take internal thoughts and feelings into account.

These theories represent the systematic application of principles of learning to the analysis and treatment of behaviors. Behaviors determine feelings. Thus, changing behaviors will also change or eliminate undesired feelings. The goal is to modify behavior.

The focus is on observable behavior—a target symptom, a problem behavior, or an environmental condition, rather than on the personality of a client.

There are two fundamental classes of behavior: respondent and operant.

1. Respondent: involuntary behavior (anxiety, sexual response) that is automatically elicited by certain behavior. A stimulus elicits a response

2. Operant: voluntary behavior (walking, talking) that is controlled by its consequences in the environment

Best known applications of behavior modification are sexual dysfunction, phobic disorders, compulsive behaviors (i.e., overeating, smoking), and training of persons with intellectual disabilities and/or autism spectrum disorder.

It is impractical for those using behavior modification to observe behavior when clients are not in residential inpatient settings offering 24-hour care. Thus, social workers train clients to observe and monitor their own behaviors. For example, clients can monitor their food intake or how many cigarettes they smoke. Client self-monitoring has advantages (i.e., inexpensive, practical, and therapeutic) and disadvantages (i.e., clients can collect inadequate and inaccurate information or can resist collecting any at all).

There are several behavioral paradigms.

A. RESPONDENT OR CLASSICAL CONDITIONING (Pavlov): Learning occurs as a result of pairing previously neutral (conditioned) stimulus with an unconditioned (involuntary) stimulus so that the conditioned stimulus eventually elicits the response normally elicited by the unconditioned stimulus.

Unconditioned Stimulus ⟶ Unconditioned Response
Unconditioned Stimulus + Conditioned Stimulus ⟶ Unconditioned Response
Conditioned Stimulus ⟶ Conditioned Response

B. OPERANT CONDITIONING (B. F. Skinner): Antecedent events or stimuli precede behaviors, which, in turn, are followed by consequences. Consequences that increase the occurrence of the behavior are referred to as reinforcing consequences; consequences that decrease the occurrence of the behavior are referred to as punishing consequences. Reinforcement aims to increase behavior frequency, whereas punishment aims to decrease it.

Antecedent ⟶ Response/Behavior ⟶ Consequence

Operant Techniques:

1. **Positive reinforcement**: Increases probability that behavior will occur—praising, giving tokens, or otherwise rewarding positive behavior

2. **Negative reinforcement**: Behavior increases because a negative (aversive) stimulus is removed (i.e., remove shock)

3. **Positive punishment**: Presentation of undesirable stimulus following a behavior for the purpose of decreasing or eliminating that behavior (i.e., hitting, shocking)

4. **Negative punishment**: Removal of a desirable stimulus following a behavior for the purpose of decreasing or eliminating that behavior (i.e., removing something positive, such as a token or dessert)

Specific Behavioral Terms:

1. **Aversion therapy**: Any treatment aimed at reducing the attractiveness of a stimulus or a behavior by repeated pairing of it with an aversive stimulus. **An example of this is treating alcoholism with antabuse.**

2. **Biofeedback**: Behavior training program that teaches a person how to control certain functions such as heart rate, blood pressure, temperature, and muscular tension. Biofeedback is often used for attention-deficit/hyperactivity disorder (ADHD) and anxiety disorders.

3. **Extinction**: Withholding a reinforcer that normally follows a behavior. Behavior that fails to produce reinforcement will eventually cease.

4. **Flooding**: A treatment procedure in which a client's anxiety is extinguished by prolonged real or imagined exposure to highintensity feared stimuli.

5. **In vivo desensitization**: Pairing and movement through a hierarchy of anxiety, from least to most anxiety provoking situations; takes place in "real" setting.

6. **Modeling**: Method of instruction that involves an individual (the model) demonstrating the behavior to be acquired by a client.

7. **Rational emotive therapy (RET)**: A cognitively oriented therapy in which a social worker seeks to change a client's irrational beliefs by argument, persuasion, and rational reevaluation and by teaching a client to counter self-defeating thinking with new, nondistressing self-statements.

8. **Shaping**: Method used to train a new behavior by prompting and reinforcing successive approximations of the desired behavior.

9. **Systematic desensitization**: An anxiety-inhibiting response cannot occur at the same time as the anxiety response. Anxiety-producing stimulus is paired with relaxation-producing response so that eventually an anxiety-producing stimulus produces a relaxation response. At each step a client's reaction of fear or dread is overcome by pleasant feelings engendered as the new behavior is reinforced by receiving a reward. The reward could be a compliment, a gift, or relaxation.

10. **Time out**: Removal of something desirable—negative punishment technique.

11. **Token economy**: A client receives tokens as reinforcement for performing specified behaviors. The tokens function as currency within the environment and can be exchanged for desired goods, services, or privileges.

THE INDICATORS OF NORMAL AND ABNORMAL PHYSICAL, COGNITIVE, EMOTIONAL, AND SEXUAL DEVELOPMENT THROUGHOUT THE LIFESPAN

Human growth, development, and learning become progressively complex over time and are influenced through a variety of experiences and interactions. Growth, development, and learning proceed in predictable patterns reflecting increasingly complex levels of organization across the life course. Each developmental stage has distinctive characteristics; however, each builds from the experiences of earlier stages. The domains of development are integrated within the child, so when one area is affected, other areas are also affected. Development proceeds at varying rates from child to child, as well as across developmental domains for individual children, reflecting the unique nature of each. Because growth and development are generally predictable, social workers should know the milestones of healthy development and the signs of potential delay or disability.

Child Development

Child development refers to the physical, mental, and socioemotional changes that occur between birth and the end of adolescence, as a child progresses from dependency to increasing autonomy. It is a continuous process with a predictable sequence, yet having a unique course. Individuals do not progress at the same rate, and each stage is affected by the preceding types of development. Because these developmental changes may be strongly influenced by genetic factors and events during prenatal life, genetics and prenatal development are usually included as part of the study of child development.

Infants and Toddlers (Age 0–3)
Healthy Growth and Development

- Physical—grows at a rapid rate, especially brain size
- Mental—learns through senses, exploring, playing, communicates by crying, babbling, then "baby talk," simple sentences
- Social–Emotional—seeks to build trust in others, dependent, beginning to develop a sense of self

Key Health Care Issues

- Communication—provide security, physical closeness; promote healthy parent–child bonds
- Health—keep immunizations/checkups on schedule; provide proper nutrition, sleep, skin care, oral health, routine screenings
- Safety—ensure a safe environment for exploring, playing, sleeping

Examples of Age-Specific Care for Infants and Toddlers

- Involve child and parent(s) in care during feeding, diapering, and bathing
- Provide safe toys and opportunities for play

- Encourage child to communicate—smile, talk softly
- Help parent(s) learn about proper child care

Young Children (Age 4–6)
Healthy Growth and Development

- Physical—grows at a slower rate; improving motor skills; dresses self, toilet trained
- Mental—begins to use symbols; improving memory; vivid imagination, fears; likes stories
- Social–Emotional—identifies with parent(s); becomes more independent; sensitive to others' feelings

Key Health Care Issues

- Communication—give praise, rewards, clear rules
- Health—keep immunizations/checkups on schedule; promote healthy habits (good nutrition, personal hygiene, etc.)
- Safety—promote safety habits (use bike helmets, safety belts, etc.)

Examples of Age-Specific Care for Young Children

- Involve parent(s) and child in care—let child make some food choices
- Use toys and games to teach child and reduce fear
- Encourage child to ask questions, play with others, and talk about feelings
- Help parent(s) teach child safety rules

Older Children (Age 7–12)
Healthy Growth and Development

- Physical—grows slowly until a "spurt" at puberty
- Mental—understands cause and effect, can read, write, do math; active, eager learner
- Social–Emotional—develops greater sense of self; focuses on school activities, negotiates for greater independence

Key Health Care Issues

- Communication—help child to feel competent, useful
- Health—keep immunizations/checkups on schedule; give information on alcohol, tobacco, other drugs, sexuality
- Safety—promote safety habits (playground safety, resolving conflicts peacefully, etc.)

Examples of Age-Specific Care for Older Children

- Allow child to make some care decisions (in which arm do you want vaccination?)
- Build self-esteem—ask child to help you do a task, recognize achievements, and so on
- Guide child in making healthy, safe lifestyle choices
- Help parent(s) talk with child about peer pressure, sexuality, alcohol, tobacco, and other drugs

Adolescent Development

The development of children ages 13 through 18 years old is a critical time as children develop the ability to understand abstract ideas, such as higher math concepts, and develop moral philosophies, including rights and privileges, and move toward a more mature sense of themselves and their purpose.

Healthy Growth and Development

- Physical—grows in spurts; matures physically; able to reproduce
- Mental—becomes an abstract thinker (goes beyond simple solutions, can consider many options, etc.); chooses own values
- Social–Emotional—develops own identity; builds close relationships; tries to balance peer group with family interests; concerned about appearances, challenges authority

Key Health Care Issues

- Communication—provide acceptance, privacy; build teamwork, respect
- Health—encourage regular checkups; promote sexual responsibility; advise against substance abuse; update immunizations
- Safety—discourage risk-taking (promote safe driving, violence prevention, etc.)

Examples of Age-Specific Care for Adolescents

- Treat more as an adult than child—avoid authoritarian approaches
- Show respect—be considerate of how treatment may affect relationships
- Guide teen in making positive lifestyle choices (i.e., correct misinformation from teen's peers)
- Encourage open communication between parent(s), teen, and peers

Adult Development

Adult development refers to the changes that occur in biological, psychological, and interpersonal domains of human life from the end of adolescence until the end of life. These changes may be gradual or rapid, and can reflect positive, negative, or no change from previous levels of functioning.

Young Adults (Age 18–35)
Healthy Growth and Development

- Physical—reaches physical and sexual maturity, nutritional needs are for maintenance, not growth

- Mental—acquires new skills, information; uses these to solve problems

- Social–Emotional—seeks closeness with others; sets career goals; chooses lifestyle, community; starts own family

Key Health Care Issues

- Communication—be supportive and honest; respect personal values

- Health—encourage regular checkups; promote healthy lifestyle (proper nutrition, exercise, weight, etc.); inform about health risks (heart disease, cancer, etc.); update immunizations

- Safety—provide information on hazards at home, work

Examples of Age-Specific Care for Young Adults

- Support the person in making health care decisions

- Encourage healthy and safe habits at work and home

- Recognize commitments to family, career, community (time, money, etc.)

Middle Age Adults (Age 36–64)
Healthy Growth and Development

- Physical—begins to age; experiences menopause (women); may develop chronic health problems

- Mental—uses life experiences to learn, create, solve problems

- Social–Emotional—hopes to contribute to future generations; stays productive, avoids feeling "stuck" in life; balances dreams with reality; plans retirement; may care for children and parents

Key Health Care Issues

- Communication—keep a hopeful attitude; focus on strengths, not limitations

- Health—encourage regular checkups and preventive exams; address age-related changes; monitor health risks; update immunizations

- Safety—address age-related changes (effects on sense, reflexes, etc.)

Examples of Age-Specific Care for Middle Age Adults

- Address worries about future—encourage talking about feelings, plans, and so on

- Recognize the person's physical, mental, and social abilities/contributions

- Help with plans for a healthy active retirement

Older Adults (Age 65–79)
Healthy Growth and Development

- Physical—ages gradually; natural decline in some physical abilities, senses
- Mental—continues to be an active learner, thinker; memory skills may start to decline
- Social–Emotional—takes on new roles (grandparent, widow or widower, etc.); balances independence, dependence; reviews life

Key Health Care Issues

- Communication—give respect; prevent isolation; encourage acceptance of aging
- Health—monitor health closely; promote physical, mental, social activity; guard against depression, apathy; update immunizations
- Safety—promote home safety; especially preventing falls

Examples of Age-Specific Care for Older Adults

- Encourage the person to talk about feelings of loss, grief, and achievements
- Provide information, materials, and so on, to make medication use and home safe
- Provide support for coping with any impairments (avoid making assumptions about loss of abilities)
- Encourage social activity with peers, as a volunteer, and so on

Elders (Age 80 and Older)
Healthy Growth and Development

- Physical—continues to decline in physical abilities; at increasing risk for chronic illness, major health problems
- Mental—continues to learn; memory skills and/or speed of learning may decline; confusion often signals illness or medication problem
- Social–Emotional—accepts end of life and personal losses; lives as independently as possible

Key Health Care Issues

- Communication—encourage the person to express feelings, thoughts, avoid despair; use humor, stay positive
- Health—monitor health closely, promote self-care; ensure proper nutrition, activity level, rest; reduce stress, update immunizations
- Safety—prevent injury, ensure safe living environment

Examples of Age-Specific Care for Adults Ages 80 and Older

- Encourage independence—provide physical, mental, and social activities

- Support end-of-life decisions—provide information, resources, and so on
- Assist the person in self-care—promote medication safety; provide safety grips, ramps, and so on

THEORIES OF SEXUAL DEVELOPMENT THROUGHOUT THE LIFESPAN

Many people cannot imagine that everyone—babies, children, teens, adults, and older adults—are sexual beings. Some inappropriately believe that sexual activity is reserved for early and middle adulthood. Teens often feel that adults are too old for sexual intercourse. Sexuality, though, is much more than sexual intercourse. Humans are sexual beings throughout life.

Sexuality in infants and toddlers—Children are sexual even before birth. Males can have erections while still in the uterus, and some boys are born with an erection. Infants touch and rub their genitals because it provides pleasure. Little boys and girls can experience orgasm from masturbation, although boys will not ejaculate until puberty. By about age 2, children know their own gender. They are aware of differences in the genitals of males and females and in how males and females urinate.

Sexuality in children (age 3–7)—Preschool children are interested in everything about their world, including sexuality. They may practice urinating in different positions. They are highly affectionate and enjoy hugging other children and adults. They begin to be more social and may imitate adult social and sexual behaviors, such as holding hands and kissing. Many young children play "doctor" during this stage, looking at other children's genitals and showing theirs. This is normal curiosity. By age 5 or 6, most children become more modest and private about dressing and bathing.

Children of this age are aware of marriage and understand living together, based on their family experience. They may role play about being married or having a partner while they "play house." Most young children talk about marrying and/or living with a person they love when they get older. Most sex play at this age happens because of curiosity.

Sexuality in preadolescent youth (age 8–12)—Puberty, the time when the body matures, begins between the ages of 9 and 12 for most children. Girls begin to grow breast buds and pubic hair as early as 9 or 10. Boys' development of the penis and testicles usually begins between 10 and 11. Children become more self-conscious about their bodies at this age and often feel uncomfortable undressing in front of others, even a same-sex parent.

Masturbation increases during these years. Preadolescent boys and girls do not usually have much sexual experience, but they often have many questions. They usually have heard about sexual intercourse, homosexuality, rape, and incest, and they want to know more about all these things. The idea of actually having sexual intercourse, however, is unpleasant to most preadolescent boys and girls.

Same-gender sexual behavior can occur at this age. Boys and girls tend to play with friends of the same gender and are likely to explore sexuality with them. Same-gender sexual behavior is unrelated to a child's sexual orientation.

Some group dating occurs at this age. Preadolescents may attend parties that have guests of both genders, and they may dance and play kissing games. By age 12 or 13, some young adolescents may pair off and begin dating and/or "making out." Young women are usually older when they begin voluntary sexual intercourse. However, many very young teens do practice sexual behaviors other than vaginal intercourse, such as petting to orgasm and oral sex.

Sexuality in adolescent youth (age 13–19)—Once youth have reached puberty and beyond, they experience increased interest in romantic and sexual relationships and in genital sex behaviors. As youth mature, they experience strong emotional attachments to romantic partners and find it natural to express their feelings within sexual relationships. There is no way to predict how a particular teenager will act sexually. Overall, most adolescents explore relationships with one another, fall in and out of love, and participate in sexual intercourse before the age of 20.

Adult sexuality—Adult sexual behaviors are extremely varied and, in most cases, remain part of an adult's life until death. At around age 50, women experience menopause, which affects their sexuality in that their ovaries no longer release eggs and their bodies no longer produce estrogen. They may experience several physical changes. Vaginal walls become thinner and vaginal intercourse may be painful because there is less vaginal lubrication and the entrance to the vagina becomes smaller. Many women use estrogen replacement therapy to relieve physical and emotional side effects of menopause. Use of vaginal lubricants can also make vaginal intercourse easier. Most women are able to have pleasurable sexual intercourse and to experience orgasm for their entire lives.

Adult men also experience some changes in their sexuality, but not at such a predictable time as with menopause in women. Men's testicles slow testosterone production after age 25 or so. Erections may occur more slowly once testosterone production slows. Men also become less able to have another erection after an orgasm and may take up to 24 hours to achieve and sustain another erection. The amount of semen released during ejaculation also decreases, but men are capable of fathering a baby even when they are in their 80s and 90s. Some older men develop an enlarged or cancerous prostate gland. If the doctors deem it necessary to remove the prostate gland, a man's ability to have an erection or an orgasm is normally unaffected.

Although adult men and women go through some sexual changes as they age, they do not lose their desire or their ability for sexual expression. Even among the very old, the need for touch and intimacy remains, although the desire and ability to have sexual intercourse may lessen.

THEORIES OF SPIRITUAL DEVELOPMENT THROUGHOUT THE LIFESPAN

Many models attempt to explain the impact of spirituality and/or religious beliefs on behavior. Many of them describe this impact along a continuum as follows, with some individuals changing during their life course and others remaining at the same point.

Individuals are unwilling to accept a will greater than their own.

Behavior is chaotic, disordered, and reckless. Individuals tend to defy and disobey, and are extremely egoistic. They lack empathy for others. Very young children can be at this stage. Adults who do not move beyond this point in the continuum may engage in criminal activity because they cannot obey rules.

Individuals have blind faith in authority figures and see the world as divided simply into good and evil and right and wrong.

Children who learn to obey their parents and other authority figures move to this point in the continuum. Many "religious" people who have blind faith in a spiritual being and do not question its existence may also be at this point. Individuals who are good, law-abiding citizens may never move further in the continuum.

Scientific skepticism and questioning are critical, because an individual does not accept things on faith, but only if convinced logically.

Many people working in a scientific and technical field may question spiritual or supernatural forces because they are difficult to measure or prove scientifically. Those who do engage in this skepticism move away from the simple, official doctrines.

The individual starts enjoying the mystery and beauty of nature and existence.

The individual develops a deeper understanding of good and evil, forgiveness and mercy, compassion and love. Religiousness and spirituality differ significantly from other points in the continuum and things are not accepted on blind faith or out of fear. The individual does not judge people harshly or seek to inflict punishment on them for their transgressions. This is the stage of loving others as one loves oneself, losing attachment to ego, and forgiving enemies.

Basic principles of all models move from the "egocentric," which are associated particularly with childhood, to "conformist," and eventually to "integration" or "universal."

THEORIES OF RACIAL, ETHNIC, AND CULTURAL DEVELOPMENT THROUGHOUT THE LIFESPAN

Ethnicity refers to the idea that one is a member of a particular cultural, national, or racial group that may share culture, religion, race, language, or place of origin. Two people can share the same race but have different ethnicities.

The meaning of **race** is not fixed; it is related to a particular social, historical, and geographic context. The way races are classified has changed in the public mind over time; for example, at one time racial classifications were based on ethnicity or nationality, religion, or minority language groups. Today, society classifies people into different races primarily based on skin color.

Cultural identity is often defined as the identity of a group or culture of individuals who are influenced by their self-identification with groups or cultures. Certain ethnic and racial identities may also bestow privilege.

Cultural, racial, and ethnic identities are important. They may instill feelings of shared commitment and values and a sense of belonging that may otherwise be missing.

Cultural, racial, and ethnic identities are passed from one generation to the next through customs, traditions, language, religious practice, and cultural values. Current events, mainstream media, and popular literature also influence cultural, racial, and ethnic identities.

Cultural, racial, and ethnic identities play a particularly large role among minority youth because they experience the contrasting and dominant culture of the majority ethnic group. Youth who belong to the majority ethnic culture may not even recognize or acknowledge their cultural, racial, and ethnic identities.

Following is a three-stage model for adolescent cultural and ethnic identity development. These stages do not correspond to specific ages, but can occur at any time. Individuals may spend their entire lives at a particular stage.

- The first stage, **unexamined cultural, racial, and ethnic identity**, is characterized by a lack of exploration of culture, race, and ethnicity and cultural, racial, and ethnic differences —they are rather taken for granted without much critical thinking. This is usually the stage reserved for childhood when cultural, racial, and ethnic ideas provided by parents, the community, or the media are easily accepted. Children at this stage tend not to be interested in culture, race, or ethnicity and are generally ready to take on the opinions of others.

■ The second stage of the model is referred to as the **cultural, racial, and ethnic identity search** and is characterized by the exploration and questioning of culture, race, and ethnicity in order to learn more about them and to understand the implications of belonging. During this stage, there is questioning of where beliefs come from and why they are held. For some, this stage may arise from a turning point in their lives or from a growing awareness of other cultures, races, and ethnicities. It can also be a very emotional time.

■ Finally, the third stage of the model is **cultural, racial, and ethnic identity achievement**. Ideally, people at this stage have a clear sense of their cultural, racial, and ethnic identity and are able to successfully navigate it in the contemporary world, which is undoubtedly very interconnected and intercultural. The acceptance of cultural, racial, and ethnic identity may play a significant role in important life decisions and choices, influencing attitudes and behavior. This usually leads to an increase in self-confidence and positive psychological development.

The classic model of cultural, racial, and ethnic identity development refers to identity statuses rather than stages, because stages imply a linear progression of steps that may not occur for all.

■ **Preencounter**: At this point, there is a lack of conscious awareness of culture, race, or ethnicity and how it may affect life.

■ **Encounter**: An encounter takes place that provokes thought about the role of cultural, racial, and ethnic identification in life. This may be a negative or positive experience related to culture, race, and ethnicity. For minorities, this experience is often a negative one in which they experience discrimination for the first time.

■ **Immersion–Emersion**: After an encounter that forces confrontation with cultural, racial, and ethnic identity, a period of exploration follows. There is a search for information and learning occurs through interaction with others from the same cultural, racial, or ethnic groups.

■ **Internalization and Commitment**: At this point, a secure sense of identity has developed and there is comfort socializing both within and outside the group with which the person identifies.

THE EFFECTS OF PHYSICAL, MENTAL, AND COGNITIVE DISABILITIES THROUGHOUT THE LIFESPAN

The impacts of disabilities on human development are extremely varied depending upon the manifestations of the disability and when it occurs during the life course. Some disabilities are short-term, whereas others are lifelong. Critical to mitigating the negative impacts is the development of coping skills that strengthen a client's ability to deal with limitations. Support (formal and informal) is also critical.

There may also be positive effects of disabilities because familial bonds may be stronger or individuals may develop skills to compensate for other tasks that cannot be performed.

Disability is a normal phenomenon in the sense that it exists in all societies. Although medical explanations remain primary in defining disability, the history of disability took an important turn in the latter half of the 20th century that has significantly influenced responses to it. Disability rights scholars and activists rejected the medical explanation for disability, since such explanations of permanent deficit did not advance social justice, equality of opportunity, and rights as citizens. Rather, these leaders proposed the intolerance and rigidity of social institutions, rather than medical conditions, as the explanation for disability. Words such as "inclusion," "participation," and "nondiscrimination" were introduced into the disability literature and reflected the notions that people who did not fit within the majority were disabled by stigma, prejudice, marginalization, segregation, and exclusion. This notion of disability requires the modification of societal structures to include all, rather than "fixing" individuals with varying abilities.

There must be policies, procedures, regulations, and legislation which provide accommodations for children and adults with disabilities. These disabilities may be related to mental and/or physical conditions. These conditions do not need to be severe or permanent. Social workers must ensure that these accommodations are available and the rights of those with disabilities are respected.

THE INTERPLAY OF BIOLOGICAL, PSYCHOLOGICAL, SOCIAL, AND SPIRITUAL FACTORS

Human development is a lifelong process beginning before birth and extending to death. At each moment in life, every human being is in a state of personal evolution. Physical changes largely drive the process, as our cognitive abilities advance and decline in response to the brain's growth in childhood and reduced functioning in old age. Psychosocial–spiritual development is also significantly influenced by physical growth, as changing body and brain, together with environment, shape a client's identity and relationships with other people.

Thus, development is the product of the elaborate interplay of biological, psychological, social, and spiritual influences. As children develop physically, gaining greater psychomotor control and increased brain function, they become more sophisticated cognitively—that is, more adept at thinking about and acting upon their environment. These physical and cognitive changes, in turn, allow them to develop psychosocially and spiritually, forming individual identities and relating effectively and appropriately with other people.

BASIC HUMAN NEEDS

Maslow's hierarchy of needs implies that clients are motivated to meet certain needs. When one need is fulfilled, a client seeks to fulfill the next one, and so on. This hierarchy is often depicted as a pyramid. This five stage model can be divided into basic (or deficiency) needs (i.e., physiological, safety, social, and esteem) and growth needs (self-actualization).

1. Deficiency needs—also known as D-Needs

2. Growth needs—also known as "being needs" or B-Needs

Deficiency Needs:

- Physiological
- Safety
- Social
- Esteem

Maslow called these needs "deficiency needs" because he felt that these needs arise due to deprivation. The satisfaction of these needs helps to "avoid" unpleasant feelings or consequence.

Growth Needs:

- Self-actualization

These needs fall on the highest level of Maslow's pyramid. They come from a place of growth rather than from a place of "lacking."

A client must satisfy lower-level basic needs before moving on to meet higher-level growth needs. After meeting lower levels of needs, a client can reach the highest level of self-actualization, but few people do so.

Every client is capable and has the desire to move up the hierarchy toward a level of self-actualization. Unfortunately, progress is often disrupted by failure to meet lower level needs. Life experiences, including divorce and loss of job, may cause a client to fluctuate between levels of the hierarchy.

Physiological needs: These needs maintain the physical organism. These are biological needs such as food, water, oxygen, and constant body temperature. If a person is deprived of these needs, the person will die.

Safety needs: There is a need to feel safe from harm, danger, or threat of destruction. Clients need regularity and some predictability.

Social needs: Friendship, intimacy, affection, and love are needed—from one's work group, family, friends, or romantic relationships.

Esteem needs: People need a stable, firmly based level of self-respect and respect from others.

Self-actualization needs: There is a need to be oneself, to act consistently with whom one is. Self-actualization is an ongoing process. It involves developing potential, becoming, and being what one is capable of being. It makes possible true objectivity—dealing with the world as it is, rather than as one needs it to be. You are free to really do what you want to do. There are moments when everything is right (peak experience); a glimmer of what it is like to be complete. One is in a position to find one's true calling (i.e., being an artist, writer, musician). Only 1% of the population consistently operates at this level.

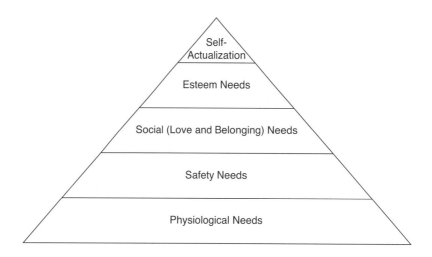

On the examination, Maslow's hierarchy of needs is often not explicitly asked about, but it can be applied when asked about the order of prioritizing problems or issues with a client. A client with an acute medical problem should focus on getting a medical evaluation first; a victim of domestic violence should prioritize medical and safety issues; and a refugee must initially meet basic survival needs (shelter, food, income, clothing, etc.) before working on fulfilling higher level needs.

THE PRINCIPLES OF ATTACHMENT AND BONDING

Attachment theory originated with the seminal work of John Bowlby. Bowlby defined attachment as a lasting psychological connectedness between human beings that can be understood within an *evolutionary* context in which a caregiver provides safety and security for a child. Bowlby suggests that children come into the world biologically preprogrammed to form attachments with others, because this will help them to survive. They initially form only one primary attachment (monotropy) and this attachment figure acts as a secure base for exploring the world. Disrupting this attachment process can have severe consequences because the critical period for developing attachment is within the first 5 years of life.

There is another major theory of attachment that suggests attachment is a set of *learned behaviors*. The basis for the learning of attachments is the provision of food. A child will initially form an attachment to whoever feeds it. This child learns to associate the feeder (usually the mother) with the comfort of being fed and, through the process of classical conditioning, comes to find contact with the mother comforting. The child also finds that certain behaviors (i.e., crying, smiling) bring desirable responses from others and through the process of operant conditioning learns to repeat these behaviors in order to get the things wanted.

In both of these theoretical approaches, parents have important impacts on their children's attachment system. Insecure attachment systems have been linked to psychiatric disorders and can result in clients reacting in a hostile and rejecting manner as children or adults.

These theories are, however, criticized because there are cultural influences that may impact on attachment and the ways in which children interact with caregivers. Much of Bowlby and others' work has not fully considered these differences.

Psychodynamic

Psychodynamic theories emphasize the influence of the unconscious mind and childhood experiences on personality.

Humanist

Humanist theories emphasize the importance of free will and individual experience in the development of personality. Humanist theorists emphasized the concept of self-actualization, which is an innate need for personal growth that motivates behavior.

Trait

Trait theories posit that the personality is made up of a number of broad traits. A trait is basically a relatively stable characteristic that causes an individual to behave in certain ways.

THEORIES OF CONFLICT

Conflict theory, derived from the works of Karl Marx, posits that society is fragmented into groups that compete for social and economic resources. Social order is maintained by consensus among those with the greatest political, economic, and social resources.

According to conflict theory, inequality exists because those in control of a disproportionate share of society's resources actively defend their advantages. The masses are bound by coercion by those in power. This perspective emphasizes social control, not consensus and conformity. Groups and individuals advance their own interests, struggling over control of societal resources.

There is great attention paid to class, race, and gender in this perspective since they relate to the most pertinent and enduring struggles in society.

Conflict theorists challenge the status quo, encourage social change, and believe rich and powerful people force social order on the poor and the weak. Conflict theorists note that unequal groups usually have conflicting values and agendas, causing them to compete against one another. This constant competition between groups forms the basis for the ever-changing nature of society.

FACTORS INFLUENCING SELF-IMAGE (E.G., CULTURE, RACE, RELIGION/SPIRITUALITY, AGE, DISABILITY, TRAUMA)

Self-image is how clients define themselves, which is often tied to physical description (i.e., tall, thin), social roles (i.e., mother, student), personal traits (i.e., worthy, generous), and/or existential beliefs (i.e., one with the world, a spiritual being). It is how clients see themselves.

Self-esteem refers to the extent to which a client accepts or approves of this definition. Self-esteem always involves a degree of evaluation that may produce positive or negative feelings. Thus, self-image and self-esteem are linked throughout the life cycle.

Generally, self-esteem is relatively high in childhood, drops during adolescence, rises gradually throughout adulthood, and then declines sharply in old age.

Childhood: Young children have relatively high self-esteem, which gradually declines over childhood. This high self-image may be because children's self-views are unrealistically positive. As children develop cognitively, they begin to base their self-evaluations on external feedback and social comparisons, and thus form a more balanced and accurate appraisal of their academic competence, social skills, attractiveness, and other personal characteristics.

Adolescence: Self-esteem continues to decline during adolescence, perhaps due to a decrease in body image and other problems associated with puberty, as well as the increasing ability to think abstractly coupled with more academic and social challenges.

Adulthood: Self-esteem increases gradually throughout adulthood, peaking sometime around the late 60s. This increase is tied to assuming positions of power and status that might promote feelings of self-worth. Adulthood also brings an increasing level of maturity and adjustment, as well as emotional stability.

Older Adulthood: Self-esteem declines in old age, beginning to drop around age 70. This decline may be due to loss of employment due to retirement, loss of a spouse or friends, and/or health problems.

Overall, males and females follow essentially the same course during the life cycle. However, there are some interesting gender differences. Although boys and girls report similar levels of self-esteem during childhood, a gender gap emerges by adolescence, with adolescent boys having higher self-esteem than adolescent girls. This gender gap persists throughout adulthood, and then narrows and perhaps even disappears in old age.

Individuals tend to maintain their ordering relative to one another, with those who have relatively high self-esteem at one point in time tending to have relatively high self-esteem years later.

BODY IMAGE AND ITS IMPACT (E.G., IDENTITY, SELF-ESTEEM, RELATIONSHIPS, HABITS)

Body image is the way one perceives and relates to one's body, and how one thinks that one is seen by others.

Body image affects nearly everyone from time to time. Body image is not only influenced by the perceptions of others, but by the media and cultural forces as well. Senses are bombarded by an onslaught of mixed messages about how one "should" look or think about one's body.

Having a healthy body image is a key to well-being, both mentally and physically. A positive body image means that, most of the time, one has a realistic perception of, and feels comfortable with, one's looks.

Factors associated with positive body image:

■ Acceptance and appreciation of natural body shape and body differences

■ Self-worth not tied to appearance

■ Confidence in and comfort with body

■ An unreasonable amount of time is not spent worrying about food, weight, or calories

■ Judgment of others is not made related to their body weight, shape, and/or eating or exercise habits

■ Knowing physical appearance says very little about character and value as a person

Factors of negative body image:

■ Distorted perception of shape or body parts, unlike what they really are

■ Believing only other people are attractive and that body size or shape is a sign of personal failure

■ Feeling body doesn't measure up to family, social, or media ideals

■ Ashamed, self-conscious, and anxious about body

■ Uncomfortable and awkward in body

■ Constant negative thoughts about body and comparisons to others

Some possible effects of a negative body image:

■ Emotional distress

■ Low self-esteem

■ Unhealthy dieting habits

■ Anxiety

■ Depression

■ Eating disorders

■ Social withdrawal or isolation

PARENTING SKILLS AND CAPACITIES

Although there are very few actual cause-and-effect links between specific actions of parents and later behavior of children, there are four distinct parenting styles that seem to impact behavior later in life.

Authoritarian Parenting

Children are expected to follow the strict rules established by the parents. Failure to follow such rules usually results in punishment. Authoritarian parents fail to explain the reasoning behind these rules.

Authoritarian parenting styles generally lead to those who are obedient and proficient, but are lower in happiness, social competence, and self-esteem.

Authoritative Parenting

Like authoritarian parents, those with an authoritative parenting style establish rules and guidelines that their children are expected to follow. However, this parenting style is much more democratic. Authoritative parents are responsive to their children and willing to listen to questions. When children fail to meet the expectations, these parents are more nurturing and forgiving rather than punishing.

Authoritative parenting styles generally tend to result in those who are happy, capable, and successful.

Permissive Parenting

Permissive parents have very few demands on their children. These parents rarely discipline their children and are generally nurturing and communicative with their children, often taking on the status of a friend more than that of a parent.

Permissive parenting often results in children who rank low in happiness and self-regulation, experiencing problems with authority and tending to perform poorly in school.

Uninvolved Parenting

An uninvolved parenting style is characterized by few demands, low responsiveness, and little communication. Although these parents fulfill basic needs, they are generally detached from their children's lives.

Those who have experienced uninvolved parenting styles rank lowest across all life domains. They tend to lack self-control, have low self-esteem, and are less competent than their peers.

THE EFFECTS OF ADDICTION AND SUBSTANCE ABUSE ON INDIVIDUALS, FAMILIES, GROUPS, ORGANIZATIONS, AND COMMUNITIES

There are biopsychosocial–spiritual–cultural impacts of substance abuse or dependence on clients themselves. Clients who use drugs experience a wide array of physical effects other than those expected. The excitement or high that results from the use of cocaine is followed by a "crash": a period of anxiety, fatigue, depression, and an acute desire for more cocaine to alleviate these continued feelings. Marijuana and alcohol interfere with motor control and are factors in many automobile accidents. Users of hallucinogenic drugs may experience flashbacks, which are unwanted recurrences of the drug's effects weeks or months after use. Sudden abstinence from certain drugs results in withdrawal symptoms. For example, heroin withdrawal can cause vomiting, muscle cramps, convulsions, and delirium. With the continued use of substances that are physically addictive, tolerance develops; that is, constantly increasing amounts of the drug are needed to duplicate the initial effect.

Substance abuse or dependence also impacts mental health because it causes irrational behavior, violence, and lapses in memory. Chronic use of some substances can cause long-lasting changes in the brain, which may lead to paranoia, depression, aggression, and hallucinations.

In addition, because the purity and dosage of illegal drugs are uncontrolled, drug overdose is a constant risk. Many drug users also engage in criminal activity, such as burglary and prostitution, to raise money to buy drugs.

Substance use can disrupt family life and destroy relationships. A client's preoccupation with the substance, plus its impacts on mood and performance, can lead to relationship/marital problems. A client may spend more time on getting and using substances than attending to relationships with others. Drug use can also create destructive patterns of codependency. Codependency occurs when a partner/spouse or members of the family, out of love or fear of consequences, inadvertently enables a client to continue using substances by covering up, supplying money, or denying there is a problem.

In addition, substance abuse or dependence can result in accidental injury, disability, legal involvement, and/or loss of income or employment, which negatively impacts on those who are friends or family members of a client. Neglect of friends and family, as well as anger that can lead to verbal assaults or physical violence, are also seen as a result of substance abuse or dependence.

Clients who are using or dependent on substances may also tend to neglect "old" relationships and find those who also engage in similar behaviors.

FEMINIST THEORY

Feminist theory analyzes the status of women and men in society with the purpose of using that knowledge to better women's lives. Feminist theorists question the differences between women and men, including how race, class, ethnicity, sexuality, nationality, and age intersect with gender. Themes that are studied include discrimination, objectification (especially sexual objectification), oppression, stereotyping, and so on. Feminist theory is used in the fields of social work, sociology, economics, education, and others.

Feminism is a political, cultural, or economic movement aimed at establishing equal rights and legal protection for women.

THE IMPACT OF OUT-OF-HOME PLACEMENT (E.G., HOSPITALIZATION, FOSTER CARE, RESIDENTIAL CARE, CRIMINAL JUSTICE SYSTEM) ON CLIENTS/CLIENT SYSTEMS

The use of out-of-home placement is generally viewed as an intervention that only occurs when there is a health or safety risk in the home. This risk can be due to the individual who is being removed (caused by a medical or behavioral health issue of the individual being removed) or family members (caused by child abuse or neglect, medical or behavioral health issues of a family member, etc.). Often, out-of-home placement occurs after in-home interventions have been tried and failed.

Individuals who are placed outside of their homes often experience significant life problems. Determining whether these issues are directly caused by the removal is difficult as these individuals are likely to be at-risk for such problems prior to the placements.

For example, children who are removed from their homes due to abuse and/or neglect typically use mental health or other social services more than before they were placed away from their parents. These children often report a high level of stress, which may manifest in substance abuse, chronic aggressive or destructive behavior, suicidal ideation or acting out, and/or patterns of runaway behavior. Academic problems are also common among these children.

For all those leaving their homes, regardless of age, there is a disruption of emotional bonds with other family members, which is often accompanied by rage, grief, sadness, and/or despair.

BASIC PRINCIPLES OF HUMAN GENETICS

Social workers in all settings must educate themselves about the process of genetic inheritance and understand the primary reasons that clients seek genetic testing and counseling. Minimally, a social worker must understand the types of genetic conditions, including single gene disorders, chromosome anomalies, and multifactorial disorders, and the effect of harmful environmental toxins on development. Furthermore, an understanding of the patterns of inheritance between generations (autosomal dominant, autosomal recessive, and X-linked recessive) is essential in working with families.

It is important that social workers be educated about the specific application of skills to genetic cases. Social workers are already trained to view people from a biopsychosocial–spiritual–cultural perspective. In order to identify the patterns of disease in a family, a social worker may need to develop a genogram as part of the assessment.

Because a client's genetic test produces information about the whole family, the biology of a genetic condition must be thoroughly understood and explained to a client and the client's family in order to make informed decisions about whether or not to be tested. Sensitivity to the principle of self-determination is essential in the process of informing clients and family members.

Social workers must take care to ensure that clients are fully informed about all aspects of genetic testing. Social workers should provide counseling before and after the decision to have a genetic test and after the test itself.

THE FAMILY LIFE CYCLE

The emotional and intellectual stages from childhood to retirement as a member of a family are called the "family life cycle." In each stage, clients face challenges in family life that allow the building or gaining of new skills.

Not everyone passes through these stages smoothly. Situations such as severe illness, financial problems, or the death of a loved one can have an effect. If skills are not learned in one stage, they can be learned in later stages.

Stage 1: Family of origin experiences

Main tasks

- Maintaining relationships with parents, siblings, and peers
- Completing education
- Developing the foundations of a family life

Stage 2: Leaving home

Main tasks

- Differentiating self from family of origin and parents and developing adult-to-adult relationships with parents
- Developing intimate peer relationships
- Beginning work, developing work identity, and financial independence

Stage 3: Premarriage stage

Main tasks

- Selecting partners
- Developing a relationship
- Deciding to establish own home with someone

Stage 4: Childless couple stage

Main tasks

- Developing a way to live together both practically and emotionally
- Adjusting relationships with families of origin and peers to include partner

Stage 5: Family with young children

Main tasks

- Realigning family system to make space for children
- Adopting and developing parenting roles
- Realigning relationships with families of origin to include parenting and grandparenting roles
- Facilitating children to develop peer relationships

Stage 6: Family with adolescents

Main tasks

- Adjusting parent–child relationships to allow adolescents more autonomy
- Adjusting family relationships to focus on midlife relationship and career issues
- Taking on responsibility of caring for families of origin

Stage 7: Launching children

Main tasks

- Resolving midlife issues
- Negotiating adult-to-adult relationships with children
- Adjusting to living as a couple again
- Adjusting to including in-laws and grandchildren within the family circle
- Dealing with disabilities and death in the family of origin

Stage 8: Later family life

Main tasks

- Coping with physiological decline in self and others
- Adjusting to children taking a more central role in family maintenance

- Valuing the wisdom and experience of the elderly
- Dealing with loss of spouse and peers
- Preparing for death, life review, and reminiscence

Mastering the skills and milestones of each stage allows successful movement from one stage of development to the next. If not mastered, clients are more likely to have difficulty with relationships and future transitions. Family life cycle theory suggests that successful transitioning may also help to prevent disease and emotional or stress-related disorders.

The stress of daily living, coping with a chronic medical condition, or other life crises can disrupt the normal life cycle. Ongoing stress or a crisis can delay the transition to the next phase of life.

FAMILY DYNAMICS AND FUNCTIONING AND THE EFFECTS ON INDIVIDUALS, FAMILIES, GROUPS, ORGANIZATIONS, AND COMMUNITIES

Family dynamics are the patterns of relating or interactions between family members. Each family system and its dynamics are unique, although there are some common patterns. All families have some helpful and some unhelpful dynamics.

Even where there is little or no present contact with family, there is almost always an influence on a client by dynamics in previous years. Family dynamics often have a strong influence on the way individuals see themselves, others, and the world, and influence their relationships, their behaviors, and their well-being.

An understanding of the impact of family dynamics on a client's selfperception may help social workers pinpoint and respond to the driving forces behind her or his current needs.

Healthy functioning is characterized by:

- Treating each family member as an individual
- Having regular routines and structure
- Being connected to extended family, friends, and the community
- Having realistic expectations
- Spending quality time, which is characterized by fun, relaxed, and conflict-free interactions
- Ensuring that members take care of their own needs and not just the family needs
- Helping one another through example and direct assistance

Family dynamics significantly impact a client's biological, psychological, and social functioning in both positive and negative ways. Having a close-knit and supportive family provides emotional support, ensures economic well-being, and increases overall health. However, the opposite is also true. When family life is characterized by stress and conflict, well-being can be poor.

Social support is one of the main ways that family positively impacts well-being. Social relationships, such as those found in close families, have been demonstrated to decrease the likelihood of negative outcomes, such as chronic disease, disability, mental illness, and death.

Though good familial relations and social support serve as protective factors and improve overall well-being and health, studies have shown that not all familial relations positively impact these areas. Problematic and nonsupportive familial interactions have a negative impact. For example, growing up in an unsupported, neglectful, or violent home is associated with poor physical health and development.

THEORIES OF COUPLES DEVELOPMENT

Although relationships vary significantly, there are some predictable stages that characterize intimate relationships. Couples interactions follow a developmental model, much like those that explain individual growth throughout the life course.

Stage 1: Romance

The first stage of couples development begins when individuals are introduced and learn that they have common interests and are attracted to one another. Much of this stage consists of conversations and dates to learn more about the other partner. The focus of this stage is attachment. Like early stages of child development, the infancy of couples development is filled with passion, nurturing, and selfless attention to the needs of others. Differences are minimized and partners place few demands on each other. This romantic bond is the foundation that is critical to the health of the relationship in the future.

In this first stage, members engage in *symbiotic or mutualistic relationships*—often putting the needs of others before their own. Individuals who are coupling do not see themselves as unique—much like babies identifying themselves as part of their mothers or caregivers. Differentiation and learning to balance and support the separate needs of others happens in later stages but is not present initially.

Stage 2: Power Struggle

Soon individuals who are engaged in intimate relationships see that they have differences from their mates. These unique qualities result in unique needs that require an ongoing process of defining oneself and managing conflict, which threatens intimacy. As the coupled individuals begin to notice differences and annoyances that were once overlooked, there can be greater separation and loss of romance resulting from self-expression. This stage differs as individuals focus on differences rather than similarities, which was the hallmark of the initial romantic stage.

Time away from each other is often needed for the partners, and the bliss associated with the initial stage of couples development dissolves. *Differentiation*, or seeing oneself as distinct within a relationship, must be managed so that these new feelings do not result in breakups as the illusion of "being one" fades. Critical effort must be made to balance the desire for self-discovery with the desire for intimacy. To "survive" this stage, individuals must acknowledge differences, learn to share power, forfeit fantasies of complete harmony, and accept partners without the need to change them.

Stage 3: Stability

This stage in couples development is characterized by the redirection of personal attention, time, and activities away from partners and toward one's self. Individuals focus on personal needs in a manner that is respectful of others. Autonomy and individuality are key. Relationships are seen as more mature as disagreements can occur with both parties "winning." There is acceptance that partners are different from one another, and power struggles to minimize these differences are avoided.

Margaret Mahler described *practicing* as a subphase of separation-individuation in infant development. Practicing occurs when toddlers begin to explore on their own but still see themselves as part of their mothers/caregivers. The stability stage of couples development mirrors this subphase as partners learn to live independent lives while still identifying as and seeing the value of being part of an intimate relationship.

Another subphase of separation-individuation identified by Mahler, "*rapprochement*," also relates to the stability stage of couples development. Often, partners who have been successful in achieving a well-defined sense of self in relationships will have crises that will threaten their identities or separateness. They may rely more heavily on companionship and intimacy, seeking more comfort and support from each other. Thus, the stability stage is a time when there is still some back and forth between intimacy and independence with the ultimate goal being intimacy that does not sacrifice separateness.

Stage 4: Commitment

While the commitment stage of couples development is when marriage is ideal, it often occurs earlier in the romance stage, perhaps explaining the high rates of divorce caused by the inability to resolve power struggles. Individuals who have stabilized are able to embrace the reality that both partners are human, resulting in shortcomings in all relationships. Partners acknowledge that they want to be with each other and that the good outweighs the bad. Although much work has been done in building relationships, there is still more needed to effectively function in the next and last stage of couplehood.

Stage 5: Co-Creation

Constancy is the hallmark of this last stage. Just like children who are able to internalize and maintain images of their mothers/caregivers and use them to soothe in stressful moments, couples in this stage are able to do something similar. Each partner is able to value and respect the separateness of the other. The foundation of the relationship is no longer personal need, but the appreciation and love of the other and the support and respect for *mutual growth*.

Often, couples in this stage work on projects together, such as businesses, charities, and/or families. This stage aims to make a contribution beyond the relationship itself. Like Erik Erikson's stage of psychosocial functioning in middle adulthood, which focuses on the crisis of generativity versus stagnation, this stage of couples development aims to create or nurture things that are enduring, often by creating positive change that benefits other people. Success leads to feelings of usefulness and accomplishment.

As with Erikson's and other theories of development, stages are not linear. Lessons learned help couples move forward, but couples can revert back to prior stages, especially those including power struggles.

Same gender couples also go through these developmental stages but have unique challenges that impact relationship formation. For example, heterosexual couples have a much wider variety of public role models for their partnerships than their same gender peers. In addition, there may be heightened concerns by partners about acceptance of their mates or even the very existence of their intimate relationships by their respective families.

THE IMPACT OF PHYSICAL AND MENTAL ILLNESS ON FAMILY DYNAMICS

Physical illness and/or disability places a set of extra demands on the family system. An illness and/or disability can consume a lot of a family's resources of time, energy, and money, so that other individual and family needs may go unmet.

Day-to-day assistance may lead to exhaustion and fatigue, taxing the physical and emotional energy of family members. There can be emotional strain, including worry, guilt, anxiety, anger, and uncertainty about the cause or prognosis of the disability, about the future, about the needs of other family members, and about whether the individual is getting enough assistance.

There can be a financial burden associated with getting health, education, and social services; buying or renting equipment and devices; making accommodations to the home; transportation; and acquiring medications and/or special food. The person or family may be eligible for payment or reimbursement from an insurance company and/or a publicly funded program such as Medicaid or Supplemental Security Income. However, knowing about services and programs and then working to become eligible is another major challenge faced by families.

Working through eligibility issues and coordinating among different providers is a challenge faced by families for which they may want a social worker to assist.

Many communities still lack programs, facilities, and resources that allow for the full inclusion of persons with disabilities. Families often report that one burden comes from dealing with people in the community whose attitudes and behaviors are judgmental, stigmatizing, and rejecting.

There are differential impacts on families. The degree to which a physical illness and/or disability limits activities or functions of daily living or the ages of individuals or parents when an illness/disability emerges are important factors that may impact on adjustment.

The impact of mental illness on family dynamics also can be profound. Mental illness of a family member affects all aspects of family functioning, including physical, financial, and emotional well-being. These impacts often depend upon the relationship of family members to a person with a mental illness. For those closest, there can be considerable time spent addressing some of the practical impacts of mental illness, such as financial problems and disruptions to daily life. This time commitment can result in family members giving up things they care about or missing appointments needed for their own health or well-being.

When mental illness is first diagnosed, family members may deny that there is a continuing illness. If there is a crisis, family members may be upset about what is happening, but the desire to put the incident "behind them" often emerges once the episode is over. Thus, family members may believe that the symptomatic behavior of the mental illness will never return. Some family members often do understand the reality of the illness, whereas others do not. This can cause problems and tension within the family, as well as isolation and loss of meaningful relationships with those who are not supportive of the illness.

Due to the stigma sometimes associated with mental illness, family members may often be reluctant to discuss it with others because they do not know how other people will react. Isolation can also occur because family members may be reluctant to invite anyone to the home for fear of the presence of unpredictable behavior and/or the fear that the activity may be a stressor, triggering behavior related to the illness. This isolation causes families to withdraw from previous relationships to protect both themselves and their loved ones.

Families may have little knowledge about mental illness. They may inappropriately believe that it is a condition that is totally disabling. Without correct information, families may become very pessimistic about the future. They may need assistance from social workers in learning how to manage the illness and to plan for the future.

It is difficult for anyone to deal with strange thinking and bizarre and unpredictable behavior. Family members may be bewildered, frightened, and exhausted. Even when stabilized, those with mental illness may have apathy and lack of motivation that can be frustrating to family members. Family members may become angry and frustrated as they struggle to get back to a routine that previously they took for granted. If the illness is not stable, families go from crisis to crisis, feeling that they have no control over what is happening. Family life can be unsettled and unpredictable. It becomes very difficult, often impossible, to plan for family outings or vacations. The needs of those with mental illness take over the attention of families and siblings can feel that their needs are put off or ignored.

PSYCHOLOGICAL DEFENSE MECHANISMS AND THEIR EFFECTS ON BEHAVIOR AND RELATIONSHIPS

To manage internal conflicts, people use defense mechanisms. **Defense mechanisms** are behaviors that protect people from anxiety. Defense mechanisms are automatic, involuntary, and usually unconscious psychological activities to exclude unacceptable thoughts, urges, threats, and impulses from awareness for fear of disapproval, punishment, or other negative outcomes. Defense mechanisms are sometimes confused with coping strategies, which are voluntary.

The following are some defense mechanisms (the list of defense mechanisms is huge, and there is no theoretical consensus on the exact number).

1. **Acting Out**—emotional conflict is dealt with through actions rather than feelings (i.e., instead of talking about feeling neglected, a person will get into trouble to get attention)

2. **Compensation**—enables one to make up for real or fancied deficiencies (i.e., a person who stutters becomes a very expressive writer; a short man assumes a cocky, overbearing manner)

3. **Conversion**—repressed urge is expressed as a disturbance of body function, usually of the sensory, voluntary nervous system (as pain, deafness, blindness, paralysis, convulsions, tics)

4. **Decompensation**—deterioration of existing defenses

5. **Denial**—primitive defense; inability to acknowledge true significance of thoughts, feelings, wishes, behavior, or external reality factors that are consciously intolerable

6. **Devaluation**—a defense mechanism frequently used by persons with borderline personality disorder in which a person attributes exaggerated negative qualities to self or another. It is the split of primitive idealization

7. **Dissociation**—a process that enables a person to split mental functions in a manner that allows the expression of forbidden or unconscious impulses without taking responsibility for the action, either because the person is unable to remember the disowned behavior, or because it is not experienced (i.e., pathologically expressed as fugue state, amnesia, or dissociative neurosis, or normally expressed as daydreaming)

8. **Displacement**—directing an impulse, wish, or feeling toward a person or situation that is not its real object, thus permitting expression in a less threatening situation (i.e., a man angry at his boss kicks his dog)

9. **Idealization**—overestimation of an admired aspect or attribute of another

10. **Identification**—universal mechanism in which individuals pattern themselves after significant others. Plays a major role in personality development, especially superego development

11. **Identification With the Aggressor**—mastering anxiety by identifying with a powerful aggressor (such as an abusing parent) to counteract feelings of helplessness and to feel powerful oneself. Usually involves behaving like the aggressor (i.e., abusing others after one has been abused oneself)

12. **Incorporation**—primitive mechanism in which psychic representation of a person is (or parts of a person are) figuratively ingested

13. **Inhibition**—loss of motivation to engage in (usually pleasurable) activity avoided because it might stir up conflict over forbidden impulses

14. **Introjection**—loved or hated external objects are symbolically absorbed within self (converse of projection; i.e., in severe depression, unconscious unacceptable hatred is turned toward self)

15. **Intellectualization**—when the person avoids uncomfortable emotions by focusing on facts and logic. Emotional aspects are completely ignored as being irrelevant. Jargon is often used as a device of intellectualization. By using complex terminology, the focus is placed on the words rather than the emotions

16. **Isolation of Affect**—unacceptable impulse, idea, or act is separated from its original memory source, thereby removing the original emotional charge associated with it

17. **Projection**—primitive defense; attributing one's disowned attitudes, wishes, feelings, and urges to some external object or person

18. **Projective Identification**—a form of projection utilized by persons with borderline personality disorder—unconsciously perceiving others' behavior as a reflection of one's own identity

19. **Rationalization**—third line of defense; not unconscious. Giving believable explanation for irrational behavior; motivated by unacceptable unconscious wishes or by defenses used to cope with such wishes

20. **Reaction Formation**—person adopts affects, ideas, attitudes, or behaviors that are opposites of those harbored consciously or unconsciously (i.e., excessive moral zeal masking strong, but repressed asocial impulses or being excessively sweet to mask unconscious anger)

21. **Regression**—partial or symbolic return to more infantile patterns of reacting or thinking. Can be in service to ego (i.e., as dependency during illness)

22. **Repression**—key mechanism; expressed clinically by amnesia or symptomatic forgetting serving to banish unacceptable ideas, fantasies, affects, or impulses from consciousness

23. **Splitting**—defensive mechanism associated with borderline personality disorder in which a person perceives self and others as "all good" or "all bad." Splitting serves to protect the good objects. A person cannot integrate the good and bad in people

24. **Sublimation**—potentially maladaptive feelings or behaviors are diverted into socially acceptable, adaptive channels (i.e., a person who has angry feelings channels them into athletics)

25. **Substitution**—unattainable or unacceptable goal, emotion, or object is replaced by one more attainable or acceptable

26. **Symbolization**—a mental representation stands for some other thing, class of things, or attribute. This mechanism underlies dream formation and some other symptoms (such as conversion reactions, obsessions, compulsions) with a link between the latent meaning of the symptom and the symbol; usually unconscious

27. **Turning Against Self**—defense to deflect hostile aggression or other unacceptable impulses from another to self

28. **Undoing**—a person uses words or actions to symbolically reverse or negate unacceptable thoughts, feelings, or actions (i.e., a person compulsively washing hands to deal with obsessive thoughts)

ADDICTION THEORIES AND CONCEPTS

There are many risk factors for alcohol and other drug abuse, including, but not limited to:

1. *Family*: Parents, siblings, and/or spouse use substances; family dysfunction (i.e., inconsistent discipline, poor parenting skills, lack of positive family rituals and routine); family trauma (i.e., death, divorce)

2. *Social*: Peers use drugs and alcohol; social or cultural norms condone use of substances; expectations about positive effects of drugs and alcohol; drugs and alcohol are available and accessible

3. *Psychiatric*: Depression, anxiety, low self-esteem, low tolerance for stress; other mental health disorders; feelings of desperation; loss of control over one's life

4. *Behavioral*: Use of other substances; aggressive behavior in childhood; impulsivity and risk-taking; rebelliousness; school-based academic or behavioral problems; poor interpersonal relationships

Different models are believed to explain the causes of substance abuse.

1. *Biopsychosocial model*: There are a wide variety of reasons why people start and continue using substances. This model provides the most comprehensive explanation for the complex nature of substance abuse disorders. It incorporates hereditary predisposition, emotional and psychological problems, social influences, and environmental problems.

2. *Medical model*: Addiction is considered a chronic, progressive, relapsing, and potentially fatal medical disease

   - Genetic causes: Inherited vulnerability to addiction, particularly alcoholism
   - Brain reward mechanisms: Substances act on parts of the brain that reinforce continued use by producing pleasurable feelings
   - Altered brain chemistry: Habitual use of substances alters brain chemistry and continued use of substances is required to avoid feeling discomfort from a brain imbalance

3. *Self-medication model*: Substances relieve symptoms of a psychiatric disorder and continued use is reinforced by relief of symptoms.

4. *Family and environmental model*: Explanation for substance abuse can be found in family and environmental factors such as behaviors shaped by family and peers, personality factors, physical and sexual abuse, disorganized communities, and school factors.

5. *Social model*: Drug use is learned and reinforced from others who serve as role models. A potential substance abuser shares the same values and activities as those who use substances. There are no controls that prevent use of substances. Social, economic, and political factors, such as racism, poverty, sexism, and so on, contribute to the cause.

Whatever the root causes, a client's substance abuse problem must be addressed before other psychotherapeutic issues. A social worker should also rule out symptoms being related to a substance abuse problem before attributing them to a psychiatric issue.

Substance Use Disorder

A substance use disorder is characterized by the problematic use of substances such as alcohol, drugs (both legal and illegal), or other addictive substances. It is a complex condition that involves a pattern of behaviors in which individuals continue to use the substance despite experiencing negative consequences in various areas of their life, including physical health, mental well-being, social relationships, and work or school performance.

A substance use disorder is typically categorized into different levels of severity, ranging from mild to moderate to severe, based on the number of symptoms and their impact on an individual's life. Some common substances associated with substance use disorders include alcohol, opioids, stimulants, cannabis, and sedatives.

Symptoms of a substance use disorder can include:

1. **Loss of control:** Individuals find it challenging to limit their use of the substance, often consuming more than intended or over longer periods than intended.

2. **Craving:** There is a strong desire or urge to use the substance.

3. **Physical dependence:** The body becomes accustomed to the substance, leading to withdrawal symptoms when its use is reduced or stopped.

4. **Tolerance:** Over time, more of the substance is needed to achieve the desired effects.

5. **Neglect of activities:** Important activities such as work, school, and social interactions are neglected due to substance use.

6. **Continued use despite consequences:** Despite experiencing negative consequences like health problems, relationship issues, legal troubles, or financial difficulties, individuals continue to use the substance.

7. **Failed attempts to quit:** There are repeated unsuccessful attempts to cut down or control substance use.

8. **Time spent obtaining and using the substance:** A significant amount of time is spent obtaining, using, or recovering from the effects of the substance.

9. **Reduced social and recreational activities:** Participation in previously enjoyed activities decreases due to substance use.

Treatment for substance use disorders often involves a combination of medical, psychological, and social interventions. These can include detoxification, counseling, therapy (such as cognitive-behavioral therapy), support groups (like Alcoholics Anonymous or Narcotics Anonymous), and in some cases, medication. The approach to treatment can vary based on the substance involved, the severity of the disorder, and the individual's specific needs.

Non-Substance-Related Disorders

There are many other addictions that involve the use of something besides drugs and alcohol. An addiction is any behavior that a client feels powerless to control and interferes with the client's normal daily life. Addictions can have serious physical, emotional, and psychological consequences.

Sexual addiction is often misunderstood because, although it is perfectly acceptable to enjoy sexual activity, letting desires dictate daily life can cause shame and embarrassment. Sexual addiction often involves compulsive and promiscuous sexual behavior, porn addiction, and/or excessive masturbation.

Though essential for survival, food can also be the focus of addiction. Consuming excessive amounts of food is used by some to fill voids related to loneliness, shame, or lack of self-worth. This addiction can result in obesity or the development of an eating disorder. Some clients who have eating disorders also get addicted to exercise, such as running, to control their weight. Computer usage is also related to other addictions, such as online gambling and shopping.

Essentially, people can become addicted, dependent, or compulsively obsessed with any activity, substance, object, or behavior that gives pleasure. These activities, substances, objects, or behaviors produce beta-endorphins in the brain, producing a "high," leading to an addictive cycle. Those who are addicted will become obsessed with an activity, substance, object, or behavior and will seek it out, often to the detriment of work or interpersonal relationships. They will compulsively engage in the activity even if they do not want to do so. Cessation of the activity results in withdrawal symptoms of irritability, craving, and restlessness. Those with addictions do not appear to have control as to when, how long, or how much they will continue the activity, use of the substance or object, or behavior (loss of control). Individuals with addictive behaviors deny problems resulting from the addiction, even though others can see the negative effects. They usually have low self-esteem because there are psychological factors associated with other addictions as well.

Goals of Treatment

1. Abstinence from substances

2. Maximizing life functioning

3. Preventing or reducing the frequency and severity of relapse

The harm reduction model refers to any program, policy, or intervention that seeks to reduce or minimize the adverse health and social consequences associated with substance use without requiring a client to discontinue use. This definition recognizes that many substance users are unwilling or unable to abstain from use at any given time and that there is a need to provide them with options that minimize the harm that continued drug use causes to themselves, to others, and to the community.

Recovery is an ongoing process, and relapse occurs when attitudes, behaviors, and values revert to what they were during active drug or alcohol use. Relapse most frequently occurs during early stages of recovery, but it can occur at any time. Prevention of relapse is a critical part of treatment.

Stages of Treatment

1. Stabilization: Focus is on establishing abstinence, accepting a substance abuse problem, and committing oneself to making changes.

2. Rehabilitation/habilitation: Focus is on remaining substance-free by establishing a stable lifestyle, developing coping and living skills, increasing supports, and grieving loss of substance use.

3. Maintenance: Focus is on stabilizing gains made in treatment, relapse prevention, and termination.

A social worker should be aware of the signs and symptoms of use, as well as withdrawal. For example, use of cocaine can be associated with dilated pupils, hyperactivity, restlessness, perspiration, anxiety, and impaired judgment.

Delirium tremens (DTs) is a symptom associated with alcohol withdrawal that includes hallucinations, rapid respiration, temperature abnormalities, and body tremors.

Wernicke's encephalopathy and Korsakoff's syndrome are disorders associated with chronic abuse of alcohol. They are caused by a thiamine (vitamin B_1) deficiency resulting from the chronic consumption of alcohol. A person with Korsakoff's syndrome has memory problems. Treatment is administration of thiamine.

Treatment Approaches

1. *Medication-assisted treatment* interventions assist with interfering with the symptoms associated with use. For example, methadone, a synthetic narcotic, can be legally prescribed. A client uses it to detox from opiates or on a daily basis as a substitute for heroin. Antabuse is a medication that produces highly unpleasant side effects (flushing, nausea, vomiting, hypotension, and anxiety) if a client drinks alcohol; it is a form of "aversion therapy." Naltrexone is a drug used to reduce cravings for alcohol; it also blocks the effects of opioids.

2. *Psychosocial or psychological interventions* modify maladaptive feelings, attitudes, and behaviors through individual, group, marital, or family therapy. These therapeutic interventions also examine the roles that are adopted within families in which substance abuse occurs; for example, the "family hero," "scapegoat," "lost child," or "mascot" (a family member who alleviates pain in the family by joking around).

3. *Behavioral therapies* ameliorate or extinguish undesirable behaviors and encourage desired ones through behavior modification.

4. *Self-help groups* (Alcoholics Anonymous, Narcotics Anonymous) provide mutual support and encouragement while becoming abstinent or in remaining abstinent. Twelve-step groups are utilized throughout all phases of treatment. After completing formal treatment, the recovering person can continue attendance indefinitely as a means of maintaining sobriety.

SYSTEMS AND ECOLOGICAL PERSPECTIVES AND THEORIES

A system is a whole comprising component parts that work together. Applied to social work, systems theory views human behavior through larger contexts, such as members of families, communities, and broader society.

Important to this theory is the concept that when one thing changes within a system, the whole system is affected.

Systems tend toward equilibrium and can have closed or open boundaries.

Applications to Social Work

1. Social workers need to understand interactions between the micro, mezzo, and macro levels.

2. Problems at one part of a system may be manifested at another.

3. Ecomaps and genograms can help to understand system dynamics.

4. Understanding "person-in-environment" (PIE) is essential to identifying barriers or opportunities for change.

5. Problems and change are viewed within larger contexts.

Some System Theory Terms

Closed system	Uses up its energy and dies
Differentiation	Becoming specialized in structure and function
Entropy	Closed, disorganized, stagnant; using up available energy
Equifinality	Arriving at the same end from different beginnings
Homeostasis	Steady state
Input	Obtaining resources from the environment that are necessary to attain the goals of the system
Negative entropy	Exchange of energy and resources between systems that promote growth and transformation
Open system	A system with cross-boundary exchange
Output	A product of the system that exports to the environment
Subsystem	A major component of a system made up of two or more interdependent components that interact in order to attain their own purpose(s) and the purpose(s) of the system in which they are embedded
Suprasystem	An entity that is served by a number of component systems organized in interacting relationships
Throughput	Energy that is integrated into the system so it can be used by the system to accomplish its goals

ROLE THEORIES

A role is defined as the collection of expectations that accompany a particular social position. Clients have multiple roles in their lives; in different contexts or with different people, such as being students, friends, employees, spouses, or parents.

Each of these roles carries its own expectations about appropriate behavior, speech, attire, and so on. What might be rewarded in one role would be unacceptable for another (e.g., competitive behavior is rewarded for an athlete but not a preschool teacher). Roles range from specific, in that they only apply to a certain setting, to diffuse, in that they apply across a range of situations. For example, gender roles influence behavior across many different contexts. Role theory examines how these roles influence a wide array of psychological outcomes, including behavior, attitudes, cognitions, and social interaction.

There are some important terms used in role theory.

- *Role ambiguity*: lack of clarity of role
- *Role complementarity*: the role is carried out in an expected way (i.e., parent–child; social worker–client)

- *Role discomplementarity*: the role expectations of others differ from one's own
- *Role reversal*: when two or more individuals switch roles
- *Role conflict*: incompatible or conflicting expectations

When assessing, social workers view problems as differences between clients' behaviors and the expectations of others with regard to roles.

THEORIES OF GROUP DEVELOPMENT AND FUNCTIONING

Humans are small group beings. Group work is a method of social work that helps individuals to enhance their social functioning through purposeful group experiences, as well as to cope more effectively with their personal, group, or community problems. In group work, **individuals help each other** in order to influence and change personal, group, organizational, and community problems.

A social worker focuses on helping each member change the environment or behavior through interpersonal experience. Members help each other change or learn social roles in the particular positions held or desired in the social environment.

A therapeutic group provides a unique microcosm in which members, through the process of interacting with each other, gain more knowledge and insight into themselves for the purpose of making changes in their lives. The goal of the group may be a major or minor change in personality structure or changing a specific emotional or behavioral problem.

A social worker helps members come to agreement regarding the purpose, function, and structure of a group. A group is the major helping agent.

Individual self-actualization occurs through:

- Release of feelings that block social performance
- Support from others (not being alone)
- Orientation to reality and check out own reality with others
- Reappraisal of self

Some types of groups include:

- Groups centered on a shared problem
- Counseling groups
- Activity groups
- Action groups
- Self-help groups
- Natural groups
- Closed versus open groups
- Structured groups
- Crisis groups
- Reference groups (similar values)

Psychodrama is a treatment approach in which roles are enacted in a group context. Members of the group re-create their problems and devote themselves to the role dilemmas of each member.

Despite the differences in goals or purposes, all groups have common characteristics and processes.

The stages of group development are:

1. Preaffiliation—development of trust (known as forming)

2. Power and control—struggles for individual autonomy and group identification (known as storming)

3. Intimacy—utilizing self in service of the group (known as norming)

4. Differentiation—acceptance of each other as distinct individuals (known as performing)

5. Separation/termination—independence (known as adjourning)

Groups help through:

- Instillation of hope
- Universality
- Altruism
- Interpersonal learning
- Self-understanding and insight

Factors affecting group cohesion include:

- Group size
- Homogeneity: similarity of group members
- Participation in goal and norm setting for group
- Interdependence: dependent on one another for achievement of common goals
- Member stability: frequent change in membership results in less cohesiveness

Key Concepts

Groupthink is when a group makes faulty decisions because of group pressures. Groups affected by groupthink ignore alternatives and tend to take irrational actions that dehumanize other groups. A group is especially vulnerable to groupthink when its members are similar in background, when the group is insulated from outside opinions, and when there are no clear rules for decision making.

There are eight causes of groupthink:

1. Illusion of invulnerability—excessive optimism is created that encourages taking extreme risks

2. Collective rationalization—members discount warnings and do not reconsider their assumptions

3. Belief in inherent morality—members believe in the rightness of their cause and ignore the ethical or moral consequences of their decisions

4. Stereotyped views of those "on the out"—negative views of the "enemy" make conflict seem unnecessary

5. Direct pressure on dissenters—members are under pressure not to express arguments against any of the group's views

6. Self-censorship—doubts and deviations from the perceived group consensus are not expressed

7. Illusion of unanimity—the majority view and judgments are assumed to be unanimous

8. Self-appointed "mindguards"—members protect the group and the leader from information that is problematic or contradictory to the group's cohesiveness, views, and/or decisions

Group polarization occurs during group decision making when discussion strengthens a dominant point of view and results in a shift to a more extreme position than any of the members would adopt on their own. These more extreme decisions are toward greater risk if individuals' initial tendencies are to be risky and toward greater caution if individuals' initial tendencies are to be cautious.

THEORIES OF SOCIAL CHANGE AND COMMUNITY DEVELOPMENT

There is no one way to define community development. Over the years, community development has been defined as an occupation, a movement, an approach, and a set of values. It has been labeled the responsibility of social workers because it is seen as the most practical framework for creating lasting change for clients.

Community development has been used to the benefit of communities of place, of interest, and of identity. But despite these differences, there are certain principles, characteristics, and values that underpin nearly every definition of community development—neighborhood work aimed at improving the quality of community life through the participation of a broad spectrum of people at the local level.

Community development is a **long-term** commitment. It is not a quick fix to address a community's problems, nor is it a time-limited process. It aims to address imbalances in power and bring about change founded on social justice, equality, and inclusion. Its key purpose is to build communities based on justice, equality, and mutual respect.

Community development is ultimately about getting community members **working together** in collective action to tackle problems that many individuals may be experiencing or to help in achieving a shared dream that many individuals will benefit from.

THE DYNAMICS OF INTERPERSONAL RELATIONSHIPS

Family theory provides a theoretical and therapeutic base for dealing with family-related situations; it is also useful in understanding and managing individual problems by determining the extent to which such problems are related to family issues. A family systems approach argues that in order to understand a family system, a social worker must look at the family as a whole, rather than focusing on its members.

People do not exist in a vacuum. They live, play, go to school, and work with other people. Most anthropologists agree that, next to their peculiar tendency to think and use tools, one of the distinguishing characteristics of human beings is that they are social creatures. The social group that seems to be most universal and pervasive in the way it shapes human behavior is the family. For social workers, the growing awareness of the crucial impact of families on clients has led to the development of family systems theory.

Family systems theory searches for the causes of behavior, not in the individual alone, but in the interactions among the members of a group. The basic rationale is that all parts of the family are interrelated. Further, the family has properties of its own that can be known only by looking at the relationships and interactions among all members.

The family systems approach is based on several basic assumptions:

- Each family is more than a sum of its members.

- Each family is unique, due to the infinite variations in personal characteristics and cultural and ideological styles.

- A healthy family has flexibility, consistent structure, and effective exchange of information.

- The family is an interactional system whose component parts have constantly shifting boundaries and varying degrees of resistance to change.

- Families must fulfill a variety of functions for each member, both collectively and individually, if each member is to grow and develop.

- Families strive for a sense of balance or **homeostasis**.

- Negative feedback loops are those patterns of interaction that maintain stability or constancy while minimizing change. Negative feedback loops help to maintain homeostasis. Positive feedback loops, in contrast, are patterns of interaction that facilitate change or movement toward either growth or dissolution.

- Families are seen as being goal oriented. The concept of **equifinality** refers to the ability of the family system to accomplish the same goals through different routes.

- The concept of hierarchies describes how families organize themselves into various smaller units or **subsystems** that are comprised by the larger family system. When the members or tasks associated with each subsystem become blurred with those of other subsystems, families have been viewed as having difficulties. For example, when a child becomes involved in marital issues, difficulties often emerge that require intervention.

- Boundaries occur at every level of the system and between subsystems. Boundaries influence the movement of people and the flow of information into and out of the system. Some families have very open boundaries where members and others are allowed to freely come and go without much restriction; in other families, there are tight restrictions on where family members can go and who may be brought into the family system. Boundaries also regulate the flow of information in a family. In more closed families, the rules strictly regulate what information may be discussed and with whom. In contrast, information may flow more freely in families that have more permeable boundaries.

■ The concept of interdependence is critical in the study of family systems. Individual family members and the subsystems comprised by the family system are mutually influenced by and are mutually dependent upon one another. What happens to one family member, or what one family member does, influences other family members.

Genograms are diagrams of family relationships beyond a family tree allowing a social worker and client to visualize hereditary patterns and psychological factors. They include annotations about the medical history and major personality traits of each family member. Genograms help uncover intergenerational patterns of behavior, marriage choices, family alliances and conflicts, the existence of family secrets, and other information that will shed light on a family's present situation.

MODELS OF FAMILY LIFE EDUCATION IN SOCIAL WORK PRACTICE

Family life education aims to strengthen individual and family life through a family perspective. Social workers are well suited to work with a client within the family context, which is essential for such a model.

Much of family life education is delivered through parenting classes, premarriage education, marriage enrichment programs, and/or family financial planning courses. All of these activities focus on improving a client's quality of life individually and, equally as important, within the client's family unit.

Social workers use a strengths perspective, as well as their knowledge of human development, systems and social role theories, and ecological or "person-in-environment (PIE)" influences, when engaging in family life education.

When conducting family life education, a social worker must be aware of the social worker's own cultural values and norms with regard to material covered and not impose these beliefs on others or be judgmental.

STRENGTHS-BASED AND RESILIENCE THEORIES

The strengths perspective is based on the assumption that clients have the capacity to grow, change, and adapt (**humanistic approach**). Clients also have the knowledge that is important in defining and solving their problems (clients or families are experts about their own lives and situations); they are resilient and survive and thrive despite difficulties.

Strength is any ability that helps an individual (or family) to confront and deal with a stressful life situation and to use the challenging situation as a stimulus for growth. Individual strengths include, but are not limited to, cognitive abilities, coping mechanisms, personal attributes, interpersonal skills, or external resources. Families may have other strengths such as kinship bonds, community supports, religious connections, flexible roles, strong ethnic traditions, and so on.

Strengths vary from one situation to another and are contextual. What may be an appropriate strength or coping mechanism in one situation may not be appropriate in another. Ideally, in a given situation, a client selects an appropriate way to cope by drawing from a repertoire of coping mechanisms or strengths. The appropriateness of a particular coping mechanism may vary according to life course stage, developmental tasks, kinds of stressors, situation, and so on. Having a variety of coping mechanisms and resources enables flexibility in the way a client copes with stresses.

The strengths perspective focuses on understanding clients (or families) on the basis of their strengths and resources (internal and external) and mobilizing the resources to improve their situations. There is a systematic assessment of all the strengths and resources available to meet desired goals.

Methods to enhance strengths include:

- Collaboration and partnership between a social worker and client
- Creating opportunities for learning or displaying competencies
- Environmental modification—environment is both a resource and a target of intervention

THE IMPACT OF STRESS, TRAUMA, AND VIOLENCE

Emotional and psychological trauma is the result of extraordinarily stressful events that destroy a sense of security, making a client feel helpless and vulnerable in a dangerous world.

Traumatic experiences often involve a threat to life or safety, but **any situation that leaves a client feeling overwhelmed and alone can be traumatic, even if it does not involve physical harm**. It is not the objective facts that determine whether an event is traumatic, but a subjective emotional experience of the event.

An event will most likely lead to emotional or psychological trauma if:

- It happened unexpectedly
- There was not preparation for it
- There is a feeling of having been powerless to prevent it

- It happens repeatedly
- Someone was intentionally cruel
- It happened in childhood

Emotional and psychological trauma can be caused by onetime events or ongoing, relentless stress.

Not all potentially traumatic events lead to lasting emotional and psychological damage. Some clients rebound quickly from even the most tragic and shocking experiences. Others are devastated by experiences that, on the surface, appear to be less upsetting.

A number of risk factors make clients susceptible to emotional and psychological trauma. Clients are more likely to be traumatized by a stressful experience if they are already under a heavy stress load or have recently suffered a series of losses.

Clients are also more likely to be traumatized by a new situation if they have been traumatized before—especially if the earlier trauma occurred in childhood. Experiencing trauma in childhood can have a severe and long-lasting effect. Children who have been traumatized see the world as a frightening and dangerous place. When childhood trauma is not resolved, this fundamental sense of fear and helplessness carries over into adulthood, setting the stage for further trauma.

CRISIS INTERVENTION THEORIES

A "crisis" is an acute disruption of psychological homeostasis in which a client's usual coping mechanisms fail and there is evidence of distress and functional impairment. While there are many theories used to explain and address crises, there are seven critical stages through which clients typically pass on the road to crisis stabilization, resolution, and mastery. These stages are essential, sequential, and sometimes overlapping in the process of crisis intervention:

1. *Plan and conduct a thorough biopsychosocial–spiritual–cultural and lethality/imminent danger assessment.*

   A social worker must conduct a biopsychosocial–spiritual–cultural assessment covering a client's environmental supports and stressors, medical needs and medications, current use of drugs and alcohol, and internal and external coping methods and resources. Assessing lethality is first and foremost.

2. *Make psychological contact and rapidly establish the collaborative relationship.*

   In a crisis, a social worker must do this quickly, generally as part of assessment.

3. *Identify the major problems, including crisis precipitants.*

   A social worker should determine from a client why things have "come to a head." There is usually a "last straw," but a social worker should also find out what other problems a client is concerned about.

   It can also be useful to prioritize the problems in terms of which problems a client wants to work on first.

4. *Encourage an exploration of feelings and emotions.*

   A social worker should validate a client's feelings and emotions and let the client vent about the crisis. The use of active listening skills, paraphrasing, and probing questions is essential. A social worker should also challenge maladaptive beliefs.

5. *Generate and explore alternatives and new coping strategies.*

   A social worker and a client must come up with a plan for what will help improve the current situation. Brainstorming possibilities and finding out what has been helpful in the past are critical.

6. *Restore functioning through implementation of an action plan.*

   This stage represents a shift from a crisis to a resolution. A client and a worker will begin to take the steps negotiated in the previous stage. This is also where a client will begin to make meaning of the crisis event.

7. *Plan follow-up.*

   Follow-up can take many forms as it can involve phone or in-person visits at specific intervals. A postcrisis evaluation may look at a client's current functioning and assess a client's progress.

THEORIES OF TRAUMA-INFORMED CARE

Trauma-informed care organizations, programs, and services are based on an understanding of the vulnerabilities or triggers of trauma survivors that traditional service delivery approaches may exacerbate, so that these services and programs can be more supportive and avoid re-traumatization.

Trauma-informed care also can be viewed as an overarching philosophy and approach based on the understanding that many clients have suffered traumatic experiences and providers must be responsible for being sensitive to this issue, regardless of whether clients are being treated specifically for the trauma. Therefore, social workers should initially approach all of their clients as if they have a trauma history, regardless of the services for which the clients are being seen.

It is important for social workers to understand trauma and how it affects people regardless of their diagnoses or identified needs. Thus, in everyday practice, social workers need to recognize how the organizations, programs, and environments in which they practice could potentially act as trauma triggers for their clients and should make every effort to minimize these triggers.

An important component of trauma-informed care is recognizing trauma's centrality to clients and how this plays into their perception of physical and emotional safety, relationships, and behaviors. When trauma goes unrecognized, it can be difficult to understand clients' behaviors or attitudes, and social workers may be tempted to assign unfounded pathologies to clients. Clients even may end up being barred from services as a result of what appears to be bizarre behavior or unfounded beliefs. Often, however, clients' otherwise challenging behavior is provoked by a legitimate trigger that easily could have been avoided.

THE IMPACT OF THE ENVIRONMENT (E.G., SOCIAL, PHYSICAL, CULTURAL, POLITICAL, ECONOMIC) ON INDIVIDUALS, FAMILIES, GROUPS, ORGANIZATIONS, AND COMMUNITIES

Social workers must be knowledgeable about human behavior across the life course, the range of social systems in which people live, and the ways social systems promote or deter people in maintaining or achieving health and well-being. Social workers should apply theories and knowledge to understand biological, social, cultural, psychological, and spiritual development.

The ecological perspective is rooted in systems theory, which views coping as a transactional process that reflects the "PIE" relationship. Using this perspective, the focus of intervention is the interface between a client (person, family, group, etc.) and a client's environment. The ecological perspective is also concerned with the issues of power and privilege and how they are withheld from some groups, imposing enormous stress on affected individuals.

Environmental factors can have strong positive or negative impacts on development.

THE EFFECTS OF LIFE EVENTS, STRESSORS, AND CRISES ON INDIVIDUALS, FAMILIES, GROUPS, ORGANIZATIONS, AND COMMUNITIES

Crisis is an essential component in the understanding of human growth and development. It has important implications for quality of life and subjective well-being. Crisis situations are viewed as unusual, mostly negative events that tend to disrupt the normal life of a person.

A crisis is an upset to a steady state. When a stressful event becomes a crisis, the individual or family is vulnerable and feels mounting anxiety, tension, and disequilibrium. *A precipitating cause of a crisis does not have to be a major event.* It may be the "last straw" in a series of events that exceed a client's ability to cope.

An individual or family, at this point, may be emotionally overtaxed, hopeless, and incapable of effective functioning or making good choices and decisions. The person or family is at a "critical turning point" of coping effectively or not effectively.

The way in which life crises are addressed—whether surviving trauma, parental divorce, or a personal loss—has a very significant role to play in determining quality of life. When crises are understood, dealt with, and overcome, clients emerge as healthier and happier.

PERSON-IN-ENVIRONMENT (PIE) THEORY

The PIE perspective highlights the importance of understanding individual behavior in light of the environmental contexts in which a client lives and acts. The perspective has historical roots in the social work profession.

The PIE classification system was developed as an alternative to the commonly used disease and moral models (i.e., *DSM, International Statistical Classification of Diseases and Related Health Problems* [ICD], civil or penal codes) to implement social work philosophy and area of expertise. PIE is client-centered, rather than agency-centered.

The PIE classification system is field-tested and examines social role functioning, the environment, mental health, and physical health.

COMMUNICATION THEORIES AND STYLES

Communication theory involves the ways in which information is transmitted; the effects of information on human systems; how people receive information from their own feelings, thoughts, memories, physical sensations, and environments; how they evaluate this information; and how they subsequently act in response to the information.

Effective communication skills are one of the most crucial components of a social worker's job. Every day, social workers must communicate with clients to gain information, convey critical information, and make important decisions. Without effective communication skills, a social worker may not be able to obtain or convey that information, thereby causing detrimental effects on clients.

One cannot not communicate. Even when one is silent one is communicating, and another person is reacting to the silence. **Silence** is very effective when faced with a client who is experiencing a high degree of emotion, because the silence indicates acceptance of these feelings.

On the other hand, silence on the part of a client can indicate a reluctance to discuss a subject. A social worker should probe further with a client who is silent for an unusually long period of time. If people do not communicate clearly, mutual understanding, acceptance, or rejection of the communication will not occur, and relationship problems can arise.

Some communication styles can serve to inhibit effective communication with clients.

1. Using "shoulds" and "oughts" may be perceived as moralizing or sermonizing by a client and elicit feelings of resentment, guilt, or obligation. In reaction to feeling judged, a client may oppose a social worker's pressure to change.

2. Offering advice or solutions prematurely, before thorough exploration of the problem, may cause resistance because a client is not ready to solve the problem.

3. Using logical arguments, lecturing, or arguing to convince a client to take another viewpoint may result in a power struggle with a client. A better way of helping a client is to assist in exploring options in order to make an informed decision.

4. Judging, criticizing, and blaming are detrimental to a client, as well as to the therapeutic relationship. A client could respond by becoming defensive or, worse yet, internalizing the negative reflections.

5. Talking to a client in professional jargon and defining a client in terms of the client's diagnosis may result in a client internalizing the view of being "sick."

6. Providing reassurance prematurely or without a genuine basis is often for a social worker's benefit rather than a client's. It is a social worker's responsibility to explore and acknowledge a client's feelings, no matter how painful they are. A client may also feel that a social worker does not understand the client's situation.

7. Ill-timed or frequent interruptions disrupt the interview process and can annoy clients. Interruptions should be purposive, well-timed, and done in such a way that they do not disrupt the flow of communication.

8. It is counterproductive to permit excessive social interactions rather than therapeutic interactions. In order for a client to benefit from the helping relationship, the client has to self-disclose about problematic issues.

9. Social workers must provide structure and direction to the therapeutic process on a moment-to-moment basis in order to maximize the helping process. Passive or inactive social workers may miss fruitful moments that could be used for client benefit. Clients may lose confidence in social workers who are not actively involved in the helping process.

The following are some communication concepts that are critical to social work practice.

Acceptance

An acknowledgment of "what is." Acceptance does not pass judgment on a circumstance and allows clients to let go of frustration and disappointment, stress and anxiety, regret and false hopes. Acceptance is the practice of recognizing the limits of one's control. Acceptance is not giving up or excusing other people's behavior and allowing it to continue. Acceptance is not about giving in to circumstances that are unhealthy or uncomfortable. The main thing that gets in the way of acceptance is wanting to be in control.

Cognitive dissonance
Arises when a person has to choose between two contradictory attitudes and beliefs. The most dissonance arises when two options are equally attractive. Three ways to reduce dissonance are to (a) reduce the importance of conflicting beliefs, (b) acquire new beliefs that change the balance, or (c) remove the conflicting attitude or behavior. This theory is relevant when making decisions or solving problems.

Context
The circumstances surrounding human exchanges of information.

Double bind
Offering two contradictory messages and prohibiting the recipient from noticing the contradiction.

Echolalia
Repeating noises and phrases. It is associated with catatonia, autism spectrum disorder, schizophrenia, and other disorders.

Information
Anything people perceive from their environments or from within themselves. People act in response to information.

Information processing
Responses to information that are mediated through one's perception and evaluation of knowledge received.

Information processing block
Failure to perceive and evaluate potentially useful new information.

Metacommunication
The context within which to interpret the content of the message (i.e., nonverbal communication, body language, vocalizations).

Nonverbal communications
Facial expression, body language, and posture can be potent forms of communication.

In communication, there are two types of content, manifest and latent. Manifest content is the concrete words or terms contained in a communication, whereas latent content is that which is not visible, the underlying meaning of words or terms.

Relying just on the manifest content to understand client experiences or problems may result in not really understanding their meaning to individuals.

There are social work techniques such as clarifying, paraphrasing, confronting, and interpreting that can assist social workers in developing a better understanding of the meaning of clients' communication.

In addition, therapeutic techniques, such as psychoanalysis, focus on the hidden meaning of fantasies or dreams.

PSYCHOANALYTIC AND PSYCHODYNAMIC APPROACHES

Psychodynamic theories explain the origin of the personality. Although many different psychodynamic theories exist, they all emphasize unconscious motives and desires, as well as the importance of childhood experiences in shaping personality.

Psychoanalytic Theory

Originally developed by Sigmund Freud, a client is seen as the product of his past and treatment involves dealing with the repressed material in the unconscious. According to psychoanalytic theory, personalities arise because of attempts to resolve conflicts between unconscious sexual and aggressive impulses and societal demands to restrain these impulses.

Freud believed that behavior and personality derive from the constant and unique interaction of conflicting psychological forces that operate at **three different levels of awareness:** the preconscious, the conscious, and the unconscious.

The **conscious** contains all the information that a client is paying attention to at any given time.

The **preconscious** contains all the information outside of a client's attention but readily available if needed—thoughts and feelings that can be brought into consciousness easily.

The **unconscious** contains thoughts, feelings, desires, and memories of which clients have no awareness but that influence every aspect of their day-to-day lives.

Freud proposed that personalities have three components: the id, the ego, and the superego.

- **Id:** A reservoir of instinctual energy that contains biological urges such as impulses toward survival, sex, and aggression. The id is unconscious and operates according to the **pleasure principle**, the drive to achieve pleasure and avoid pain.
- **Ego:** The component that manages the conflict between the id and the constraints of the real world. Some parts of the ego are unconscious, whereas others are preconscious or conscious. The ego operates according to the reality principle—the awareness that gratification of impulses has to be delayed in order to accommodate the demands of the real world. The ego's role is to prevent the id from gratifying its impulses in socially inappropriate ways.

Ego-Syntonic/Ego-Dystonic:

- Syntonic = behaviors "insync" with the ego (no guilt)
- Dystonic = behavior "dis-n-sync" with the ego (guilt)

The ego's job is to determine the best course of action based on information from the id, reality, and the superego. When the ego is comfortable with its conclusions and behaviors, a client is said to be ego-syntonic. However, if a client is bothered by some behaviors, the client would be ego-dystonic (ego alien).

Inability of the ego to reconcile the demands of the id, the superego, and reality produces conflict that leads to a state of psychic distress known as anxiety.

Ego strength is the ability of the ego to effectively deal with the demands of the id, the superego, and reality. Those with little ego strength may feel torn between these competing demands, whereas those with too much ego strength can become too unyielding and rigid. Ego strength helps maintain emotional stability and cope with internal and external stress.

- **Superego:** The moral component of personality. It contains all the moral standards learned from parents and society. The superego forces the ego to conform not only to reality, but also to its ideals of morality. Hence, the superego causes clients to feel guilty when they go against society's rules.

Psychosexual Stages of Development

Freud believed that personality solidifies during childhood, largely before age 5. He proposed five stages of psychosexual development: the oral stage, the anal stage, the phallic stage, the latency stage, and the genital stage. He believed that at each stage of development, children gain sexual gratification or sensual pleasure from a particular part of their bodies. Each stage has special conflicts, and children's ways of managing these conflicts influence their personalities.

If a child's needs in a particular stage are gratified too much or frustrated too much, the child can become fixated at that stage of development. **Fixation** is an inability to progress normally from one stage into another. When the child becomes an adult, the fixation shows up as a tendency to focus on the needs that were overgratified or overfrustrated.

Freud believed that the crucially important **Oedipus complex** also developed during the phallic stage. The Oedipus complex refers to a male child's sexual desire for his mother and hostility toward his father, whom he considers to be a rival for his mother's love. Freud thought that a male child who sees a naked girl for the first time believes that her penis has been cut off. The child fears that his own father will do the same to him for desiring his mother—a fear called **castration anxiety**. Because of this fear, the child represses his longing for his mother and begins to identify with his father. The child's acceptance of his father's authority results in the emergence of the superego.

Stage	Age	Sources of pleasure	Result of fixation
Oral	Birth to roughly 12 months	Activities involving the mouth, such as sucking, biting, and chewing	Excessive smoking, overeating, or dependence on others
Anal	Age 2, when the child is being toilet trained	Bowel movements	An overly controlling (anal-retentive) personality or an easily angered (anal-expulsive) personality
Phallic	Age 3–5	Genitals	Guilt or anxiety about sex
Latency	Age 5 to puberty	Sexuality is latent, or dormant, during this period	No fixations at this stage
Genital	Begins at puberty	The genitals; sexual urges return	No fixations at this stage

In psychoanalytic psychotherapy, the primary technique used is analysis (of dreams, resistances, transferences, and free associations).

Individual Psychology

Alfred Adler, a follower of Freud and a member of his inner circle, eventually broke away from Freud and developed his own school of thought, which he called "individual psychology." Adler believed that the **main motivations for human behavior are not sexual or aggressive urges, but striving for perfection**. He pointed out that children naturally feel weak and inadequate in comparison to adults. This normal feeling of inferiority drives them to adapt, develop skills, and master challenges. Adler used the term "**compensation**" to refer to the attempt to shed normal feelings of inferiority.

However, some people suffer from an exaggerated sense of **inferiority**. Such people overcompensate, which means that, rather than try to master challenges, they try to cover up their sense of inferiority by focusing on outward signs of superiority such as status, wealth, and power.

Healthy individuals have a broad social concern and want to contribute to the welfare of others. Unhealthy people are those who are overwhelmed by feelings of inferiority.

The aim of therapy is to develop a more adaptive lifestyle by overcoming feelings of inferiority and self-centeredness and to contribute more toward the welfare of others.

Self Psychology

This approach defines the self as the central organizing and motivating force in personality. As a result of receiving empathic responses from early caretakers (self-objects), a child's needs are met and the child develops a strong sense of selfhood. "Empathic failures" by caretakers result in a lack of self-cohesion.

The objective of self psychology is to help a client develop a greater sense of self-cohesion. Through therapeutic regression, a client reexperiences frustrated self-object needs.

Three self-object needs are:

- **Mirroring:** behavior validates the child's sense of a perfect self.

- **Idealization:** child borrows strength from others and identifies with someone more capable.

- **Twinship/Twinning:** child needs an alter ego for a sense of belonging.

Ego Psychology

Ego psychology focuses on the rational, conscious processes of the ego. Ego psychology is based on an assessment of a client as presented in the present (here and now). Treatment focuses on the ego functioning of a client, because healthy behavior is under the control of the ego. It addresses:

- Behavior in varying situations

- Reality testing: perception of a situation

- Coping abilities: ego strengths

- Capacity for relating to others

The goal is to maintain and enhance the ego's control and management of stress and its effects.

Object Relations Theory

Object relations theory, which was a focus of Margaret Mahler's work, is centered on relationships with others. According to this theory, lifelong relationship skills are strongly rooted in early attachments with parents, especially mothers. Objects refer to people, parts of people, or physical items that symbolically represent either a person or part of a person. Object relations, then, are relationships to those people or items.

Age	Phase	Subphase	Characteristics
0–1 month	**Normal autism**		First few weeks of life. The infant is detached and self-absorbed. Spends most of the time sleeping. Mahler later abandoned this phase, based on new findings from her infant research.
1–5 months	**Normal symbiotic**		The child is now aware of the mother, but there is not a sense of individuality. The infant and the mother are one, and there is a barrier between them and the rest of the world.
5–9 months	**Separation/ Individuation**	Differentiation/ Hatching	The infant ceases to be ignorant of the differentiation between the infant and the mother. Increased alertness and interest for the outside world. Using the mother as a point of orientation.
9–15 months		Practicing	Brought about by the infant's ability to crawl and then walk freely; the infant begins to explore actively and becomes more distant from the mother.
15–24 months		Rapprochement	The infant once again becomes close to the mother. The child realizes that physical mobility demonstrates psychic separateness from the mother. The toddler may become tentative, wanting the mother to be in sight so that, through eye contact and action, the toddler can explore the world. The risk is that the mother will misread this need and respond with impatience or unavailability. This can lead to an anxious fear of abandonment in the toddler.
24–38 months	**Object Constancy**		Describes the phase when the child understands that the mother has a separate identity and is truly a separate individual. Provides the child with an image that helps supply the child with an unconscious level of guiding support and comfort. Deficiencies in positive internalization could possibly lead to a sense of insecurity and low self-esteem issues in adulthood.

THE IMPACT OF CAREGIVING ON FAMILIES

Although caregiving is at the heart of family functioning, the dynamics of families can be greatly altered when family members experience physical illness or disability. For example, when a primary family caregiver becomes ill or disabled, family roles must shift to redistribute the tasks that this family member is unable to perform. This redistribution includes both instrumental and emotional tasks, as the family may face a loss of both financial and emotional support that was provided by the primary family caregiver.

When a child is ill or disabled, parents can be overwhelmed by the added responsibilities to typical childrearing. In addition, healthy siblings may also feel the strain and may feel that they should not "burden" parents any further, so they ignore their own emotional and/or physical needs.

The stage when physical illness or disability occurs within the life course can also have differential impacts. For example, parents of children born ill or disabled may be more accepting of the situation than those who are faced with the illness or disability of children that occurs later. At any time, it is a major challenge for a family to tend to its members' individual developmental needs and meet the caregiving demands of a serious illness or disability. Some families may be paralyzed at the time of the illness or onset of the disability. Crisis intervention may be needed to stabilize the situation and develop coping skills.

Addressing the grief or loss that can accompany chronic illness or disability may also be needed. In addition, families may seek help from social workers to identify critical resources because they are not able to meet family members' needs and/or their own without them. Lastly, illness and disability can be isolating for an individual, as well as the individual's family.

THE DYNAMICS AND EFFECTS OF LOSS, SEPARATION, AND GRIEF

Loss, separation, and grief are expressed differently, but it is essential that they involve mourning to allow healing. Loss, separation, and grief can be caused by death, disability, divorce, relocation, family conflict, and other life events. Loss is universal, but the reactions to it are not. Mourning is the expression of grief such as crying, talking to others, sharing stories, looking at photos, etc. Grief is not only expressed through emotion. It includes physical, behavioral, cognitive, social, and spiritual reactions. Responses to loss, separation, and grief are influenced by gender, culture, race, spirituality, and ethnicity. Instead of encouraging mourning, people often discourage showing emotions associated with loss, separation, and grief by telling others to "be strong." While people mourn in different ways, there are needs which exist such as:

- Acknowledging the reality of the loss or separation
- Embracing the pain of the loss
- Remembering the relationships that existed
- Developing a new self-identity
- Searching for meaning
- Receiving ongoing support from others

There is growth which can result from grief, but it is often not readily apparent and cannot be achieved immediately. There is no predefined timeframe for grief as it is processed differently by each person. Grief is a reaction to any loss, not just death. Emotional reactions can include but are not limited to sadness, guilt, loneliness, and yearning. Sometimes the emotions associated with grief can be intense and at other times, they can wane. However, they can return quickly and strongly, often without warning. There are often mourning rituals and customs around loss, separation, and grief.

Although most people retain or return to the levels of functioning prior to the loss, separation, or grief, a significant proportion struggle with protracted grief. Grieving can be thought of as a developmental process with phases which focus on reacting (focusing on safety, trust, and survival), reconstructing (focusing on validation and understanding), and reorienting (focusing on self-reinvention), though the process is not always linear.

Concepts of Abuse and Neglect

INDICATORS AND DYNAMICS OF ABUSE AND NEGLECT THROUGHOUT THE LIFESPAN

There are various forms of abuse and neglect: **physical abuse** (infliction of physical injury); **sexual abuse** (inappropriate exposure or sexual contact, activity, or behavior without consent); **psychological abuse** (emotional/verbal/mental injury); and **neglect** (failing to meet physical, emotional, or other needs).

Different forms of abuse occur separately, but are often seen in combinations. Psychological abuse almost always accompanies other forms of abuse.

Indicators and Dynamics of Sexual Abuse

Physical or anatomical signs/injuries associated with the genital and rectal areas are signs of physical or sexual abuse. Behavioral signs include any extreme changes in behavior, including regression, fears and anxieties, withdrawal, sleep disturbances, and/or recurrent nightmares. If the victim is a child, the child may also show an unusual interest in sexual matters or know sexual information inappropriate for the child's age group. Sexual promiscuity, sexual victimization, and prostitution can also be signs.

Some factors influencing the effect of sexual abuse include:

- Age of the victim (at time of abuse and time of assessment)
- Extent and duration of sexual abuse
- Relationship of offender to victim
- Reaction of others to the abuse
- Other life experiences

Immediately after disclosing the abuse, an individual is at risk for:

- Disbelief by others (especially if victim is a child or perpetrator is a spouse/partner of an adult)

- Being rejected by others
- Being blamed for the abuse and the consequences of disclosing the sexual abuse

For a child, one of the most significant factors contributing to adjustment after sexual abuse is the level of parental support.

Some of the effects of sexual abuse can be:

- Aversive feelings about sex; overvaluing sex; sexual identity problems; and/or hyper-sexual behaviors
- Feelings of shame and guilt or feeling responsible for the abuse, which are reflected in self-destructive behaviors (such as substance abuse, self-mutilation, suicidal ideation and gestures, and acts that aim to provoke punishment)
- Lack of trust, unwillingness to invest in others; involvement in exploitive relationships; angry and acting-out behaviors
- Perceived vulnerability and victimization; phobias; sleep and eating problems

Indicators and Dynamics of Psychological Abuse and Neglect

Psychological abuse/neglect is sustained, repetitive, and inappropriate behavior aimed at threatening, isolating, discrediting, belittling, teasing, humiliating, bullying, confusing, and/or ignoring. Psychological abuse/neglect can be seen in constant criticism, belittling, teasing, ignoring or withholding of praise or affection, and placing excessive or unreasonable demands, including expectations above what is appropriate.

It can impact intelligence, memory, recognition, perception, attention, imagination, and moral development. Individuals who have been psychologically abused are likely to be fearful, withdrawn, and/or resentful, distressed, and despairing. They are likely to feel unloved, worthless, and unwanted, or only valued in meeting another's needs.

Those who are victims of psychological abuse and neglect often:

- Avoid eye contact and experience deep loneliness, anxiety, and/or despair
- Have a flat and superficial way of relating, with little empathy toward others
- Have a lowered capacity to engage appropriately with others
- Engage in bullying, disruptive, or aggressive behaviors toward others
- Engage in self-harming and/or self-destructive behaviors (i.e., cutting, physical aggression, reckless behavior showing a disregard for self and safety, drug taking)

Indicators and Dynamics of Physical Abuse and Neglect

Physical abuse is defined as nonaccidental trauma or physical injury caused by punching, beating, kicking, biting, or burning. It is the most visible form of abuse because there are usually physical signs.

With a child, physical abuse can result from inappropriate or excessive physical discipline. Indicators of physical abuse include:

- Unexplained bruises or welts on the face, lips, mouth, torso, back, buttocks, or thighs, sometimes reflecting the shape of the article used to inflict them (electric cord, belt buckle, etc.)
- Unexplained burns from a cigar or cigarette, especially on soles, palms, back, or buttocks—sometimes patterned like an electric burner, iron, or similar
- Unexplained fractures to the skull, nose, or facial structure
- Unexplained lacerations or abrasions to the mouth, lips, gums, eyes, and/or external genitalia

Behavioral indicators include being wary of individuals (parent or caretaker if a child is being abused) and behavioral extremes (aggressiveness or withdrawal), as well as fear related to reporting injury.

THE EFFECTS OF PHYSICAL, SEXUAL, AND PSYCHOLOGICAL ABUSE ON INDIVIDUALS, FAMILIES, GROUPS, ORGANIZATIONS, AND COMMUNITIES

Abuse and neglect have both immediate and long-term consequences. The impacts are often influenced by various factors including the extent and type of abuse or neglect, whether it was continual or infrequent, the age at which it occurred, the relationship to the perpetrator (if abuse), and how the abuse or neglect was discovered and addressed upon disclosure. Client personality traits, inner strength, and support systems also influence the effects.

For many, the impacts of abuse and neglect will not be immediately evident. Physical injuries, if there are any, are usually temporary. The more damaging and lasting impacts are those that result from impaired language, cognitive, and physical development due to the abuse and neglect. Children who have been abused and neglected are at risk of academic problems and school failure due to difficulty following rules, being respectful, staying in their seats and keeping on-task, temper tantrums, and/or difficult peer relationships.

In addition, social and emotional problems, poor relationships, substance use and dependency, risky or violent behaviors, and delinquency are manifestations of abuse and neglect. The psychological consequences of abuse and neglect include isolation, fear, inability to trust, low self-esteem, anxiety, depression, and hopelessness. These difficulties can lead to relationship problems and the possibility of antisocial behavioral traits.

It is important to note that not all those who have been abused and neglected will experience physical, behavioral, and/or psychological problems—though they are more likely. Thus, a lack of these problems should not be used as evidence that abuse or neglect did not occur.

THE INDICATORS, DYNAMICS, AND IMPACT OF EXPLOITATION ACROSS THE LIFESPAN (E.G., FINANCIAL, IMMIGRATION STATUS, SEXUAL TRAFFICKING)

Exploitation is treating a person badly in order to benefit from the person's resources or work. It is when someone uses a situation to gain unfair advantage. Exploitation is more common when there is a power differential between parties due to social status, abilities, income, education, job position, and so on.

Social workers have ethical mandates not to exploit clients, supervisees, students, and others who they come in contact with in their work.

They also may be asked to assess exploitation of clients by others and intervene when needed. For example, a form of maltreatment sometimes seen with older adults is financial/material exploitation or unauthorized use of an older person's resources. Individuals may befriend an older person to gain trust so that the older adult's money or items of value can be inappropriately used for the individual's wants or needs and not the care of the older adult.

On a macro level, it is also important to see the relationship between discrimination and exploitation of individuals. When individuals are not provided the same access to social rewards, they are inherently exploited. Most social problems are aggravated by the status of particular groups in the society, including that:

- There is a greater prevalence of poverty among people of color and female household heads.

- Poverty decreases the opportunities for employment, education, goods, and so on.

- Poverty creates greater stresses that lead to physical and mental illnesses, family breakdown, inability to work, and other problems.

- Discrimination creates deficits in social power.

THE CHARACTERISTICS OF PERPETRATORS OF ABUSE, NEGLECT, AND EXPLOITATION

Many individuals with these characteristics do not commit acts of abuse. However, some factors are more likely to be present in those who commit abusive acts. Thus, having one of these risk factors does not mean that an individual will become an abuser, but an abuser is likely to have one or more of these risk factors.

A past history of violent behavior is the best predictor of future violence. Each prior act of violence increases the chance of future episodes of violence. In addition, those who suffered some form of abuse as children are more likely to be perpetrators of abuse as adults.

Risk factors include:

1. History of owning weapons and using them against others
2. Criminal history; repetitive antisocial behavior
3. Drug and alcohol use (substance use is associated with the most violent crimes)
4. Psychiatric disorder with coexisting substance abuse
5. Certain psychiatric symptoms such as psychosis, intense suspiciousness, anger, and/or unhappiness
6. Personality disorders (borderline and antisocial personality disorders)
7. History of impulsivity; low frustration tolerance; recklessness; inability to tolerate criticism; entitlement

8. Angry affect without empathy for others—high anger scores associated with increased chance of violence

9. Environmental stressors: lower socioeconomic status or poverty; job termination

A social worker should take all reports of abuse and all threats for harm seriously. A social worker can distinguish between static and dynamic risk factors.

Static risk factors: These are factors that cannot be changed by interventions such as past history of violent behavior or demographic information.

Dynamic risk factors: These are factors that can be changed by interventions such as change in living situation, treatment of psychiatric symptoms, abstaining from drug and alcohol use, access to weapons, and so on. Each client presents with a unique set of risk factors that require an individualized plan.

Some of the risk factors include the following:

- *Stressors*: history of abuse; isolated with lack of social supports; low sense of self-competence and self-esteem; financial problems
- *Poor skills*: rigid, authoritarian; low intelligence quotient (IQ); poor self-control; poor communication, problem-solving, and interpersonal skills
- *Family issues*: marital discord, imbalanced relationship with marital partner (dominant or noninvolved); domestic violence; substance abuse

The victim is often blamed for the abuse by the perpetrator.

Interventions to reduce dynamic risk factors include:

- Pharmacological interventions
- Substance use treatment
- Psychosocial interventions
- Removal of weapons
- Increased level of supervision

3

Diversity, Social/ Economic Justice, and Oppression

THE EFFECT OF DISABILITY ON BIOPSYCHOSOCIAL FUNCTIONING THROUGHOUT THE LIFESPAN

With increased age comes increased likelihood of disability as people live longer and do not encounter fatal diseases. Unfortunately, this positive association between age and disability sometimes leads to a negative image of aging. Given that the aging process often results in some type of disability, examinations of differences in aging outcomes have not centered around whether disabilities will occur, but rather when they will happen, how many will occur, and how severe they will be.

Disability occurs when physical or mental health declines associated with aging, illness, or injury restrict ability to perform activities of daily living (ADLs). Mobility impairment is often tied to disability because being able to ambulate and/or use one's upper extremities are critical to engaging in many activities that allow independence.

The most common causes of disability among older adults are chronic diseases, injuries, mental impairment, and/or malnutrition. Major chronic conditions related to disability include cardiovascular diseases, hypertension, stroke, diabetes, cancer, chronic obstructive pulmonary disease, musculoskeletal conditions including arthritis and osteoporosis, mental health conditions such as dementia and depression, and blindness and visual impairment. Injuries can be due to accidents and/or falls.

There is a relationship between disability and poverty. Poverty can lead to malnutrition, poor or no health services, and/or unsafe living conditions that can result in increased risk for disability. Disability can also result in loss of income and, thus, a greater likelihood of living in poverty.

Interestingly, happiness and well-being tend to be high among older adults overall despite declines in physical and mental health and the onset of disability for some. This discrepancy is due to the fact that not all disability leads to dependence. If the consequences of disability can be reduced or eliminated altogether, its negative effects on quality of life can be minimized.

The environment and improvements in lifestyle are critical. The environment plays an important role in the impact of disability on the lives of older adults, with those remaining outside of institutional settings—such as nursing homes—being more productive and satisfied.

In addition, environments based on accessible design promote independent living, which can result in good quality of life for those who are older and/or have disabilities.

Improvements in lifestyle and health behaviors include better nutrition, quitting or reducing smoking, less obesity, and greater physical activity. Benefits from exercise, even when begun later in life, can postpone and/or minimize disability.

THE EFFECT OF CULTURE, RACE, AND ETHNICITY ON BEHAVIORS, ATTITUDES, AND IDENTITY

Cultural, racial, and ethnic groups are diverse and behaviors, attitudes, and identities of their members change over time. Understanding the effects cannot be achieved by learning facts about specific populations or attending trainings on cultural competence. Working with those from diverse cultural, racial, and/or ethnic groups is a developmental process that begins with awareness and commitment and evolves into skill building and culturally responsive behavior.

Social workers must recognize the importance of culture, race, and/or ethnicity on behaviors, attitudes, and identity. Clients do not share the same beliefs and practices or perceive, interpret, or encounter similar experiences in the same way. Social workers must recognize that people have ethnocentric views that are shaped by their culture, race, and/or ethnicity. It is often difficult to appreciate differences and to address these differences effectively, because many people tend to see things solely from their own culture-bound perspectives.

The following listing describes some effects of culture, race, and/or ethnicity, as well as factors which can contribute to behavioral, attitudinal, and identity differences.

Language and Communication

Language is a key element of culture but speaking the same language does not necessarily mean the sharing of the same cultural beliefs. Conversely, those who share an ethnicity do not automatically share a language. Families who immigrated to this country several generations earlier may identify with their culture of origin but no longer be able to speak its language.

Styles of communication and nonverbal methods of communication are also important aspects of cultural groups. Issues such as the use of direct versus indirect communication, appropriate personal space, social parameters for and displays of physical contact, use of silence, preferred ways of moving, meaning of gestures, degree to which arguments and verbal confrontations are acceptable, degree of formality expected in communication, and amount of eye contact expected are all culturally defined and reflect very basic cultural, racial, and/or ethnic differences. More specifically, the relative importance of nonverbal messages varies greatly from culture to culture.

Geographic Location

Cultural groups form within communities and among people who interact meaningfully with each other. Any culture is subject to local adaptations. For example, clients coming from a geographic area—even if they come from different ethnicities—can have a great deal in common, whereas individuals from the same ethnicity who were raised in different geographic locales can have very different experiences and, consequently, attitudes.

Geography can strongly affect substance use and abuse, mental health and well-being, and access to and use of behavioral health services. Even among members of the same culture, race, and/or ethnicity, these factors differ across geographic areas.

Worldview, Values, and Traditions

There are many ways of conceptualizing how culture influences behaviors, attitudes, and identity. Culture can be seen as a frame through which to look at the world, beliefs and practices that can be used to explain why people do what they do, sets of values and traditions to delineate one group of people from another, and so on. Cultural groups define the values, worldviews, and traditions of their members, from food preferences to appropriate leisure activities.

Family and Kinship

Although families are important in all cultural groups, concepts of and attitudes toward family are culturally defined and can vary in a number of ways, including the relative importance of particular family ties, family inclusiveness, hierarchies within families, and how family roles and behaviors are defined. In some cultural groups, family is limited to the nuclear family, whereas in other groups, the idea of family typically includes many other blood or marital relations. Some cultural groups clearly define roles for different family members and carefully prescribe methods of behaving toward one another based on specific relationships. Despite culture, family dynamics may change as the result of internal or external forces. Acculturation can significantly affect family roles and dynamics among immigrant families, causing the dissolution of longstanding cultural hierarchies and traditions, resulting in potential conflict between spouses or different generations of a family.

Gender Roles

Gender roles are largely cultural constructs; diverse cultural groups have different understandings of the proper roles, attitudes, and behaviors for those of different genders. Culturally defined gender has a strong effect on behaviors, attitudes, and identity. Some cultural groups identify gender as binary—male and female—while others do not.

Socioeconomic Status and Education

Socioeconomic status (SES) affects culture in several ways, namely through the accumulation of material wealth, access to opportunities, and use of resources. Education is also an important factor related to SES, with higher levels of education associated with increased income. Discrimination and historical racism have led to lasting inequalities in SES. Poverty results in limited access to resources, increased stress, and enhanced vulnerabilities to substance use and mental illness.

Health disparities are defined as differences in the incidence, prevalence, morbidity, and burden of diseases and other adverse health conditions that exist between specific groups. There are longstanding health disparities between cultural, racial, and ethnic groups. The causes of these historical inequalities include lack of insurance coverage and persistent discrimination, as well as distrust of the service delivery system by certain groups. Social determinants of health are conditions that affect functioning and quality-of-life outcomes, including access to educational, economic, and vocational training; job opportunities; transportation; healthcare services; emerging technologies; availability of community-based resources, basic resources to meet daily living needs, language services, and social support; exposure to crime; community and concentrated poverty; and residential segregation.

Immigration and Migration

Immigration is stressful, though the reasons for migrating and the legal status of immigrants affect the degree of stress. Immigrants who are refugees from war, famine, oppression, and other dangerous environments are more vulnerable to psychological distress. They are likely to have left behind painful and often life-threatening situations in their countries of origin and are likely to be impacted by these experiences.

For immigrants, there may be conflicts in identities—wanting to fit in with new cultures while also wanting to retain the values of their cultures of origin. Cultural identification may change over time and vary from group to group. Adaptation and acculturation can be a source of conflict within families, especially when parents and children adapt or acculturate at different rates.

For documented residents, the process of adaptation tends to be smoother than for those who are undocumented. However, they can have concerns surrounding the renewal of visas and obtainment of citizenship. Undocumented persons may be wary of deportation, are less likely to seek social services, and frequently encounter hostility. There are numerous variables that contribute to or influence well-being, quality of life, cultural adaptation, and the development of resilience.

Immigration nearly always includes separation from family and culture and can involve a grieving process resulting from these losses, as well as changes in socioeconomic status, physical environment, social support, and/or cultural practices. For immigrant families, disruption of roles and norms often occurs. Clients who are migrants (e.g., seasonal workers) pose a particular set of challenges as they are particularly marginalized and underserved due to lack of childcare, insurance, access to regular health care, and transportation. High rates of alcohol use, alcohol use disorders, and binge drinking, often occur as a response to stress or boredom associated with the migrant lifestyle.

Sexuality

Attitudes toward sexuality and toward sexual identity or orientation are culturally defined. Each culture determines how to conceptualize specific sexual behaviors, the degree to which they accept same-gender relationships, and the types of sexual behaviors considered acceptable or not. Diverse views and attitudes about appropriate gender norms and behavior exist between cultural, racial, and/or ethnic groups. Sexual behaviors considered acceptable for one gender can be considered unacceptable for another. Other factors that can vary across cultural groups include the appropriate age for sexual activity, the rituals and actions surrounding sexual activity, the use of birth control, the level of secrecy or openness related to sexual acts, the role of sex workers, attitudes toward sexual dysfunction, and the level of sexual freedom in choosing partners.

Perspectives on Health, Illness, and Healing

Behaviors and attitudes related to health, illness, and healing vary across racial, ethnic, and cultural groups. In general, cultural groups differ in how they define and determine health and illness; who is able to diagnose and treat an illness; their beliefs about the causes of illness; and their remedies, treatments, and healing practices for illness. In addition, there are complex rules about which members of a community or family can make decisions about health care across cultural groups. Mental disorders or symptoms may be socially defined norms. For instance, in some societies, those who hear voices can be considered to have greater access to the spirit world and to be blessed in some way. Furthermore, there are mental disorders that only present in a specific cultural group or locality. Other specific examples of cultural differences relate to the use of health care and alternative approaches to medical diagnoses and treatments.

Religion and Spirituality

Religious traditions or spiritual beliefs are often very important factors associated with culture, race, and ethnicity. However, members of religious groups can be racially or ethnically diverse. It is important to distinguish between spirituality and religion. Some clients are willing to think of themselves as spiritual but not necessarily religious. Religion is organized, with each religion having its own set of beliefs and practices designed to organize and further its members' spirituality. Spirituality, on the other hand, is typically conceived of as a personal matter involving a search for meaning; it does not require an affiliation with any religious group. People can have spiritual experiences or develop their own spirituality outside of the context of an organized religion.

THE EFFECTS OF DISCRIMINATION AND STEREOTYPES ON BEHAVIORS, ATTITUDES, AND IDENTITY

The negative impacts of discrimination can be seen on both the micro and macro levels. Exposure to discrimination is linked to anxiety and depression as well as other mental health and behavioral problems. In addition, there may be physical effects such as diabetes, obesity, and high blood pressure. These health problems may be caused by not maintaining healthy behaviors (such as physical activity) or engaging in unhealthy ones (such as smoking and alcohol or drug abuse).

On a macro level, discrimination also restricts access to the resources and systems needed for good health, education, employment, social support, and participation in sports, cultural, and civic activities. Discrimination and intolerance can also create a climate of despondence, apprehension, and fear within a community. The social and economic effects of discrimination on one generation may flow on to affect future generations, which can lead to cycles of poverty and disadvantage through those generations.

THE INFLUENCE OF SEXUAL ORIENTATION ON BEHAVIORS, ATTITUDES, AND IDENTITY

Sexuality is a crucial part of who we are. Sexual orientation, sexual behavior, and sexual identity are three parts of sexuality that can help to understand the term better.

> **Sexual orientation** refers to an individual's pattern of physical and emotional arousal toward other persons. People do not choose their sexual orientation—it is simply part of who they are.
>
> **Sexual behavior** refers to sexual contacts or actions. It is important to realize that people's sexual orientation may not fit perfectly with their sexual behavior (what they do sexually). There are many factors that shape or determine sexual behavior and sexual orientation is only one of those factors. Sexual behavior can be influenced by peer pressure, family expectations, cultural expectations, religious beliefs, and so on.
>
> **Sexual identity** also may be very different from an individual's sexual orientation. Sexual identity is about the way people present their sexual preferences. People may have private sexual identities, which may be different from their public identities. Even private sexual identities can differ from sexual orientation or attractions. Many people who experience same-sex attraction and/or have sexual contact with others of the same sex do not see themselves as homosexual or bisexual.

Sexual orientation often does not fit "neatly" into a label or category. People's attractions can be complicated and often are not clear. Clients may be struggling to determine what feels right for them.

Sexual orientation can be fluid with attractions changing over time. Some people take a while to figure out these attractions. That does not mean people "grow out of" their sexual attractions or that one set of feelings was a stage, it just means people change. *It is important to not use labels and let individuals define their own sexual orientation.*

THE IMPACT OF TRANSGENDER AND TRANSITIONING PROCESS ON BEHAVIORS, ATTITUDES, IDENTITY, AND RELATIONSHIPS

"Transgender" is a term for people whose gender identity, expression, or behavior is different from those typically associated with their assigned sex at birth. "Trans" is sometimes used as shorthand for "transgender."

People might realize they are trans (that their gender identity does not align with their birth sex designation) at any point in their lives. Some people may first experience an internal sense of identity that does not match their external characteristics in early childhood. Others report realizing this in puberty or later. Societal gender norms and expectations may contribute to realization of their true gender identity. These assumptions can also contribute to dysphoria, as people might first attempt to conform to societal expectations by expressing gender identities they do not have. Feelings of distress frequently arise, during which people realize that they cannot meet these gender norms as they do not match their identities.

Transition is a time when individuals begin living as the gender with which they identify rather than the gender they were assigned at birth, which often includes changing one's first name and dressing and grooming differently. Transitioning may or may not also include medical and legal aspects, including taking hormones, having surgery, or changing identity documents (e.g., driver's license, Social Security record) to reflect one's gender identity. Medical and legal steps are costly and, therefore, unaffordable.

Transition, whether social, through hormone therapy, through surgery, or through some combination, often improves feelings of dysphoria, though it may not relieve them completely. The goal of many is for their gender to be perceived correctly by others, which is often referred to as "passing." Typically, people transition to align their physical appearance and characteristics with their gender identities. Many people begin the process after years of dysphoria and distress, and transitioning may help them feel as if they are finally able to be their true selves.

Transitioning can have significant psychological, social, and physical benefits. Anxiety and depression caused by gender dysphoria may diminish as dysphoria improves. Individuals who no longer have to make uncomfortable adjustments—such as hiding unwanted physical characteristics—may not only feel better physically but may have greater confidence and self-esteem.

People's reasons for choosing to transition, and the goals they have regarding transition, are personal and unique. Some individuals may not pursue certain aspects of transition, whether through personal choice, lack of resources, or lack of access. There is no single "right" way to transition. Gender identity does not depend on whether they have had surgery or if they are taking hormones.

Friends and family members who may have little to no understanding of gender transition or of what it means to be trans may ask invasive questions or say things that are invalidating or hurtful, regardless of intention. They may also find people's true genders difficult to accept. "You'll always be _____ to me," a mother might say, without the intention of harm. But this type of remark may be invalidating and cause distress.

Social work services can help individuals who are transgender as they consider and move through the transitioning process. They can also help family members by creating safe spaces where they can ask questions, develop a better understanding of what it means to be transgender, and learn more about what transition entails.

SYSTEMIC (INSTITUTIONALIZED) DISCRIMINATION (E.G., RACISM, SEXISM, AGEISM)

Social workers should not practice, condone, facilitate, or collaborate with any form of discrimination on the basis of race, ethnicity, national origin, color, sex, sexual orientation, gender identity or expression, age, marital status, political belief, religion, immigration status, or mental or physical disability (*NASW Code of Ethics—Discrimination*).

Discrimination can occur at the individual or institutional level. Individual discrimination is when an individual is treated differently whereas institutionalized discrimination refers to policies or practices that discriminate against a group of people based on these characteristics (achievement gaps in education, residential segregation, etc.).

Social workers are charged with challenging discriminatory practices and upholding the belief of equal rights for all.

THE PRINCIPLES OF CULTURALLY COMPETENT SOCIAL WORK PRACTICE

Cultural awareness involves working in conjunction with natural, informal support and helping networks within a minority community (neighborhoods, churches, spiritual leaders, healers, etc.). It extends the concept of self-determination to the community. Only when a community recognizes and owns a problem does it take responsibility for creating solutions that fit the context of the culture.

Social workers should promote conditions that encourage respect for cultural and social diversity and promote policies and practices that demonstrate respect for difference, support the expansion of cultural knowledge and resources, advocate for programs and institutions that demonstrate cultural awareness, and promote policies that safeguard the rights of all people.

Social workers should act to prevent and eliminate domination of, exploitation of, and discrimination against any person, group, or class on the basis of race, ethnicity, national origin, color, sex, sexual orientation, gender identity or expression, age, marital status, political belief, religion, immigration status, and mental or physical disability.

Since every client's cultural experiences are different, services must be delivered using a flexible and individualized approach. Social workers should be aware of ethical standards on cultural awareness and social diversity.

1. Social workers should understand culture and its function in human behavior and society, recognizing the strengths that exist in all cultures.

2. Social workers should have a knowledge base of their clients' cultures and be able to demonstrate competence in the provision of services that are sensitive to clients' cultures and to differences among people and cultural groups. *When social workers are from different racial or cultural backgrounds than their clients, they must clearly understand how these differences impact the problem-solving process.*

3. Social workers should obtain education about and seek to understand the nature of social diversity and oppression with respect to race, ethnicity, national origin, color, sex, sexual orientation, gender identity or expression, age, marital status, political belief, religion, immigration status, and mental or physical disability.

4. Social workers should also not use derogatory language in their written or verbal communications to or about clients. Social workers should use accurate and respectful language in all communications to and about clients (*NASW Code of Ethics—Derogatory Language*).

Social workers should be aware of terminology related to cultural barriers and goals.

Ethnocentrism: an orientation that holds one's own culture, ethnic, or racial group as superior to others

Stratification: structured inequality of entire categories of people who have unequal access to social rewards (e.g., ethnic stratification, social stratification)

Pluralism: a society in which diverse members maintain their own traditions while cooperatively working together and seeing others' traits as valuable (cultural pluralism—respecting and encouraging cultural difference)

Social workers must possess specific knowledge about the cultural groups with whom they work, including diverse historical experiences, adjustment styles, socioeconomic backgrounds, learning styles, cognitive skills, and/or specific cultural customs. This knowledge must include theories and principles concerning human behavior development, psychopathology, therapy, rehabilitation, and community functioning because they relate to cultural group members. Institutions, class, culture, and language barriers that prevent ethnic group members from accessing or using services must be identified and addressed.

Some approaches within organizations to promote cultural diversity include recruiting multiethnic staff, including cultural awareness requirements in job descriptions and performance/promotion measures, reviewing demographic trends for the geographic area served to determine service needs, creating service delivery systems that are more appropriate to the diversity of the target population, and advocating for clients as major stakeholders in the development of service delivery systems to ensure they are reflective of their cultural heritage.

SEXUAL ORIENTATION CONCEPTS

"Sexual orientation" is a term used to describe patterns of emotional, romantic, and sexual attraction—and a sense of personal and social identity based on those attractions. Sexual orientation exists along a continuum, with exclusive attraction to the opposite sex on one end of the continuum and exclusive attraction to the same sex on the other.

There are a bunch of identities associated with sexual orientation:

- People who are attracted to a different gender (e.g., women who are attracted to men or men who are attracted to women) often call themselves straight or heterosexual.

- People who are attracted to people of the same gender often call themselves gay or homosexual. Gay women may prefer the term "lesbian."

- People who are attracted to both men and women often call themselves bisexual.

- People whose attractions span across many different gender identities (male, female, transgender, genderqueer, intersex, etc.) may call themselves pansexual or queer.

- People who are unsure about their sexual orientation may call themselves questioning or curious.

- People who do not experience sexual attraction often call themselves asexual.

It is also important to note that some people don't think any of these labels describe them accurately. Some people don't like the idea of labels at all. Other people feel comfortable with certain labels and not others.

Social workers must let clients identify and use their own labels to describe their own sexual orientations.

GENDER AND GENDER IDENTITY CONCEPTS

A gender role is a theoretical construct that refers to a set of social and behavioral norms that, within a specific culture, are widely considered to be socially appropriate for individuals of a specific sex. Socially accepted gender roles differ widely between different cultures. Gender role theory asserts that observed gender differences in behavior and personality characteristics are, at least in part, socially constructed, and therefore the product of socialization experiences; this contrasts with other models of gender, which assert that gender differences are "essential" to biological sex. Thus, there is a debate over the environmental or biological causes for the development of gender roles.

Gender role theory posits that boys and girls learn to perform one's biologically assigned gender through particular behaviors and attitudes. Gender role theory emphasizes the environmental causes of gender roles and the impact of socialization, or the process of transferring norms, values, beliefs, and behaviors to group members, in learning how to behave as a male or a female. Social role theory proposes that the social structure is the underlying force in distinguishing genders and that sex-differentiated behavior is driven by the division of labor between two sexes within a society. The division of labor creates gender roles, which, in turn, lead to gendered social behavior.

Gender has several definitions. It usually refers to a set of characteristics that are either seen to distinguish between male and female, one's biological sex, or one's gender identity. Gender identity is the gender(s), or lack thereof, a person self-identifies as; it is not based on biological sex, either real or perceived, nor is it always based on sexual orientation. There are two main genders, masculine (male) and feminine (female), although in some cultures there are more genders. Gender roles refer to the set of attitudes and behaviors socially expected from those with a particular gender identity.

Gender identity usually conforms to anatomic sex in both heterosexual and homosexual individuals. However, individuals who identify as transgender feel themselves to be of a gender different from their biological sex; their gender identity does not match their anatomic or chromosomal sex.

Sexual orientation and gender identity are distinct with those who are transgender exhibiting the same full range of possible sexual orientations and interests of those who are not transgender.

It is important to let individuals define their own gender identity. For some, gender is not just about being male or female; in fact, identity can change every day or even every few hours. **Gender fluidity**, when gender expression shifts between masculine and feminine, can be displayed in dress, expression, and self-description.

There are lots of misconceptions about gender fluidity. Gender fluidity is also not the equivalent of transgender, in which a person's gender identity is different from the one assigned at birth. It is the belief that gender exists on a spectrum and is not binary with the ability to change at any time.

It is important for social workers to use proper "gender pronouns" when working with clients as it is a sign of mutual respect between the parties. A "gender pronoun" is the pronoun that a person chooses to use to be referred to in a sentence or conversation. Some people do not use pronouns at all, using their names as pronouns instead. It is not possible to know people's gender pronouns by looking at them. Gender pronouns can also change over time to match shifts in gender identity.

Being referred to with the wrong pronoun results in feeling disrespected, invalidated, dismissed, alienated, and/or dysphoric. Being misgendered can be a source of great distress. It is also important to use the correct pronouns for the safety of a person. Using incorrect pronouns can "out" someone or expose someone's identity without consent.

Asking about and correctly using gender pronouns is one of the most basic ways to show respect for gender identity. Clients determine quickly if they feel respected. Social workers must set an example by asking about and correctly using gender pronouns, educating others about pronoun privilege. Pronoun privilege occurs when one does not have to worry about which pronoun is going to be used based on gender perception.

Gender pronouns can include, but are not limited to:

- he/him/his (masculine pronouns)
- she/her/hers (feminine pronouns)
- they/them/theirs (neutral pronouns)—can be used in the singular and a common gender-neutral pronoun, often used when unsure what pronoun someone uses
- ze/zir/zirs (neutral pronouns)
- ze/hir/hirs (neutral pronouns)

Asking about gender pronouns can occur by using one of the following questions:

- "What gender pronouns should I use to refer to you?"
- "What are your gender pronouns?"
- "I don't want to make any assumptions, so what gender pronouns do you use?"
- "How should I refer to you in conversations?"

SOCIAL AND ECONOMIC JUSTICE

Social work is a profession aimed at helping people address their problems and match them with the resources they need to lead healthy and productive lives. One of the most important values of the social work profession is social and economic justice. Social justice is the view that everyone deserves equal economic, political, and social rights and opportunities.

Economic justice is a component of social justice. It is a set of moral principles for building economic institutions, the ultimate goal of which is to create an opportunity for each person to create a sufficient material foundation upon which to have a dignified, productive, and creative life.

Social workers promote social justice and social change with and on behalf of clients who are individuals, families, groups, organizations, and/or communities.

Social workers aim to open the doors of access and opportunity for all, particularly those in greatest need.

Social workers also apply social justice principles to structural problems in the social service agencies in which they work. Armed with the long-term goal of empowering clients, they use knowledge of existing legal principles and organizational structure to suggest changes to protect clients, who are often powerless and underserved.

THE EFFECT OF POVERTY ON INDIVIDUALS, FAMILIES, GROUPS, ORGANIZATIONS, AND COMMUNITIES

Clients who are poor often do not have resources to meet their basic needs. There are many social problems that contribute to and result from poverty, including, but not limited to, little or no education, poor basic nutrition and hygiene, disability or illness, unemployment, substance abuse, and homelessness.

Family income has selective but, in some instances, quite substantial impacts on child and adolescent well-being. Family income appears to be more strongly related to children's ability and achievement than to their emotional outcomes.

Children who live in extreme poverty or who live below the poverty line for multiple years appear, all other things being equal, to suffer the worst outcomes. The timing of poverty also seems to be important for certain outcomes. Children who experience poverty during their preschool and early school years have lower rates of school completion than children and adolescents who experience poverty only in later years. Although more research is needed, findings to date suggest that interventions during early childhood may be most important in reducing poverty's impact on children.

Social workers must also consider the implications on the biopsychosocial–spiritual–cultural aspects of well-being. Medical care may be neglected in order to meet other needs. Coping skills are needed when there are dramatic changes in income and opportunities to adapt and return to economic stability are critical.

Wealth is often poorly distributed. A small minority has the majority of the money, causing major societal tensions and divisions. There are the "haves" and the "have nots." Communities are often homogeneous—with those comprised of poor people being segregated from those living above the poverty line. Communities comprised of those who are poor have fewer opportunities and resources to assist their members, leading to a greater likelihood that they will not be able to break out of the cycle that originally resulted in their economic insecurity. Thus, those born into poverty often remain there throughout their life course.

THE IMPACT OF SOCIAL INSTITUTIONS ON SOCIETY

Many social institutions exist within our society. They have many functions including satisfying individuals' basic needs, defining and promoting dominant social values, defining and promoting individual roles, creating permanent patterns of social behavior, and supporting other social institutions.

The five basic institutions are family, religion, government, education, and economics. Some of the functions of each of these institutions include the following.

Family

- To control and regulate sexual behavior
- To provide for new members of society (children)
- To provide for the economic and emotional maintenance of individuals
- To provide for primary socialization of children

Religion

- To provide solutions for the unexplained
- To support the normative structure of the society
- To provide a psychological diversion from unwanted life situations
- To sustain the existing class structure
- To promote and prevent social change

Government

- To create norms via laws and enforce them
- To adjudicate conflict via the courts
- To provide for the welfare of members of society
- To protect society from external threats

Education

- To transmit culture
- To prepare for jobs and roles
- To evaluate and select competent individuals
- To transmit functional skills

Economics

- To provide methods for the production and distribution of goods and services
- To enable individuals to acquire goods and services that are produced

CRIMINAL JUSTICE SYSTEMS

Social work is an essential component of the criminal justice system. For the most part, social work practice as performed in the various criminal (and juvenile) justice systems is referred to as criminal justice social work, correctional social work, or forensic social work.

Criminal justice social workers serve as frontline staff and administrators in criminal justice settings. There are many thousands of social workers employed in criminal justice settings, serving criminal justice populations, or both.

In the United States, the criminal justice system encompasses a broad spectrum of public and private agencies and settings including, but not limited to, federal and state correctional facilities; city and county jails; federal, state, and city parole and probation agencies; federal, state, and local court systems (including drug courts and mental health courts); community-based nonprofit agencies; faith-based agencies; and primary health and behavioral health care providers.

Schools of social work prepare their graduates to address the complex psychosocial needs of individuals in the criminal justice system. Social work is adapting to the evolving changes in the country's philosophy on the best ways to balance the sometimes conflicted dichotomy between the need for public safety and the need to address the biopsychosocial needs of offenders. The ethical challenge to social workers is to weigh the needs of the justice system against those of the offender. The social worker should take on the challenge by participating in legislative action to mold social policy to create a balance between the justice system and the offender. Thus, the social worker can help the justice system provide more effective services to the offender, their families, and their communities as professionals by participating in the process of public policy development.

Two competing, dichotomous schools of thought drive the discussion related to crime prevention. One, the pro-punishment school of thought, postulates that punishment is the means to preventing; whereas the positivist (pro-treatment) philosophy suggests that some instances of criminal behavior are determined by factors, such as mental illness, that offenders find difficult to control. Therefore, treatment becomes a means of preventing future criminal behaviors. Social work has historically been strongly associated with the positivist school of thought of crime prevention. Social work must recognize its professional obligation both to the offender and to the community (from a public safety perspective) and participate in the process of developing crime reduction policies that reflect social work's commitment to both the offender and the community.

THE IMPACT OF GLOBALIZATION ON CLIENTS/CLIENT SYSTEMS (E.G., INTERRELATEDNESS OF SYSTEMS, INTERNATIONAL INTEGRATION, TECHNOLOGY, ENVIRONMENTAL OR FINANCIAL CRISES, EPIDEMICS)

Globalization has had a profound effect on social work practice, changing service delivery; creating new social problems for practitioners to address, such as human trafficking and environmental issues; and producing demands for indigenization, or the development of locality specific forms of theory and practice. **Globalization** refers to an interconnectedness of persons across the world.

The current globalization of the economy requires that social workers broaden their horizons and view many domestic social justice issues within a global framework. Social workers can benefit from knowing how the issues in their town or nation are played out in other towns and nations. There is so much to learn of innovative practices and of possible solutions to social problems that never would have been imagined without an international exchange of information. Globalization has the potential to transport traditional social policy analysis into an ever-widening international arena. Social workers must help people to influence their own governments to consider human rights issues in foreign relations. Contained in the *Universal Declaration of Human Rights* are principles germane to the alleviation of oppression and injustice. Social workers recognize the benefits and disadvantages of globalization for the most vulnerable people in the world, focusing especially on how the economic and environmental consequences affect social relationships and individual opportunity.

Content Area I: Practice Questions

The following section has 46 unique practice questions that assess retention of material related to human development, diversity, and behavior in the environment. The number of questions reflects the approximate proportion of a typical exam (27%) devoted to this content.

1. An 11-year-old child would like to start helping around the house with chores. She approaches her mother many times, but is told she cannot assist because "she won't do it right." During several attempts to do things on her own, she is scolded. According to psychosocial development theory, she may experience doubts in her abilities due to a crisis in which of the following stages?

   A. Industry versus inferiority
   B. Initiative versus guilt
   C. Autonomy versus shame/doubt

2. Which of the following is an example of role discomplementarity?

   A. A husband complains that his wife does not take responsibility for keeping the house clean and a wife is upset that her husband does not financially provide for the family.
   B. A woman states that she does not like working and wants to quit her job
   C. A man struggles to fit in time at home with his family due to his hectic work schedule

3. Which of the following is last level of cognition?

   A. Synthesis
   B. Knowledge
   C. Evaluation

4. Which of the following is an example of role reversal?

   A. A mother who shares her 11-year-old daughter's clothes and collects stuffed animals
   B. A mother with relationship problems who is repeatedly emotionally comforted by her 11-year-old daughter
   C. A mother who arranges a date for her 11-year-old daughter

(See answers next page.)

1. **A.** Industry versus inferiority—From age 6 to puberty, children begin to develop a sense of pride in their accomplishments. If children are encouraged and reinforced for their initiative, they begin to feel industrious and feel confident in their ability to achieve goals. If this initiative is not encouraged and is restricted, children begin to feel inferior, doubting their abilities.

Question Assesses

Content Area I—Human Development, Diversity, and Behavior in the Environment; Human Growth and Development (Competency); Theories of Human Development Throughout the Lifespan (e.g., Physical, Social, Emotional, Cognitive, and Behavioral) (KSA)

2. **A.** Role discomplementarity results when roles conflict or when the role expectations of others differ from one's own. In this situation, the husband and wife do not have the same expectations with regard to the tasks for which each other should be responsible.

Question Assesses

Content Area I—Human Development, Diversity, and Behavior in the Environment; Human Growth and Development (Competency); Role Theories (KSA)

3. **C.** The six levels of cognition are, in sequential order—knowledge, comprehension, application, analysis, synthesis, and evaluation. Teaching techniques should match the cognitive objective, such as knowing specific facts, theories, or information (knowledge) or creating something new/integrating it into a solution (synthesis). Learning aimed at judging the quality of something is known as evaluation.

Question Assesses

Content Area I—Human Development, Diversity, and Behavior in the Environment; Human Growth and Development (Competency); Theories of Human Development Throughout the Lifespan (e.g., Physical, Social, Emotional, Cognitive, and Behavioral) (KSA)

4. **B.** A role reversal is when two people switch or reverse roles. In this answer, the mother is emotionally dependent and the child is the comforter. These behaviors are usually reversed in a parent–child relationship. The other response choices may relate to roles, but are not reversals.

Question Assesses

Content Area I—Human Development, Diversity, and Behavior in the Environment; Human Growth and Development (Competency); Role Theories (KSA)

5. Which **BEST** defines echolalia?

   A. Mimicking another's speech
   B. Spontaneous movement
   C. Repetitive movements

6. A man who is having problems at work finds that he is yelling at his children more and has begun to have marital issues with his wife. Which defense mechanism is the husband **MOST** likely using?

   A. Reaction formation
   B. Projection
   C. Displacement

7. A woman complains that her 7-year-old son "makes things up and exaggerates." He often adds information when recalling experiences and talks about knights and dragons being part of his everyday world. The woman is angry about this behavior and worried that it is an indication of some mental health problem. In order to **BEST** assist in this situation, the social worker should:

   A. Explain that the behaviors are associated with the preoperational thought stage of cognitive development
   B. Conduct a mental status examination on the child
   C. Determine whether this behavior is a concern to others, including his teachers

8. Which of the following stage of psychosexual development occurs during the first year of life?

   A. Genital
   B. Latency
   C. Oral

9. Most models of spiritual development move from an individual being egocentric to eventually becoming a(n):

   A. Conformist
   B. Integrated being
   C. Dichotomous thinker

(*See answers next page.*)

5. **A.** Echolalia is repeating noises and phrases. It is sometimes associated with catatonia, autism spectrum disorder, schizophrenia, and other disorders.

Question Assesses

Content Area I—Human Development, Diversity, and Behavior in the Environment; Human Growth and Development (Competency); Communication Theories and Styles (KSA)

6. **C.** Displacement is directing an impulse, wish, or feeling toward another person or situation that is less threatening. The man unconsciously realizes that he cannot express his anger on the job or it may have negative consequences, so he goes home and yells at his wife and children.

Question Assesses

Content Area I—Human Development, Diversity, and Behavior in the Environment; Human Growth and Development (Competency); Psychological Defense Mechanisms and Their Effects on Behavior and Relationships (KSA)

7. **A.** Magical thinking is a hallmark of Piaget's preoperational thought stage. Understanding that children learn through this process, and that it is typical, may assist the mother in better coping with this behavior. There is no indication that there are any mental health issues, so the social worker should not see the child or take other action based on this report alone.

Question Assesses

Content Area I—Human Development, Diversity, and Behavior in the Environment; Human Growth and Development (Competency); Theories of Human Development Throughout the Lifespan (e.g., Physical, Social, Emotional, Cognitive, and Behavioral) (KSA)

8. **C.** Freud's psychosexual stages are oral, anal, phallic, latency, and genital. They begin in infancy and proceed through puberty into adulthood. The oral stage occurs from birth until about a child's first birthday. It involves sucking, biting, and chewing. Fixation during this stage can result in overeating, dependence on others, or the need for oral stimuli such as through excessive smoking.

Question Assesses

Content Area I—Human Development, Diversity, and Behavior in the Environment; Human Growth and Development (Competency); Communication Theories and Styles (KSA)

9. **B.** Individuals usually begin unwilling to accept a will greater than their own and are extremely egotistical. They then move to conforming and having blind faith. In this second stage, things are seen dichotomously—as right or wrong. Individuals then come to develop a deeper understanding of good and evil and do not accept blind faith, but integrate their beliefs into their larger worldview and behaviors.

Question Assesses

Content Area I—Human Development, Diversity, and Behavior in the Environment; Human Growth and Development (Competency); Theories of Spiritual Development Throughout the Lifespan (KSA)

10. A client has just been diagnosed with terminal cancer. Using a systems approach, the social worker should:

    A. Develop a plan for long-term care aimed at meeting the client's medical needs
    B. Work with the client on addressing the impacts of this prognosis on psychological and spiritual well-being
    C. Reexamine the treatment goals to see if they are still relevant or need to be revised given this health information

11. According to Freud, an adolescent in puberty is in which stage of psychosexual development?

    A. Genital
    B. Phallic
    C. Anal

12. A client is very worried about her financial situation. She buys a new car and tells the social worker that she made the purchase "because the car is much less likely to break down and will save money in the long run." What is **MOST** likely the basis of this client's statement?

    A. Ego-syntonic beliefs
    B. A double bind
    C. Cognitive dissonance

13. Which of the following represents the order of client needs within a hierarchy?

    A. Physiological, safety, social, esteem, and self-actualization
    B. Physiological, safety, esteem, social, and self-actualization
    C. Safety, physiological, social, esteem, and self-actualization

14. Which of the following is the basic premise of groupthink?

    A. Groups make faulty decisions because they ignore alternatives due to group pressures
    B. Groups with similar membership tend to be more cohesive and effective
    C. Groups come up with creative solutions to problems using their diverse perspectives

(*See answers next page.*)

10. **B.** A systems approach states that all parts of well-being are interrelated or interconnected. Thus, a change in physical health will impact on psychological and spiritual functioning. The treatment should not focus on just the health issues, but ensure that these other areas are considered.

Question Assesses

Content Area I—Human Development, Diversity, and Behavior in the Environment; Human Growth and Development (Competency); Systems and Ecological Perspectives and Theories (KSA)

11. **A.** The genital stage begins in puberty and the source of pleasure is the genitals. Sexual urges return after being dormant during the latency stage, which begins at about age 5.

Question Assesses

Content Area I—Human Development, Diversity, and Behavior in the Environment; Human Growth and Development (Competency); Psychoanalytic and Psychodynamic Approaches (KSA)

12. **C.** Cognitive dissonance is a state of conflict in the mind, whereby two opposing views are present at the same time. It suggests that the mind naturally wants to eliminate dissonance whenever possible and does so by justifying or changing attitudes and beliefs. Cognitive dissonance is extremely powerful, so justification is used to reduce it.

Question Assesses

Content Area I—Human Development, Diversity, and Behavior in the Environment; Human Growth and Development (Competency); Communication Theories and Styles (KSA)

13. **A.** According to Maslow's hierarchy of needs, the needs of individuals are ordered as physiological, safety, social, esteem, and self-actualization.

Question Assesses

Content Area I—Human Development, Diversity, and Behavior in the Environment; Human Growth and Development (Competency); Basic Human Needs (KSA)

14. **A.** Groupthink is when a group makes faulty decisions based on group pressures. Groups affected by groupthink ignore alternatives and tend to take irrational actions. A group is especially vulnerable to groupthink when its members are similar in background, when the group is insulated from outside opinions, and when there are no clear rules for decision making.

Question Assesses

Content Area I—Human Development, Diversity, and Behavior in the Environment; Human Growth and Development (Competency); Theories of Group Development and Functioning (KSA)

15. Which of the following stages is often described as "a midlife crisis" where individuals struggle between guiding the next generation and becoming self-absorbed?

    A. Generativity versus stagnation
    B. Ego integrity versus despair
    C. Identity versus role confusion

16. A client is very distressed because she is physically attracted to individuals of the same gender. She has become increasingly upset by these desires and wants to find ways to eliminate them. Which **BEST** describes the feelings that the client is experiencing?

    A. Latent
    B. Ego alien
    C. Ego-syntonic

17. A client learns that her medical problem is a genetic condition and would like to learn more about the chances of passing it on to her children as she is contemplating becoming pregnant. Which of the following conditions could the client possess?

    A. Type 2 diabetes
    B. Sickle cell disease
    C. Heart disease

18. Which of the following is associated with negative body image?

    A. Not linking self-worth to appearance
    B. Lack of worry about food or weight
    C. Physical appearance tied to personal value

19. A mother states that her 12-year-old son is now able to stay home alone because he is aware of dangers, meets his basic needs, and problem-solves when needed. This child has reached which stage of cognitive development?

    A. Formal operations
    B. Concrete operations
    C. Preoperational

(*See answers next page.*)

15. **A.** Generativity versus stagnation—During middle adulthood, individuals should develop a sense of being a part of the bigger picture, as well as giving back to society. By failing to achieve these objectives, individuals become stagnant and self-absorbed.

Question Assesses

Content Area I—Human Development, Diversity, and Behavior in the Environment; Human Growth and Development (Competency); Theories of Human Development Throughout the Lifespan (e.g., Physical, Social, Emotional, Cognitive, and Behavioral) (KSA)

16. **B.** "Ego alien" means these feelings are experienced as being alien to the ego and not consistent with the client's interests, conflicting with the rest of her view of herself.

Question Assesses

Content Area I—Human Development, Diversity, and Behavior in the Environment; Human Growth and Development (Competency); Psychoanalytic and Psychodynamic Approaches (KSA)

17. **B.** Sickle cell disease is a group of inherited red blood cell disorders. Common health problems such as heart disease and type 2 diabetes do not have a single genetic cause—they are influenced by lifestyle and environmental factors, such as exercise, diet, or pollutant exposures.

Question Assesses

Content Area I—Human Development, Diversity, and Behavior in the Environment; Human Growth and Development (Competency); Basic Principles of Human Genetics (KSA)

18. **C.** If a client believes that physical appearance is linked to personal value, negative body image is likely to emerge. A client's self-worth should not be defined by appearance.

Question Assesses

Content Area I—Human Development, Diversity, and Behavior in the Environment; Human Growth and Development (Competency); Body Image and Its Impact (e.g., Identity, Self-Esteem, Relationships, and Habits) (KSA)

19. **A.** Piaget defined four stages of cognitive development. They are sensorimotor, preoperational, concrete operations, and formal operations. The formal operations stage begins at about age 11 and is characterized by a higher level of abstraction, assuming adult roles, and thinking hypothetically.

Question Assesses

Content Area I—Human Development, Diversity, and Behavior in the Environment; Human Growth and Development (Competency); Theories of Human Development Throughout the Lifespan (e.g., Physical, Social, Emotional, Cognitive, and Behavioral) (KSA)

20. Which of the following is **MOST** important when implementing a token economy?

    A. Points or rewards must be consistently given when the desired behavior is exhibited
    B. A substantial number of points or rewards must be taken away for undesirable behavior
    C. Rewards must be past reinforcers of the desired behavior

21. Which of the following is the **BEST** definition of rapprochement?

    A. A technique used to confront a client in a nonthreatening way
    B. A feeling experienced by clients who have not formed emotional attachments to others
    C. A stage in childhood development in which a small child needs reassurance from a caregiver

22. According to self psychology, which of the following is **MOST** important for children to develop a strong sense of self?

    A. Environment with others like themselves in order to feel "belonging"
    B. Physical touch from others to demonstrate care and nurturing
    C. Coping skills to control aggressive drives

23. Which of the following statements is accurate about psychodynamic treatment modalities or approaches?

    A. They are good for use in a managed care environment where change has to occur in a limited time period
    B. They use dynamic intervention methods that are hands on, such as play therapy
    C. They emphasize unconscious motives and desires, as well as the importance of childhood experiences, in shaping personality

24. A married couple reports that they feel disconnected from one another and rarely speak or provide each other with any kind of support. Which **BEST** describes the reasons for these feelings?

    A. Negative entropy
    B. Entropy
    C. Equifinality

(*See answers next page.*)

20. **A.** Token economies must include consistent reinforcement of desired behaviors. Some token economies do not include the removal of points for undesirable behavior. They only provide points or rewards when the targeted behavior is exhibited. Even when points are deducted for undesired behavior, it is usually done in a manner in which the client does not lose a substantial number because this may make the client feel hopeless or that the lost points cannot be regained by exhibiting positive behavior in the future. Rewards should be of value to the client but they do not need to be past reinforcers.

Question Assesses

Content Area I—Human Development, Diversity, and Behavior in the Environment; Human Growth and Development (Competency); Theories of Human Development Throughout the Lifespan (e.g., Physical, Social, Emotional, Cognitive, and Behavioral) (KSA)

21. **C.** This stage in object relations theory generally occurs prior to the second birthday when a small child wants to once again become closer to the caregiver, realizing that mobility causes separateness. The child realizes that the caregiver is a separate entity and needs reassurance.

Question Assesses

Content Area I—Human Development, Diversity, and Behavior in the Environment; Human Growth and Development (Competency); Psychoanalytic and Psychodynamic Approaches (KSA)

22. **A.** As a result of receiving empathic responses from early caretakers, a child's needs are met and the child develops a strong sense of self. The needs of a child are mirroring, idealization, and twinship. Twinship is described in the correct answer.

Question Assesses

Content Area I—Human Development, Diversity, and Behavior in the Environment; Human Growth and Development (Competency); Psychoanalytic and Psychodynamic Approaches (KSA)

23. **C.** Psychodynamic theories explain the origin of the personality. Although many different psychodynamic theories exist, they all emphasize unconscious motives and desires, as well as the importance of childhood experiences in shaping personality.

Question Assesses

Content Area I—Human Development, Diversity, and Behavior in the Environment; Human Growth and Development (Competency); Psychoanalytic and Psychodynamic Approaches (KSA)

24. **B.** Entropy is a closed system, whereas negative entropy is the opposite (an exchange of energy and resources to promote growth). In this example, the married couple is not using personal resources to ensure the health of their relationship.

Question Assesses

Content Area I—Human Development, Diversity, and Behavior in the Environment; Human Growth and Development (Competency); Systems and Ecological Perspectives and Theories (KSA)

25. Which of the following is a physical symptom of trauma?

    A. Flashbacks
    B. Feeling disconnected
    C. Muscle tension

26. A client has recently learned that her child has been diagnosed with a life-threatening condition that will substantially affect her abilities in the future. For an hour, she talks to the social worker in detail about the medical condition without showing any emotion. Which of the following defense mechanisms **BEST** describes the client's response?

    A. Devaluation
    B. Substitution
    C. Intellectualization

27. A social work administrator is part of a management team who decides to close an agency program due to financial pressures. The management team receives many letters from program supporters asserting that this program is essential for other agency operations. The team does not consider other alternatives and closes the program anyway, only to encounter major problems in agency operations weeks later. Which **BEST** describes the actions by the management team?

    A. Groupthink
    B. Homogeneity
    C. Group polarization

28. Which of the following statements is accurate about sexual development of individuals?

    A. Children are not sexual before birth
    B. Humans are sexual beings throughout life
    C. Adults lose their desire for sexual expression later in life

29. A client who is meeting with a social worker reports that her child unexpectedly died in an accident several years ago. When questioned about the loss, the client shows little emotion. To understand the impact of the death on the client's current functioning, the social worker should **FIRST**:

    A. Assess changes in her life circumstances before and after the death
    B. Ask her about the circumstances which caused the death
    C. Reassure her that discussing the death will help with healing

(*See answers next page.*)

25. **C.** All of the options are signs of trauma, but muscle tension is the only physical symptom.

Question Assesses

Content Area I—Human Development, Diversity, and Behavior in the Environment; Human Growth and Development (Competency); The Impact of Stress, Trauma, and Violence (KSA)

26. **C.** Intellectualization is when a person avoids uncomfortable emotions by focusing on facts and logic. In this instance, the client is not dealing with the emotions associated with this recent diagnosis, but instead focused on the rational medical details of the condition.

Question Assesses

Content Area I—Human Development, Diversity, and Behavior in the Environment; Human Growth and Development (Competency); Psychological Defense Mechanisms and Their Effects on Behavior and Relationships (KSA)

27. **A.** Groupthink is when a group makes faulty decisions because of group pressures. Groups affected by groupthink ignore alternatives and tend to take irrational actions that dehumanize other groups. A group is especially vulnerable to groupthink when its members are similar in background, when the group is insulated from outside opinions, and when there are no clear rules for decision making.

Question Assesses

Content Area I—Human Development, Diversity, and Behavior in the Environment; Human Growth and Development (Competency); Theories of Group Development and Functioning (KSA)

28. **B.** Humans are sexual throughout the life course. Children are sexual even before birth, with males sometimes having erections in the uterus. Although there may be physiological changes that occur in older adults, they do not lose their desire to be sexual.

Question Assesses

Content Area I—Human Development, Diversity, and Behavior in the Environment; Human Growth and Development (Competency); Theories of Sexual Development Throughout the Lifespan (KSA)

29. **A.** Grief can be manifested in many ways. For some, the mourning process is protracted and for others, it is not. The lack of emotion by the client in the scenario may or may not be a problem. The client may have acknowledged the reality of the loss and been able to find meaning in her life despite the death. The question is focused on understanding the impact of the death on the client's current functioning. To assess or evaluate the effects, it is necessary to determine her level of functioning before and after the death. Without information about the client's well-being before the death, it is impossible to determine whether there have been issues due to unresolved grief.

Question Assesses

Content Area I—Human Development, Diversity, and Behavior in the Environment; Human Growth and Development (Competency); The Dynamics and Effects of Loss, Separation, and Grief (KSA)

30. A client who is suffering from depression asks a social worker to read her journal. After reading the journal, the social worker identifies major themes of her writings including feeling isolated, not understood, and rejected by her family. The social worker speaks with the client about these issues and they decide to include them as treatment goals. These goals are based on which of the following in the journal?

   A. Latent content
   B. Manifest content
   C. Explicit communication

31. A client sees a woman get brutally beaten and killed during an incident of domestic violence. Shortly after the incident, the client reports the inability to see. Which of the following defense mechanisms is the client **MOST** likely experiencing?

   A. Conversion
   B. Compensation
   C. Reaction formation

32. A woman has strong feelings of resentment toward her sister. These feelings are rooted in her childhood and she has always believed that her sister was a mean person. However, throughout her childhood, she reports being inseparable from her sister and "doing everything together." She also reports buying a necklace for her recently that states "Best Sister Ever." Which of the following defense mechanisms is the client **MOST** likely experiencing?

   A. Splitting
   B. Projective identification
   C. Reaction formation

33. A husband complains that his wife nags him too much about working around the house. Once she stops this behavior, he begins to spend more time on house maintenance. Which of the following **BEST** describes the reason for the husband's behavioral change?

   A. Shaping
   B. Negative reinforcement
   C. Positive reinforcement

34. A client who struggles with alcoholism is prescribed a medication that makes him feel sick every time he drinks while taking it. Which type of operant technique is the use of this medicine?

   A. Extinction
   B. Aversion therapy
   C. In vivo desensitization

(See answers next page.)

30. **A.** In communication, there are two types of content, manifest and latent. Manifest content is the concrete words or terms contained in the journal. Explicit and overt communication also refers to the actual statements made by the client in the journal. Latent content is that which is not visible, such as the underlying meaning or themes of the words or terms used.

Question Assesses

Content Area I—Human Development, Diversity, and Behavior in the Environment; Human Growth and Development (Competency); Communication Theories and Styles (KSA)

31. **A.** Conversion is when mental conflict or disturbance is transferred into a physical symptom to relieve anxiety. The loss of eyesight after witnessing the incident may have resulted from this trauma.

Question Assesses

Content Area I—Human Development, Diversity, and Behavior in the Environment; Human Growth and Development (Competency); Psychological Defense Mechanisms and Their Effects on Behavior and Relationships (KSA)

32. **C.** Reaction formation is when a client adopts attitudes or engages in behaviors that are the opposite of unconscious belief. The behavior of the woman growing up and recently is in contrast to the way in which she feels about her sister.

Question Assesses

Content Area I—Human Development, Diversity, and Behavior in the Environment; Human Growth and Development (Competency); Psychological Defense Mechanisms and Their Effects on Behavior and Relationships (KSA)

33. **B.** In negative reinforcement, behavior increases because negative (aversive) stimulus (i.e., nagging) is removed. The word "negative" does not mean bad, but rather "removal." In positive reinforcement, a behavior increases because of the introduction (positive) of something desirable to reward it.

Question Assesses

Content Area I—Human Development, Diversity, and Behavior in the Environment; Human Growth and Development (Competency); Theories of Human Development Throughout the Lifespan (e.g., Physical, Social, Emotional, Cognitive, and Behavioral) (KSA)

34. **B.** Aversion therapy or treatment is aimed at reducing the attractiveness of a stimulus or a behavior by pairing it with an aversive stimulus. An example of this technique is treating alcoholism with Antabuse.

Question Assesses

Content Area I—Human Development, Diversity, and Behavior in the Environment; Human Growth and Development (Competency); Theories of Human Development Throughout the Lifespan (e.g., Physical, Social, Emotional, Cognitive, and Behavioral) (KSA)

35. During a session, a client is reporting on her daily activities during the last week. She looks down at the ground, not making eye contact. She also pauses repeatedly with periods of silence. The social worker should:

    A. Ask the client if there is something that is bothering her
    B. Listen attentively to show acceptance of her feelings
    C. Accept this behavior as part of her communication style

36. Which of the following is important to understanding cultural, racial, and ethnic identity development?

    A. The ways in which races have been defined have been fixed over time
    B. Ethnic and racial identities do not confer privilege
    C. Cultural, racial, and ethnic identity is passed from one generation to the next

37. A social worker notices what appears to be burns on a child's arm and asks the child about these markings. The child responds that "grandma burned me, but mommy isn't going to let me go over there anymore." The social worker should:

    A. Document the conversation in the file
    B. Report the conversation immediately to child protective services
    C. Check the child regularly in the future for burns or bruises

38. When reporting suspected abuse of a client, which of the following factors is **MOST** important?

    A. The client must give assent to the reporting of the abuse when feasible
    B. The identity of the perpetrators must be provided so a proper investigation can be conducted
    C. The report must be made as soon as possible to the abuse hotline

(*See answers next page.*)

35. **A.** There is no indication that this behavior is typical. Nonverbal communication can be very powerful. Her behavior may be the result of something that she is reluctant to discuss. Asking her if something is bothering her will give the client an opening to disclose it to the social worker.

Question Assesses

Content Area I—Human Development, Diversity, and Behavior in the Environment; Human Growth and Development (Competency); Communication Theories and Styles (KSA)

36. **C.** Cultural, racial, and ethnic identities are passed on through customs, traditions, language, religious practice, and values. Racial definitions have changed over time—they were once based on ethnicity or nationality, religion, and so on, but are now primarily defined by skin color. Some races and cultures have inherent privilege.

Question Assesses

Content Area I—Human Development, Diversity, and Behavior in the Environment; Human Growth and Development (Competency); Theories of Racial, Ethnic, and Cultural Development Throughout the Lifespan (KSA)

37. **B.** Social workers are mandatory reporters and must not delay in reporting or investigating such an incident themselves. All suspected abuse situations should be reported to the child protection agency immediately.

Question Assesses

Content Area I—Human Development, Diversity, and Behavior in the Environment; Concepts of Abuse and Neglect (Competency); Indicators and Dynamics of Abuse and Neglect Throughout the Lifespan (KSA)

38. **C.** Suspected child abuse must be reported to the authorities (e.g., the child protection agency) immediately. Many jurisdictions have hotline systems to make such reports easier. While the *NASW Code of Ethics*—states that best practice is to disclose the need to make such reports to clients when feasible, assent (the willingness to have these reports made) and consent (a legal term authorizing their report) are not needed. If a social worker suspects abuse, the social worker has a duty to report it as soon as possible.

Question Assesses

Content Area I—Human Development, Diversity, and Behavior in the Environment; Concepts of Abuse and Neglect (Competency); Indicators and Dynamics of Abuse and Neglect Throughout the Lifespan (KSA)

39. A child in an after-school program comes into a social worker's office and shows the social worker a burn that appears to have been caused by an iron. The child reports that her mother did it as punishment because she was "being bad." The social worker's colleague overhears the child and tells the social worker that the child has lied many times in the past. The social worker should:

   A. Ask the colleague to discuss the incident with the social worker and the agency director
   B. Report the incident to the child protection agency
   C. Investigate the incident to see if the child is telling the truth

40. What immediate action must be taken when a parent is diagnosed with factitious disorder imposed on another for acts toward their children?

   A. Child(ren) must be removed from the parent's care to ensure protection from harm
   B. An evaluation must be completed to assess the ability to fulfill parenting responsibilities
   C. Support services must be provided to meet the basic needs of all family members

41. A social worker employed in a youth recreation program is concerned as a child who developed a severe rash on her arm has not returned to the program after the agency director stated that she needed medical clearance. When contacting the mother, the social worker learns that she has not brought her young child to a doctor "for years" and does not plan to do so. The BEST response for the social worker is to:

   A. Determine what occurred to cause the mother's resistance
   B. Speak to the agency director about reconsidering the child's participation
   C. Report the incident to the authorities

42. Which of the following is an example of social stratification?

   A. A child is not included in group activities in school because of poor social skills
   B. Children who are violent are segregated from their peers
   C. Children from affluent households receive a better public education than those from low-income households

(See answers next page.)

39. **B.** A social worker is a mandatory reporter and must contact the child protection agency that is trained to conduct the investigation and determine the child's credibility. The social worker must report even when a colleague or supervisor does not have the same reasonable suspicion.

Question Assesses

Content Area I—Human Development, Diversity, and Behavior in the Environment; Concepts of Abuse and Neglect (Competency); Indicators and Dynamics of Abuse and Neglect Throughout the Lifespan (KSA)

40. **A.** Factitious disorder imposed on another is a mental health disorder in which caregivers make up or causes an illness or injury in persons under their care, such as a children, elderly adults, or persons who have disabilities. Because vulnerable people are the victims, it is a form of abuse. Most instances are between mothers and children. Caregivers may lie about symptoms, change test results to make victims appear ill, or physically harm to produce symptoms. *Victims need to be protected. They need to be immediately removed from direct care and may require medical care to treat complications from injuries, infections, medicines, surgeries, or tests.*

Question Assesses

Content Area I—Human Development, Diversity, and Behavior in the Environment; Concepts of Abuse and Neglect (Competency); Indicators and Dynamics of Abuse and Neglect Throughout the Lifespan (KSA)

41. **C.** Failing to provide appropriate health care, including dental care and refusal of care or ignoring medical recommendations, is considered neglect and should be reported to the authorities immediately for further investigation. It is not the role of the social worker to investigate the allegations. As there are many names for child protection organizations, generic terms such as "the authorities" may be used in examination questions.

Question Assesses

Content Area I—Human Development, Diversity, and Behavior in the Environment; Concepts of Abuse and Neglect (Competency); Indicators and Dynamics of Abuse and Neglect Throughout the Lifespan (KSA)

42. **C.** Stratification refers to structured inequality of entire categories of people in society who have unequal access to social rewards. Stratification applies to individuals based on ethnic and racial background, social status, and/or other factors.

Question Assesses

Content Area I—Human Development, Diversity, and Behavior in the Environment; Diversity, Social/Economic Justice, and Oppression (Competency); The Principles of Culturally Competent Social Work Practice (KSA)

43. Which of the following is an essential part of culturally informed intervention planning?

    A. Use of individual versus group treatment modalities
    B. Incorporation of alternative treatment approaches
    C. Need for informed consent procedures

44. Which of the following statements is accurate with regard to gender identity and/or sexual orientation?

    A. Pansexual refers to being attracted to individuals outside or independent of gender
    B. Individuals who cross-dress usually identify as homosexual
    C. Sexual orientation and gender identity are related

45. Which of the following is a form of institutional discrimination?

    A. Providing translation services rather than having agency paperwork available in all languages
    B. Offering therapy and other services only on Saturdays
    C. Referring a client to another social worker based on cultural background

46. Which of the following practice is **MOST** likely to promote cultural diversity within an organization?

    A. Ensuring that personnel represent the broader community
    B. Incorporating cultural competence requirements in hiring decisions
    C. Appointing diverse personnel to decision-making positions

(*See answers next page.*)

43. **B.** A social worker should consider the cultural appropriateness of different treatment approaches, beyond just whether treatment should be individual or group modalities. Informed consent procedures used may vary depending upon client culture, but the need for informed consent is universal.

Question Assesses

Content Area I—Human Development, Diversity, and Behavior in the Environment; Diversity, Social/Economic Justice, and Oppression (Competency); The Effect of Culture, Race, and Ethnicity on Behaviors, Attitudes, and Identity (KSA)

44. **A.** Pansexuality refers to being attracted to an individual, independent or blind to gender. Most individuals who cross-dress are not homosexual or attracted to those of the same sex. Sexual orientation and gender identity are unique.

Question Assesses

Content Area I—Human Development, Diversity, and Behavior in the Environment; Diversity, Social/Economic Justice, and Oppression (Competency); Sexual Orientation Concepts (KSA); Gender and Gender Identity Concepts (KSA)

45. **B.** Institutional discrimination is when the policies or practices of an agency are discriminatory to a group of people. Saturday services will preclude those who observe this day as the Sabbath. Social workers may refer individuals to others based on cultural factors for appropriate therapeutic reasons. If the reason for the referral is simply based on cultural background, this may be a form of discrimination, but is not institutional discrimination unless it is a repeated practice or policy. Forms cannot be printed in all languages so translation services are useful to meet the needs of linguistically diverse client populations.

Question Assesses

Content Area I—Human Development, Diversity, and Behavior in the Environment; Diversity, Social/Economic Justice, and Oppression (Competency); Systemic (Institutionalized) Discrimination (e.g., Racism, Sexism, and Ageism) (KSA)

46. **C.** While all response choices listed are important, only appointing diverse personnel to decision-making positions will help increase diversity within an organization as they will be in positions to ensure that varied viewpoints are considered. Just because personnel represent the broader community or cultural competence requirements are used in hiring decisions does not mean that an organization will be diverse or that those from diverse backgrounds will be in positions of power.

Question Assesses

Content Area I—Human Development, Diversity, and Behavior in the Environment; Diversity, Social/Economic Justice, and Oppression (Competency); The Principles of Culturally Competent Social Work Practice (KSA)

Practice Questions

Content Area I: Human Development, Diversity, and Behavior in the Environment (27%)

Competency	Question Numbers	Number of Questions	Number Correct	Percentage Correct	Area Requiring Further Study?
1. Human Growth and Development	1, 2, 3, 4, 5, 6, 7, 8, 9, 10, 11, 12, 13, 14, 15, 16, 17, 18, 19, 21, 22, 23, 24, 25, 26, 27, 28, 29, 31, 32, 33, 34, 35, 36	36	___/36	___%	
2. Concepts of Abuse and Neglect	37, 38, 39, 40, 41	5	___/5	___%	
3. Diversity, Social/ Economic Justice, and Oppression	42, 43, 44, 45, 46	5	___/5	___%	

Content Area II: Assessment and Intervention Planning (24%)

4

Biopsychosocial History and Collateral Data

THE COMPONENTS OF A BIOPSYCHOSOCIAL ASSESSMENT

The biopsychosocial–spiritual–cultural history is a tool that provides information on the current/presenting issue or issues; a client's past and present physical health, including developmental milestones; a client's emotional functioning; educational or vocational background; cultural issues; spiritual and religious beliefs; environmental issues; and social functioning. Each issue may be reviewed for its relationship and/or impact with the presenting issue.

The *biological section* assesses a client's medical history, developmental history, current medications, substance abuse history, and family history of medical illnesses. Issues related to medical problems should be explored because mental health symptoms can exacerbate them. Referrals should be made to address medical concerns that are not being treated. Clients who are on medications should have care coordinated with the treating provider, and more should be known about the medications because side effects can also mask or exacerbate psychiatric symptoms or illnesses.

The *psychological section* assesses a client's present psychiatric illness or symptoms, history of the current psychiatric illness or symptoms, past or current psychosocial stressors, and mental status. Exploration of how the problem has been treated in the past, past or present psychiatric medications, and the family history of psychiatric and substance-related issues is also included.

The *social section* focuses on client systems and unique client context, and may identify strengths and/or resources available for treatment planning. Included are sexual identity issues or concerns, personal history, family of origin history, support system, abuse history, education, legal history, marital/relationship status and concerns, work history, and risks.

The assessment should also include information about a client's spiritual beliefs, as well as the client's cultural traditions.

THE COMPONENTS AND FUNCTION OF THE MENTAL STATUS EXAMINATION

A mental status examination is a structured way of observing and describing a client's current state of mind under the domains of appearance, attitude, behavior, mood and affect, speech, thought process, thought content, perception, cognition, insight, and judgment. A mental status examination is a necessary part of any client assessment no matter what the presenting problem. It should be documented in the record either in list form or in narrative form. The following client functions should be included:

1. *Appearance*—facial expression, grooming, dress, gait, and so on

2. *Orientation*—awareness of time and place, events, and so on

3. *Speech pattern*—slurred, pressured, slow, flat tone, calm, and so on

4. *Affect/mood*—mood as evidenced in both behavior and client's statements (sad, jittery, manic, placid, etc.)

5. *Impulsive/potential for harm*—impulse control with special attention to potential suicidality and/or harm to others

6. *Judgment/insight*—ability to predict the consequences of behavior, to make "sensible" decisions, to recognize a contribution to a problem

7. *Thought processes/reality testing*—thinking style and ability to know reality, including the difference between stimuli that are coming from inside oneself and those that are coming from outside oneself (statements about delusions, hallucinations, and conclusions about whether or not a client is psychotic would appear here)

8. *Intellectual functioning/memory*—level of intelligence and of recent and remote memory functions

A paragraph about mental status in the record might read as follows:

> "Client is a 43-year-old woman who looks older than her stated age. She is well groomed and appropriately dressed for a professional interview. She is well oriented. Her speech is slow as if it is painful to talk. She has had occasional thoughts of 'ending it all,' but has not made any suicidal plans or preparations. She talks about future events with expectation to be alive. She is aware that she is 'depressed' and recognizes that the source of some of the feeling comes from 'inside moods' although she often refers to the difficulties of her situation. Her thoughts are organized. She is not psychotic."

BIOPSYCHOSOCIAL RESPONSES TO ILLNESS AND DISABILITY

The ways in which clients experience chronic illness or disability are influenced by numerous factors including:

- Personal characteristics (such as gender, race, age, coping style, past experience)
- Social and family supports
- Socioeconomic status
- Culture
- Environment (physical, social, and political)
- Activities (restrictions on those related to daily living, work, school, social)
- Personal goals

The responses to illness or disability are dependent on the interplay between these factors. Limitations faced may not be due to the illness or disability, but instead the environment. In addition, societal attitudes may influence their responses with norms focused more on the limitations than on actual functioning.

Clients also vary in terms of their personal resources such as tolerance of symptoms, functional capabilities, coping strategies, and social supports. Consequently, social workers must assess biopsychosocial responses individually. The health condition or disability is only one factor that determines clients' abilities to function effectively.

BIOPSYCHOSOCIAL FACTORS RELATED TO MENTAL HEALTH

It is not possible to understand mental health and the onset or course of mental disorders without knowing about biological, psychological, and social factors and how they interact across the lifespan.

Biological Factors

There is clear evidence to support the role that genes play as a factor in the development of psychiatric disorders. New information also keeps emerging about how brain structure and functioning relate to the existence of mental disorders. It is thought that brain growth in utero or early life can be affected by exposure to adverse factors, leading to changes in brain structure that increase the risk of development of particular mental disorders.

A social worker must use a systems approach in assessment of client mental health. A change in one aspect of a client's life—such as loss of a job, diagnosis of a physical illness, and so on—can affect the client's mental health. Conversely, mental health problems can have a dramatic impact on earnings, role fulfillment, friendships and social relationships, and even physical health.

Psychological Factors

Personality, relating to others and reacting to the world, includes a wide range of psychological responses to cope with different situations. Psychoanalytic, cognitive, and behavioral theories have all had an influence on how personality is understood, its impact on mental disorders, and how it can be influenced in treatment.

Social Factors

Social factors can influence mental health in dramatic ways and it is necessary to investigate social factors thoroughly to fully understand mental health and disorder. Factors such as socioeconomic situation, age, gender, social networks, level of support, life events, migration, and culture can all play a role in influencing the onset and course of mental illnesses.

THE INDICATORS OF PSYCHOSOCIAL STRESS

Psychosocial stress results when there is a perceived threat (real or imagined). Examples of psychosocial stress include threats to social status, social esteem, respect, and/or acceptance within a group; threats to self-worth; or threats that are perceived as uncontrollable.

Psychosocial stress can be caused by upsetting events, such as natural disasters, sudden health problems or death, and/or breakups or divorce.

Although current upsetting events certainly create stress, events from the past can also still affect clients. Social workers should assess the impacts of events such as childhood abuse, bullying, discrimination, violence, and/or trauma.

Often, psychosocial stress is not caused by single events, but by ongoing problems such as caring for a parent or child with disabilities.

Stress may manifest itself in many different ways, such as high blood pressure, sweating, rapid heart rate, dizziness, and/or feelings of irritability or sadness.

When psychosocial stress triggers a stress response, the body releases a group of stress hormones that lead to a burst of energy, as well as other changes in the body. The changes brought about by stress hormones can be helpful in the short term, but can be damaging in the long run.

It is essential that clients learn to manage psychosocial stress so that the stress response is only triggered when necessary and not for prolonged states of chronic stress.

BASIC MEDICAL TERMINOLOGY

Social workers must recognize the relationship between physical well-being and mental status. Social workers should always rule out medical etiology before making psychiatric diagnoses. A **differential diagnosis** is a systematic diagnostic method used to identify the presence of an entity where multiple alternatives are possible.

Social workers must know the major body systems and medical conditions associated with them that can affect psychological functioning and mood.

1. *Circulatory System*

   The circulatory system is the body's transport system. It is made up of a group of organs that transport blood throughout the body. The heart pumps the blood and the arteries and veins transport it.

2. *Digestive System*

   The digestive system is made up of organs that break down food into protein, vitamins, minerals, carbohydrates, and fats, which the body needs for energy, growth, and repair.

3. *Endocrine System*

   The endocrine system is made up of a group of glands that produce the body's long-distance messengers, or hormones. Hormones are chemicals that control body functions, such as metabolism, growth, and sexual development.

4. *Immune System*

   The immune system is a body's defense system against infections and diseases. Organs, tissues, cells, and cell products work together to respond to dangerous organisms (like viruses or bacteria) and substances that may enter the body from the environment.

5. *Lymphatic System*

   The lymphatic system is also a defense system for the body. It filters out organisms that cause disease, produces white blood cells, and generates disease-fighting antibodies. It also distributes fluids and nutrients in the body and drains excess fluids and protein so that tissues do not swell.

6. *Muscular System*

The muscular system is made up of tissues that work with the skeletal system to control movement of the body. Some muscles—like those in arms and legs—are voluntary, meaning that an individual decides when to move them. Other muscles, like the ones in the stomach, heart, intestines, and other organs, are involuntary. This means that they are controlled automatically by the nervous system and hormones—one often does not realize they are at work.

7. *Nervous System*

The nervous system is made up of the brain, the spinal cord, and nerves. One of the most important systems in the body, the nervous system is the body's control system. It sends, receives, and processes nerve impulses throughout the body. These nerve impulses tell muscles and organs what to do and how to respond to the environment.

8. *Reproductive System*

The reproductive system allows humans to produce children. Sperm from the male fertilizes the female's egg, or ovum, in the fallopian tube. The fertilized egg travels from the fallopian tube to the uterus, where the fetus develops over a period of 9 months.

9. *Respiratory System*

The respiratory system brings air into the body and removes carbon dioxide. It includes the nose, trachea, and lungs.

10. *Skeletal System*

The skeletal system is made up of bones, ligaments, and tendons. It shapes the body and protects organs. The skeletal system works with the muscular system to help the body move.

11. *Urinary System*

The urinary system eliminates waste from the body in the form of urine. The kidneys remove waste from the blood. The waste combines with water to form urine.

THE INDICATORS OF MENTAL AND EMOTIONAL ILLNESS THROUGHOUT THE LIFESPAN

Although the *Diagnostic and Statistical Manual of Mental Disorders (DSM)* provides a framework and criteria for applying uniform labels to psychiatric dysfunction, the process of social work assessment and diagnosis is much broader.

Diagnosis refers to the process of identifying problems, with their underlying causes and practical solutions.

A diagnosis is generally obtained after a social worker utilizes information gained through the assessment. Diagnosing includes drawing inferences and reaching conclusions based on the data available. A social worker should not diagnose if adequate information or data is not available.

A social worker must consider biological, psychological, and social factors when identifying the root causes of client problems.

Diagnostic information should always be shared with clients and used to facilitate the establishment of intervention plans.

Assessment and diagnosis must be a continual part of the problem-solving process.

The assessment process must focus on client strengths and resources for addressing problems.

There are some terms and concepts that a social worker should be familiar with when making assessments and/or diagnosing.

1. *Comorbid*: existing with or at the same time; for instance, having two different illnesses at the same time

2. *Contraindicated*: not recommended or safe to use (a medication or treatment that is contraindicated would not be prescribed because it could have serious consequences)

3. *Delusion*: false, fixed belief despite evidence to the contrary (believing something that is not true)

4. *Disorientation*: confusion with regard to person, time, or place

5. *Dissociation*: disturbance or change in the usually integrative functions of memory, identity, perception, or consciousness (often seen in clients with a history of trauma)

6. *Endogenous depression*: depression caused by a biochemical imbalance rather than a psychosocial stressor or external factors

7. *Exogenous depression*: depression caused by external events or psychosocial stressors

8. *Folie à deux*: shared delusion

9. *Hallucinations*: hearing, seeing, smelling, or feeling something that is not real (auditory most common)

10. *Hypomanic*: elevated, expansive, or irritable mood that is less severe than full-blown manic symptoms (not severe enough to interfere with functioning and not accompanied by psychotic symptoms)

11. *Postmorbid*: subsequent to the onset of an illness

12. *Premorbid*: prior to the onset of an illness

13. *Psychotic*: experiencing delusions or hallucinations

THE TYPES OF INFORMATION AVAILABLE FROM OTHER SOURCES (E.G., AGENCY, EMPLOYMENT, MEDICAL, PSYCHOLOGICAL, LEGAL, OR SCHOOL RECORDS)

Assessment is ongoing within the problem-solving process. In order to ensure that all relevant information is considered, social workers often rely on information available from clients' existing records in addition to the data that they collect directly.

In order to access this information, it is critical that social workers are aware of laws governing the release of such information and get the informed consent of clients prior to requesting these documents. The consent process must make clients aware of the reasons for such requests and the benefits and risks of social workers obtaining this information.

When information is obtained, it becomes part of the client record. Though protected by the Health Insurance Portability and Accountability Act (HIPAA), these client records can be subject to subpoenas and/or court orders. Thus, inclusion of this information in their records can have some additional risks associated with the legal duty to release them if court ordered to do so.

Despite this risk, using existing employment, medical, psychological, psychiatric, and educational records can be very helpful when completing a biopsychosocial–spiritual–cultural history.

Employment records may help social workers construct clients' work histories and obtain data about income earned from their jobs. These records may be essential if clients need assistance with applying for Unemployment Insurance or other public benefits (Temporary Assistance for Needy Families [TANF], Supplemental Nutrition Assistance Program [SNAP], and so on).

Medical records are essential to ensure that client problems are not a result of health issues and to better understand the impact of past or current medical problems on client functioning.

Psychological records can be helpful as they can contain the results of any psychological testing that has been completed and whether any mental health diagnoses have been assigned. Whether or not a client has been prescribed psychotropic medications and/or received any subsequent treatment for behavioral health concerns would also be contained in psychiatric records.

When working with children, educational records are often consulted to determine performance in school and whether any problems experienced at home or elsewhere are being manifested in this setting as well. When working with adults, educational records can provide clues as to the age at which problems or difficulties began. Historical educational records are often used to diagnose adults with intellectual or developmental disabilities if they were not appropriately identified while in school.

Children with disabilities are eligible for free, appropriate public education between the ages of 3 and 21. Children with disabilities may have Individual Educational Plans (IEPs) which are revised annually. Teams composed of social workers, teachers, administrators, and other relevant school personnel typically create IEPs. Parents, and often the children, also participate. IEPs include goals, means of attaining goals, and ways of evaluating goal attainment. Children with IEPs must be educated in the "least restrictive environment." Thus, these children should either spend part or all their time in regular classrooms or in environments that are as close to this as possible while still leading to the attainment of educational goals. Services needed, such as speech therapy and others related to educational goals, are provided at no extra cost to families.

Components of a Sexual History

Some clients may not be comfortable talking about their sexual history, sex partners, or sexual practices. It is critical that social workers try to put clients at ease and let them know that taking a sexual history may be an important part of the assessment process. A history is usually obtained through a face-to-face interview, but can also be gotten from a pencil-and-paper document.

Questions included in a sexual history may vary depending upon client issues. However, they usually involve collecting information about partners (number, gender, risk factors, length of relationships), practices (risk behaviors, oral/vaginal/anal intercourse, satisfaction with practices, desire/arousal/orgasm), protection from and past history of sexually transmitted diseases (STDs; condom use), and prevention of pregnancy (if desired)/ reproductive history.

If clients are experiencing dissatisfaction or dysfunction, social workers will need to understand the reasons for dissatisfaction and/or dysfunction. Medical explanations must be ruled out before psychological factors are considered as causes. A systems perspective should be used to understand issues in this area. For example, a medical/biological condition that decreases satisfaction or causes dysfunction may heavily impact on psychological and social functioning. In addition, a psychological or social issue can lead to a lack of desire, inability to become aroused, or failure to attain orgasm.

Alcohol and/or drug use should also be considered related to concerns about desire, arousal, or orgasm because they can cause decreased interest or abilities in these areas.

Components of a Family History

Understanding a client's family history is an important part of the assessment process. A client is part of a larger family system. Thus, gaining a better understanding of the experiences of other family members may prove useful in understanding influences imposed on a client throughout the life course.

One tool used by social workers to depict a client as part of a larger family system is a **genogram**. A genogram is a graphic representation of a family tree that displays the interaction of generations within a family. It goes beyond a traditional family tree by allowing the user to analyze family, emotional, and social relationships within a group. It is used to identify repetitive patterns of behavior and to recognize hereditary tendencies. A social worker can also ask about these relationships, behaviors, and tendencies without using a genogram.

There are no set questions that must be included in a family history; often, they relate to the problem or issue experienced by a client at the time. However, they may include identifying family members':

- Ethnic backgrounds (including immigration) and traditions
- Biological ties (adoption, blended family structures, foster children)
- Occupations and educational levels
- Unusual life events or achievements
- Psychological and social histories, as well as current well-being
- Past and present substance use behaviors
- Relationships with other family members
- Roles within the immediate and larger family unit
- Losses such as those from death, divorce, or physical separation
- Current and past significant problems, including those due to medical, financial, and other issues
- Values related to economic status, educational attainment, and employment
- Coping skills or defense mechanisms

Finding out which adults and/or children get the most attention or recognition and which get the least may also provide insight.

METHODS TO OBTAIN SENSITIVE INFORMATION (E.G., SUBSTANCE ABUSE, SEXUAL ABUSE)

Clients are often reluctant to reveal sensitive information about themselves and others in their families. However, this information may be vital to understanding client problems and designing interventions that will be effective. While there is no set road map of how to elicit this information, there are some techniques that may assist.

- A social worker should start off with some open-ended and nonthreatening questions to gather needed background and get a client used to talking about the situation before having to disclose more sensitive material. This initial questioning will also give a client time to "test the waters" with a social worker and gauge the social worker's reaction as more sensitive information is provided. Trust is often needed in a therapeutic relationship before a client can be completely honest about the situation.

- A social worker should be aware of verbal and nonverbal clues when speaking with a client. A client may avoid eye contact, fail to completely answer a question, look down when speaking, or laugh nervously when feeling anxious about a topic. A social worker may want to repeat a question or probe further into this area to see if there is something undisclosed which is causing this behavior.

- A client who is engaged in couples, family, or group treatment may worry about the confidentiality of revealing sensitive information, as well as the reactions of others to such disclosure. In these instances, a social worker may want to explore with a client whether individual treatment in lieu of or in conjunction with couples, family, or group treatment may be appropriate.

- A social worker may want to review with a client the professional mandate for confidentiality and what information will be stored in a client file.

- A client may be reluctant to reveal sensitive information if the client thinks there could be negative repercussions as a result of the information being disclosed to others verbally or lack of security related to the file.

- A client is much more likely to disclose sensitive information if a social worker reacts to such disclosures with acceptance and a neutral stance, being neither judgmental nor confrontational and not interrupting when information is being gathered.

THE INDICATORS OF ADDICTION AND SUBSTANCE ABUSE

Some people are able to engage in behaviors or use substances without abusing them and/or becoming addicted.

There are signs when clients are addicted to behaviors and/or substances are being abused. These include, but are not limited to, indications that the behavior or substance use is:

- Causing problems at work, home, school, and in relationships
- Resulting in neglected responsibilities at school, work, or home (i.e., flunking classes, skipping work, neglecting children)

- Dangerous (i.e., driving while on drugs, using dirty needles, having unprotected sex, binging/purging despite medical conditions)

- Causing financial and/or legal trouble (i.e., arrests, stealing to support shopping, gambling, or drug habit)

- Causing problems in relationships, such as fights with partner or family members or loss of old friends

- Creating tolerance (more of the behavior or substance is needed to produce the same impact)

- Out of control or causing a feeling of being powerless

- Life-consuming, resulting in abandoned activities that used to be enjoyed

- Resulting in psychological issues such as mood swings, attitude changes, depression, and/or paranoia

Signs of Drug Use

- Marijuana: glassy, red eyes; loud talking, inappropriate laughter followed by sleepiness; loss of interest, motivation; weight gain or loss

- Cocaine: dilated pupils; hyperactivity; euphoria; irritability; anxiety; excessive talking followed by depression or excessive sleeping at odd times; may go long periods of time without eating or sleeping; weight loss; dry mouth and nose

- Heroin: contracted pupils; no response of pupils to light; needle marks; sleeping at unusual times; sweating; vomiting; coughing, sniffling; twitching; loss of appetite

THE INDICATORS OF SOMATIZATION

Somatization is the unconscious process by which psychological distress is expressed as physical symptoms. Somatic symptoms often occur as reactions to stressful situations and are not considered abnormal if they occur sporadically. However, some clients experience continuing somatic symptoms and even seek medical care for them.

Persistent somatization is associated with considerable distress and disability. Somatization may lead to overutilization of medical care, including unnecessary medical tests, and even increased hospitalization rates.

Not all somatizing clients are motivated by an unconscious wish to adopt the sick role, as is observed in clients with factitious disorder. Clients may vary in their degree of conviction that their symptoms are caused by a physical illness or disease. Clients may also present in multiple ways, including having multiple unexplained somatic symptoms, exhibiting predominantly illness worry or hypochondriacal beliefs, and/or displaying somatization as a manifestation of a variety of mental disorders.

CO-OCCURRING DISORDERS AND CONDITIONS

Co-occurring disorders and conditions are present when there are two or more disorders occurring at the same time. For example, clients may have one or more disorders relating to the use of alcohol and/or other drugs, as well as one or more mental disorders. In order for a disorder or condition to be co-occurring, it must be independent and not symptomatology resulting from the other disorder(s)/condition(s).

Co-occurring disorders used to be called "dual diagnoses" or "dual disorders." Just as the field of treatment for substance use and mental disorders has evolved to become more precise, so too has the terminology used to describe clients with both substance use and mental disorders. Many clients with severe mental illness are further impaired by substance use disorders. However, co-occurring can also be used to describe clients with other conditions, such as those with physical and/or intellectual disabilities.

Though co-occurring, disorders and conditions may not be equivalent in severity, chronicity, and/or degree of impairment in functioning. For example, disorders or conditions may each be severe or mild, or one may be more severe than the other. The severity of both disorders or conditions may also change over time.

Compared with clients who have a single disorder or condition, clients with co-occurring disorders or conditions often require longer treatment, have more crises, and progress more gradually in treatment. Integrated treatment or treatment that considers the presence of all the disorders or conditions at the same time is associated with lower costs and better outcomes.

SYMPTOMS OF NEUROLOGIC AND ORGANIC DISORDERS

Neurologic and organic symptoms are those that are caused by disorders that affect part or all of the nervous system or are biologically based. These symptoms can vary greatly. For example, the nervous system controls many different body functions. Symptoms can, but do not have to, be associated with pain, including headache and back pain. Neurologic symptoms can also include muscle weakness or lack of coordination, abnormal sensations in the skin, and disturbances of vision, taste, smell, and hearing.

They may be minor (such as a foot that has fallen asleep) or life threatening (such as coma due to stroke).

Some Common Neurologic Symptoms

Pain

- Back pain
- Neck pain
- Headache
- Pain along a nerve pathway (as sciatica)

Muscle malfunction

- Weakness
- Tremor (rhythmic shaking of a body part)
- Paralysis
- Involuntary (unintended) movements (such as tics)
- Clumsiness or poor coordination
- Muscle spasms

Changes in sensation

- Numbness of the skin
- Tingling or a "pins-and-needles" sensation
- Hypersensitivity to light touch
- Loss of sensation for touch, cold, heat, or pain

Other symptoms

- Vertigo
- Loss of balance
- Slurred speech (dysarthria)

Changes in consciousness

- Fainting
- Confusion or delirium
- Seizures (ranging from brief lapses in consciousness to severe muscle contractions and jerking throughout the body)

Changes in cognition (mental ability)

- Difficulty understanding language or using language to speak or write (aphasia)
- Poor memory
- Inability to recognize familiar objects (agnosia) or familiar faces (prosopagnosia)
- Inability to do simple arithmetic (acalculia)

Changes in the senses

- Disturbances of smell and taste
- Partial or complete loss of vision
- Double vision
- Deafness
- Ringing or other sounds originating in the ears (tinnitus)

Organic brain syndrome is a term used to describe physical disorders that impair mental function. The most common symptoms are confusion; impairment of memory, judgment, and intellectual function; and agitation. Disorders that cause injury or damage to the brain and contribute to organic brain syndrome include, but are not limited to, alcoholism, Alzheimer's disease, fetal alcohol spectrum disorders (FASDs), Parkinson's disease, and stroke.

Elderly clients are at high risk for depression, as well as cognitive disorders, the latter of which can be chronic (as in dementia) or acute (as in delirium). Some patients have both affective (mood) and cognitive disorders. Clarifying the diagnosis is the first step to effective treatment, but this can be particularly difficult because elderly clients often have medical comorbidities that can contribute to cognitive and affective changes.

	Delirium	Dementia	Depression
Alertness	Altered level of consciousness; alertness may fluctuate	May vary	May vary
Motor behavior	Fluctuates; lethargy or hyperactivity	May vary	Psychomotor behavior may be agitated or unaffected
Attention	Impaired and fluctuates	Usually normal	Usually normal, but may be distractible
Awareness	Impaired, reduced	Clear	Clear
Course	Acute; responds to treatment	Chronic, with deterioration over time	Chronic; responds to treatment
Progression	Abrupt	Slow but stable	Varies
Orientation	Fluctuates in severity; usually impaired	May be impaired	May be selective disorientation
Memory	Recent and immediate impaired	Recent and remote impaired	Selective or patchy impairment
Thinking	Disorganized, distorted, incoherent; slow or accelerated	Difficulty with abstraction; thoughts impoverished; difficulty finding words; poor judgment	Intact, but may voice hopelessness and self-deprecation
Instrumental activities of daily living (IADLs)	May be intact or impaired	May be intact early; impaired ADLs as disease progresses	May be intact or impaired
Stability	Variable, hour-to-hour	Fairly stable	Some variability
Emotions	Irritable, aggressive, fearful	Labile, apathetic, irritable	Flat, unresponsive, or sad; may be irritable
Activities of daily living (ADLs)	May be intact or impaired	May be intact early, impaired as disease progresses	May neglect basic self-care

THE INDICATORS OF SEXUAL DYSFUNCTION

Sexual dysfunction is a problem associated with sexual desire or response. Many issues can be included under the term "sexual dysfunction." For example, for men, sexual dysfunction may include erectile dysfunction and premature or delayed ejaculation. For women, sexual dysfunction may refer to pain during sexual intercourse.

Problems may be caused by psychological factors, physical conditions, or a combination of both. It is essential that a medical examination be the first step in treating sexual dysfunction in order to identify medications or medical conditions that are the causes of the problems. Many of the symptoms can be addressed medically. However, sexual dysfunction can also be due to childhood sexual abuse, depression, anxiety, stressful life events, and/or other psychological issues. Treatment may also be needed to assist with coping with the signs and symptoms; these include, but are not limited to:

- Premature or delayed ejaculation in men
- Erectile disorder (not being able to get or keep an erection)
- Pain during sex
- Lack or loss of sexual desire
- Difficulty having an orgasm
- Vaginal dryness

METHODS USED TO ASSESS TRAUMA

Trauma is the response that a client has to an extremely negative event. Although trauma is a normal reaction to a horrible event, the effects can be so severe that they interfere with a client's ability to live life. Thus, a social worker is needed to treat the stress and dysfunction caused by the traumatic event and to restore a client to a previous emotional state.

Emotional reactions are the common effects of trauma. Impacts of trauma on clients' self-image include, but are not limited to:

- Anxiety
- Denial
- Agitation
- Irritability or rage
- Flashbacks or intrusive memories
- Feeling disconnected from the world
- Unrest in certain situations
- Being "shut down"
- Being very passive
- Feeling depressed

- Guilt/shame/self-blame
- Unusual fears
- Impatience
- Having a hard time concentrating
- Wanting to hurt oneself
- Being unable to trust anyone
- Feeling unlikable
- Feeling unsafe

Trauma often manifests physically, including both physiological and behavioral symptoms. Behavioral manifestations of trauma include, but are not limited to:

- Insomnia or fatigue
- Using harmful substances
- Keeping to oneself
- Overworking
- Lethargy
- Eating problems
- Drug or alcohol use
- Needing to do certain things over and over
- Always having to have things a certain way
- Doing strange or risky things

Clients may have anxiety or panic attacks and be unable to cope in certain circumstances. Social workers must often work with clients to address the underlying emotional impacts of the trauma in order for clients to make behavioral changes.

Clients who experience trauma often believe that they cannot trust, the world is not safe, and they are powerless to change their circumstances. Beliefs about themselves, others, and the world diminish their sense of competency. Thus, clients view themselves as powerless or "damaged" and have trouble feeling hopeful.

Clients who have experienced trauma may display intense emotions toward others, such as friends or family members. Clients can also emotionally retreat from these individuals, choosing to isolate themselves. Thus, trauma can be difficult for those who are close to clients as well.

THE INDICATORS OF TRAUMATIC STRESS AND VIOLENCE

Stress is a typical response to feeling overwhelmed or threatened. Fight, flight, and freeze are survival responses to protect individuals from danger. Individuals react and respond to stress in different ways. There are many disadvantages to a stressful lifestyle that creates constant feelings of being overwhelmed, as well as physiological stimulation. Interventions aimed at social and lifestyle changes can usually restore physiological and psychological balance in order to address stress.

This is not the case when traumatization occurs. Traumatization is when a client experiences neurological distress that does not go away or when the client is not able to return to a state of equilibrium. Traumatization can lead to mental, social, emotional, and physical disability. Like stress, trauma is also experienced differently by different individuals.

There are many indicators of traumatic stress and violence, including:

1. Addictive behaviors related to drugs, alcohol, sex, shopping, and gambling

2. An inability to tolerate conflicts with others or intense feelings

3. A belief of being bad, worthless, without value or importance

4. Dichotomous "all or nothing" thinking

5. Chronic and repeated suicidal thoughts/feelings

6. Poor attachment

7. Dissociation

8. Eating disorders—anorexia, bulimia, and overeating

9. Self-blame

10. Intense anxiety and repeated panic attacks

11. Depression

12. Self-harm, self-mutilation, self-injury, or self-destruction

13. Unexplained, but intense, fears of people, places, or things

When trauma or violence occurs during childhood, children may have problems regulating their behaviors and emotions. They may be clingy and fearful of new situations, easily frightened, difficult to console, aggressive, impulsive, sleepless, delayed in developmental milestones, and/or regressing in functioning and behavior.

In order to practice competently in this area, social workers must:

1. Realize the widespread impact of trauma and understand potential paths for recovery

2. Recognize the signs and symptoms of trauma in clients, families, staff, and other systems

3. Respond by fully integrating knowledge about trauma into social work policies, procedures, and practices

4. Seek to actively resist retraumatization

COMMON PSYCHOTROPIC AND NON-PSYCHOTROPIC PRESCRIPTIONS AND OVER-THE-COUNTER MEDICATIONS AND THEIR SIDE EFFECTS

Psychotropic medications affect brain chemicals associated with mood and behavior. Psychotropic drugs are prescribed to treat a variety of mental health problems and typically work by changing the amounts of important chemicals in the brain called neurotransmitters. Psychotropic drugs are usually prescribed by psychiatrists, though other physicians and professionals may be allowed to prescribe them in certain jurisdictions. Psychotropic drugs may be needed to treat disorders such as schizophrenia or bipolar disorder, but are often combined with other supports, such as that from family and friends, therapy, lifestyle changes, and other treatment protocols, to ensure healthy everyday living.

Antipsychotics

Used for the treatment of schizophrenia and mania

Typical

Haldol (haloperidol)

Haldol Decanoate (long-acting injectable)

Loxitane (loxapine)

Mellaril (thioridazine)

Moban (molindone)

Navane (thiothixene)

Prolixin (fluphenazine)

Serentil (mesoridazine)

Stelazine (trifluoperazine)

Thorazine (chlorpromazine)

Trilafon (perphenazine)

Atypical

Abilify (aripiprazole)

Clozaril (clozapine)

Geodon (ziprasidone)

Risperdal (risperidone)

Seroquel (quetiapine)

Zyprexa (olanzapine)

With Clozaril, there is an increased risk of agranulocytosis that requires blood monitoring. Some antipsychotics are available in injectable forms; these are useful for clients who are noncompliant with oral medications.

Tardive dyskinesia (abnormal, involuntary movements of the tongue, lips, jaw, and face, as well as twitching and snakelike movement of the extremities and occasionally the trunk) may result from taking high doses of antipsychotic medications over a long period of time. Symptoms may persist indefinitely after discontinuation of these medications. Thus, antipsychotic use should be closely monitored and prescribed at low doses if possible.

Antimanic Agents (Mood Stabilizers)

Used for the treatment of bipolar disorder

Depakene (valproic acid, divalproex sodium), Depakote sprinkles

Lamictal (lamotrigine)

Lithium (lithium carbonate), Eskalith, Lithobid

Tegretol (carbamazepine), Carbotrol

Topamax (topiramate)

There is a small difference between toxic and therapeutic levels (narrow therapeutic index) that necessitates periodic checks of blood levels of lithium. Also, there is a need for periodic checks of thyroid and kidney functions, because lithium can affect the functioning of these organs.

Antidepressants

Used for the treatment of depressive disorders

Selective Serotonin Reuptake Inhibitors (SSRIs)

Celexa (citalopram)

Lexapro (escitalopram)

Luvox (fluvoxamine)

Paxil (paroxetine)

Prozac (fluoxetine)

Zoloft (sertraline)

Tricyclics

Anafranil (clomipramine)

Asendin (amoxapine)

Elavil (amitriptyline)

Norpramin (desipramine)

Pamelor (nortriptyline)

Sinequan (doxepin)

Surmontil (trimipramine)

Tofranil (imipramine)

Vivactil (protriptyline)

Monoamine Oxidase Inhibitors (MAOIs)

Nardil (phenelzine)

Parnate (tranylcypromine)

There are dietary restrictions of foods that contain high levels of tyramine (generally food that has been aged). Foods to avoid may include beer, ale, wine (particularly Chianti), cheese (except cottage and cream cheese), smoked or pickled fish (herring), beef or chicken liver, summer (dry) sausage, fava or broad bean pods (Italian green beans), and yeast vitamin supplements (brewer's yeast).

Others

Desyrel (trazodone)

Effexor (venlafaxine)

Remeron (mirtazapine)

Serzone (nefazodone)

Wellbutrin (bupropion)

Antianxiety Drugs

Used for the treatment of anxiety disorders

Ativan (lorazepam)

Buspar (buspirone)

Klonopin (clonazepam)

Valium (diazepam)

Xanax (alprazolam)

Benzodiazepines are a class of drugs primarily used for treating anxiety, but they also are effective in treating several other conditions.

There is a high abuse potential of these drugs and they can be dangerous when combined with alcohol or illicit substances. It is critical to look for signs of impaired motor or other functioning.

Stimulants

Used for the treatment of attention-deficit/hyperactivity disorder

Adderall (amphetamine, mixed salts)

Concerta (methylphenidate, long acting)

Dexedrine (dextroamphetamine)

Dexedrine Spansules (dextroamphetamine, long acting)

Metadate (methylphenidate, long acting)

Ritalin (methylphenidate)

Common Prescription Medications

Many people take at least one prescription medication, with more than half taking two or more. The most commonly prescribed include the following medications.

Advair Diskus is a prescription used to treat asthma and chronic obstructive pulmonary disease (COPD).

Crestor is a lipid-lowering agent taken orally.

Cymbalta is a selective serotonin and norepinephrine reuptake inhibitor (SSNRI) for oral administration used to treat depression, anxiety, and pain caused by nerve damage.

Diovan is used to treat heart disease or heart failure.

Hydrocodone/acetaminophen is the most popular painkiller used to treat moderate to severe pain. Hydrocodone, a narcotic analgesic, relieves pain through the central nervous system, and it also is used to stop or prevent coughing. This drug can become habit-forming when used over an extended period of time.

Levothyroxine sodium is used to treat hypothyroidism, a condition where the thyroid gland does not produce enough of the thyroid hormone. This drug also is used to treat thyroid cancer and to help shrink an enlarged thyroid gland.

Lantus is a sterile solution of insulin glargine for use as a subcutaneous injection for diabetes.

Lisinopril (which used to be sold under the brand names Zestril and Prinivil) is a high blood pressure medication. Its main function is to block chemicals in the body that trigger the tightening of blood vessels. Lisinopril also is used to help treat heart failure.

Lyrica is used to control seizures, as well as treat nerve pain and fibromyalgia.

Metoprolol, the generic version of Lopressor, is used to treat high blood pressure and also helps reduce the risk of repeated heart attacks. Metoprolol also treats heart failure and heart pain or angina.

Nexium is used to treat symptoms of gastroesophageal reflux disease (GERD) and other conditions involving excessive stomach acid.

Simvastatin (generic form of Zocor) is prescribed to treat high cholesterol and is typically recommended in conjunction with diet changes. This drug is believed to have a variety of benefits including helping to prevent heart attacks and strokes.

Synthroid is a prescription, man-made thyroid hormone that is used to treat hypothyroidism.

Ventolin solution is used in inhalers for asthma.

Vyvanse is used to treat hyperactivity and impulse control disorders.

5 Assessment Methods and Techniques

THE FACTORS AND PROCESSES USED IN PROBLEM FORMULATION

In both micro and macro practice, social workers must work with clients to identify the problem(s) to be addressed. Problem identification concerns determining the problem targeted for intervention. Although this seems straightforward, it is often difficult to isolate the issue that, when addressed, will result in a change in the symptomology of a client and/or client system.

Part of problem identification is determining the issue in exact definable terms, when it occurs, and its magnitude. When doing macro practice, a social worker may often need to get consensus from the group regarding whether there is agreement as to the nature of the problem and its occurrence and magnitude.

It is often useful in problem identification to determine that which is not the problem. Such a technique will ensure that these elements are not grouped in with those that are targeted and will assist in narrowing down the focus.

The problem should always be considered within the person-in-environment perspective and using a strengths-based approach. It should not blame a client and/or client system for its existence.

METHODS OF INVOLVING CLIENTS/CLIENT SYSTEMS IN PROBLEM IDENTIFICATION (E.G., GATHERING COLLATERAL INFORMATION)

Social workers focus on assisting clients to identify problems and areas of strength, as well as increasing problem-solving strategies.

It is essential that, throughout the problem-solving process, social workers view clients as experts in their lives.

Clients should be asked about what they would like to see changed in their lives and clients' definitions of problems should be accepted.

Clients should be asked about what will be different in their lives when their problems are solved. Social workers should listen carefully for, and work hard to respect, the directions in which clients want to go with their lives (their goals) and the words they use to express these directions.

Clients should be asked about the paths that they would like to take to make desired changes. Clients' perceptions should be respected and clients' inner resources (strengths) should be maximized as part of treatment.

Use of Collateral Sources

Social workers often use collateral sources—family, friends, other agencies, physicians, and so on—as informants when collecting information to effectively treat clients. These sources can provide vital information because other professionals or agencies may have treated clients in the past. Family members and friends may also provide important information about the length or severity of issues or problems.

Collateral information is often used when the credibility and validity of information obtained from a client or others are questionable. For example, child custody cases are inherently characterized by biased data within an adversarial process. Thus, it is often necessary to evaluate the integrity of information gathered through use of collateral information.

However, social workers should always assess the credibility of collateral informants, because data from more neutral parties has higher integrity. In addition, informants who have greater access to key information may produce more valid data.

When an account by a collateral informant agrees with information gathered from a client, it enhances the trustworthiness of the data collected.

Using multiple information sources (or triangulation) is an excellent method for social workers to have accurate accounts upon which to make assessments or base interventions.

It is essential that a social worker get a client's informed consent prior to reaching out to collateral sources. However, they can be a valuable source of data to supplement that obtained directly from a client, as well as provide contextual or background information that a client may not know.

TECHNIQUES AND INSTRUMENTS USED TO ASSESS CLIENTS/CLIENT SYSTEMS

There are many psychological tests in existence for assessment and diagnostic purposes. The following are a few of the most well known.

Beck Depression Inventory

The Beck Depression Inventory (BDI) is a 21-item test, presented in multiple-choice formats, that assesses the presence and degree of depression in adolescents and adults.

The Minnesota Multiphasic Personality Inventory

The Minnesota Multiphasic Personality Inventory (MMPI) is an objective verbal inventory designed as a personality test for the assessment of psychopathology consisting of 550 statements, 16 of which are repeated.

Myers–Briggs Type Indicator

The Myers–Briggs Type Indicator (MBTI) is a forced-choice, self-report inventory that attempts to classify individuals along four theoretically independent dimensions. The first dimension is a general attitude toward the world, either extraverted (E) or introverted (I). The second dimension, perception, is divided between sensation (S) and intuition (N). The third dimension is that of processing. Once information is received, it is processed in either a thinking (T) or feeling (F) style. The final dimension is judging (J) versus perceiving (P).

Rorschach Inkblot Test

Client responses to inkblots are used to assess perceptual reactions and other psychological functioning. It is one of the most widely used projective tests.

Stanford–Binet Intelligence Scale

The Stanford–Binet Intelligence Scale is designed for the testing of cognitive abilities. It provides verbal, performance, and full scale scores for children and adults.

Thematic Apperception Test

The Thematic Apperception Test (TAT) is another widely used projective test. It consists of a series of pictures of ambiguous scenes. Clients are asked to make up stories or fantasies concerning what is happening, has happened, and is going to happen in the scenes, along with a description of their thoughts and feelings. The TAT provides information on a client's perceptions and imagination for use in the understanding of a client's current needs, motives, emotions, and conflicts, both conscious and unconscious. Its use in clinical assessment is generally part of a larger battery of tests and interview data.

Wechsler Intelligence Scale

The Wechsler Intelligence Scale (WISC) is designed as a measure of a child's intellectual and cognitive ability. It has four index scales and a full scale score.

METHODS TO INCORPORATE THE RESULTS OF PSYCHOLOGICAL AND EDUCATIONAL TESTS INTO ASSESSMENT

Social workers use both tests and assessments to help formulate diagnoses and to guide treatment for their clients.

Psychological tests are instruments used to measure an assortment of mental abilities and characteristics, such as personality, achievement, intelligence, and neurological functioning. They often take the form of questionnaires. They may be written, verbal, or pictorial tests (like the famous Rorschach test that uses inkblot images). The tests may also be referred to as scales, surveys, screens, checklists, assessments, measures, inventories, and so on.

Educational tests measure cognitive (thinking) abilities and academic achievement. These measurements provide a profile of strengths and weaknesses that accurately identify areas for academic remediation and insight into the best learning strategies. They provide details into the learning process that will provide clients, family members, and school staff the best learning strategies. Educational assessments provide the necessary documentation for the legal purposes of establishing the presence of disabilities, but they do not guarantee that their findings will be accepted by schools and/or accommodations provided. Reaching decisions to have educational testing is often arrived at after a period of struggle, distress, and different efforts at improving the educational process with limited success.

Social work assessment is a more comprehensive process that may utilize the results from educational and psychological tests, but can also involve interviewing a client and/or family, reviewing a client's history, checking existing records, and consulting with previous or concurrent providers.

Some common tests are:

- *Achievement/aptitude tests*: typically used in education, measure how much clients know (have *achieved*) in a certain subject or subjects, or have ability (*aptitude*) to learn
- *Intelligence tests*: measure intelligence quotient (IQ)
- *Job/occupational tests*: match interests with careers
- *Personality tests*: measure basic personality traits/characteristics
- *Neuropsychological tests*: assess and measure cognitive functioning (e.g., how a particular problem with the brain affects recall, concentration, etc.)
- *Specialized clinical tests*: investigate areas of clinical interest, such as anxiety, depression, posttraumatic stress disorder, and so on

RISK ASSESSMENT METHODS

Social workers are often called upon to assess risks of clients to themselves and others. Such assessments are not easy, because there are no indicators that definitively predict whether a client will act on feelings or desires to do self-harm. A social worker must review all assessment data in order to determine the appropriate level of care and a treatment plan. Such an assessment must include examining risk and protective factors, as well as the presence of behavioral warning signs. Such an assessment may include examining:

- Frequency, intensity, and duration of suicidal or violent thoughts
- Access to or availability of method(s)
- Ability or inability to control suicidal/violent thoughts
- Ability not to act on thoughts

- Factors making a client feel better or worse
- Consequences of actions
- Deterrents to acting on thoughts
- Whether client has been using drugs or alcohol to cope
- Measures a client requires to maintain safety

In situations where a client is seen to be a danger to self or others, a social worker may limit a client's right to self-determination and seek involuntary treatment such as commitment to an inpatient setting. If a client is deemed to be a danger to others, a social worker should consider this as a "duty to warn" situation (under the Tarasoff decision), and notify the authorities as well as the party in danger.

THE INDICATORS AND RISK FACTORS OF THE CLIENT'S/CLIENT SYSTEM'S DANGER TO SELF AND OTHERS

There are risk factors that must be considered in any assessment, because they are linked to a risk of suicide or violence.

Danger to Self: Suicide

Risk Factors

- History of previous suicide attempt (best predictor of future attempt; medical seriousness of attempt is also significant)
- Lives alone; lack of social supports
- Presence of psychiatric disorder—depression (feeling hopeless), anxiety disorder, personality disorder (*A client is also at greater risk after being discharged from the hospital or after being started on antidepressants as the client may now have the energy to implement a suicide plan.*)
- Substance abuse
- Family history of suicide
- Exposure to suicidal behavior of others through media or peers
- Losses—relationship, job, financial, social
- Presence of firearm or easy access to other lethal methods

Some Protective Factors

- Effective and appropriate clinical care for mental, physical, and substance use disorders
- Easy access to a variety of clinical interventions and support (i.e., medical and mental health care)
- Restricted access to highly lethal methods

- Family and community support
- Learned coping and stress reduction skills
- Cultural and religious beliefs that discourage suicide and support self-preservation

Some Behavioral Warning Signs

- Change in eating and sleeping habits
- Drug and alcohol use
- Unusual neglect of personal appearance
- Marked personality change
- Loss of interest in pleasurable activities
- Not tolerating praise or rewards
- Giving away belongings
- Isolation from others
- Taking care of legal and other issues
- Dramatic increase in mood (might indicate a client has made a decision to end life)
- Verbalizes threats to die by suicide or feelings of despair and hopelessness
  - "I'm going to kill myself."
  - "I wish I were dead."
  - "My family would be better off without me."
  - "The only way out for me is to die."
  - "It's just too much for me to put up with."
  - "Nobody needs me anymore."

Danger to Others: Violence

Most aggressive children or children with behavioral disorders do not become serious violent offenders.

Risk Factors

- Youth who become violent before age 13 generally commit more crimes, and more serious crimes, for a longer time; these youth exhibit a pattern of escalating violence throughout childhood, sometimes continuing into adulthood.
- Serious violence is associated with drugs, guns, and other risky behaviors.
- Involvement with delinquent peers and gang membership are two of the most powerful predictors of violence.

Some Protective Factors

- Effective programs combine components that address both individual risks and environmental conditions; building individual skills and competencies; changes in peer groups

- Interventions that target change in social context appear to be more effective, on average, than those that attempt to change individual attitudes, skills, and risk behaviors

- Effective and appropriate clinical care for mental, physical, and substance abuse disorders

- Easy access to a variety of clinical interventions and support (i.e., medical and mental health care)

- Restricted access to highly lethal methods

- Family and community support

- Learned coping and stress reduction skills

Some Behavioral Warning Signs

- Drug and alcohol use

- Marked personality changes

- Angry outbursts

- Preoccupation with killing, war, violence, weapons, and so on

- Isolation from others

- Obtaining guns or other lethal methods

METHODS TO ASSESS THE CLIENT'S/CLIENT SYSTEM'S STRENGTHS, RESOURCES, AND CHALLENGES (E.G., INDIVIDUAL, FAMILY, GROUP, ORGANIZATION, COMMUNITY)

Clients typically seek social work services for help with problems or difficulties. As a result, the assessment generally focuses on the problems. This focus can lead to an overemphasis on client pathology and dysfunction without the same attention to client strengths, capabilities, and achievements. Information on both strengths and challenges are needed to get a full understanding of the client situation.

Social workers must be sensitive to client strengths and skillful in using them to achieve service goals. Social workers who do not attend to client strengths will not be able to determine clients' potential for growth and the steps needed to get there. Often clients are experiencing self-doubt or poor self-esteem. To assist with helping clients view themselves more positively, social workers must be able to emphasize their strengths.

Strengths which may be overlooked include clients:

- Facing problems by seeking help—rather than denying them

- Taking risks by sharing problems with social workers

- Persevering under difficult situations

- Being resourceful

- Meeting family and financial obligations

- Seeking to understand the actions of others

- Functioning in stressful situations

  Considering alternative courses of action

Methods to identify more about client strengths, resources, and challenges can be obtained by:

- Seeking exceptions—determining when the problem does not exist or occur (locations, times, contexts)

- Scaling the problem—identifying the severity of the problem on a scale from 1 to 10 according to the client

- Scaling motivation—estimating the degree to which client feels hopeful about resolution

- Miracle question—having the client determine what would be different if problem did not exist

When conducting community assessments, it is essential for social workers to identify strengths and challenges. Strengths are positive features of the community that can be leveraged to develop solutions to problems. Strengths can include organizations, people, partnerships, facilities, funding, policies, regulations, and culture.

A social worker should consider the current assets that are already in existence to promote the quality of life of community members. For example, organizations that provide after-school programs that help youth graduate on time would be included in a community assessment focused on keeping kids in school. In some instances, a social worker may want to look at experiences of other communities with similar demographics that have successfully addressed similar problems. Examining the presence and utilization of strengths in these communities can assist a social worker in determining if similar assets can be found in its target community.

A social worker must also develop an informed understanding of the gaps or needs that exist within a community. These needs serve as challenges that can affect a large or small number of community members. If community needs affect a large number of community members, there may be more support for addressing them. Collaboration and community building are essential in addressing community challenges.

There are a number of methods for data collection related to community strengths and challenges including interviews, observation, and surveys. Ensuring that the data collection procedures are robust is essential in conducting a complete and accurate community assessment.

METHODS TO ASSESS MOTIVATION, RESISTANCE, AND READINESS TO CHANGE

Motivation and resistance exist along a continuum of readiness. When assessing motivation and resistance of a client, it is important to determine what stage of change a client is in. This will provide a social worker with appropriate clinical strategies to use to address these issues. If social workers push clients at a faster pace than they are ready to take, the therapeutic alliance may break down.

A lack of motivation and resistance are often found in *precontemplation* and *contemplation* before making the decision to change. There can also be motivational challenges during preparation, action, and maintenance, but they are more easily addressed. When resistance occurs in these latter stages of change, a social worker should reassess the problem and appropriateness of the intervention to ensure that there have not been new developments in a client's life that need to be considered. They may be distracting a client from making progress or serving as barriers to making real change.

In precontemplation, a client is unaware, unable, and/or unwilling to change. In this stage, there is the greatest resistance and lack of motivation. It can be characterized by arguing, interrupting, denial, ignoring the problem, and/or avoiding talking or thinking about it. A client may not even show up for appointments and does not agree that change is needed.

A social worker can best deal with lack of motivation and resistance in this stage by establishing a rapport, acknowledging resistance or ambivalence, keeping conversation informal, trying to engage a client, and recognizing a client's thoughts, feelings, fears, and concerns.

In contemplation, a client is ambivalent or uncertain regarding behavior change; thus, behaviors are unpredictable. In this stage, a client may be willing to look at the pros and cons of behavior change, but is not committed to working toward it.

A social worker can best deal with lack of motivation and resistance in this stage by emphasizing a client's free choice and responsibility, as well as discussing the pros and cons of changing. It is also useful to discuss how change will assist a client in achieving life goals. Fear can be reduced by producing examples of change and clarifying what change is and is not.

METHODS TO ASSESS THE CLIENT'S/CLIENT SYSTEM'S COMMUNICATION SKILLS

Social workers must involve clients in every aspect of treatment. In order to do so, social workers must assess clients' communication skills and determine effective methods to gather needed information, as well as to ensure that clients understand data that is presented to them. Thus, the expressive and receptive communication of clients must be considered.

As many clients may have experienced trauma, it is essential that social workers understand how such experiences may impact on clients' communication styles and patterns. Much of communication is also cultural and should be viewed within the context of clients' backgrounds and experiences.

Silence is a form of communication and should be considered by a social worker when used by a client.

Social workers should understand how to communicate with clients who are upset and angry, as well as how some wording choices and tones can be upsetting to clients based on their ethnic backgrounds and/or past experiences, such as victimization.

METHODS TO ASSESS THE CLIENT'S/CLIENT SYSTEM'S COPING ABILITIES

Social workers can learn a lot about clients' difficulties by determining how clients have attempted to cope with their problems in the past. The coping abilities that clients employ give valuable clues about their levels of stress and functioning. Investigation may indicate that clients have few coping abilities, but rely on rigid patterns that are unhelpful or cause further problems. Some clients follow avoidance pattern by immersing themselves in work, withdrawing, or using drugs or alcohol. Others attempt to cope by being aggressive or acting out. Lastly, others become dependent and rely on family members or friends to manage difficulties for them.

Exploring how clients have attempted to cope with problems may reveal that they have struggled with the same or similar problems in the past. As they are no longer able to manage, it is important to find out what has changed ("why now?"). In order to assess coping skills, social workers might want to ask about the extent to which clients:

- Turn to work or other substitute activities to take their minds off things
- Get upset and let their emotions out
- Get advice from others about what to do
- Concentrate on doing something about their problems
- Put their trust in high beings
- Laugh about their situations
- Discuss their feelings with others
- Use alcohol or drugs to make themselves feel better
- Pretend that their problems do not exist
- Seek out others who have similar experiences

THE INDICATORS OF CLIENT'S/CLIENT SYSTEM'S STRENGTHS AND CHALLENGES

Strength is the capacity to cope with difficulties, to maintain functioning under stress, to return to equilibrium in the face of significant trauma, to use external challenges to promote growth, and to be resilient by using social supports.

There is not a single approach to the assessment of strengths. However, social workers can view all of these areas as strengths or protective factors that can assist clients when they experience challenges. These characteristics can also be abilities that need to be bolstered as a focus of treatment.

Cognitive and Appraisal Skills

- Intellectual/cognitive ability
- Creativity and curiosity
- Initiative, perseverance, and patience
- Common sense
- Ability to anticipate problems
- Realistic appraisal of demands and capacities
- Ability to use feedback

Defenses and Coping Mechanisms

- Ability to regulate impulses and affect
- Self-soothing
- Flexible; can handle stressors

Temperamental and Dispositional Factors

- Belief in trustworthiness of others
- Belief in justice

- Self-esteem and self-worth
- Sense of mastery, confidence, and optimism
- Ability to tolerate ambiguity and uncertainty
- Ability to make sense of negative events
- Sense of humor
- Lack of hostility, anger, and anxiety
- Optimistic and open
- Ability to grieve
- Lack of helplessness
- Responsibility for decisions
- Sense of direction, mission, and purpose

Interpersonal Skills and Supports

- Ability to develop/maintain good relationships
- Ability to confide in others
- Problem-solving skills
- Capacity for empathy
- Presence of an intimate relationship
- Sense of security

Other Factors

- Supportive social institutions, such as church
- Good physical health
- Adequate income
- Supportive family and friends

METHODS TO ASSESS EGO STRENGTHS

Ego strength is the ability of the ego to effectively deal with the demands of the id, the super-ego, and reality. It is a basis for resilience and helps maintain emotional stability by coping with internal and external stress.

Traits usually considered to be indicators of positive ego strength include tolerance of pain associated with loss, disappointment, shame, or guilt; forgiveness of others, with feelings of compassion rather than anger; persistence and perseverance in the pursuit of goals; and/or openness, flexibility, and creativity in learning to adapt. Those with positive ego strength are less likely to have psychiatric crises.

Other indicators of positive ego strength include clients:

- Acknowledging their feelings—including grief, insecurity, loneliness, and anxiety
- Not getting overwhelmed by their moods
- Pushing forward after loss and not being paralyzed by self-pity or resentment
- Using painful events to strengthen themselves
- Knowing that painful feelings will eventually fade
- Empathizing with others without trying to reduce or eliminate their pain

- Being self-disciplined and fighting addictive urges
- Taking responsibility for actions
- Holding themselves accountable
- Not blaming others
- Accepting themselves with their limitations
- Setting firm limits even if it means disappointing others or risking rejection
- Avoiding people who drain them physically and/or emotionally

PLACEMENT OPTIONS BASED ON ASSESSED LEVEL OF CARE

Social workers must assess the client's needed level of care, with the belief that there should be a continuum of intensity depending upon the level of crisis. Clients should enter treatment at a level appropriate to their needs and then step up to more intense treatment or down to less intense treatment as needed. An effective continuum of care features successful transfer of a client between levels of care.

Levels of care for behavioral health services, for example, vary from early intervention services/outpatient services to intensive outpatient/partial hospitalization to residential/inpatient services.

Early intervention or outpatient services are appropriate unless a client is experiencing crisis or at risk for residential/inpatient services, which may then warrant a step up to intensive outpatient or partial hospitalization. The goal is to serve clients in the least restrictive environment, while ensuring health and safety.

THE USE OF THE *DIAGNOSTIC AND STATISTICAL MANUAL OF MENTAL DISORDERS* BY THE AMERICAN PSYCHIATRIC ASSOCIATION

The *Diagnostic and Statistical Manual of Mental Disorders* (*DSM*) is used by social workers and other mental health professionals as an authoritative guide to the diagnosis of mental disorders. The *DSM* contains descriptions, symptoms, and other criteria for diagnosing mental disorders.

A social worker might give a client an ***other specified diagnosis*** if the client is missing one or two of the symptoms that are necessary for a diagnosis. For example, a diagnosis of generalized anxiety disorder (GAD) requires that the client experience anxiety more days than not. A social work might see that a client has all the other symptoms of that disorder and that anxiety is interfering with life, but the anxiety might not show up on enough days to technically count as GAD. In that case, the client could be diagnosed with other specified anxiety disorder. The social worker would add a note to the diagnosis explaining the reason that the diagnosis is not GAD.

An ***unspecified diagnosis*** is used when a social worker has determined that a client's challenges fall within a certain group of disorders, but it's not clear exactly which diagnosis in that group best suits the client. The main difference is that an ***unspecified diagnosis*** doesn't include detailed information or the reason that the criteria for a specific diagnosis are not met.

Specifiers are extensions to a diagnosis that further clarify the course, severity, or special features of the client disorders or illnesses. Specifiers allow for a more specific diagnosis that will help social workers select more effective treatment for clients.

Neurodevelopmental Disorders

Intellectual Developmental Disorders

Intellectual developmental disorder (intellectual disability)
This disorder involves limitations in intellectual functioning (such as reasoning, problem-solving, and learning) and adaptive behavior. It begins during the developmental period and impacts an individual's ability to independently function in daily life.

> Specify current severity: Mild, Moderate, Severe, and Profound

Global developmental delay

Unspecified intellectual developmental disorder (intellectual disability)

Communication Disorders

This category includes disorders such as language disorder (difficulties in language expression or comprehension) and speech sound disorder (pronunciation difficulties), among others. These disorders impact effective communication skills.

Language disorder

Speech sound disorder

Childhood-onset fluency disorder (stuttering)
> Note: Later-onset cases are diagnosed as adult-onset fluency disorder.

Social (pragmatic) communication disorder
This disorder involves difficulties in using and understanding verbal and nonverbal communication for social purposes. Individuals struggle to effectively use language in social contexts.

Unspecified communication disorder

Autism Spectrum Disorder

Autism spectrum disorder (ASD)
ASD is characterized by difficulties in social communication and interaction, as well as restricted and repetitive patterns of behavior, interests, or activities. Symptoms vary widely in severity, and early intervention is crucial for improving outcomes.

> Specify current severity: Requiring very substantial support, Requiring substantial support, Requiring support
> Specify if: With or without accompanying intellectual impairment, With or without accompanying language impairment
> Specify if: Associated with a known genetic or other medical condition or environmental factor; Associated with a neurodevelopmental, mental, or behavioral problem
> Specify if: With catatonia

Attention-Deficit/Hyperactivity Disorder

Attention-deficit/hyperactivity disorder (ADHD)
ADHD is marked by persistent patterns of inattention, hyperactivity, and impulsivity that can interfere with daily functioning and development. It commonly starts in childhood and may persist into adulthood.

Specify if: In partial remission

Specify current severity: Mild, Moderate, and Severe

Specify whether: Combined presentation, Predominantly inattentive presentation, Predominantly hyperactive/impulsive presentation, other specified attention-deficit/hyperactivity disorder, unspecified attention-deficit/hyperactivity disorder

Specific Learning Disorder

Specific learning disorder

Individuals with this disorder struggle with specific academic skills, such as reading, writing, or mathematics, despite having average or above-average intelligence. These difficulties significantly interfere with academic achievement or daily activities.

Specify current severity: Mild, Moderate, and Severe

Specify if: With impairment in reading (specify if with word reading accuracy, reading rate or fluency, and reading comprehension); With impairment in written expression (specify if with spelling accuracy, grammar and punctuation accuracy, clarity or organization of written expression); With impairment in mathematics (specify if with number sense, memorization of arithmetic facts, accurate or fluent calculation, accurate math reasoning)

Motor Disorders

This category includes disorders such as developmental coordination disorder (difficulty with motor coordination and physical tasks) and Tourette's disorder (presence of both motor and vocal tics).

Developmental coordination disorder

Stereotypic movement disorder

Specify if: With self-injurious behavior, Without self-injurious behavior

Specify if: Associated with a known genetic or other medical condition, neurodevelopmental disorder, or environmental factor

Specify current severity: Mild, Moderate, and Severe

Tic disorders

Apart from Tourette's disorder, this category includes persistent (chronic) motor or vocal tic disorder (single or multiple motor or vocal tics present for more than a year) and provisional tic disorder (tics present for less than a year).

Tourette's disorder

Persistent (chronic) motor or vocal tic disorder

Specify if: With motor tics only, With vocal tics only

Provisional tic disorder

Other specified tic disorder

Unspecified tic disorder

Other Neurodevelopmental Disorders

Other specified neurodevelopmental disorder

Unspecified neurodevelopmental disorder

Schizophrenia Spectrum and Other Psychotic Disorders

The following specifiers apply to schizophrenia spectrum and other psychotic disorders where indicated:

Specify if: The following course specifiers are only to be used after a 1-year duration of the disorder: First episode, currently in acute episode; First episode, currently in partial remission; First episode, currently in full remission; Multiple episodes, currently in acute episode; Multiple episodes, currently in partial remission; Multiple episodes, currently in full remission; Continuous; Unspecified

Specify if: With catatonia

Specify current severity of delusions, hallucinations, disorganized speech, abnormal psychomotor behavior, negative symptoms, impaired cognition, depression, and mania symptoms

Schizotypal (personality) disorder

Delusional disorder

Individuals with this disorder have non-bizarre delusions (false beliefs that could be plausible) that are present for at least 1 month. These delusions significantly impact their daily lives, but other aspects of functioning remain relatively intact.

Specify whether: Erotomanic type, Grandiose type, Jealous type, Persecutory type, Somatic type, Mixed type, and Unspecified type

Specify if: With bizarre content

Brief psychotic disorder

This disorder is characterized by the sudden onset of psychotic symptoms such as hallucinations, delusions, disorganized speech, or grossly disorganized or catatonic behavior. The duration is brief, lasting less than 1 month, with eventual return to full premorbid functioning.

Specify if: With marked stressor(s), Without marked stressor(s), With peripartum onset

Schizophreniform disorder

Similar to schizophrenia, this disorder involves the presence of symptoms like delusions, hallucinations, disorganized speech, and/or negative symptoms. However, the duration of these symptoms is shorter, lasting between 1 and 6 months.

Specify if: With good prognostic features, Without good prognostic features

Schizophrenia

Schizophrenia is a complex disorder characterized by a range of symptoms including delusions (false beliefs), hallucinations (false sensory perceptions), disorganized thinking and speech, grossly disorganized or catatonic behavior, and negative symptoms (diminished emotional expression or motivation). These symptoms significantly impair an individual's ability to function in daily life.

Schizoaffective disorder

This disorder combines symptoms of schizophrenia (hallucinations, delusions) with prominent mood episodes (depression or mania). These mood episodes occur alongside periods of psychosis but are not solely due to mood disturbances.

Specify whether: Bipolar type, Depressive type

Substance/medication-induced psychotic disorder
Psychotic symptoms (hallucinations, delusions, etc.) emerge due to substance intoxication, withdrawal, or after exposure to a medication. These symptoms are not better explained by a primary psychotic disorder.
    Specify if: With onset during intoxication, With onset during withdrawal, With onset after medication use

Psychotic disorder due to another medical condition
Psychotic symptoms arise as a direct result of a medical condition (such as a neurological disorder or endocrine disorder). The symptoms are not better explained by another primary psychotic disorder.
    Specify whether: With delusions, With hallucinations

Catatonia associated with another mental disorder (catatonia specifier)
Catatonic symptoms, such as motoric immobility or excessive motor activity, are present in the context of another mental disorder (e.g., mood disorders, schizophrenia).

Catatonic disorder due to another medical condition
Catatonic symptoms are directly caused by a medical condition, such as neurodevelopmental or neurological disorders.

Unspecified catatonia
Diagnosis is applied when the catatonic symptoms are present and causing distress or impairment, but they do not neatly fit into any of the more specific diagnostic categories within the catatonia-related disorders.

Other specified schizophrenia spectrum and other psychotic disorder
This diagnosis includes presentations of psychotic symptoms that do not fit neatly into the other defined categories but still warrant clinical attention.

Unspecified schizophrenia spectrum and other psychotic disorder
This diagnosis is used when the symptoms do not meet criteria for any specific psychotic disorder but still cause significant distress or impairment.

Bipolar and Related Disorders

The following specifiers apply to bipolar and related disorders where indicated:
    Specify: With anxious distress (specify current severity: mild, moderate, moderate-severe, and severe); With mixed features; With rapid cycling; With melancholic features; With atypical features; With mood-congruent psychotic features; With mood incongruent psychotic features; With catatonia; With peripartum onset; With seasonal pattern
    Specify: With anxious distress (specify current severity: mild, moderate, moderate-severe, and severe); With mixed features; With rapid cycling; With peripartum onset; With seasonal pattern

Bipolar I disorder

This disorder involves the occurrence of at least one manic episode, which is a distinct period of abnormally elevated or irritable mood, along with potential episodes of major depressive or hypomanic episodes. The manic episode may include symptoms such as increased energy, decreased need for sleep, racing thoughts, and risky behavior.

Current or most recent episode manic: Mild, Moderate, Severe, With psychotic features, In partial remission, In full remission, Unspecified, Current or most recent episode hypomanic, In partial remission, In full remission, Unspecified

Current or most recent episode depressed: Mild, Moderate, Severe, With psychotic features, In partial remission, In full remission, Unspecified

Current or most recent episode unspecified

Bipolar II disorder

This disorder is characterized by at least one major depressive episode and at least one hypomanic episode. Hypomania is similar to mania but with less severe symptoms and less impairment in daily functioning.

Specify current or most recent episode: Hypomanic, Depressed

Specify course if full criteria for a mood episode are not currently met: In partial remission, In full remission

Specify severity if full criteria for a major depressive episode are currently met: Mild, Moderate, and Severe

Cyclothymic disorder

Individuals with this disorder experience numerous periods of hypomanic symptoms and depressive symptoms that do not meet the criteria for major depressive or manic episodes. These mood fluctuations are chronic and persist for at least two years in adults (one year in children and adolescents).

Specify if: With anxious distress (specify current severity: Mild, Moderate, Moderate-Severe, and Severe)

Substance/medication-induced bipolar and related disorder

Mood episodes (manic, depressive, or mixed) are caused by substance intoxication, withdrawal, or medication effects. The symptoms are not better explained by a primary mood disorder.

Specify if: With onset during intoxication, With onset during withdrawal, With onset after medication use

Bipolar and related disorder due to another medical condition

Mood disturbances, including manic or depressive symptoms, are directly attributed to the physiological effects of a medical condition, such as a neurological disorder or endocrine disorder.

Specify if: With manic features, With manic- or hypomanic-like episode, With mixed features

Other specified bipolar and related disorder
This diagnosis includes presentations of bipolar symptoms that do not fit neatly into the other defined categories but still warrant clinical attention. This could involve atypical symptom patterns or specific circumstances.

Unspecified bipolar and related disorder
This diagnosis is used when the symptoms do not meet criteria for any specific bipolar or related disorder but still cause significant distress or impairment.

Unspecified mood disorder
Diagnosis is applied when a person experiences mood-related symptoms that don't align with the specific criteria for disorders such as major depressive disorder, bipolar disorder, or others within the mood disorder category.

Depressive Disorders

Disruptive mood dysregulation disorder
This diagnosis is typically made in children and adolescents who experience severe and frequent temper outbursts that are out of proportion to the situation. The mood between outbursts is persistently irritable or angry. It is a way to differentiate this pattern from early-onset bipolar disorder.

Major depressive disorder (MDD)
Also known as clinical depression, MDD involves persistent feelings of sadness, loss of interest or pleasure in activities (anhedonia), and a range of other symptoms such as changes in appetite or sleep patterns, fatigue, feelings of worthlessness or guilt, difficulty concentrating, and even thoughts of death or suicide. To receive a diagnosis, a person must experience these symptoms for at least two weeks.

> Specify: With anxious distress (specify current severity: mild, moderate, moderate-severe, and severe); With mixed features; With melancholic features; With atypical features; With mood-congruent psychotic features; With mood-incongruent psychotic features; With catatonia; With peripartum onset; With seasonal pattern
> Single episode: Mild, Moderate, Severe, With psychotic features, In partial remission, In full remission, Unspecified
> Recurrent episode: Mild, Moderate, Severe, With psychotic features, In partial remission, In full remission, Unspecified

Persistent depressive disorder
This disorder involves chronic low-grade depression lasting for at least two years in adults (one year in children or adolescents). The symptoms are less severe than in MDD but are still impactful, and they can include changes in appetite or sleep, fatigue, low self-esteem, and difficulty making decisions.

> Specify: With anxious distress (specify current severity: mild, moderate, moderate-severe, and severe); With atypical features
> Specify if: In partial remission, In full remission
> Specify if: Early onset, Late onset

Specify if: With pure dysthymic syndrome; With persistent major depressive episode; With intermittent major depressive episodes, with current episode; With intermittent major depressive episodes, without current episode
Specify current severity: Mild, Moderate, and Severe

Premenstrual dysphoric disorder
This disorder involves severe mood disturbances that occur in the week before menstruation and improve shortly after menstruation begins. Symptoms include mood swings, irritability, anxiety, and physical symptoms like bloating or fatigue.

Substance/medication-induced depressive disorder
Depressive symptoms arise due to substance intoxication, withdrawal, or as a side effect of a medication. These symptoms are not better explained by a primary depressive disorder.
Specify if: With onset during intoxication, With onset during withdrawal, With onset after medication use

Depressive disorder due to another medical condition
Depressive symptoms emerge as a direct result of a medical condition, such as a neurological disorder or endocrine disorder. The symptoms are not better explained by another primary depressive disorder.
Specify if: With depressive features, With major depressive—like episode, With mixed features

Other specified depressive disorder
This diagnosis includes presentations of depressive symptoms that do not fit neatly into the other defined categories but still warrant clinical attention. This could involve atypical symptom patterns or specific circumstances.

Unspecified depressive disorder
This diagnosis is used when the symptoms do not meet criteria for any specific depressive disorder but still cause significant distress or impairment.

Unspecified mood disorder
Diagnosis is often applied when the presentation of symptoms is not well-defined or when the symptoms are atypical.

Anxiety Disorders

Separation anxiety disorder
Primarily diagnosed in children, separation anxiety disorder involves excessive distress and anxiety related to separation from attachment figures or home. These fears go beyond what's developmentally appropriate and can impact daily functioning.

Selective mutism

Selective mutism is characterized by consistent failure to speak in specific social situations despite speaking in other settings. This typically occurs due to anxiety or discomfort.

Specific phobia

Specific phobia involves an intense and irrational fear of a specific object or situation, such as heights, animals, or flying. This fear causes immediate anxiety and may lead to avoidance behavior.

      Specify if: Animal, Natural environment, Blood-injection-injury, Fear of blood, Fear of injections and transfusions, Fear of other medical care, Fear of injury, Situational, Other

Social anxiety disorder

People with social anxiety disorder experience intense fear and anxiety in social situations due to a fear of being judged, embarrassed, or humiliated. This fear leads to avoidance of social interactions.

      Specify if: Performance only

Panic disorder

Panic disorder involves recurrent and unexpected panic attacks, which are intense periods of fear or discomfort that reach a peak within minutes. Panic attacks can be accompanied by physical symptoms such as heart palpitations, sweating, trembling, and a fear of losing control or dying.

      Panic attack specifier

Agoraphobia

Agoraphobia is marked by a fear of situations where escape might be difficult or help might not be available if a panic attack or other distressing symptoms occur. Individuals often avoid places or situations that trigger this fear.

Generalized anxiety disorder (GAD)

GAD is characterized by excessive and persistent worry and anxiety about various life situations or events, often without a specific trigger. This worry is difficult to control and is associated with physical symptoms such as restlessness, muscle tension, and fatigue.

Substance/medication-induced anxiety disorder

Anxiety symptoms arise due to substance intoxication, withdrawal, or as a side effect of medication. These symptoms are not better explained by a primary anxiety disorder.

      Specify if: With onset during intoxication, With onset during withdrawal, With onset after medication use

Anxiety disorder due to another medical condition

Anxiety symptoms emerge as a direct result of a medical condition, such as a neurological disorder or endocrine disorder. The symptoms are not better explained by another primary anxiety disorder.

Other specified anxiety disorder
This diagnosis includes presentations of anxiety symptoms that do not fit neatly into the other defined categories but still warrant clinical attention. This could involve atypical symptom patterns or specific circumstances.

Unspecified anxiety disorder
This diagnosis is used when the symptoms do not meet criteria for any specific anxiety disorder but still cause significant distress or impairment.

Obsessive-Compulsive and Related Disorders

The following specifier applies to obsessive-compulsive and related disorders where indicated:
    Specify if: With good or fair insight, With poor insight, With absent insight/delusional beliefs

Obsessive-compulsive disorder (OCD)
OCD is characterized by the presence of obsessions and/or compulsions. Obsessions are intrusive and distressing thoughts, images, or urges that cause significant anxiety. Compulsions are repetitive behaviors or mental acts performed to alleviate the distress caused by obsessions. These behaviors are often time-consuming and interfere with daily life.
    Specify if: Tic-related

Body dysmorphic disorder (BDD)
Individuals with BDD have an intense preoccupation with perceived flaws or defects in their physical appearance, which are not noticeable to others or are very minor. This obsession leads to distress and often results in behaviors like checking mirrors excessively or seeking cosmetic procedures.
    Specify if: With muscle dysmorphia

Hoarding disorder
People with this disorder excessively accumulate and struggle to discard possessions, regardless of their value. This behavior leads to clutter that significantly impairs living spaces and daily functioning.
    Specify if: With excessive acquisition

Trichotillomania (hair-pulling disorder)
Individuals repetitively pull out their own hair, often leading to noticeable hair loss. This behavior is usually driven by tension or an urge and may be an attempt to alleviate distress.

Excoriation (skin-picking) disorder
This disorder involves recurrent and compulsive picking of one's own skin, resulting in skin lesions. This behavior is typically driven by the urge to remove perceived imperfections or relieve tension.

Substance/medication-induced obsessive-compulsive and related disorder
Obsessive-compulsive or related symptoms arise due to substance intoxication, withdrawal, or as a side effect of medication. These symptoms are not better explained by a primary obsessive-compulsive or related disorder.
> Specify if: With onset during intoxication, With onset during withdrawal, With onset after medication use

Obsessive-compulsive and related disorder due to another medical condition
Obsessive-compulsive or related symptoms emerge as a direct result of a medical condition, such as a neurological disorder or endocrine disorder. The symptoms are not better explained by another primary obsessive-compulsive or related disorder.
> Specify if: With obsessive-compulsive disorder—like symptoms, With appearance preoccupations, With hoarding symptoms, With hair-pulling symptoms, With skin-picking symptoms

Other specified obsessive-compulsive and related disorder
This diagnosis includes presentations of obsessive-compulsive or related symptoms that do not fit neatly into the other defined categories but still warrant clinical attention. This could involve atypical symptom patterns or specific circumstances.

Unspecified obsessive-compulsive and related disorder
This diagnosis is used when the symptoms do not meet criteria for any specific obsessive-compulsive or related disorder but still cause significant distress or impairment.

Trauma- and Stressor-Related Disorders

Reactive attachment disorder
Typically diagnosed in children, this disorder involves significantly disturbed and developmentally inappropriate social interactions due to early neglect, deprivation, or other forms of trauma. Children with this disorder may struggle to form appropriate emotional bonds.
> Specify if: Persistent
> Specify current severity: Severe

Disinhibited social engagement disorder
Also diagnosed in children, this disorder manifests as a pattern of overly familiar behavior with unfamiliar individuals, often due to a history of neglect or multiple caregivers. Children with this disorder may lack appropriate social boundaries.
> Specify if: Persistent
> Specify current severity: Severe

Posttraumatic stress disorder (PTSD)
PTSD occurs after exposure to traumatic events, causing symptoms like intrusive memories, nightmares, flashbacks, avoidance of reminders, negative changes in mood and cognition, and increased arousal. Symptoms may significantly impair daily functioning.
> Specify whether: With dissociative symptoms
> Specify if: With delayed expression
> Posttraumatic stress disorder in individuals older than 6 years
> Posttraumatic stress disorder in children 6 years and younger

Acute stress disorder
Similar to PTSD, acute stress disorder involves symptoms like intrusion, negative mood, dissociation, avoidance, and arousal, but these symptoms arise immediately after exposure to a traumatic event and last up to a month, while PTSD symptoms present slower and last longer, especially if not treated.

Adjustment disorders
These are characterized by emotional or behavioral symptoms that arise in response to an identifiable stressor. Symptoms may include sadness, anxiety, or behavior changes. The stressor's impact exceeds what is typically expected in relation to the event.
> Specify if: Acute, Persistent (chronic)
> Specify whether: With depressed mood, With anxiety, With mixed anxiety and depressed mood, With disturbance of conduct, With mixed disturbance of emotions and conduct, Unspecified

Prolonged grief disorder
This diagnosis refers to an intense and prolonged form of grief that extends beyond the expected period of mourning. It is characterized by a persistent and severe longing for the deceased individual, along with emotional pain and difficulty adapting to life without them.

Other specified trauma- and stressor-related disorder
This diagnosis includes presentations of trauma- or stressor-related symptoms that do not fit neatly into the other defined categories but still warrant clinical attention. This could involve atypical symptom patterns or specific circumstances.

Unspecified trauma- and stressor-related disorder
This diagnosis includes presentations of trauma- or stressor-related symptoms that do not fit neatly into the other defined categories but still warrant clinical attention. This could involve atypical symptom patterns or specific circumstances.

Dissociative Disorders

Dissociative identity disorder (DID)
Formerly known as multiple personality disorder, DID involves the presence of two or more distinct identity states that control an individual's behavior, thoughts, and feelings. Gaps in memory, awareness, and personal information are common between these identity states.

Dissociative amnesia

This disorder involves memory gaps related to personal information, often about traumatic or stressful events. It can be localized (specific time period), selective (specific events), generalized (overall identity and life history), or continuous (ongoing inability to recall new information).

    Specify if: With dissociative fugue

Depersonalization/derealization disorder

Depersonalization is characterized by feelings of detachment from oneself, as if observing from outside the body. Derealization involves a sense of unreality or detachment from the surroundings. These experiences are distressing and can impair daily functioning.

Other specified dissociative disorder

This diagnosis includes presentations of dissociative symptoms that do not fit neatly into the other defined categories but still warrant clinical attention. This could involve atypical symptom patterns or specific circumstances.

Unspecified dissociative disorder

This diagnosis is used when the symptoms do not meet criteria for any specific dissociative disorder but still cause significant distress or impairment.

Somatic Symptom and Related Disorders

Somatic symptom disorder

This disorder involves excessive and distressing thoughts, feelings, and behaviors related to physical symptoms. Individuals may have a preoccupation with their symptoms and experience significant distress or impairment due to these concerns.

    Specify if: With predominant pain
    Specify if: Persistent
    Specify current severity: Mild, Moderate, and Severe

Illness anxiety disorder

Formerly known as hypochondriasis, this disorder involves excessive worry about having a serious illness, despite minimal or no medical evidence to support the belief. Individuals often misinterpret normal bodily sensations as signs of a severe medical condition.

    Specify whether: Care-seeking type, Care-avoidant type

Functional neurological symptom disorder (conversion disorder)

This disorder involves neurological symptoms that can't be explained by a medical condition. These symptoms may resemble those of a neurological disorder, such as paralysis or blindness, but they are not caused by a physiological issue.

Specify if: Acute episode, Persistent
Specify if: With psychological stressor (specify stressor), Without psychological stressor
Specify symptom type: With weakness or paralysis, With abnormal movement, With swallowing symptoms, With speech symptom, With attacks or seizures, With anesthesia or sensory loss, With special sensory symptom, With mixed symptoms

Psychological factors affecting other medical conditions
A disorder that is diagnosed when a general medical condition is adversely affected by psychological or behavioral factors; the factors may precipitate or exacerbate the medical condition, interfere with treatment, or contribute to morbidity and mortality.
Specify current severity: Mild, Moderate, Severe, and Extreme

Factitious disorder
Specify: Single episode, Recurrent episodes

Factitious disorder imposed on self
In this disorder, individuals intentionally falsify, exaggerate, or induce physical or psychological symptoms in themselves for the purpose of assuming a "sick role." There is no apparent external reward, such as financial gain.

Factitious disorder imposed on another
Formerly known as Munchausen syndrome by proxy, in this disorder, individuals falsify, exaggerate, or induce physical or psychological symptoms in another person, often someone under their care, to assume a caregiver role. There is no apparent external reward.

Other specified somatic symptom and related disorder
This diagnosis includes presentations of somatic and related symptoms that do not fit neatly into the other defined categories but still warrant clinical attention. This could involve atypical symptom patterns or specific circumstances.

Unspecified somatic symptom and related disorder
This diagnosis is used when the symptoms do not meet criteria for any specific somatic symptom and related disorder but still cause significant distress or impairment.

Feeding and Eating Disorders

These disorders involve disruptions in eating behaviors, such as avoidant/restrictive food intake disorder (extreme pickiness) and can lead to nutritional deficiencies or developmental problems.
The following specifiers apply to feeding and eating disorders where indicated:
Specify if: In remission
Specify if: In partial remission, In full remission
Specify current severity: Mild, Moderate, Severe, and Extreme

Pica

Pica involves eating non-nutritive, non-food substances over a period of at least one month, and the behavior is developmentally inappropriate. Common substances ingested might include paper, clay, hair, cloth, or string.

> *In children*
> *In adults*

Rumination disorder

This disorder involves the repeated regurgitation of food, which may be re-chewed, re-swallowed, or spit out. It's not due to a medical condition and lasts for at least one month.

Avoidant/restrictive food intake disorder (ARFID)

ARFID involves an extreme limitation in food intake, often due to sensory sensitivities, concerns about adverse consequences, or lack of interest in eating. It is not driven by concerns about weight or body shape.

Anorexia nervosa

Anorexia involves severe restriction of food intake, leading to significantly low body weight. Fear of gaining weight and distorted body image are common. It often involves intense efforts to control weight through dieting, excessive exercise, or other behaviors.

> Specify whether: Restricting type, Binge-eating/purging type

Bulimia nervosa

Bulimia involves recurrent episodes of binge eating followed by compensatory behaviors like vomiting, excessive exercise, or laxative use to prevent weight gain. It's often characterized by a cycle of bingeing and purging.

Binge-eating disorder (BED)

BED involves recurrent episodes of eating large amounts of food in a short period, with a sense of lack of control during the binge. Unlike bulimia, there are no regular compensatory behaviors.

Other specified feeding or eating disorder

This diagnosis includes presentations of feeding and eating symptoms that do not fit neatly into the other defined categories but still warrant clinical attention. This could involve atypical symptom patterns or specific circumstances.

Unspecified feeding or eating disorder

This diagnosis is used when the symptoms do not meet criteria for any specific feeding and eating disorder but still cause significant distress or impairment.

Elimination Disorders

Enuresis

Enuresis refers to the repeated involuntary urination in inappropriate places, typically occurring during sleep (nocturnal enuresis) or during waking hours (diurnal enuresis). The behavior is considered developmentally inappropriate and typically occurs in children who are old enough to have bladder control.

> Specify whether: Nocturnal only, Diurnal only, Nocturnal and diurnal

Encopresis

Encopresis involves the repeated involuntary passage of feces in inappropriate places, often after the age when bowel control is expected. This behavior is not due to a medical condition and typically occurs in children.

> Specify whether: With constipation and overflow incontinence, Without constipation and overflow incontinence

Other specified elimination disorder
> *With urinary symptoms*
>
> This subcategory would include cases where the individual experiences problematic patterns related to urination, but the symptoms do not meet the criteria for enuresis or other well-defined disorders. The symptoms might involve issues with urgency, frequency, or other urinary difficulties.
>
> *With fecal symptoms*
>
> This subcategory would include cases where the individual experiences problematic patterns related to bowel movements or feces, but the symptoms do not meet the criteria for encopresis or other specific disorders. The symptoms might involve issues with soiling, discomfort, or other fecal-related difficulties.

Unspecified elimination disorder
> *With urinary symptoms*
> *With fecal symptoms*

Sleep–Wake Disorders

> The following specifiers apply to sleep–wake disorders where indicated:
> > Specify if: Episodic, Persistent, and Recurrent
> > Specify if: Acute, Subacute, and Persistent
> > Specify current severity: Mild, Moderate, and Severe

Insomnia disorder

Insomnia involves difficulty falling asleep, staying asleep, or experiencing non-restorative sleep, despite having adequate opportunity for sleep. This pattern leads to significant daytime distress or impairment.

> Specify if: With mental disorder, With medical condition, With another sleep disorder

Hypersomnolence disorder

Individuals with hypersomnolence experience excessive daytime sleepiness, which often results in prolonged sleep episodes during the day. Despite getting sufficient sleep, they struggle to stay awake and alert.

> Specify if: With mental disorder, With medical condition, With another sleep disorder

Narcolepsy

Narcolepsy is characterized by excessive daytime sleepiness and sudden, uncontrollable episodes of falling asleep during the day. It may also involve cataplexy (sudden loss of muscle tone), sleep paralysis, and hallucinations during sleep onset or upon awakening.

Specify whether: Narcolepsy with cataplexy or hypocretin deficiency (type 1); narcolepsy without cataplexy and either without hypocretin deficiency or hypocretin unmeasured (type 2); narcolepsy with cataplexy or hypocretin deficiency due to a medical condition; narcolepsy without cataplexy and without hypocretin deficiency due to a medical condition

Breathing-related sleep disorders

This category includes sleep disorders caused by disrupted breathing patterns, such as obstructive sleep apnea, central sleep apnea, and sleep-related hypoventilation disorders. These disorders often lead to disrupted sleep and excessive daytime sleepiness.

Obstructive sleep apnea hypopnea

Central sleep apnea

Specify current severity

Specify whether: Idiopathic central sleep apnea, Cheyne-Stokes breathing, Central sleep apnea comorbid with opioid use

Sleep-related hypoventilation

Specify current severity

Specify whether: Idiopathic hypoventilation, Congenital central alveolar hypoventilation, Comorbid sleep-related hypoventilation

Circadian rhythm sleep–wake disorders

Circadian rhythm sleep–wake disorders involve disruptions in the sleep–wake schedule due to misalignment with the body's natural circadian rhythms. Conditions like delayed sleep phase disorder and shift work disorder are examples.

Specify whether: Delayed sleep phase type (specify if: Familial, Overlapping with non-24-hour sleep–wake type); Advanced sleep phase type (specify if: Familial); Irregular sleep-wake type; Non-24-hour sleep–wake type; Shift work type; Unspecified type

Parasomnias

Parasomnias are abnormal behaviors or experiences during sleep or during transitions between sleep stages. Examples include sleepwalking, sleep terrors, nightmares, and REM sleep behavior disorder.

Non-rapid eye movement sleep arousal disorders

Specify whether: Sleepwalking type (specify if: With sleep-related eating, With sleep-related sexual behavior [sexsomnia]), Sleep terror type

Nightmare disorder
> Specify if: During sleep onset
> Specify if: With mental disorder, With medical condition, With another sleep disorder

Rapid eye movement sleep behavior disorder

Restless legs syndrome

Substance/medication-induced sleep disorder
> Specify whether: Insomnia type, Daytime sleepiness type, Parasomnia type, and Mixed type
> Specify if: With onset during intoxication, With onset during withdrawal, With onset after medication use

Other specified insomnia disorder
This diagnosis is used when an individual experiences symptoms of insomnia that do not meet the full criteria for insomnia disorder, but still warrant clinical attention. This might include atypical patterns of difficulty falling asleep, staying asleep, or experiencing non-restorative sleep that cause distress or impairment. The symptoms may not fit all the specific criteria for insomnia disorder, but they are still significant enough to require assessment and possible intervention.

Unspecified insomnia disorder
This diagnosis is used when an individual experiences symptoms of insomnia causing distress or impairment, but the specific nature of the symptoms or their relationship to other sleep disorders is not fully understood. In other words, the symptoms meet the general criteria for insomnia, but they do not meet criteria for any specific subtype or diagnosis within the insomnia disorder category.

Other specified hypersomnolence disorder
This diagnosis is used when an individual experiences excessive daytime sleepiness that does not meet the full criteria for hypersomnolence disorder, but the symptoms still require clinical attention. This could involve atypical patterns of daytime sleepiness, sleep attacks, or difficulty staying awake during appropriate waking hours.

Unspecified hypersomnolence disorder
This diagnosis is used when an individual experiences significant excessive daytime sleepiness causing distress or impairment, but the specific nature of the symptoms or their relationship to other sleep disorders is not fully understood. The symptoms meet the general criteria for excessive daytime sleepiness, but they do not meet criteria for any specific subtype or diagnosis within the hypersomnolence disorder category.

Other specified sleep–wake disorder
This diagnosis includes presentations of sleep–wake symptoms that do not fit neatly into the other defined categories but still warrant clinical attention. This could involve atypical symptom patterns or specific circumstances.

Unspecified sleep–wake disorder

This diagnosis includes presentations of sleep–wake symptoms that do not fit neatly into the other defined categories but still warrant clinical attention. This could involve atypical symptom patterns or specific circumstances.

Sexual Dysfunctions

The following specifiers apply to sexual dysfunctions where indicated:
Specify whether: Lifelong, Acquired
Specify whether: Generalized, Situational
Specify current severity: Mild, Moderate, and Severe

Delayed ejaculation

Delayed ejaculation involves a significant delay or absence of ejaculation during sexual activity, despite adequate sexual arousal and stimulation. This issue causes distress or impairment.

Erectile disorder

Erectile disorder (previously known as erectile dysfunction) involves persistent difficulty achieving or maintaining an erection sufficient for satisfactory sexual performance. The issue causes distress or impairment.

Female orgasmic disorder

This disorder involves a delay, absence, or reduced intensity of orgasm during sexual activity, even when arousal and stimulation are adequate. The difficulty in achieving orgasm causes distress or impairment.
Specify if: Never experienced an orgasm under any situation

Female sexual interest/arousal disorder

This disorder involves a persistent or recurrent deficiency in sexual interest, thoughts, or arousal. Individuals may have difficulty becoming sexually aroused or maintaining arousal during sexual activity, leading to distress or impairment.

Genito-pelvic pain/penetration disorder

This disorder involves persistent or recurrent pain during intercourse, difficulty with vaginal penetration, or fear or anxiety about pain during sexual activity. The pain or fear causes distress or impairment.

Male hypoactive sexual desire disorder

This disorder involves a persistent or recurrent lack of interest in sexual activity, often accompanied by reduced sexual thoughts or fantasies. The lack of sexual desire causes distress or impairment in the individual's life.

Premature (early) ejaculation
Premature ejaculation involves the recurrent ejaculation before or shortly after penetration during sexual activity, often with minimal sexual stimulation. The timing of ejaculation causes distress or impairment.

Substance/medication-induced sexual dysfunction
Diagnosis refers to the development of sexual dysfunction as a result of substance use or medication. This category recognizes that certain substances and medications can have a direct impact on sexual function, leading to changes in sexual desire, arousal, and performance.
Specify if: With onset during intoxication, With onset during withdrawal, With onset after medication use

Other specified sexual dysfunction
This diagnosis includes presentations of sexual dysfunction symptoms that do not meet the criteria for any specific sexual dysfunction but still warrant clinical attention. This could involve atypical symptom patterns or specific circumstances.

Unspecified sexual dysfunction
This diagnosis is used when the symptoms of sexual dysfunction cause distress or impairment, but the specific nature of the dysfunction or its relationship to other sexual disorders is not fully understood.

Gender Dysphoria

Gender dysphoria is a diagnostic category that pertains to individuals whose emotional and psychological identity as male, female, or another gender does not align with their birth-assigned sex. This category replaced the previous diagnosis of gender identity disorder and reflects a more affirming and understanding approach to individuals experiencing gender incongruence.
The following specifier and note apply to gender dysphoria where indicated:
Specify if: With a disorder/difference of sex development

Gender dysphoria

Gender dysphoria in children
This diagnosis is given when a child experiences a marked incongruence between their experienced/expressed gender and their assigned sex at birth. The child may express a desire to be of a different gender, to be treated as a different gender, or assert that they are of a different gender.

Gender dysphoria in adolescents and adults
Similar to the diagnosis in children, this diagnosis is given when adolescents and adults experience a marked incongruence between their experienced/expressed gender and their assigned sex at birth. The individual may experience significant distress related to the incongruence and may seek social, hormonal, or surgical interventions to bring their body and gender identity into alignment.
Specify if: Posttransition

Other specified gender dysphoria

This diagnosis is used when an individual's gender-related experiences do not fully meet the criteria for gender dysphoria in children, adolescents, or adults, but they still warrant clinical attention. This could include atypical patterns of gender identity, expression, or incongruence that do not align with the specific criteria of other diagnoses. The individual may experience some degree of distress or impairment related to their gender identity.

Unspecified gender dysphoria

This category is used when an individual's gender-related experiences do not fully meet the criteria for gender dysphoria in children, adolescents, or adults, but they still warrant clinical attention. This could include atypical patterns of gender identity, expression, or incongruence that do not align with the specific criteria of other diagnoses. The individual may experience some degree of distress or impairment related to their gender identity.

Disruptive, Impulse-Control, and Conduct Disorders

Oppositional defiant disorder (ODD)

ODD involves a pattern of defiant, hostile, and disobedient behavior directed toward authority figures. Individuals with ODD may often argue with adults, refuse to comply with rules, and deliberately annoy others. This behavior is consistent and causes significant distress or impairment in social, academic, or occupational functioning.
Specify current severity: Mild, Moderate, and Severe

Intermittent explosive disorder

This disorder involves recurrent episodes of impulsive and aggressive behavior, often out of proportion to the situation. Individuals may have difficulty controlling their anger, leading to verbal or physical aggression that is not premeditated. These outbursts cause distress and impairment.

Conduct disorder

Conduct disorder is characterized by persistent patterns of behavior that violate the rights of others or societal norms. These behaviors may include aggression toward people or animals, destruction of property, deceitfulness, and serious violations of rules. Conduct disorder can range from mild to severe and is often a precursor to antisocial personality disorder in adulthood.
Specify if: With limited prosocial emotions
Specify current severity: Mild, Moderate, and Severe
Specify whether: Childhood-onset type, Adolescent-onset type, Unspecified onset

Antisocial personality disorder (ASPD)

ASPD is a personality disorder characterized by a pattern of disregard for the rights of others, impulsivity, deceitfulness, irritability, aggressiveness, and lack of remorse. Individuals with ASPD may engage in illegal activities, lie or manipulate others for personal gain, and have difficulty forming meaningful relationships. This disorder typically emerges in late childhood or adolescence and continues into adulthood. It is often associated with a history of conduct disorder during childhood.

Pyromania
Pyromania is a rare impulse-control disorder characterized by an urge to deliberately set fires for pleasure, gratification, or relief. Individuals with pyromania are often fascinated by fire and may experience a sense of excitement or relief while setting fires. This behavior is not driven by financial gain, political ideology, or a desire for revenge.

Kleptomania
Kleptomania is another impulse-control disorder characterized by recurrent acts of stealing objects that are not needed for personal use or monetary gain. Individuals with kleptomania may experience tension before committing the theft and a sense of relief or gratification afterward. The stolen items are typically of little or no value to the individual.

Other specified disruptive, impulse-control, and conduct disorder
This diagnosis is used when an individual's symptoms do not fully meet the criteria for any specific disorder within this category but still warrant clinical attention. This could involve atypical symptom patterns or specific circumstances.

Unspecified disruptive, impulse-control, and conduct disorder
This diagnosis is used when an individual's symptoms cause distress or impairment, but the specific nature of the symptoms or their relationship to other disorders is not fully understood.

Substance-Related and Addictive Disorders

Substance-related disorders
Substance use disorders (SUDs): These disorders involve problematic and repeated use of substances such as alcohol, drugs, or medications. Symptoms include an inability to control use, spending excessive time seeking or using the substance, neglecting responsibilities, cravings, and withdrawal symptoms when not using the substance. Severity ranges from mild to severe, and treatment involves counseling, therapy, and sometimes medication.

Substance-induced intoxication: This occurs when using a substance leads to temporary changes in behavior, mood, cognition, or perception. Intoxication can vary depending on the substance, ranging from euphoria to confusion, and can sometimes result in dangerous behaviors or accidents.

Substance-induced withdrawal: This involves physical and psychological symptoms that occur when a person stops using a substance that has reached dependency. Symptoms can include nausea, tremors, anxiety, irritability, and in severe cases, seizures, or hallucinations.

Substance-induced mental disorders: These are mental health conditions triggered by substance use. For instance, substance-induced anxiety or substance-induced depressive disorder can emerge as a result of using certain substances. The symptoms of these disorders usually resolve once the substance use stops.

Substance-induced sleep disorders: Substance use can disrupt sleep patterns and lead to sleep disorders. This may involve insomnia, hypersomnia (excessive sleepiness), or other sleep-related problems triggered by substance consumption.

Alcohol-Related Disorders

Alcohol is a depressant that affects the central nervous system. In small amounts, it can lead to relaxation and lowered inhibitions. However, in larger amounts, it can cause impaired judgment, slowed reaction times, slurred speech, memory impairment, and motor coordination difficulties. Long-term heavy use can lead to liver damage, cognitive deficits, addiction, and various physical and mental health problems.

Alcohol use disorder

This is a specific type of substance use disorder related to alcohol consumption. It involves problematic drinking patterns, such as excessive consumption, unsuccessful attempts to cut down, and continued use despite negative consequences.

> Specify if: In a controlled environment
>
> Specify current severity/remission: Mild (In early remission, In sustained remission), Moderate (In early remission, In sustained remission), Severe (In early remission, In sustained remission)

Alcohol intoxication

> *With mild use disorder*
> *With moderate or severe use disorder*
> *Without use disorder*

Alcohol withdrawal

> *Without perceptual disturbances*
> > *With mild use disorder*
> > *With moderate or severe use disorder*
> > *Without use disorder*

> *With perceptual disturbances*
> > *With mild use disorder*
> > *With moderate or severe use disorder*
> > *Without use disorder*

Alcohol-induced mental disorders

> Specify: With onset during intoxication, With onset during withdrawal
> Specify if: Acute, Persistent
> Specify if: Hyperactive, Hypoactive, and Mixed level of activity

Alcohol-induced psychotic disorder
    With mild use disorder
    With moderate or severe use disorder
    Without use disorder

Alcohol-induced bipolar and related disorder
    With mild use disorder
    With moderate or severe use disorder
    Without use disorder

Alcohol-induced depressive disorder
    With mild use disorder
    With moderate or severe use disorder
    Without use disorder

Alcohol-induced anxiety disorder
    With mild use disorder
    With moderate or severe use disorder
    Without use disorder

Alcohol-induced sleep disorder
    Specify whether Insomnia type
    With mild use disorder
    With moderate or severe use disorder
    Without use disorder

Alcohol-induced sexual dysfunction
    Specify if: Mild, Moderate, and Severe
    With mild use disorder
    With moderate or severe use disorder
    Without use disorder

Alcohol intoxication delirium
    With mild use disorder
    With moderate or severe use disorder
    Without use disorder

Alcohol withdrawal delirium
    With mild use disorder
    With moderate or severe use disorder
    Without use disorder

Alcohol-induced major neurocognitive disorder
> Specify if: Persistent
> *Amnestic-confabulatory type*
>> *With moderate or severe use disorder*
>> *Without use disorder*
> *Nonamnestic-confabulatory type*
>> *With moderate or severe use disorder*
>> *Without use disorder*

Alcohol-induced mild neurocognitive disorder
> Specify if: Persistent
> *With mild use disorder*
> *With moderate or severe use disorder*
> *Without use disorder*

Unspecified alcohol-related disorder

Caffeine-Related Disorders

Caffeine-related disorders refer to a set of conditions that are related to the consumption of caffeine, a stimulant found in various beverages, foods, and medications.

Caffeine intoxication

Caffeine withdrawal

Caffeine-induced mental disorders
> Specify: With onset during intoxication, With onset during withdrawal, With onset after medication use

> *Caffeine-induced anxiety disorder*

> *Caffeine-induced sleep disorder*
> Specify whether: Insomnia type, Daytime sleepiness type, Mixed type

Unspecified caffeine-related disorder

Cannabis-Related Disorders

Cannabis, often referred to as marijuana, has both depressant and mild hallucinogenic effects. It can lead to relaxation, altered perception of time, and euphoria. Common short-term effects include bloodshot eyes, increased heart rate, dry mouth, and impaired memory and coordination. Long-term use can lead to cognitive impairment, respiratory issues, and potential addiction.

Cannabis use disorder
This disorder involves problematic use of marijuana or cannabis products, leading to impairment or distress. Symptoms include unsuccessful attempts to quit, increased tolerance, and reduced engagement in important activities.
> Specify if: In a controlled environment
> Specify current severity/remission: Mild (In early remission, In sustained remission), Moderate (In early remission, In sustained remission), Severe (In early remission, In sustained remission)

Cannabis intoxication
 Without perceptual disturbances
  With mild use disorder
  With moderate or severe use disorder
  Without use disorder
 With perceptual disturbances
  With mild use disorder
  With moderate or severe use disorder
  Without use disorder

Cannabis withdrawal
 With mild use disorder
 With moderate or severe use disorder
 Without use disorder

Cannabis-induced mental disorders
 Specify: With onset during intoxication, With onset during withdrawal, With onset after medication use
 Specify if: Acute, Persistent
 Specify if: Hyperactive, Hypoactive, and Mixed level of activity

Cannabis-induced psychotic disorder
 With mild use disorder
 With moderate or severe use disorder
 Without use disorder

Cannabis-induced anxiety disorder
 With mild use disorder
 With moderate or severe use disorder
 Without use disorder

Cannabis-induced sleep disorder
 Specify whether: Insomnia type, Daytime sleepiness type, and Mixed type
 With mild use disorder
 With moderate or severe use disorder
 Without use disorder

Cannabis intoxication delirium
 With mild use disorder
 With moderate or severe use disorder
 Without use disorder

Pharmaceutical cannabis receptor agonist-induced delirium

Unspecified cannabis-related disorder

Hallucinogen-Related Disorders

Hallucinogens can alter perception, thoughts, and feelings. They can cause hallucinations, sensory distortions, and profound changes in consciousness. Short-term effects can vary widely, but long-term effects are less well-defined. However, some users may experience persistent changes in perception or emotional states.

Phencyclidine use disorder
Specify if: In a controlled environment
Specify current severity/remission: Mild (In early remission, In sustained remission), Moderate (In early remission, In sustained remission), Severe (In early remission, In sustained remission)

Other hallucinogen use disorder
Specify the particular hallucinogen
Specify if: In a controlled environment
Specify current severity/remission: Mild (In early remission, In sustained remission), Moderate (In early remission, In sustained remission), Severe (In early remission, In sustained remission)

Phencyclidine intoxication
With mild use disorder
With moderate or severe use disorder
Without use disorder

Other hallucinogen intoxication
With mild use disorder
With moderate or severe use disorder
Without use disorder

Hallucinogen persisting perception disorder

Phencyclidine-induced mental disorders
Specify: With onset during intoxication, With onset after medication use

Phencyclidine-induced psychotic disorder
With mild use disorder
With moderate or severe use disorder
Without use disorder

Phencyclidine-induced bipolar and related disorder
With mild use disorder
With moderate or severe use disorder
Without use disorder

Phencyclidine-induced depressive disorder
With mild use disorder
With moderate or severe use disorder
Without use disorder

Phencyclidine-induced anxiety disorder
    With mild use disorder
    With moderate or severe use disorder
    Without use disorder

Phencyclidine intoxication delirium
    Specify if: Acute, Persistent
    Specify if: Hyperactive, Hypoactive, and Mixed level of activity

    With mild use disorder
    With moderate or severe use disorder
    Without use disorder

Hallucinogen-induced mental disorders
    Specify: With onset during intoxication, With onset after medication use
    Specify if: Acute, Persistent
    Specify if: Hyperactive, Hypoactive, and Mixed level of activity

    Other hallucinogen-induced psychotic disorder
        With mild use disorder
        With moderate or severe use disorder
        Without use disorder

    Other hallucinogen-induced bipolar and related disorder
        With mild use disorder
        With moderate or severe use disorder
        Without use disorder

    Other hallucinogen-induced depressive disorder
        With mild use disorder
        With moderate or severe use disorder
        Without use disorder

    Other hallucinogen-induced anxiety disorder
        With mild use disorder
        With moderate or severe use disorder
        Without use disorder

    Other hallucinogen intoxication delirium
        With mild use disorder
        With moderate or severe use disorder
        Without use disorder

    Ketamine or other hallucinogen-induced delirium

Unspecified phencyclidine-related disorder

Unspecified hallucinogen-related disorder

Inhalant-Related Disorders

Inhalants are volatile substances that produce chemical vapors that can be inhaled to induce a psychoactive, or mind-altering, effect. Short-term effects can include dizziness, confusion, impaired coordination, and nausea. Long-term use can lead to serious neurological and other health-related consequences.

Inhalant use disorder
>   Specify the particular inhalant
>   Specify if: In a controlled environment
>   Specify current severity/remission: Mild (In early remission, In sustained remission), Moderate (In early remission, In sustained remission), Severe (In early remission, In sustained remission)

Inhalant intoxication
>   *With mild use disorder*
>   *With moderate or severe use disorder*
>   *Without use disorder*

Inhalant-induced mental disorders
>   Specify: With onset during intoxication

>   *Inhalant-induced psychotic disorder*
>   >   *With mild use disorder*
>   >   *With moderate or severe use disorder*
>   >   *Without use disorder*

>   *Inhalant-induced depressive disorder*
>   >   *With mild use disorder*
>   >   *With moderate or severe use disorder*
>   >   *Without use disorder*

>   *Inhalant-induced anxiety disorder*
>   >   *With mild use disorder*
>   >   *With moderate or severe use disorder*
>   >   *Without use disorder*

>   *Inhalant intoxication delirium*
>   >   Specify if: Acute, Persistent
>   >   Specify if: Hyperactive, Hypoactive, and Mixed level of activity
>   >   *With mild use disorder*
>   >   *With moderate or severe use disorder*
>   >   *Without use disorder*

>   *Inhalant-induced major neurocognitive disorder*
>   >   Specify if: Persistent
>   >   *With mild use disorder*
>   >   *With moderate or severe use disorder*
>   >   *Without use disorder*

Inhalant-induced mild neurocognitive disorder
 Specify if: Persistent
 With mild use disorder
 With moderate or severe use disorder
 Without use disorder

Unspecified inhalant-related disorder

Opioid-Related Disorders

Opioids are central nervous system depressants that induce pain relief, relaxation, and euphoria. Short-term effects include pain relief, drowsiness, and constipation. Long-term use can lead to physical dependence, respiratory depression, increased risk of overdose, and potential addiction.

Opioid use disorder
 Specify if: On maintenance therapy, In a controlled environment
 Specify current severity/remission: Mild (In early remission, In sustained remission), Moderate (In early remission, In sustained remission), Severe (In early remission, In sustained remission)

Opioid intoxication
 Without perceptual disturbances
  With mild use disorder
  With moderate or severe use disorder
  Without use disorder
 With perceptual disturbances
  With mild use disorder
  With moderate or severe use disorder
  Without use disorder

Opioid withdrawal
 With mild use disorder
 With moderate or severe use disorder
 Without use disorder

Opioid-induced mental disorders
 Specify: With onset during intoxication, With onset during withdrawal, With onset after medication use.
 Specify if: Acute, Persistent
 Specify if: Hyperactive, Hypoactive, and Mixed level of activity

 Opioid-induced depressive disorder
  With mild use disorder
  With moderate or severe use disorder
  Without use disorder

Opioid-induced anxiety disorder
 With mild use disorder
 With moderate or severe use disorder
 Without use disorder

Opioid-induced sleep disorder
 Specify whether: Insomnia type, Daytime sleepiness type, and Mixed type
 With mild use disorder
 With moderate or severe use disorder
 Without use disorder

Opioid-induced sexual dysfunction
 Specify if: Mild, Moderate, and Severe
 With mild use disorder
 With moderate or severe use disorder
 Without use disorder

Opioid intoxication delirium
 With mild use disorder
 With moderate or severe use disorder
 Without use disorder

Opioid withdrawal delirium
 With mild use disorder
 With moderate or severe use disorder
 Without use disorder

Opioid-induced delirium
 When opioid medication taken as prescribed
 During withdrawal from opioid medication taken as prescribed

Unspecified opioid-related disorder

Sedative-, Hypnotic-, or Anxiolytic-Related Disorders

These substances are commonly prescribed medications that are used to manage anxiety, promote sleep, or induce relaxation. However, when used inappropriately or excessively, they can lead to negative consequences and potential addiction.

Sedatives: These are substances that have a calming effect and can help reduce anxiety and induce relaxation. They may also be referred to as "tranquilizers." Common sedatives include benzodiazepines like diazepam (Valium) and lorazepam (Ativan).

Hypnotics: Hypnotics are substances that promote sleep. They are often prescribed for individuals with insomnia or sleep disorders. Common hypnotics include medications like zolpidem (Ambien) and eszopiclone (Lunesta).

Anxiolytics: Anxiolytics are substances used to manage anxiety. They help alleviate feelings of anxiety and tension. Benzodiazepines and certain other medications can also fall under this category

Sedative, hypnotic, or anxiolytic use disorder
    Specify if: In a controlled environment
    Specify current severity/remission: Mild (In early remission, In sustained remission), Moderate (In early remission, In sustained remission), Severe (In early remission, In sustained remission)

Sedative, hypnotic, or anxiolytic intoxication
    With mild use disorder
    With moderate or severe use disorder
    Without use disorder

Sedative, hypnotic, or anxiolytic withdrawal
    Without perceptual disturbances
        With mild use disorder
        With moderate or severe use disorder
        Without use disorder
    With perceptual disturbances
        With mild use disorder
        With moderate or severe use disorder
        Without use disorder

Sedative-, hypnotic-, or anxiolytic-induced mental disorders
    Specify: With onset during intoxication, With onset during withdrawal, With onset after medication use.
    Specify if: Acute, Persistent
    Specify if: Hyperactive, Hypoactive, and Mixed level of activity

    Sedative-, hypnotic-, or anxiolytic-induced psychotic disorder
        With mild use disorder
        With moderate or severe use disorder
        Without use disorder

    Sedative-, hypnotic-, or anxiolytic-induced bipolar and related disorder
        With mild use disorder
        With moderate or severe use disorder
        Without use disorder

Sedative-, hypnotic-, or anxiolytic-induced depressive disorder
    With mild use disorder
    With moderate or severe use disorder
    Without use disorder

Sedative-, hypnotic-, or anxiolytic-induced anxiety disorder
    With mild use disorder
    With moderate or severe use disorder
    Without use disorder

Sedative-, hypnotic-, or anxiolytic-induced sleep disorder
    Specify whether: Insomnia type, Daytime sleepiness type, Parasomnia type, and Mixed type
    With mild use disorder
    With moderate or severe use disorder
    Without use disorder

Sedative-, hypnotic-, or anxiolytic-induced sexual dysfunction
    Specify if: Mild, Moderate, and Severe
    With mild use disorder
    With moderate or severe use disorder
    Without use disorder

Sedative-, hypnotic-, or anxiolytic intoxication delirium
    With mild use disorder
    With moderate or severe use disorder
    Without use disorder

Sedative-, hypnotic-, or anxiolytic withdrawal delirium
    With mild use disorder
    With moderate or severe use disorder
    Without use disorder

Sedative-, hypnotic-, or anxiolytic-induced delirium
    When sedative, hypnotic, or anxiolytic medication taken as prescribed
    During withdrawal from sedative, hypnotic, or anxiolytic medication taken as prescribed

Sedative-, hypnotic-, or anxiolytic-induced major neurocognitive disorder
    Specify if: Persistent
    With moderate or severe use disorder
    Without use disorder

Sedative-, hypnotic-, or anxiolytic-induced mild neurocognitive disorder
> Specify if: Persistent
> *With mild use disorder*
> *With moderate or severe use disorder*
> *Without use disorder*

Unspecified sedative-, hypnotic-, or anxiolytic-related disorder

Stimulant-Related Disorders

Stimulants increase alertness, energy, and focus. They can cause heightened heart rate, increased blood pressure, and intense euphoria. Short-term effects include increased energy and reduced appetite. Long-term use can lead to cardiovascular issues, anxiety, paranoia, and addiction.

Stimulant use disorder
> Specify if: In a controlled environment
> Specify current severity/remission: Mild (amphetamine-type substance, cocaine, other or unspecified stimulant), Mild in early remission (amphetamine-type substance, cocaine, other or unspecified stimulant), Mild in sustained remission (amphetamine-type substance, cocaine, other or unspecified stimulant), Moderate (amphetamine-type substance, cocaine, other or unspecified stimulant), Moderate in early remission (amphetamine-type substance, cocaine, other or unspecified stimulant), Moderate in sustained remission (amphetamine-type substance, cocaine, other or unspecified stimulant), Severe (amphetamine-type substance, cocaine, other or unspecified stimulant), Severe in early remission (amphetamine-type substance, cocaine, other or unspecified stimulant), Severe in sustained remission (amphetamine-type substance, cocaine, other or unspecified stimulant)

Stimulant intoxication
> Specify the particular intoxicant

> *Without perceptual disturbances*
>> *Amphetamine-type substance or other stimulant intoxication*
>>> *With mild use disorder*
>>> *With moderate or severe use disorder*
>>> *Without use disorder*
>> *Cocaine intoxication*
>>> *With mild use disorder*
>>> *With moderate or severe use disorder*
>>> *Without use disorder*
> *With perceptual disturbances*
>> *Amphetamine-type substance or other stimulant intoxication*
>>> *With mild use disorder*
>>> *With moderate or severe use disorder*
>>> *Without use disorder*
>> *Cocaine intoxication*
>>> *With mild use disorder*

> > *With moderate or severe use disorder*
> > *Without use disorder*

> *Stimulant withdrawal*
> > Specify the particular substance that causes the withdrawal syndrome
> > > *Amphetamine-type substance or other stimulant withdrawal*
> > > > *With mild use disorder*
> > > > *With moderate or severe use disorder*
> > > > *Without use disorder*
> > > *Cocaine withdrawal*
> > > > *With mild use disorder*
> > > > *With moderate or severe use disorder*
> > > > *Without use disorder*

> *Stimulant-induced mental disorders*
> > Specify: With onset during intoxication, With onset during withdrawal, With onset after medication use
> > Specify if: Acute, Persistent
> > Specify if: Hyperactive, Hypoactive, and Mixed level of activity

> > *Amphetamine-type substance (or other stimulant)-induced psychotic disorder*
> > > *With mild use disorder*
> > > *With moderate or severe use disorder*
> > > *Without use disorder*

> > *Cocaine-induced psychotic disorder*
> > > *With mild use disorder*
> > > *With moderate or severe use disorder*
> > > *Without use disorder*

> > *Amphetamine-type substance (or other stimulant)-induced bipolar and related disorder*
> > > *With mild use disorder*
> > > *With moderate or severe use disorder*
> > > *Without use disorder*

> > *Cocaine-induced bipolar and related disorder*
> > > *With mild use disorder*
> > > *With moderate or severe use disorder*
> > > *Without use disorder*

> > *Amphetamine-type substance (or other stimulant)-induced depressive disorder*
> > > *With mild use disorder*
> > > *With moderate or severe use disorder*
> > > *Without use disorder*

> > *Cocaine-induced depressive disorder*
> > > *With mild use disorder*
> > > *With moderate or severe use disorder*
> > > *Without use disorder*

Amphetamine-type substance (or other stimulant)-induced anxiety disorder
    With mild use disorder
    With moderate or severe use disorder
    Without use disorder

Cocaine-induced anxiety disorder
    With mild use disorder
    With moderate or severe use disorder
    Without use disorder

Amphetamine-type substance (or other stimulant)-induced obsessive-compulsive and related disorder
    With mild use disorder
    With moderate or severe use disorder
    Without use disorder

Cocaine-induced obsessive-compulsive and related disorder
    With mild use disorder
    With moderate or severe use disorder
    Without use disorder

Amphetamine-type substance (or other stimulant)-induced sleep disorder
Specify whether: Insomnia type, Daytime sleepiness type, and Mixed type
    With mild use disorder
    With moderate or severe use disorder
    Without use disorder

Cocaine-induced sleep disorder
Specify whether: Insomnia type, Daytime sleepiness type, and Mixed type
    With mild use disorder
    With moderate or severe use disorder
    Without use disorder

Amphetamine-type substance (or other stimulant-induced sexual dysfunction
Specify if: Mild, Moderate, and Severe
    With mild use disorder
    With moderate or severe use disorder
    Without use disorder

Cocaine-induced sexual dysfunction
Specify if: Mild, Moderate, and Severe
    With mild use disorder
    With moderate or severe use disorder
    Without use disorder

Amphetamine-type substance (or other stimulant) intoxication delirium
    With mild use disorder
    With moderate or severe use disorder
    Without use disorder

Cocaine intoxication delirium
    With mild use disorder
    With moderate or severe use disorder
    Without use disorder

Amphetamine-type (or other stimulant) medication-induced delirium
Amphetamine-type substance (or other stimulant)-induced mild neurocognitive disorder
Specify if: Persistent
    With mild use disorder
    With moderate or severe use disorder
    Without use disorder

Cocaine-induced mild neurocognitive disorder
Specify if: Persistent
    With mild use disorder
    With moderate or severe use disorder
    Without use disorder

Unspecified stimulant-related disorder
    Amphetamine-type substance or other stimulant
    Cocaine

Tobacco-Related Disorders

Tobacco products, which contain nicotine, are stimulants. Nicotine causes a quick release of adrenaline, leading to increased heart rate, increased blood pressure, and a sense of alertness. Regular use can lead to addiction and long-term health issues, including respiratory problems and various forms of cancer.

Tobacco use disorder
    Specify if: On maintenance therapy, In a controlled environment
    Specify current severity/remission: Mild, Moderate (In early remission, In sustained remission), and Severe (In early remission, In sustained remission)

Tobacco withdrawal

Tobacco-induced mental disorders
    Tobacco-induced sleep disorder, With moderate or severe use disorder
    Specify whether: Insomnia type, Daytime sleepiness type, and Mixed type
    Specify: With onset during withdrawal, With onset after medication use

Unspecified tobacco-related disorder

Other (or Unknown) Substance–Related Disorders

Other (or unknown) substance use disorder
    Specify if: In a controlled environment
    Specify current severity/remission: Mild (In early remission, In sustained remission), Moderate (In early remission, In sustained remission), and Severe (In early remission, In sustained remission)

Other (or unknown) substance intoxication
    Without perceptual disturbances

With mild use disorder
With moderate or severe use disorder
Without use disorder
With perceptual disturbances
    With mild use disorder
    With moderate or severe use disorder
    Without use disorder

Other (or unknown) substance withdrawal
  Without perceptual disturbances
    With mild use disorder
    With moderate or severe use disorder
    Without use disorder
  With perceptual disturbances
    With mild use disorder
    With moderate or severe use disorder
    Without use disorder

Other (or unknown) substance-induced mental disorders
Specify: With onset during intoxication, With onset during withdrawal, With onset after medication use
Specify if: Acute, Persistent
Specify if: Hyperactive, Hypoactive, and Mixed level of activity

  Other (or unknown) substance-induced psychotic disorder
    With mild use disorder
    With moderate or severe use disorder
    Without use disorder

  Other (or unknown) substance-induced bipolar and related disorder
    With mild use disorder
    With moderate or severe use disorder
    Without use disorder

  Other (or unknown) substance-induced depressive disorder
    With mild use disorder
    With moderate or severe use disorder
    Without use disorder

  Other (or unknown) substance-induced anxiety disorder
    With mild use disorder
    With moderate or severe use disorder
    Without use disorder

  Other (or unknown) substance-induced obsessive-compulsive and related disorder
    With mild use disorder
    With moderate or severe use disorder
    Without use disorder

  Other (or unknown) substance-induced sleep disorder
Specify whether: Insomnia type, Daytime sleepiness type, Parasomnia type, and Mixed type

With mild use disorder
With moderate or severe use disorder
Without use disorder

Other (or unknown) substance-induced sexual dysfunction
Specify if: Mild, Moderate, and Severe
With mild use disorder
With moderate or severe use disorder
Without use disorder

Other (or unknown) substance intoxication delirium
With mild use disorder
With moderate or severe use disorder
Without use disorder

Other (or unknown) substance withdrawal delirium
With mild use disorder
With moderate or severe use disorder
Without use disorder

Other (or unknown) medication-induced delirium
When other (or unknown) medication taken as prescribed
During withdrawal from other (or unknown) medication taken as prescribed

Other (or unknown) substance-induced major neurocognitive disorder
Specify if: Persistent
With mild use disorder
With moderate or severe use disorder
Without use disorder

Other (or unknown) substance-induced mild neurocognitive disorder
Specify if: Persistent
With mild use disorder
With moderate or severe use disorder
Without use disorder

Unspecified other (or unknown) substance–related disorder

Non-Substance-Related Disorders

Gambling disorder
Specify if: Episodic, Persistent
Specify if: In early remission, In sustained remission
Specify current severity: Mild, Moderate, and Severe

Neurocognitive Disorders

Neurocognitive disorders refer to a group of conditions characterized by a significant decline in cognitive functioning (thinking abilities, memory, reasoning, perception, and more) that goes beyond what might be expected due to normal aging. These disorders reflect impairments that impact a person's ability to perform everyday activities independently.

Delirium

    Specify if: Acute, Persistent

    Specify if: Hyperactive, Hypoactive, and Mixed level of activity

    Specify whether: Substance intoxication delirium; Substance withdrawal delirium; Medication-induced delirium

Delirium due to another medical condition

Delirium due to multiple etiologies

Other specified delirium

Unspecified delirium

Major and Mild Neurocognitive Disorders

    Specify whether due to (any of the following medical etiologies): Alzheimer's disease, frontotemporal degeneration, lewy body disease, vascular disease, traumatic brain injury, substance/medication use, HIV infection, prion disease, Parkinson's disease, Huntington's disease, another medical condition, multiple etiologies, unspecified etiology

    Specify current severity: Mild, Moderate, and Severe. This specifier applies only to major neurocognitive disorders (including probable and possible).

    Specify: Without behavioral disturbance, With behavioral disturbance. For all mild neurocognitive disorders, substance/medication-induced major neurocognitive disorder, and unspecified neurocognitive disorder, behavioral disturbance cannot be coded but should still be recorded.

Major or mild neurocognitive disorder due to Alzheimer's disease

    Major neurocognitive disorder due to probable Alzheimer's disease

        With behavioral disturbance

        Without behavioral disturbance

    Major neurocognitive disorder due to possible Alzheimer's disease

        With behavioral disturbance

        Without behavioral disturbance

    Mild neurocognitive disorder due to Alzheimer's disease

Major or mild frontotemporal neurocognitive disorder

    Major neurocognitive disorder due to probable frontotemporal degeneration

        With behavioral disturbance

Without behavioral disturbance
Major neurocognitive disorder due to possible frontotemporal degeneration
With behavioral disturbance
Without behavioral disturbance
Mild neurocognitive disorder due to frontotemporal degeneration

Major or mild neurocognitive disorder with Lewy bodies
Major neurocognitive disorder with probable Lewy bodies
With behavioral disturbance
Without behavioral disturbance
Major neurocognitive disorder with possible Lewy bodies
With behavioral disturbance
Without behavioral disturbance
Mild neurocognitive disorder with Lewy bodies

Major or mild vascular neurocognitive disorder
Major neurocognitive disorder probably due to vascular disease
With behavioral disturbance
Without behavioral disturbance
Major neurocognitive disorder possibly due to vascular disease
With behavioral disturbance
Without behavioral disturbance
Mild neurocognitive disorder due to vascular disease

Major or mild neurocognitive disorder due to traumatic brain injury
Major neurocognitive disorder due to traumatic brain injury
With behavioral disturbance
Without behavioral disturbance
Mild neurocognitive disorder due to traumatic brain injury

Substance/medication-induced major or mild neurocognitive disorder
Specify if: Persistent
Substance/medication-induced major neurocognitive disorder
Substance/medication-induced mild neurocognitive disorder

Major or mild neurocognitive disorder due to HIV infection
Major neurocognitive disorder due to HIV infection
With behavioral disturbance
Without behavioral disturbance
Mild neurocognitive disorder due to HIV infection

Major or mild neurocognitive disorder due to prion disease
Major neurocognitive disorder due to prion disease

With behavioral disturbance
Without behavioral disturbance
Mild neurocognitive disorder due to prion disease

Major or mild neurocognitive disorder due to Parkinson's disease
Major neurocognitive disorder probably due to Parkinson's disease
With behavioral disturbance
Without behavioral disturbance
Major neurocognitive disorder possibly due to Parkinson's disease
With behavioral disturbance
Without behavioral disturbance
Mild neurocognitive disorder due to Parkinson's disease

Major or mild neurocognitive disorder due to Huntington's disease
Major neurocognitive disorder due to Huntington's disease
With behavioral disturbance
Without behavioral disturbance
Mild neurocognitive disorder due to Huntington's disease

Major or mild neurocognitive disorder due to another medical condition
Major neurocognitive disorder due to another medical condition
With behavioral disturbance
Without behavioral disturbance
Mild neurocognitive disorder due to another medical condition

Major or mild neurocognitive disorder due to multiple etiologies
Major neurocognitive disorder due to multiple etiologies
With behavioral disturbance
Without behavioral disturbance
Mild neurocognitive disorder due to multiple etiologies

Unspecified neurocognitive disorder

Personality Disorders

Each personality disorder involves a distinct pattern of thinking, feeling, and behaving that differs from societal norms and causes significant impairment in daily life.

Cluster A Personality Disorders

Paranoid personality disorder—a pattern of distrust and suspicion of others, interpreting their motives as malevolent, without justification

Schizoid personality disorder—detachment from social relationships, limited emotional expression, and preference for solitary activities

Schizotypal personality disorder—eccentric behavior, odd beliefs or magical thinking, and discomfort with close relationships, along with perceptual distortions

Cluster B Personality Disorders

Antisocial personality disorder—disregard for others' rights, lack of empathy, manipulative behavior, impulsivity, and a history of conduct problems

Borderline personality disorder—instability in relationships, self-image, and emotions, marked by impulsivity, self-destructive behavior, and intense fear of abandonment

Histrionic personality disorder—attention-seeking behavior, strong emotions, and exaggerated expressions, often seeking reassurance and approval

Narcissistic personality disorder—grandiosity, a need for admiration, lack of empathy, and a sense of entitlement

Cluster C Personality Disorders

Avoidant personality disorder—extreme social inhibition, feelings of inadequacy, and hypersensitivity to negative evaluation, leading to avoidance of social interactions

Dependent personality disorder—excessive need to be cared for, submissive behavior, fear of separation, and difficulty making decisions independently

Obsessive-compulsive personality disorder—preoccupation with orderliness, perfectionism, and control, often at the expense of flexibility and interpersonal relationships

Other Personality Disorders

Personality change due to another medical condition
  Specify whether: Labile type, Disinhibited type, Aggressive type, Apathetic type, Paranoid type, Other type, Combined type, Unspecified type

Other specified personality disorder—traits of one or more personality disorders that do not align with any specific category but cause significant distress or impairment

Unspecified personality disorder—when personality traits cause distress or impairment but do not fit the criteria for any specific personality disorder

Paraphilic Disorders

Paraphilic disorders refer to a group of mental health conditions characterized by atypical sexual interests or behaviors that are outside the cultural norm and may cause distress, impairment, or harm to oneself or others. These disorders involve recurrent and intense sexual fantasies, urges, or behaviors that center around non-human objects, non-consenting individuals, suffering or humiliation, or other unconventional preferences. Not all unconventional sexual interests are considered disorders; only those that lead to distress, impairment, or harm are diagnosed as paraphilic disorders.

  The following specifier applies to paraphilic disorders where indicated:
  Specify if: In a controlled environment, In full remission

Voyeuristic disorder
Arousal is derived from secretly observing others undressing or engaging in sexual activities without their knowledge or consent.

Exhibitionistic disorder
Arousal is achieved through exposing one's genitals to others without their consent, often seeking reactions or shock.
>   Specify whether: Sexually aroused by exposing genitals to prepubertal children, Sexually aroused by exposing genitals to physically mature individuals, Sexually aroused by exposing genitals to prepubertal children and to physically mature individuals

Frotteuristic disorder
Arousal is obtained from touching or rubbing against non-consenting individuals in crowded situations.

Sexual masochism disorder
Arousal is linked to experiencing pain, humiliation, or suffering during sexual activities.
>   Specify if: With asphyxiophilia

Sexual sadism disorder
Arousal is derived from inflicting pain, humiliation, or suffering on others during sexual activities.

Pedophilic disorder
Sexual attraction is directed toward prepubescent children.
>   Specify whether: Exclusive type, Nonexclusive type
>   Specify if: Sexually attracted to males, Sexually attracted to females, Sexually attracted to both
>   Specify if: Limited to incest

Fetishistic disorder
Arousal is achieved from non-human objects or specific body parts that are not typically sexual.
>   Specify: Body part(s), Nonliving object(s), Other

Transvestic disorder
Arousal is gained from cross-dressing, mainly in males, which causes distress or impairment.
>   Specify if: With fetishism, With autogynephilia

Other specified paraphilic disorder
Atypical sexual interests cause distress but don't fit established categories.

Unspecified paraphilic disorder
Distressful sexual interests don't meet criteria for specific paraphilic disorders.

Medication-Induced Movement Disorders and Other Adverse Effects of Medication

These are involuntary and abnormal movements, like tardive dyskinesia or akathisia, triggered by certain medications, often antipsychotics.

Medication-induced parkinsonism
    Antipsychotic medication—and other dopamine receptor blocking agent-induced parkinsonism
    Other medication-induced parkinsonism

Neuroleptic malignant syndrome
Medication-induced acute dystonia
Medication-induced acute akathisia
Tardive dyskinesia
Tardive dystonia
Tardive akathisia
Medication-induced postural tremor

Other medication-induced movement disorder

Antidepressant discontinuation syndrome
    Initial encounter
    Subsequent encounter
    Sequelae

Other adverse effect of medication
    Initial encounter
    Subsequent encounter
    Sequelae

THE INDICATORS OF BEHAVIORAL DYSFUNCTION

"Normal" and "abnormal" depend on the person, place, and situation, and are largely shaped by social standards. Definitions of "normal" change with societal standards and norms. Normality is often viewed as good, whereas abnormality is seen as bad. When people do not conform to what is perceived as "normal," they are often given a number of negative labels, including unusual, sick, or disabled. These labels can lead to that individual being marginalized, or stigmatized.

The most comprehensive attempt to distinguish normality from abnormality is the *DSM*. The *DSM* shows how normality has changed throughout history and how it often involves value judgments. The *DSM* explicitly distinguishes mental disorders and nondisordered conditions.

METHODS TO DEVELOP, REVIEW, AND IMPLEMENT CRISIS PLANS

A crisis is defined as an acute *disruption of psychological homeostasis (steady state) in which usual coping mechanisms fail* and there exists evidence of distress and functional impairment. The subjective reaction to a stressful life is a compromised stability and ability to cope or function.

Given such a definition, it is imperative that social workers have a framework or blue-print to guide them in responding. When confronted by clients in crisis, social workers need to address their distress, impairment, and instability by operating in a logical and orderly process. Social workers can easily exacerbate crises with well-intentioned, but haphazard responding. Comprehensive plans allow for responses that are active and directive, but do not take problem ownership away from clients. Finally, plans should meet clients where they are at, assessing their levels of risk, mobilizing client resources, and moving strategically to stabilize the crisis and improve functioning.

The development, review, and implementation of crises plans require actions aimed at crisis stabilization, resolution, and mastery. Social workers should:

1. Plan and conduct a thorough biopsychosocial and lethality/imminent danger assessment.
2. Make psychological contact and rapidly establish the collaborative relationship.
3. Identify the major problems, including crisis precipitants.
4. Encourage an exploration of feelings and emotions.
5. Generate and explore alternatives and new coping strategies.
6. Restore functioning through implementation of an action plan.
7. Plan follow-up and "booster" sessions.

THE PRINCIPLES AND FEATURES OF OBJECTIVE AND SUBJECTIVE DATA

A social worker uses both objective and subjective data throughout the problem-solving process. For example, in assessment, a social worker must understand the "facts" related to a client's situation (objective data), but also how those "facts" are perceived by the client through descriptions of feelings, experiences, and perceptions (subjective data). It is not the objective facts that determine whether an event is traumatic, but a subjective emotional experience of the event. Thus, having a client describe the meaning of an event is critically important.

Treatment plans are often developed and progress is often assessed based upon objective and subjective data gathered by a social worker. For example, in health care, a **SOAP format** is often used.

S (Subjective): The subjective component is a client's report of how the client has been doing since the last visit and/or what brought the client into treatment.

O (Objective): In health care, the objective component includes vital signs (temperature, blood pressure, pulse, and respiration), documentation of any physical examinations, and results of laboratory tests. In other settings, this section may include other objective indicators of problems such as disorientation, failing school, legal issues, and so forth.

A (Assessment): A social worker pulls together the objective and subjective findings and consolidates them into a short assessment.

P (Plan): The plan includes what will be done as a consequence of the assessment.

Lastly, in evaluation, subjective reports of a client, in conjunction with objective indicators of progress, should be used to determine when goals or objectives have been met and whether new goals or objectives should be set. Client self-monitoring (subjective data) is a good way to involve a client so the client can see and track progress toward goal attainment.

BASIC AND APPLIED RESEARCH DESIGN AND METHODS

Social work research needs a design or a structure before data collection or analysis can commence. The function of a research design is to ensure that the evidence or data collected enables the research questions to be answered. Research design is different from the method by which data are collected. Many research methods texts confuse research designs with methods. It is not uncommon to see research design treated as a mode of data collection rather than as a logical structure of the inquiry.

Research design is a blueprint, with the research problem determining the type of design used. The research process will:

1. Identify the research problem clearly and justify its selection.

2. Review previously published literature associated with the problem area.

3. Clearly and explicitly specify hypotheses (i.e., research questions) central to the problem selected.

4. Effectively describe the data that will be necessary for an adequate test of the hypotheses and explain how such data will be obtained.

5. Describe the methods of analysis that will be applied to the data in determining whether or not the hypotheses are true or false.

Types of Research

There are three broad types of research—*experimental, quasi-experimental*, and *pre-experimental*. Randomized experiments, also called "experimental," are the most rigorous. When randomization of subjects or groups is neither practical nor feasible, quasi-experimental approaches can be used. Quasi-experimental research uses intervention and comparison groups, but assignment to the groups is nonrandom. Pre-experimental studies contain intervention groups only and lack comparison/control groups, making them the weakest.

Single-Subject Research

Single-subject research aims to determine whether an intervention has the intended impact on a client, or on many clients who form a group. The most common single-subject research is *pre- and post-test* or *single-case study* (AB) in which there is a comparison of behavior before treatment (baseline; denoted by an "A") and behavior after the start of treatment (intervention; denoted by a "B"). The *reversal or multiple baseline* (ABA or ABAB) is also commonly used.

In single-subject research, a client is used as the client's own control. The focus differs from experimental research, which looks at the average effect of an intervention between groups of people.

Single-subject research is ideal for studying the behavioral change a client exhibits as a result of some treatment. When done correctly and carefully, single-subject research can show a causal effect between the intervention and the outcome.

The flexibility, simplicity, and low cost of single-subject research are also beneficial. It can be more flexible and easier to plan because it is usually smaller in scale than experimental research.

Attempts should be made to maximize both internal and external validity. **Internal validity** addresses the extent to which causal inferences can be made about the intervention and the targeted behavior. **External validity** addresses how generalizable those inferences are to the general population. Due to the small number of study participants, single-subject research tends to have poor external validity, limiting the ability to generalize the findings to a wider audience.

It is important to remember that, in some cases, it would be unethical to withdraw treatment if clients would be put at risk for harm. Also, in a crisis, treatment would not be delayed in an effort to obtain baseline data.

DATA COLLECTION AND ANALYSIS METHODS

Qualitative research usually involves collecting information through unstructured interviews, observation, and/or focus groups. Data can be collected from a single individual at a time or multiple people in group settings. Qualitative data collection methods are usually very time consuming, so they are confined to smaller samples than usually found in quantitative approaches. Quantitative research mainly collects data through the input of responses to research instruments containing questions (i.e., such as questionnaires). Information can be input either by the respondents themselves (e.g., online or mail survey) or social workers can input data (e.g., phone surveys or interviews). Methods for distributing surveys are via postal mail, phone, website, or in person. However, newer technologies have created additional delivery options, including through wireless devices such as smartphones.

Social workers can also do research using secondary data, which is information that has already been collected for other purposes. Use of existing data is efficient since time and money associated with data collection are spared. However, the completeness of existing data, as well as its reliability, may be a concern as sound research practices covering its collection may not have been used.

Data analysis procedures begin with preparation that involves cleaning the data, checking it for accuracy, coding it for analysis, developing a database, and entering the data into the computer.

Once entered into the computer, *descriptive statistics* are used to describe the basic features of the data. They provide simple summaries about the sample and the measures. Together with simple graphics analysis, they form the basis of virtually every quantitative analysis of data. Descriptive statistics describe what the data shows.

Inferential statistics are used to answer research questions or test models or hypotheses. In many cases, the conclusions from inferential statistics extend beyond the immediate data. For instance, inferential statistics determine the probability that an observed difference between groups is a dependable one or one that might have happened by chance.

In most research, analyses include both descriptive and inferential statistics. Social workers must balance the level of detail that is included in a research report with the need to avoid overwhelming readers and missing the highlighting of major findings. If too much detail is included, readers may not be able to pick out the key results. Analysis details are appropriately relegated to appendices, reserving only the most critical analysis summaries for the body of the report itself.

METHODS TO ASSESS RELIABILITY AND VALIDITY IN SOCIAL WORK RESEARCH

Reliability in social work research concerns the ability to get consistent assessments or data by reducing random errors associated with its collection. There are four main methods to assess reliability.

- *Interrater or Interobserver Reliability*

Assesses the degree to which different raters/observers give consistent estimates of the same phenomenon

- *Test–Retest Reliability*

Assesses the consistency of a measure from one time to another

- *Parallel Forms Reliability*

Assesses the consistency of the results of two tests constructed in the same way from the same content domain

- *Internal Consistency Reliability*

Assesses the consistency of results across items within a test

Validity is the degree to which what is being measured actually is what is claimed to be measured. It attempts to minimize systematic errors that may yield reliable results but do not actually assess the constructs of interest. There are different means to assess validity.

- *Face Validity*

Examines whether the assessments "on their face" measure the constructs

- *Content Validity*

Examines whether all of the relevant content domains are covered

- *Criterion-Related Validity (including predictive, concurrent, convergent, and discriminant validities)*

Examines whether constructs perform as anticipated in relation to other theoretical constructs

Predictive validity assesses whether constructs predict what they should theoretically be able to predict.

Concurrent validity assesses whether constructs distinguish between groups that should be able to be distinguished.

Convergent validity assesses the degree to which constructs are similar to (converge on) other constructs to which they should be similar.

Discriminant validity assesses the degree to which constructs are different from (diverge away from) other constructs to which they should be dissimilar.

6

Intervention Planning

METHODS TO INVOLVE CLIENTS/CLIENT SYSTEMS IN INTERVENTION PLANNING

The participation of clients in the process of identifying what is important to them now and in the future, and acting upon these priorities, is paramount. Clients' participation in the process will reduce resistance, increase motivation to change, and ensure sustainability of progress made.

In order to involve clients, social workers must continually listen to, learn about, and facilitate opportunities with clients who they are serving. Client involvement should not just occur during intervention planning, but instead during the entire problem-solving process.

In *engagement*, a social worker should be actively involved with a client in determining why treatment was sought; what has precipitated the desire to change now; the parameters of the helping relationship, including defining the roles of a social worker and client; and the expectations for treatment (what will occur and when it will happen). Client involvement is essential in determining what is important to a client now and in the future.

In *assessment*, a client is the source of providing essential information upon which to define the problem and solutions, as well as identifying collateral contacts from which gaps in data can be collected.

In *planning*, a client and social worker must develop a common understanding of a client's preferred lifestyle. Goals are developed from this common understanding in order to provide a direction to help a client move toward this lifestyle. Specific action plans are developed and agreed upon in order to specify who will do what, what and how resources will be needed and used, and timelines for implementation and review.

In planning, a social worker and client should be:

1. Defining the problem (in a well-defined, clear, and data-driven format)

2. Examining the causes of the problem and how it relates to other positive/negative aspects of a client's life

3. Generating possible solutions that will impact on the problem

4. Identifying the driving and restraining forces related to implementation of each of the possible solutions

5. Rating the driving and restraining forces related to consistency and potency

6. Prioritizing these solutions based on these ratings

7. Developing SMART objectives—Specific, Measurable, Achievable, Relevant, and Time-specific—related to the chosen solutions

8. Creating strategies and activities related to the objectives

In *intervention*, a client must be actively involved in mobilizing a support network to realize continued progress and sustainable change. A client must bring to the attention of a social worker issues that arise which may threaten goal attainment. Progress, based upon client reports, must be tracked and plans/timelines adjusted accordingly.

In *evaluation*, subjective reports of a client, in conjunction with objective indicators of progress, should be used to determine when goals or objectives have been met and whether new goals or objectives should be set. Client self-monitoring is a good way to involve a client so the client can see and track progress.

In *termination*, a client should reflect on what has been achieved and anticipate what supports are in place if problems arise again. Although this is the last phase of the problem-solving process, it still requires active involvement by both a social worker and client.

THE INDICATORS OF MOTIVATION, RESISTANCE, AND READINESS TO CHANGE

Social workers should not assume that clients are ready or have the skills needed to make changes in their lives. Clients may be oppositional, reactionary, noncompliant, and/or unmotivated. These attitudes or behaviors are often referred to as resistance.

There are indicators that a social worker should use as evidence that a client may be resistant or not ready/able to fully participate in services. These indicators include:

- Limiting the amount of information communicated to a social worker
- Silence/minimal talking during sessions
- Engaging in small talk with a social worker about irrelevant topics
- Engaging in intellectual talk by using technical terms/abstract concepts or asking questions of a social worker that are not related to client issues or problems
- Being preoccupied with past events, instead of current issues
- Discounting, censoring, or editing thoughts when asked about them by a social worker
- False promising
- Flattering a social worker in an attempt to "soften" the social worker so the client will not be pushed to act
- Not keeping appointments
- Payment delays or refusals

It is essential to determine the extent to which this resistance or these inabilities are caused by a client, a social worker, and/or the conditions present.

A client may be resistant due to feelings of guilt or shame and may not be ready to recognize or address the feelings and behaviors being brought up by a social worker. Clients may be frightened of change and may be getting some benefit from the problems that they are experiencing.

Social workers may experience a lack of readiness, as they have not developed sufficient rapport with clients. There also may not be clear expectations by clients of their role versus those of social workers. Social workers need to use interventions that are appropriate for clients.

Sometimes, a lack of readiness or ability is a result of external factors, such as changes in clients' living situations, physical health problems, lack of social support, and/or financial problems.

Whatever the causes, a social worker must address these barriers as clients will not make changes until they are ready and able.

CULTURAL CONSIDERATIONS IN THE CREATION OF AN INTERVENTION PLAN

It is essential that a social worker address cultural considerations into treatment or intervention planning. These considerations should include the identification of cross-cultural barriers, which may hinder a client's engagement and/or progress in treatment.

Social workers also have an ethical mandate to take information learned when working with individual clients and adapt agency resources to meet others who may also have similar cultural considerations and/or language assistance needs.

Social workers who provide electronic social work services must be aware of cultural and socioeconomic differences among clients and how they may use electronic technology. Social workers should assess all issues (cultural, environmental, economic, mental or physical ability, and linguistic) that may affect the delivery or use of these services.

A social worker should understand and validate each client's cultural norms, beliefs, and values. Areas in treatment or intervention planning that can be greatly influenced by cultural factors include identification of client strengths and problems, goals and objectives, and modalities of treatment.

For example, a client's culture can provide the client with strengths that can be brought to the intervention process. These strengths can include, but are not limited to:

- Supportive family and community relations
- Community and cultural events and activities
- Faith and spiritual or religious beliefs
- Multilingual capabilities
- Healing practices and beliefs
- Participation in rituals (religious, cultural, familial, spiritual, community)
- Dreams and aspirations

A culturally informed intervention plan must be based on a therapeutic relationship in which a client feels safe to explore problems within the client's cultural context.

Intervention will be most effective when it is consistent with a consumer's culture. A social worker should consider the following given their cultural appropriateness:

■ Individual versus group treatment

■ Alternative treatment approaches (yoga, aromatherapy, music, writing)

■ Medication (western, traditional, and/or alternative)

■ Family involvement

■ Location/duration of intervention

Different cultures and communities exhibit or explain symptoms in various ways. Because of this, it is important for social workers to be aware of relevant contextual information stemming from clients' cultures, races, ethnicities, religious affiliations, and/or geographical origins so social workers can more accurately diagnose client problems, as well as more effectively treat them.

The Cultural Formulation Interview Guide is included in the *DSM* to help social workers assess cultural factors influencing clients' perspectives of their symptoms and treatment options. It includes questions about clients' backgrounds in terms of their culture, race, ethnicity, religion, or geographical origin. Use of this tool provides an opportunity for clients to define their distress in their own words and then relate this distress to how others, who may not share their culture, see their problems.

THE CRITERIA USED IN THE SELECTION OF INTERVENTION/TREATMENT MODALITIES (E.G., CLIENT/CLIENT SYSTEM ABILITIES, CULTURE, LIFE STAGE)

A social worker develops an intervention plan by consulting the relevant practice research and then flexibly implementing an approach to fit a client's needs and circumstances. The intervention plan is driven by the data collected as part of assessment. Assessment is informed by current human behavior and development research that provides key information about how clients behave and research about risk and resilience factors that affect human functioning. These theories inform social workers about what skills, techniques, and strategies must be used by social workers, clients, and others for the purpose of improving well-being. These techniques and strategies are outlined in an intervention plan.

An intervention plan should be reviewed during the intervention, at termination, and, if possible, following the termination of services to make adjustments, ensure progress, and determine the sustainability of change after treatment.

THE COMPONENTS OF INTERVENTION, TREATMENT, AND SERVICE PLANS

The goals of intervention and means used to achieve these goals are incorporated in a contractual agreement between a client and a social worker. The contract (also called an intervention or service plan) may be informal or written. The contract specifies problem(s) to be worked on; the goals to reduce the problem(s); client and social worker roles in the process; the interventions or techniques to be employed; the means of monitoring progress; stipulations for renegotiating the contract; and the time, place, fee, and frequency of meetings.

PSYCHOTHERAPIES

Psychotherapy aims to treat clients with mental disorders or problems by helping them understand their illness or situation. Social workers use verbal techniques to teach clients strategies to deal with stress, unhealthy thoughts, and dysfunctional behaviors. Psychotherapy helps clients manage their symptoms better and function optimally in everyday life.

Sometimes, psychotherapy alone may be the best treatment for a client, depending on the illness and its severity. Other times, psychotherapy is combined with the use of medication or a psychopharmacological approach.

There are many kinds of psychotherapy, so social workers must determine which is best to meet a client's need. A social worker should not use a "one size fits all approach" or a particular type of psychotherapy because it is more familiar or convenient. Some psychotherapies have been scientifically tested more than others for particular disorders.

For example, cognitive behavioral therapy (CBT), a blend of cognitive and behavioral therapy, is used for depression, anxiety, and other disorders. Dialectical behavior therapy (DBT), a form of CBT developed by Marsha Linehan, was developed to treat people with suicidal thoughts and actions. It is now also used to treat people with borderline personality disorder. A social worker assures a client that the client's feelings are valid and understandable, but coaches the client to understand that they are unhealthy or disruptive and a balance must be achieved. A client understands that it is the client's personal responsibility to change the situation.

Some psychotherapies are effective with children and adolescents and can also be used with families.

THE IMPACT OF IMMIGRATION, REFUGEE, OR UNDOCUMENTED STATUS ON SERVICE DELIVERY

Social workers may have a general concept of immigration requirements, but this area of law is both complex and volatile. Laws and policies affecting the status of immigrants have evolved over time in response to various social, political, and economic pressures. Most recently, immigration policy has had an exclusionary focus that has turned toward conflating criminality and undocumented immigration status. Although immigration laws are within the exclusive purview of the federal government, some states have attempted to address concerns by passing their own measures. This situation creates legal questions and ethical dilemmas for social workers who are employed in programs or areas serving immigrants.

Professional social work standards support immigration and refugee policies that uphold and support equity and human rights, while protecting national security. The social work profession recognizes the challenge of competing claims; however, immigration policies must promote social justice and avoid racism and discrimination or profiling on the basis of race, religion, country of origin, gender, or other grounds. The impact of refugee and immigration policies on families and children have to be closely monitored. Policies that encourage family reunification and ensure that children do not grow up unduly disadvantaged by the immigration status of their parents must be enacted and upheld.

Given the great diversity and myriad needs of the growing immigrant population, it is essential that social workers understand the legal and political, as well as psychological and social, issues surrounding immigration. Undocumented immigrants represent a large and vulnerable population. When conducting individual practice with undocumented immigrants, social workers must be aware of the laws that impact service provision and the unique psychosocial stressors that are experienced by this population.

Numerous immigrant households are comprised of mixed-status families in which family members hold different legal statuses. Each status carries different benefit entitlements, services, and legal rights.

DISCHARGE, AFTERCARE, AND FOLLOW-UP PLANNING

Discharge may occur for a variety of reasons; for example, a client may have met the goals or no longer needs the services; decides not to continue to receive them from a particular social worker or in general; and/or requires a different level of care. In addition, when a social worker leaves an agency, a client may continue to receive the same service from this agency, but from another worker. Although this is not a "discharge" from services, there is careful planning and standards that need to be followed to ensure continuity of care and prevent gaps in service.

The *NASW Code of Ethics*—provides some guidance with regard to discharge or terminations, as well as aftercare and follow-up services.

Social workers should terminate services to clients and professional relationships with them when such services and relationships are no longer required or no longer serve client needs or interests (*NASW Code of Ethics—Termination of Services*).

Social workers should take reasonable steps to avoid abandoning clients who are still in need of services. Social workers should withdraw services precipitously only under unusual circumstances, giving careful consideration to all factors in the situation and taking care to minimize possible adverse effects. Social workers should assist in making appropriate arrangements for continuation of services when necessary (*NASW Code of Ethics—Termination of Services*).

Social workers in fee-for-service settings may terminate services to clients who are not paying an overdue balance if the financial contractual arrangements have been made clear to a client, if a client does not pose an imminent danger to self or others, and if the clinical and other consequences of the current nonpayment have been addressed and discussed with a client (*NASW Code of Ethics—Termination of Services*).

Social workers should not terminate services to pursue a social, financial, or sexual relationship with a client (*NASW Code of Ethics—Termination of Services*).

Social workers who anticipate the termination or interruption of services to clients should notify clients promptly and seek the transfer, referral, or continuation of services in relation to client needs and preferences (*NASW Code of Ethics—Termination of Services*).

Social workers who are leaving an employment setting should inform clients of appropriate options for the continuation of services and of the benefits and risks of the options (*NASW Code of Ethics—Termination of Services*).

It is unethical to continue to treat clients when services are no longer needed or in their best interests.

Another standard that is relevant to termination of services (*NASW Code of Ethics—Interruption of Services*) mandates that social workers should make reasonable efforts to ensure continuity of services in the event that services are interrupted by factors such as unavailability, disruptions in electronic communication, relocation, illness, disability, or death.

Social workers must involve clients and their families (when appropriate) in making their own decisions about follow-up services or aftercare. Involvement must include, at a minimum, discussion of client and family preferences (when appropriate).

Social workers are often responsible for coordination of clients' follow-up services, when needed.

A return of clients to services quickly may suggest either that they did not receive needed follow-up services or that these services were inadequate. Termination may have occurred prematurely.

Clients who are at high risk for developing problems after services have ended should receive regular assessments after discharge to determine whether services are needed or discharge plans are being implemented as planned.

Content Area II: Practice Questions

The following section has 41 unique practice questions that assess retention of material related to assessment and intervention planning. The number of questions reflects the approximate proportion of a typical exam (24%) devoted to this content.

1. A young boy is stopped by a police officer and claims that he is a member of the armed forces, though it is obvious that he is not. Which of the following **BEST** describes the boy's assertion?

   A. Dissociation
   B. Folie à deux
   C. Delusion

2. A client with a social anxiety disorder will **MOST** likely be prescribed which of the following medications to take on an ongoing basis?

   A. Zoloft (sertraline)
   B. Mellaril (thioridazine)
   C. Valium (diazepam)

3. With which of the following will a client have difficulty if diagnosed with aphasia?

   A. Using common motor skills despite normal strength
   B. Understanding language or using language to speak or write
   C. Recognizing familiar objects

4. A client is currently taking clozaril for the treatment of schizophrenia. The client is **MOST** likely going to be required to undergo what medical monitoring due to this medication use?

   A. Weight checks
   B. Blood work
   C. Dietary restrictions

(See answers next page.)

1. **C.** A delusion is a false, fixed belief despite evidence to the contrary (i.e., believing something that is not true).

   Dissociation is a change in memory, perception, or consciousness. Folie à deux is a shared delusion.

   Question Assesses

   Content Area II—Assessment and Intervention Planning; Biopsychosocial History and Collateral Data (Competency); The Indicators of Mental and Emotional Illness Throughout the Lifespan (KSA)

2. **A.** The primary medications used to treat social anxiety disorder are selective serotonin reuptake inhibitors (SSRIs), which were first developed to treat depression. They have been found to be effective in the treatment of a wider range of disorders. Zoloft (sertraline) is an SSRI.

   Benzodiazepines, such as Valium (diazepam), reduce levels of anxiety. However, they are habit-forming and sedating, so they are typically prescribed for only short-term use.

   Mellaril (thioridazine) is an antipsychotic medication for the treatment of psychosis.

   Question Assesses

   Content Area II—Assessment and Intervention Planning; Biopsychosocial History and Collateral Data (Competency); Common Psychotropic and Non-Psychotropic Prescriptions and Over-the-Counter Medications and Their Side Effects (KSA)

3. **B.** Aphasia is a change in cognition (mental ability) that is characterized by difficulty understanding language or using language to speak or write.

   Difficulty with common motor skills is known as ataxia. Inability to recognize familiar objects is labeled agnosia.

   Question Assesses

   Content Area II—Assessment and Intervention Planning; Biopsychosocial History and Collateral Data (Competency); Symptoms of neurologic and organic disorders (KSA)

4. **B.** Clozaril increases the risk of agranulocytosis (low white blood cell count). Monitoring of the white blood cell count through regular blood work is required.

   Question Assesses

   Content Area II—Assessment and Intervention Planning; Biopsychosocial History and Collateral Data (Competency); Common Psychotropic and Non-Psychotropic Prescriptions and Over-the-Counter Medications and Their Side Effects (KSA)

5. A client was referred to a mental health agency for treatment. Upon admission, he reported feeling lethargic and hopeless and had difficulty getting out of bed. Several weeks later, he states that he is sleepless, agitated, and unable to focus. Which of the following medications is the client **MOST** likely going to be prescribed?

   A. Ativan (lorazepam)
   B. Lithium (lithium carbonate)
   C. Buspar (buspirone)

6. A new client enters the office walking slowly, using a cane, and has difficulty picking up objects, swallowing, and speaking as a result of a stroke. Which of the following is the **BEST** diagnosis for this client?

   A. Agnosia
   B. Ataxia
   C. Prosopagnosia

7. If a client has a substance use disorder in addition to schizophrenia, which **BEST** describes the relationship between these two disorders?

   A. Premorbid
   B. Comorbid
   C. Contraindicated

8. A new client comes to the first appointment and is extremely anxious. She paces while in the waiting room and states that she "just needs to get some sleep." During the intake interview, the client reports that she is a recreational drug user. Based on her behavior, the client is **MOST** likely using which of the following substances?

   A. Cocaine
   B. Marijuana
   C. Oxycontin

(*See answers next page.*)

5. **B.** Ativan and Buspar are antianxiety medications. Lithium is a mood stabilizer, and this client appears to be experiencing depression upon admission, as well as mania later in treatment. A mood stabilizer is used for the treatment of bipolar disorder.

Question Assesses

Content Area II—Assessment and Intervention Planning; Biopsychosocial History and Collateral Data (Competency); Common Psychotropic and Non-Psychotropic Prescriptions and Over-the-Counter Medications and Their Side Effects (KSA)

6. **B.** Ataxia describes a lack of muscle control during voluntary movements, such as walking or picking up objects. A sign of an underlying condition, ataxia can affect movement, speech, eye movement, and swallowing.

Persistent ataxia usually results from damage to the cerebellum—the part of the brain that controls muscle coordination. Many conditions can cause ataxia, including alcohol abuse, stroke, tumor, cerebral palsy, and multiple sclerosis.

An inability to recognize familiar objects is agnosia, and an inability to recognize familiar faces is prosopagnosia.

Question Assesses

Content Area II—Assessment and Intervention Planning; Biopsychosocial History and Collateral Data (Competency); Symptoms of neurologic and organic disorders (KSA)

7. **B.** Comorbid refers to two problems, conditions, or disorders that exist at the same time—such as the presence of a mental health and substance use issue, or a mental health and medical problem.

Question Assesses

Content Area II—Assessment and Intervention Planning; Biopsychosocial History and Collateral Data (Competency); The Indicators of Mental and Emotional Illness Throughout the Lifespan (KSA)

8. **A.** Cocaine use is indicated by dilated pupils, hyperactivity, euphoria, anxiety, and excessive talking.

Marijuana use is indicated by glassy, red eyes; inappropriate laughter; and loss of interest and motivation. Oxycontin (oxycodone) is an opioid pain medication used to treat moderate to severe pain and its use is indicated by sleepiness, inattention, and loss of appetite.

Question Assesses

Content Area II—Assessment and Intervention Planning; Biopsychosocial History and Collateral Data (Competency); The Indicators of Addiction and Substance Abuse (KSA)

9. A client reports that he has experienced some "ringing" in his ears for the last week, which is causing him great distress. The social worker should **FIRST**:

   A. Refer the client for a neurological evaluation
   B. Identify whether he is reporting an auditory hallucination
   C. Explore with the client what changes in his life may have coincided with this symptom

10. A client became depressed a month ago due to the ending of her marriage. Which of the following is the **BEST** diagnosis for this client?

   A. Major depression
   B. Endogenous depression
   C. Exogenous depression

11. Which of the following **BEST** described awareness of a client diagnosed with delirium?

   A. The client is completely aware with no impairment
   B. The client has reduced or impaired awareness
   C. The client may experience periods of reduced awareness which subsist over time

12. A social worker is reviewing a client's record and sees that a client was recently taking Zoloft after being switched from Lexapro. Which of the following is the **BEST** diagnosis for this client?

   A. Major depressive disorder
   B. Schizoaffective disorder
   C. Attention-deficit/hyperactivity disorder

(*See answers next page.*)

9. **A.** "Ringing" or other sounds originating in the ears (tinnitus) can be a symptom of a neurologic or organic problem. The social worker needs to FIRST rule out a medical cause before determining other etiology.

Question Assesses

Content Area II—Assessment and Intervention Planning; Biopsychosocial History and Collateral Data (Competency); Symptoms of neurologic and organic disorders (KSA)

10. **C.** Exogenous depression is caused by external events or psychosocial stressors, such as the ending of a marriage.

Endogenous depression is caused by a biochemical imbalance rather than a psychosocial stressor or external factors.

The criteria for major depression are not explicitly stated in this scenario and, thus, cannot be considered.

Question Assesses

Content Area II—Assessment and Intervention Planning; Biopsychosocial History and Collateral Data (Competency); The Indicators of Mental and Emotional Illness Throughout the Lifespan (KSA)

11. **B.** Delirium is a medical condition that results in confusion and other disruptions in thinking and behavior, including changes in perception, attention, mood, and activity level. Awareness is impaired and reduced.

Question Assesses

Content Area II—Assessment and Intervention Planning; Biopsychosocial History and Collateral Data (Competency); Symptoms of neurologic and organic disorders (KSA)

12. **A.** These medications are antidepressants. The client may have one of the other diagnoses and/or more than one diagnosis, but is MOST likely taking these medications for depressive symptoms that are associated with major depressive disorder.

Question Assesses

Content Area II—Assessment and Intervention Planning; Biopsychosocial History and Collateral Data (Competency); Common Psychotropic and Non-Psychotropic Prescriptions and Over-the-Counter Medications and Their Side Effects (KSA)

13. When completing a mental status examination, a social worker is **MOST** likely assessing which of the following client issues?

    A. Psychiatric issues or problems
    B. Level of suicidality or lethality
    C. Judgment or insight

14. Which of the following systems in the body is responsible for the production of hormones that control metabolism and growth?

    A. Digestive
    B. Lymphatic
    C. Endocrine

15. Which type of medications places clients at risk for tardive dyskinesia?

    A. Antipsychotics
    B. Antidepressants
    C. Mood stabilizers

16. During an intake interview, a client reports that she is extremely depressed and has self-destructive thoughts. She has had prior suicide attempts, but tells the social worker not to worry as she won't "do it again." The social worker should **FIRST**:

    A. Explore with the client what is causing her depression
    B. Conduct a safety assessment
    C. Refer the client to a psychiatrist for a medication evaluation

(*See answers next page.*)

13. **C.** A mental status examination is a structured way of observing and describing a client's current state of mind, under the domains of appearance, attitude, behavior, mood and affect, speech, thought process, thought content, perception, cognition, insight, and judgment. A mental status examination is a necessary part of any client assessment no matter what the presenting problem. It is not a psychiatric evaluation and does not determine mental health problems. A mental status examination is also not a safety assessment so cannot determine danger to self or others.

Question Assesses

Content Area II—Assessment and Intervention Planning; Biopsychosocial History and Collateral Data (Competency); The Components and Function of the Mental Status Examination (KSA)

14. **C.** The endocrine system produces hormones, which are chemicals that control body functions such as metabolism, growth, and sexual development.

The digestive system is made up of organs that break down food into protein, vitamins, minerals, carbohydrates, and fats. The lymphatic system is the defense system for the body.

Question Assesses

Content Area II—Assessment and Intervention Planning; Biopsychosocial History and Collateral Data (Competency); Basic Medical Terminology (KSA)

15. **A.** Tardive dyskinesia may result from taking high doses of antipsychotic medications over a long period of time. Symptoms may persist indefinitely after discontinuation of these medications. Thus, antipsychotic use should be closely monitored and prescribed at low doses, if possible.

Question Assesses

Content Area II—Assessment and Intervention Planning; Biopsychosocial History and Collateral Data (Competency); Common Psychotropic and Non-Psychotropic Prescriptions and Over-the-Counter Medications and Their Side Effects (KSA)

16. **B.** Despite the client's report that she will not act on her thoughts, she is at risk because she has had these feelings and has acted on them in the past. The scenario does not describe the social worker taking any action yet. A safety assessment will determine the severity of the depression and whether the client is at risk for a suicide attempt. It must be done FIRST before any other action is taken.

Question Assesses

Content Area II—Assessment and Intervention Planning; Assessment Methods and Techniques (Competency); The Indicators and Risk Factors of the Client's/Client System's Danger to Self and Others

17. A social worker is appointed by the court to conduct a child custody evaluation for a couple that is divorcing. The mother reports that her husband is verbally abusive, controlling, and neglects the children when they are in his care. She reports that the children have missed a lot of school when staying with their father because he does not assist with getting them ready for school or doing their homework. The father states that his wife is lazy, irresponsible, and cannot meet the children's basic needs. He reports that the school frequently provides lunch for the children because the mother does not supply it when they are in her care. In order to **BEST** evaluate the legitimacy of the information, the social worker should:

    A. Ask the husband and wife to put their allegations in writing and sign them, attesting to their accuracy
    B. Always speak to the husband and wife together so that they are more likely to be honest
    C. Obtain information from school personnel and records after obtaining parental consent

18. A social worker employed in a hospital is asked to use a SOAP format for documentation in a client's record. After describing the subjective and objective symptoms, the social worker should then enter which of the following information?

    A. Assessment findings
    B. Active treatment received
    C. Adjustments to services needed

19. According to the *DSM*, a social worker should use which of the following when a client's presenting problem does not meet diagnostic criteria and the social worker would like to elaborate as to the reasons?

    A. Not otherwise specified
    B. Other specified
    C. Unspecified

20. Which of the following is a non-substance-related addictive disorder in the *DSM*?

    A. Gambling
    B. Shopping
    C. Eating

21. Which of the following is the **MOST** important diagnostic criterion of paraphilic disorders according to the *DSM*?

    A. Sexual attraction to children who are prepubescent
    B. Sexual desire or behavior causes significant distress in important areas of functioning
    C. Legal involvement due to sexual interests or behaviors

(See answers next page.)

17. **C.** Collateral information is often used when the credibility and validity of information obtained from a client or others is questionable. For example, child custody cases are inherently characterized by biased data within an adversarial process. Social workers should use data from neutral parties, such as the school, because this information has higher integrity.

Question Assesses

Content Area II—Assessment and Intervention Planning; Assessment Methods and Techniques (Competency); Methods of Involving Clients/Client Systems in Problem Identification (e.g., Gathering Collateral Information) (KSA)

18. **A.** SOAP stands for Subjective, Objective, Assessment, and Plan. In the assessment portion, a social worker pulls together objective and subjective findings which have already been documented in the record.

Question Assesses

Content Area II—Assessment and Intervention Planning; Assessment Methods and Techniques (Competency); The Principles and Features of Objective and Subjective Data (KSA)

19. **B.** "Other specified" (i.e., "other specified depressive disorder") categories are used when a social worker provides the reason why the condition does not qualify for a specific diagnosis (i.e., short duration). "Unspecified" is used when no additional explanation is provided as to why the disorder does not meet the usual criteria. "Not otherwise specified" is no longer used in the *DSM*.

Question Assesses

Content Area II—Assessment and Intervention Planning; Assessment Methods and Techniques (Competency); The Use of the *Diagnostic and Statistical Manual* of the American Psychiatric Association (KSA)

20. **A.** Gambling disorder is the only non-substance-related addictive disorder listed in the *DSM*.

Question Assesses

Content Area II—Assessment and Intervention Planning; Assessment Methods and Techniques (Competency); The Use of the *Diagnostic and Statistical Manual* of the American Psychiatric Association (KSA)

21. **B.** Most clients with atypical sexual interests do not have mental disorders. To be diagnosed with paraphilic disorders, the behaviors or desires must cause significant distress or impairment in social, occupational, or other important areas of functioning. These desires and/or behaviors do not need to have resulted in legal involvement or involve children.

Question Assesses

Content Area II—Assessment and Intervention Planning; Assessment Methods and Techniques (Competency); The Use of the *Diagnostic and Statistical Manual* of the American Psychiatric Association (KSA)

22. A client who has schizophrenia has not been taking his medication. He is in crisis, but does not pose a danger to himself or others. The client was recently discharged from an inpatient hospitalization after an involuntary commitment. In the social worker's opinion, the client would benefit from rehospitalization, but the client does not want to be readmitted. The social worker should:

    A. Identify community resources to meet his immediate needs
    B. Contact the hospital to see if he can be readmitted
    C. Recommend that the client be involuntarily committed to get the medication needed

23. Which of the following theoretical approaches are the basis of projective tests?

    A. Psychoanalytic
    B. Cognitive behavioral
    C. Self psychology

24. What type of disorder is trichotillomania?

    A. Anxiety disorder
    B. Trauma- and stressor-related disorder
    C. Obsessive-compulsive and related disorder

25. A client is referred to a social worker by an employee assistance program for problems at work including insubordination and not following company policies. Upon intake, the client states that he is not the one who needs help and that the social worker should be trying to "fix" his boss, who is the real problem. The client reports that his difficulties are a result of jealousy by his boss because the client "knows more and is more successful." The client dominates the conversation during the session and spends most of the time describing his achievements, including the amount of money that he earns and spends on his possessions. What is the **BEST** diagnosis for this client?

    A. Narcissistic personality disorder
    B. Histrionic personality disorder
    C. Obsessive-compulsive personality disorder

(*See answers next page.*)

22. **A.** The scenario states that the client is not a danger to himself or others, so he cannot be involuntarily committed. The social worker should not contact the hospital because the client is not agreeable to admission. The client is in crisis, so community resources aimed at meeting his immediate needs are the priority.

Question Assesses

Content Area II—Assessment and Intervention Planning; Assessment Methods and Techniques (Competency); The Indicators and Risk Factors of the Client's/Client System's Danger to Self and Others (KSA)

23. **A.** In a projective test, a client offers responses to ambiguous scenes, words, or images. This type of test emerged from a psychoanalytic approach, which suggested that clients have unconscious thoughts or urges. Projective tests are intended to uncover unconscious desires that are hidden from conscious awareness.

Question Assesses

Content Area II—Assessment and Intervention Planning; Assessment Methods and Techniques (Competency); Techniques and Instruments Used to Assess Clients/Client Systems (KSA)

24. **C.** Trichotillomania is a hair pulling disorder that was classified as an obsessive-compulsive and related disorder.

Question Assesses

Content Area II—Assessment and Intervention Planning; Assessment Methods and Techniques (Competency); The Use of the *Diagnostic and Statistical Manual* of the American Psychiatric Association (KSA)

25. **A.** There are many features of narcissistic personality disorder described, including not voluntarily coming into treatment, blaming others, having an exaggerated sense of self-importance, being absorbed by fantasies of unlimited success, constantly seeking attention, monopolizing the conversation, and bragging.

Question Assesses

Content Area II—Assessment and Intervention Planning; Assessment Methods and Techniques (Competency); The Use of the *Diagnostic and Statistical Manual* of the American Psychiatric Association (KSA)

26. A mother comes in to see a social worker because she is concerned about cognitive delays in her child. The child is far behind her peers in academic achievement. A social worker refers this child for diagnostic testing. Given the mother's concerns, the child will **MOST** likely be given which of the following assessments?

   A. Minnesota Multiphasic Personality Inventory
   B. Thematic Apperception Test
   C. Wechsler Intelligence Scale

27. A client who has been experiencing severe depression and previously expressed thoughts aimed at hurting herself appears less hopeless and to have a more positive affect. In this situation, the social worker should **FIRST**:

   A. Acknowledge the recent improvement in depressive symptoms to the client
   B. Determine the coping skills that the client is using to bring about change
   C. Conduct a suicide risk assessment

28. A client is having difficulty finding a career that is fulfilling to her. She has repeatedly taken jobs that she has quit because "they just don't fit." In order to assist the client in resolving this problem, which of the following tests may be used?

   A. Minnesota Multiphasic Personality Inventory
   B. Myers–Briggs Type Indicator
   C. Thematic Apperception Test

29. According to the Tarasoff decision, which of the following is **MOST** important for a social worker to have a duty to warn?

   A. Threat of imminent danger
   B. History of danger to others
   C. Reasonable suspicion of abuse

(*See answers next page.*)

26. **C.** The Wechsler Intelligence Scale is designed as a measure of a child's intellectual and cognitive ability.

The Minnesota Multiphasic Personality Inventory is a personality test for the assessment of psychopathology. The Thematic Apperception Test provides information on a client's perceptions and imagination, for use in the understanding of the subject's current needs, motives, emotions, and conflicts, both conscious and unconscious.

Question Assesses

Content Area II—Assessment and Intervention Planning; Assessment Methods and Techniques (Competency); Techniques and Instruments Used to Assess Clients/Client Systems (KSA)

27. **C.** A sign of a possible suicide attempt is a recent improvement in depressive symptoms. A client is also at greater risk after being discharged from the hospital or after being started on antidepressants because the client may now have the energy to implement a suicide plan. The social worker should assess the client for suicide risk immediately.

Question Assesses

Content Area II—Assessment and Intervention Planning; Assessment Methods and Techniques (Competency); The Indicators and Risk Factors of the Client's/Client System's Danger to Self and Others (KSA)

28. **B.** The Myers–Briggs Type Indicator (MBTI) attempts to describe personality features. The client may find the MBTI test useful as a way of understanding herself. The client may want to pursue careers that allow her to make use of her natural preferences.

The Minnesota Multiphasic Personality Inventory is a personality test for the assessment of psychopathology. The Thematic Apperception Test provides information on a client's perceptions and imagination, for use in the understanding of the subject's current needs, motives, emotions, and conflicts, both conscious and unconscious.

Question Assesses

Content Area II—Assessment and Intervention Planning; Assessment Methods and Techniques (Competency); Techniques and Instruments Used to Assess Clients/Client Systems (KSA)

29. **A.** Duty to warn has become an important mandate in social work. Generally, a social worker believes that a client is a danger to a third party and that the client is able to act on this danger in order for it to be considered necessary to warn and/or protect the intended victim. For example, if a client who is incarcerated and not going to be released makes a threat against someone outside the prison to whom the client does not have access, there is no imminent threat. A history of violence is not required for a social worker's duty to warn obligation. Duty to warn focuses on violence, not abuse.

Question Assesses

Content Area II—Assessment and Intervention Planning; Assessment Methods and Techniques (Competency); Risk Assessment Methods (KSA)

30. A social worker has been asked to evaluate client progress using a single-subject design. Which of the following designs has the greatest internal validity?

   A. AB
   B. ABAB
   C. BAB

31. The social worker learns from a client who is HIV positive that he is having unprotected sexual contact with his girlfriend who is unaware of his HIV status. In order to address this situation ethically, the social worker should:

   A. Tell the client that the social worker must contact the girlfriend in this situation due to the duty to warn obligation
   B. Locate the girlfriend, without informing the client to disclose the risk
   C. Make no attempt to contact the girlfriend to disclose the client's HIV status

32. A school social worker is using an intervention aimed at enhancing the social functioning of an adolescent student who is acting out. The social worker collects data daily prior to the intervention and during treatment. During the holiday break, the social worker asks the parents to write down the frequency of the behaviors each day in a journal. This journal is reviewed by the social worker upon return to school, at which time the intervention is restarted and the behavior is monitored. Which of the following single-subject designs is reflective of the social worker's intervention?

   A. AB
   B. ABA
   C. ABAB

33. Which of the following is associated with histrionic personality disorder?

   A. Flirtatious or sexually provocative behavior
   B. Suicidal or risk-taking behavior
   C. Feigning illness or malingering

(See answers next page.)

30. **B.** "A" stands for measures taken when treatment is not provided (such as during baseline) and "B" stands for measures taken when treatment is being delivered. Internal validity is the confidence that the treatment is the cause of changes in behavior seen. There are two opportunities using the ABAB design to see if the introduction of treatment coincides with changes in behavior. A baseline assessment process is desired in single-subject designs, unless the client is in crisis, which necessitates the immediate starting of treatment (BAB).

Question Assesses

Content Area II—Assessment and Intervention Planning; Assessment Methods and Techniques (Competency); Basic and Applied Research Design and Methods (KSA)

31. **C.** This situation does not fall under duty to warn. The allowance to breach confidentiality if a client poses an imminent risk to an identifiable party has not generally been applied to HIV-positive clients who are engaging in unprotected sexual activity. It is the responsibility of all sexually active adults to use "safe sex" procedures or use proper protective measures to reduce the risk of sexually transmitted conditions. Thus, if this client's girlfriend were using such measures, there would be no risk to her.

Question Assesses

Content Area II—Assessment and Intervention Planning; Assessment Methods and Techniques (Competency); Risk Assessment Methods (KSA)

32. **C.** The baseline is denoted by "A" and the intervention is denoted by "B." In the scenario, the social worker collected data prior to the onset of an intervention (AB). However, the holiday break represented a second baseline due to the interruption of treatment. It is an opportunity to see if the behavior changed once the intervention was removed. The intervention was then reinstituted upon the adolescent's return to school. This baseline and re-introduction of the intervention is also represented as an AB design. Thus, the social worker is using an ABAB design.

Question Assesses

Content Area II—Assessment and Intervention Planning; Assessment Methods and Techniques (Competency); Basic and Applied Research Design and Methods (KSA)

33. **A.** Histrionic personality disorder is a pervasive pattern of excessive emotionality and attention seeking. A client with this disorder interacts with others using inappropriate sexually seductive or provocative behavior, consistently uses physical appearance to garner attention, is highly suggestible or easily influenced by others or circumstances, and considers relationships to be more intimate than they actually are in real life.

Clients with this disorder may have difficulty achieving emotional intimacy in romantic relationships, as well as impaired relationships with friends, because of their sexually provocative behavior or their demands for constant attention.

Question Assesses

Content Area II—Assessment and Intervention Planning; Assessment Methods and Techniques (Competency); The Use of the *Diagnostic and Statistical Manual* of the American Psychiatric Association (KSA)

34. At which severity of autism spectrum disorder do individuals have noticeable difficulties with social interactions and communication?

    A. Severe
    B. Mild
    C. Moderate

35. When a social worker needs to conduct a functional assessment of a client, the *DSM* recommends using which of the following tools?

    A. World Health Organization Disability Assessment Schedule (WHODAS)
    B. Global Assessment of Functioning (GAF)
    C. Cultural Formulation Interview Guide (CFI)

36. Which of the following client emotional needs must be met during termination?

    A. Loss
    B. Hope
    C. Belonging

37. Which of the following accurately describes the relationship between expressive and receptive communication?

    A. Receptive communication usually develops at an earlier age than does expressive communication
    B. Expressive communication usually develops at an earlier age than does receptive communication
    C. Some young children develop receptive communication skills before developing expressive communication skills; for other children, it is the reverse

(*See answers next page.*)

34. **B.** Even with mild autism spectrum disorder, individuals have noticeable difficulties with social communication and interaction. However, they can still manage some level of interaction with others. The severity of the communication and socialization deficits increase in moderate and severe forms of the disorder.

Question Assesses

Content Area II—Assessment and Intervention Planning; Assessment Methods and Techniques (Competency); The Use of the *Diagnostic and Statistical Manual* of the American Psychiatric Association (KSA)

35. **A.** The WHODAS (World Health Organization Disability Assessment Schedule) is a tool developed by the World Health Organization (WHO) to assess and measure disability and functioning across various domains of life. It provides a standardized way to evaluate an individual's level of functioning, including their physical, mental, and social well-being. The WHODAS is used to assess the impact of health conditions, disabilities, and other factors on a person's ability to participate in daily activities and engage with their environment.

Question Assesses

Content Area II—Assessment and Intervention Planning; Assessment Methods and Techniques (Competency); The Use of the *Diagnostic and Statistical Manual* of the American Psychiatric Association (KSA)

36. **A.** During termination, there should be discussion of the emotional loss that may result from the ending of the therapeutic relationship. While hope and belonging are important emotional needs, they are not hallmarks of termination. Hope is often a focus at the beginning of the problem-solving process and belonging relates to the helping relationship that is more critical during the planned change effort.

Question Assesses

Content Area II—Assessment and Intervention Planning; Assessment Methods and Techniques (Competency); Discharge, Aftercare, and Follow-Up Planning (KSA)

37. **A.** Language is a system of using words to communicate. It has two parts: using words and gestures to say what is meant (expressive communication) and understanding what others say (receptive communication). Receptive communication develops earlier than does expressive communication. Infants start learning in the womb, where they hear and respond to familiar voices.

Question Assesses

Content Area II—Assessment and Intervention Planning; Assessment Methods and Techniques (Competency); Methods to Assess the Client's/Client System's Communication Skills (KSA)

38. A social worker can **BEST** help a resistant client in the precontemplation stage of change by:

    A. Examining the positives and negatives of behavior change

    B. Acknowledging a client's fears and concerns

    C. Identifying whether new developments in a client's life are causing barriers to change

39. Which **BEST** describes culturally specific ways in which individuals or communities express, experience, and communicate psychological distress or emotional suffering that must be considered when intervention planning?

    A. Cultural biases

    B. Cultural stratification

    C. Cultural concepts of distress

40. When clients are at high risk for relapse after discharge, which of the following is **MOST** important after termination?

    A. Ongoing assessments to determine whether services are needed

    B. Utilization of peer and agency supports

    C. Follow-up to monitor implementation of discharge plans

41. Which of the following components of a client contract is **MOST** critical for goal setting?

    A. Problem identification

    B. Insurance coverage

    C. Frequency of meetings

(See answers next page.)

38. **B.** Precontemplation is the first step in the change process. In precontemplation, a client is unaware, unable, and/or unwilling to change. This stage is characterized by a client arguing, interrupting, ignoring the problem, and/or avoiding talking or thinking about it. A social worker should establish a rapport, acknowledge resistance or ambivalence, try to engage a client, and recognize thoughts, feelings, fears, and concerns.

Question Assesses

Content Area II—Assessment and Intervention Planning; Assessment Methods and Techniques (Competency); Methods to Assess Motivation, Resistance, and Readiness to Change (KSA)

39. **C.** The *DSM* acknowledges that cultural factors play a significant role in shaping how mental health issues are understood and manifested across different cultural groups. Cultural concepts of distress refer to culturally specific ways in which individuals or communities express, experience, and communicate psychological distress or emotional suffering.

Question Assesses

Content Area II—Assessment and Intervention Planning; Intervention Planning (Competency); Cultural Considerations in the Creation of an Intervention Planning (KSA)

40. **C.** Clients who are at high risk for developing problems after services have ended should receive regular follow up to ensure that discharge plans are being implemented. Natural and peer supports may not be needed as the follow up may focus on psychopharmacological receipt. Also, assessment for service needs is not done typically as part of termination.

Question Assesses

Content Area II—Assessment and Intervention Planning; Intervention Planning (Competency); Discharge, Aftercare, and Follow-Up Planning (KSA)

41. **A.** The contract or service plan specifies problem(s) to be worked on, the goals to reduce the problem(s), a client's and a social worker's roles in the process, the interventions or techniques to be employed, the means of monitoring progress, stipulations for renegotiating the contract, and the time, place, fee, and frequency of meetings. All these elements depend on the diagnosis or problem. Some clients do not have insurance coverage.

Question Assesses

Content Area II—Assessment and Intervention Planning; Intervention Planning (Competency); The Components of Intervention, Treatment, and Service Plans (KSA)

Practice Questions Content Area II: Assessment and Intervention Planning (24%)					
Competency	Question Numbers	Number of Questions	Number Correct	Percentage Correct	Area Requiring Further Study?
1. Biopsychosocial History and Collateral Data	1, 2, 3, 4, 5, 6, 7, 8, 9, 10, 11, 12, 13, 14, 15	15	___/15	___%	
2. Assessment Methods and Techniques	16, 17, 18, 19, 20, 21, 22, 23, 24, 25, 26, 27, 28, 29, 30, 31, 32, 33, 34, 35, 36, 37, 38	23	___/23	___%	
3. Intervention Planning	39, 40, 41	3	___/3	___%	

Content Area III: Interventions With Clients/Client Systems (24%)

7 Intervention Processes and Techniques for Use Across Systems

THE PRINCIPLES AND TECHNIQUES OF INTERVIEWING (E.G., SUPPORTING, CLARIFYING, FOCUSING, CONFRONTING, VALIDATING, FEEDBACK, REFLECTING LANGUAGE DIFFERENCES, USE OF INTERPRETERS, REDIRECTING)

In social work, an interview is always purposeful and involves verbal and nonverbal communication between a social worker and client, during which ideas, attitudes, and feelings are exchanged. The actions of a social worker aim to gather important information and keep a client focused on the achievement of the goal.

A social work interview is designed to serve the interest of a client; therefore, the actions of a social worker during the interview must be planned and focused. Questions in a social work interview should be tailored to the specifics of a client, not generic, "one size fits all" inquiries. The focus is on the uniqueness of a client and the client's unique situation.

The purpose of the social work interview can be informational, diagnostic, or therapeutic. The same interview may serve more than one purpose.

Communication during a social work interview is interactive and interrelational. A social worker's questions will result in specific responses by a client that, in turn, lead to other inquiries. The message is formulated by a client, encoded, transmitted, received, processed, and decoded. The importance of words and messages may be implicit (implied) or explicit (evident). *A social worker should listen, being nonjudgmental, throughout a social work interview.*

There are a number of techniques that a social worker may use during an interview to assist clients.

- *Clarification*—reformulate problem in a client's words to make sure that the social worker is on the same wavelength
- *Confrontation*—calling attention to something
- *Interpretation*—pulling together patterns of behavior to get a new understanding
- *Reframing and relabeling*—stating problem in a different way so a client can see possible solutions

- *Summarization*—identifying key ideas and themes regarding client problems to provide focus and continuity to an interview
- *Universalization*—the generalization or normalization of behavior

Social workers must be proficient in the languages spoken by clients or use qualified interpreters. *It is not appropriate to use family members to interpret or provide services in which social workers are not linguistically competent as valuable information may be missed during social work interviews.* When working with interpreters, social workers should face clients and speak directly to them—not the interpreters. Social workers also should not ask for the opinions of the interpreters or have conversations with them as their focus must be on clients.

THE PHASES OF INTERVENTION AND TREATMENT

Social work aims to assist with making change on the micro, mezzo, or macro levels to enhance well-being. Despite the level of intervention, the steps that a social worker takes are similar.

Step 1	Engagement with client, group, or community
Step 2	Assessment of strengths and needs to be used in the intervention process
Step 3	Planning or design of intervention to address problem
Step 4	Intervention aimed at making change
Step 5	Evaluation of efforts
Step 6	Termination and anticipation of future needs

Usually change does not occur easily and there are stages of change that occur. Understanding these stages can help achieve goals.

Precontemplation	Denial, ignorance of the problem
Contemplation	Ambivalence, conflicted emotion
Preparation	Experimenting with small changes, collecting information about change
Action	Taking direct action toward achieving a goal
Maintenance	Maintaining a new behavior, avoiding temptation
Relapse	Feelings of frustration and failure

In order for real change to occur, all intervention steps must occur and change must be understood in these sequential stages.

PROBLEM-SOLVING MODELS AND APPROACHES (E.G., BRIEF, SOLUTION-FOCUSED METHODS OR TECHNIQUES)

The problem-solving approach is based on the belief that an inability to cope with a problem is due to some lack of motivation, capacity, or opportunity to solve problems in an appropriate way. Clients' problem-solving capacities or resources are maladaptive or impaired.

The goal of the problem-solving process is to enhance client mental, emotional, and action capacities for coping with problems and/or making accessible the opportunities and resources necessary to generate solutions to problems.

A social worker engages in the problem-solving process via the following steps:

1. Engaging
2. Assessing (includes a focus on client strengths and not just weaknesses)
3. Planning
4. Intervening
5. Evaluating
6. Terminating

Short-Term Interventions

The growing need for time-limited treatment, fueled by the widening influence of managed care in the behavioral health field, has produced a renewed focus on short-term therapy. Short-term interventions vary greatly in their duration.

Research has suggested that a social worker's and client's views on the time of treatment are more important than the duration of treatment itself. Sometimes these approaches are used because of organizational or financial constraints. In other instances, clients are choosing them over open-ended approaches. Although some have been wary of the effectiveness of these techniques to instill long-lasting change, they are being used more broadly than ever before. Some short-term interventions include a crisis intervention model and a cognitive behavioral model.

Although psychoanalysis is often thought of as long term, this was not the case with Freud's early work, and psychoanalysis did not start out this way. A number of short-term psychodynamic approaches focus on the belief that childhood experiences are the root of adult dysfunction.

METHODS TO ENGAGE AND MOTIVATE CLIENTS/CLIENT SYSTEMS

A motivational approach aims to help clients realize what needs to change and to get them to talk about their daily lives, as well as their satisfaction with current situations. Social workers want to create doubt that everything is "OK" and help clients recognize consequences of current behaviors or conditions that contribute to dissatisfaction.

It is much easier if clients believe goals can be achieved and life can be different. Sometimes clients are incapacitated by conditions that need to be addressed first (i.e., depression). Social workers can help clients think of a time when things were better or create a picture of what their lives could look like with fewer stresses.

The role of a social worker is to create an atmosphere that is conducive to change and to increase a client's intrinsic motivation, so that change arises from within rather than being imposed from without.

Motivation is a state of readiness or eagerness to change, which may fluctuate from one time or situation to another.

Some additional techniques include:

- Clearly identifying the problem or risk area
- Explaining why change is important
- Advocating for specific change
- Identifying barriers and working to remove them
- Finding the best course of action
- Setting goals
- Taking steps toward change
- Preventing relapse

Empathy is a factor that increases motivation, lowers resistance, and fosters greater long-term behavioral change.

METHODS TO ENGAGE AND WORK WITH INVOLUNTARY CLIENTS/CLIENT SYSTEMS

Social workers often find themselves providing services to those who did not choose to receive them, but instead have to do so as mandated by law, including families in the child protection system, people in the criminal justice system, and so on. Working with involuntary clients can be challenging because they may want to have no contact or may only participate because they feel that they have no other choice.

Often these situations require social workers to receive peer support or supervision to process struggles encountered, as well as reassert their professionalism, because clients may try to test and exhibit anger at social workers, who represent the mandates placed upon them.

Some methods that can be helpful in working with involuntary clients include:

- Acknowledging clients' circumstances and understanding how they came about given clients' histories
- Listening to clients' experiences in order to try to understand how they feel about intervention
- Engaging in clear communication because involuntary clients struggle to understand what is happening to them
- Making clear what the purpose of the intervention is, what clients have control over and what they do not, what is going to happen next, and what the likely consequences will be if they do not participate
- Assisting at an appropriate pace as progress may be slow
- Building trust, even on the smallest scale, by consistently being honest and up-front about the situation and why a social worker is involved
- Giving clients practical assistance when needed to help them fight for their rights
- Paying attention to what is positive in clients' behavior and celebrating achievements
- Showing empathy and viewing clients as more than the problems that brought them into services

METHODS TO OBTAIN AND PROVIDE FEEDBACK

Social workers interface with professionals and others in order to achieve the best possible outcomes for clients. Feedback is essential in order to learn what works and what can be done better.

There is no single method for social workers to seek feedback. Many factors may impact on how such feedback is solicited and incorporated into practice. However, there are some important principles that social workers should adhere to when obtaining or providing feedback.

1. Feedback may be either verbal or nonverbal, so social workers must make efforts to see what clients are trying to convey verbally or via their behavior and nonverbal cues in order to see whether interventions should be altered.

2. When social workers involve consultants or others in the feedback process related to client care, clients should provide consent.

3. Social workers should ask for feedback in difficult circumstances—not just when circumstances appear neutral or positive. It can be tempting only to ask for feedback from people who will say something positive. Sometimes the best learning can be from those who will be critical. Talking through difficult feedback in supervision is important.

4. Feedback is especially critical at key decision points (such as when transferring or terminating with clients).

5. It is important to guard against influencing people to respond in a particular way; this influence may be unintentional, because a social worker may have more influence or power than the individual from whom feedback is sought.

6. Confidentiality should be respected if the informant wants it.

7. Always be clear about why feedback is needed and what will be done with the information.

8. Documentation of feedback is essential.

9. Be aware that the feedback may be very different depending upon when it is solicited. It is critical to realize how recent events may have influenced information received. Getting feedback repeatedly at several different times may be needed to see if responses differ.

10. A social worker must make sure that the communication method is appropriate. For a younger person, texting, email, or an online questionnaire may work, whereas a face-to-face conversation may be needed for others. The language should be jargon free and issues such as language, culture, and disability may affect the ways in which people both understand and react to requests for feedback. A social worker may want to use close-ended questions and/or open ones to capture needed data.

There are varied methods for feedback. It can be formal or informal, mutual or one-way, written or verbal, personal or impersonal, and/or requested or unsolicited. Feedback can even be anonymous.

The following are some common feedback methods.

One-on-One Feedback

An individual delivering feedback to another, face-to-face, is probably the most common form. Such feedback needs to be delivered sensitively and according to the principles of the profession.

Intragroup Feedback

Individuals in a group provide feedback to the group and/or to one or more individuals within the group. If the feedback is directed to the performance of the group, it can be particularly effective.

Group-to-Group Feedback

This might take place between two groups that are working together. The feedback may go in one direction or both. The feedback might be directed at particular individuals or at the group as a whole.

Consultative Feedback

An individual or group serves as a formal or informal consultant to another (usually to a group, but occasionally to an individual). The individual or group receiving the feedback may be more apt to accept and consider the feedback, given the expertise of the consultative entity, but has no obligation to do so.

360° Feedback

This method involves feedback from all directions—supervisors, peers, subordinates, the community, and so forth. The idea is that the feedback reflects multiple viewpoints and gives a complete picture.

All models of feedback in social work practice should be supportive, use a strengths perspective (emphasizing the positives), not "attack," and focus on actions needed for change.

THE PRINCIPLES OF ACTIVE LISTENING AND OBSERVATION

Active listening skills are an essential part of building relationships and trust. The active part in the listening process can be achieved by showing interest in clients' words. Once clients notice that social workers are understanding what is said and really taking an interest, communication will be more open.

Active listening establishes trust and respect, so clients will feel comfortable confiding in social workers. Thus, it helps build a therapeutic alliance.

Active listening can also include speaking by using mirroring techniques to paraphrase and reflect back to clients what they have just said. For example, a client may say, "I hate my job and my boss yells at me all the time." An active listening response might involve saying something such as, "So you feel like your boss doesn't appreciate you or treat you with respect."

Responses need to be tailored to what clients are saying to demonstrate listening and engagement in what is being said.

Although most information that a social worker uses during assessment comes from the social work interview, direct observation of interactions between family members and the client's nonverbal behavior can produce a lot of information about emotional states and interaction patterns.

Social workers also may use observation as part of macro-level intervention in order to assess the extent of a problem/issue, driving and restraining forces for change, key policy influencers, and community members who can work as part of a task group for reform.

When functioning as an observer, a social worker can take many roles, including *complete participant* (living the experience as a participant), *participant as observer* (interacting with those who are participating), *observer as participant* (limited relationship with others participating—primarily observer), or *complete observer* (removed from activity—observer only). Observation is also a method used in scientific inquiry to collect data.

VERBAL AND NONVERBAL COMMUNICATION TECHNIQUES

In order to facilitate change through the problem-solving process, a social worker must use various verbal and nonverbal communication techniques to assist clients to understand their behavior and feelings. In addition, to ensure clients are honest and forthcoming during this process, social workers must build trusting relationships with clients. These relationships develop through effective verbal and nonverbal communication. Social workers must be adept at using both forms of communication successfully, as well as understanding them, because verbal and nonverbal cues will be used by clients throughout the problem-solving process. Insight into their meaning will produce a higher degree of sensitivity to clients' experiences and a deeper understanding of their problems.

There are many verbal and nonverbal communication methods, including:

- **Active listening**, in which social workers are sitting up straight and leaning toward clients in a relaxed and open manner. Attentive listening can involve commenting on clients' statements, asking open-ended questions, and making statements that show listening is occurring.

- **Silence** by social workers, which can show acceptance of clients' feelings and promotes introspection or time to think about what has been learned (*very effective when used with a client who is displaying a high degree of emotion*).

- **Questioning** using open- and closed-ended formats to get relevant information in a nonjudgmental manner.

- **Reflecting** or **validating** to show empathetic understanding of clients' problems. These techniques can also assist clients in understanding negative thought patterns.

- **Paraphrasing** and **clarifying** by social workers to rephrase what clients are saying in order to join together information. Clarification uses questioning, paraphrasing, and restating to ensure full understanding of clients' ideas and thoughts.

- **Reframing** by social workers shows clients that there are different perspectives and ideas that can help to change negative thinking patterns and promote change.
- Exhibiting desirable **facial expressions**, which include direct eye contact if culturally appropriate, warmth and concern reflected, and varied facial expressions.
- Using desirable **postures or gestures**, which include appropriate arm movements and attentive gestures.

There are many methods that social workers use to facilitate communication with clients. Central to the formation of a therapeutic alliance is displaying empathy. Empathy is distinguished from sympathy as the latter denotes pity or feeling bad for a client, whereas the former means that a social worker understands the ideas expressed, as well as the feelings of a client. To be empathetic, a social worker must accurately perceive a client's situation, perspective, and feelings, as well as communicate this understanding in a helpful (therapeutic) way.

A social worker should also display *genuineness* in order to build trust. Genuineness is needed in order to establish a therapeutic relationship. It involves listening to and communicating with clients without distorting their messages, as well as being clear and concrete in communications.

Another method is the use of *positive regard*, which is the ability to view a client as being worthy of caring about and as someone who has strengths and achievement potential. It is built on respect and is usually communicated nonverbally.

Communication is also facilitated by *listening, attending, suspending value judgments*, and *helping* clients develop their own resources. A social worker should always use culturally appropriate communication.

It is also essential to clearly establish *boundaries* with clients to facilitate a safe environment for change.

THE CONCEPT OF CONGRUENCE IN COMMUNICATION

Communication can be verbal and nonverbal, so an assessment of clients' communication skills must involve both. Role playing is a good way to assess and enhance clients' communication skills. It also allows a social worker to see if there is congruence between nonverbal and verbal communication.

Congruence is the matching of awareness and experience with communication. It is essential that a client is able to communicate freely and that this communication is reflective of the client's feelings. *Congruence is essential for the vitality of a relationship and to facilitate true helping as part of the problem-solving process.*

LIMIT-SETTING TECHNIQUES

Clients of all ages are frequently desperate for an environment with consistent boundaries. For this reason, it is helpful if social workers can learn limit-setting skills. Limit setting is facilitative as clients do not feel safe or accepted in a completely permissive environment.

In addition, although compassion is important for a social worker, it is important to maintain a client–social worker relationship. Understanding boundaries and being able to maintain those boundaries with clients are essential.

THE TECHNIQUE OF ROLE PLAY

Role playing is a teaching strategy that offers several advantages. Role playing in social work practice may be seen between supervisor and supervisee or social worker and client.

In all instances, role playing usually raises interest in a topic as clients are not passive recipients in the learning process. In addition, role playing teaches empathy and understanding of different perspectives as clients take on the role of another, learning and acting as that individual would in the specified setting. In role playing, participation helps embed concepts. Role playing gives clarity to information that may be abstract or difficult to understand.

The use of role playing emphasizes personal concerns, problems, behavior, and active participation. It improves interpersonal and communication skills, and enhances communication.

Role playing activities can be divided into four stages:

1. Preparation and explanation of the activity

2. Preparation of the activity

3. Role playing

4. Discussion or debriefing after the role play activity

ROLE-MODELING TECHNIQUES

Role modeling emphasizes the importance of learning from observing and imitating and has been used successfully in helping clients acquire new skills, including those associated with assertiveness.

Role modeling works well when it is combined with role play and reinforcement to produce lasting change.

There are different types of modeling, including live modeling, symbolic modeling, participant modeling, or covert modeling.

Live modeling refers to watching a real person perform the desired behavior.

Symbolic modeling includes filmed or videotaped models demonstrating the desired behavior. Self-modeling is another form of symbolic modeling in which clients are videotaped performing the target behavior.

In *participant modeling*, an individual models anxiety-evoking behaviors for a client and then prompts the client to engage in the behavior.

In *covert modeling*, clients are asked to use their imagination, visualizing a particular behavior as another describes the imaginary situation in detail.

Models in any of these forms may be presented as either a coping or a mastery model. The coping model is shown as initially fearful or incompetent, and then is shown as gradually becoming comfortable and competent performing the feared behavior. The mastery model shows no fear and is competent from the beginning of the demonstration.

TECHNIQUES FOR HARM REDUCTION FOR SELF AND OTHERS

A harm reduction approach refers to any program, policy, or intervention that seeks to reduce or minimize the adverse health and social consequences associated with an illness, condition, and/or behavior, such as substance use, without requiring a client to practice abstinence, discontinue use, or completely extinguish the behavior. This definition recognizes that many clients are unwilling or unable to abstain from behaviors or use at any given time and that there is a need to provide them with options that minimize the harm caused by their condition to themselves, to others, and to the community.

Harm reduction complements prevention approaches because it is based on the acceptance that, despite best efforts, clients will engage in behaviors such as substance use, and are unable or unwilling to stop using substances at any given time.

In addition, clients who use substances may prefer to use informal and nonclinical methods to reduce their consumption or reduce the risks associated with use. Harm reduction is practical, feasible, effective, safe, and cost-effective. Most harm reduction approaches are inexpensive, easy to implement, and have a high impact on individual and community health.

Harm reduction acknowledges the significance of ANY positive change that clients make in their lives; these interventions are designed to "meet clients where they are" currently.

Harm reduction recognizes that intervention can be seen as a continuum with the more feasible options at one end and less feasible, but desirable, ones at the other end. Though desirable, abstinence can be considered difficult to achieve. Thus, social workers should partner with clients to identify actions that can be taken to minimize impacts of their illnesses, conditions, and/or behaviors.

METHODS TO TEACH COPING AND OTHER SELF-CARE SKILLS TO CLIENTS/ CLIENT SYSTEMS

Social workers assist clients in realizing how their lives can improve and/or how they can learn from mistakes that they have made. The techniques that social workers employ are a form of informal or didactic teaching.

For example, social workers may help clients see:

- How their histories have shaped them
- Needs associated with medical and/or behavioral health conditions
- Developmental issues related to various phases across the lifespan
- The workings of systems in which they operate
- Ways of coping in various situations

A social worker must use the problem-solving process to teach clients skills needed to make changes in their lives.

In addition, social workers may collaborate with or inform clients of colleagues who may also assist with more formal teaching, such as learning to read, obtaining a driver's license, and so on.

CLIENT/CLIENT SYSTEM SELF-MONITORING TECHNIQUES

Clients are encouraged to pay attention to any subtle shift in feelings. Clients frequently keep thought or emotion logs that include three components: (a) disturbing emotional states, (b) the exact behaviors engaged in at the time of the emotional states, and (c) thoughts that occurred when the emotions emerged. In cognitive behavioral therapy, homework is often done between sessions to record these encounters. This homework involves client self-monitoring, which is central to this approach.

METHODS OF CONFLICT RESOLUTION

Management of conflict entails four steps:

1. The recognition of an existing or potential conflict
2. An assessment of the conflict situation
3. The selection of an appropriate strategy
4. Intervention

When previous attempts to resolve a conflict have only escalated the conflict, a useful technique is to structure the interactions between the parties. Structuring techniques include:

1. Decreasing the amount of contact between the parties in the early stages of conflict resolution
2. Decreasing the amount of time between problem-solving sessions
3. Decreasing the formality of problem-solving sessions
4. Limiting the scope of the issues that can be discussed
5. Using a third-party mediator

CRISIS INTERVENTION AND TREATMENT APPROACHES

A state of crisis is time limited. Brief intervention during a crisis usually provides maximum therapeutic effect. Crisis intervention is a process of actively influencing the psychosocial functioning of clients during a period of disequilibrium or crisis. *A crisis does not need to be precipitated by a major life event.* The goals are to alleviate stress and mobilize coping skills, psychological capabilities, and social resources.

The goals of crisis intervention are to (a) relieve the impact of stress with emotional and social resources, (b) return a client to a previous level of functioning (regain equilibrium), (c) help strengthen coping mechanisms during the crisis period, and (d) develop adaptive coping strategies.

Crisis intervention focuses on the here and now, is time limited (most crises last from 4 to 6 weeks), is directive, and requires high levels of activity and involvement from a social worker. A social worker sets specific goals and tasks in order to increase a client's sense of mastery and control.

METHODS AND APPROACHES TO TRAUMA-INFORMED CARE

A good trauma-informed approach is multidimensional. The following list includes several elements that indicate a good, trauma-informed program:

Environment of Care

- Soothing colors for decor and paint
- Overall quiet; soft music
- Neutral or pleasant aroma
- Individual chairs with discrete seating areas
- Individual bathroom options

Staff Appearance

- Attire connotes professionalism; easy to identify staff members
- Clothing not sexually provocative

Staff Behavior

- Clearly demonstrate proper manners and respect
- Make every effort to minimize delays
- Speak in clear, nonthreatening tones
- Make eye contact
- Smile and demonstrate a generally pleasant demeanor
- Open physical stance, nodding
- Open to change/not rigid

Organizational Understanding

- Trauma policy/philosophy in place
- Commitment to trauma-informed care articulated
- All staff/clients/family members taught about trauma and its impact
- Universal trauma screenings for all clients
- Trauma status continually assessed
- Clear organization plan for dealing with behavioral crises
- Discrete areas for calming or crisis management identified
- Feedback valued and concerted outreach efforts made

Treatment Considerations

- Treatment goals reflect consumer preferences
- Treatment integrated across disciplines
- Offering choice of treatment provider when possible
- Everyday language used
- All statements of abuse acknowledged and addressed
- Sensitivity to seating configuration and proximity of seating options
- Co-occurring treatment needs assessed and incorporated into service provided
- Culture of origin respected and incorporated into service planning
- Recognize the importance of physical boundaries and aware that touch—sometimes even a handshake—could trigger trauma
- Avoid jokes and stories that can serve as triggers

ANGER MANAGEMENT TECHNIQUES

Although everyone gets angry, clients may come to social workers because they are not able to control their anger, causing problems. Anger can also increase risk for developing physical health problems, such as heart disease, stress-related illnesses, insomnia, digestive issues, and/or headaches.

Social workers can assist clients to develop action or treatment plans to change these behaviors. Techniques for assisting clients can include one or more of the following.

Relaxation Exercises

- Deep breathing
- Meditation or repeating calming words/phrases
- Guided imagery
- Yoga
- Stretching or physical exercise

Assisting clients to practice these techniques regularly will result in using them automatically in tense situations.

Cognitive Techniques

- Replacing destructive thoughts, such as "This is the end of the world" with healthy ones like "This is frustrating, but it will pass"
- Focusing on goals as a way of finding solutions to problems

■ Using logic to get a more balanced perspective

■ Not using an "all or nothing" approach

■ Putting situations into perspective

Communication Skills

■ Slowing down speech to avoid saying something not meant or that one will regret

■ Listening to what others are saying

■ Thinking about what to say before speaking

■ Avoiding defensiveness

■ Using humor to lighten the situation

Environmental Change

■ Walking away or leaving situation

■ Avoiding people or situations in the future that evoke anger

■ Not starting conversations or entering situations that may cause anger when tired or rushed

STRESS MANAGEMENT TECHNIQUES

Stress is a psychological and/or physical reaction to life events, with most people experiencing it regularly in their own lives. When a life event is seen as a threat, it signals the release of hormones aimed at generating a response. This process has been labeled the "fight-or-flight" response.

Once the threat is gone, clients should return to typical relaxed states, but this may not happen if other threats are presented immediately thereafter. Thus, stress management is important because it provides tools to deal with threats and minimize the impacts of psychological and/or physical reactions.

The first step in stress management is for clients to monitor their stress levels and identify their stress triggers. These can be major life events, but also those associated with day-to-day life, such as job pressures, relationship problems, or financial difficulties. Positive life events, such as getting a job promotion, getting married, or having children, also can be stressful.

The second step in stress management is to assist clients in identifying what aspects of a situation they can control. Clients can make these changes, as well as benefit from stress-reduction techniques, such as deep breathing, exercise, massage, tai chi, or yoga, to manage those aspects of a situation that cannot be altered. Maintaining a healthy lifestyle is essential to helping manage stress.

Stress will always be a part of life, but assisting clients to manage it can increase their ability to cope with challenges and enhance their psychological and/or physical well-being.

COGNITIVE AND BEHAVIORAL INTERVENTIONS

Cognitive behavioral therapy (CBT) is a hands-on, practical approach to problem solving. Its goal is to change patterns of thinking or behavior that are responsible for clients' difficulties, and so change the way they feel. CBT works by changing clients' attitudes and their behavior by focusing on the thoughts, images, beliefs, and attitudes that are held (cognitive processes) and how this relates to behavior, as a way of dealing with emotional problems.

CBT can be thought of as a combination of psychotherapy and behavioral therapy. Psychotherapy emphasizes the importance of the personal meaning placed on things and how thinking patterns begin in childhood. Behavioral therapy pays close attention to the relationship between problems, behaviors, and thoughts.

This approach is active, collaborative, structured, time limited, goal oriented, and problem focused. This approach lends itself to the requirements posed by managed care companies, including brief treatment, well-delineated techniques, goal and problem oriented, and empirically supported evidence of its effectiveness.

Steps in Cognitive Restructuring

Assist clients in:

1. Accepting that their self-statements, assumptions, and beliefs determine or govern their emotional reaction to life's events
2. Identifying dysfunctional beliefs and patterns of thoughts that underlie their problems
3. Identifying situations that evoke dysfunctional cognitions
4. Substituting functional self-statements in place of self-defeating thoughts
5. Rewarding themselves for successful coping efforts

Foundational to this treatment is client self-monitoring. Clients are encouraged to pay attention to any subtle shift in feelings. Clients frequently keep thought or emotion logs that include three components: (a) disturbing emotional states, (b) the exact behaviors engaged in at the time of the emotional states, and (c) thoughts that occurred when the emotions emerged. Homework is often done between sessions to record these encounters.

STRENGTHS-BASED AND EMPOWERMENT STRATEGIES AND INTERVENTIONS

The primary mission of the social work profession is to enhance human well-being and help meet the basic human needs of all people, with particular attention to the needs and empowerment of people who are vulnerable, oppressed, and living in poverty (*NASW Code of Ethics—Preamble*).

Empowerment aims to ensure a sense of control over well-being and that change is possible. A social worker can help to empower individuals, groups, communities, and institutions.

On an individual level, social workers can engage in a process with a client aimed at strengthening self-worth by making a change in life that is based on personal desires (self-determination).

To facilitate empowerment, a social worker should:

- Establish a relationship aimed at meeting a client's needs and wishes such as access to social services and benefits or to other sources of information.

- Educate a client to improve skills, thereby increasing the ability for self-help.

- Help a client to secure resources, such as those from other organizations or agencies, as well as natural support networks, to meet needs.

- Unite a client with others who are experiencing the same issues when needed to enable social and political action.

Social workers should also use an empowerment process with groups, communities, and institutions so they may gain or regain the capacity to meet human needs, enhance overall well-being and potential, and provide individuals control over their lives to the extent possible.

A social worker needs many skills that focus on the activation of resources, the creation of alliances, and the expansion of opportunities in order to facilitate empowerment.

CLIENT/CLIENT SYSTEM CONTRACTING AND GOAL-SETTING TECHNIQUES

A social worker and client work together to develop a contract (intervention or service plan), including an agreement on its implementation or the activities used to help a client attain identified goals. Modification of the contract may be required as new information about a client's situation emerges and/or as the situation changes.

When clients seek to attain their goals, changes may need to be made to themselves, groups, families, and/or systems in the larger environment. This choice of targets is an even more complex issue than it first appears because the process of changing one system may bring about changes in others.

Change Strategies

- *Modify systems:* The decision to help a client on a one-to-one basis or in the context of a larger system must take into consideration a client's preferences and previous experiences, as well as the degree to which a client's problem is a response to forces within the larger system and whether change can be readily attained by a change in the larger system.

- *Modify individual thoughts:* A social worker may teach how to problem solve, alter self-concepts by modifying self-defeating statements, and/or make interpretations to increase a client's understanding about the relationship between events in the client's life.

- *Modify individual actions:* A social worker may use behavior modification techniques, such as reinforcement, punishment, modeling, role playing, and/or task assignments. *Modeling and role modeling are very effective methods for teaching. They should be used whenever possible.*

- Thoughts can be modified by *feedback from others* and behaviors can be modified through the *actions of others* in a system (by altering reinforcements).

- A social worker can also *advocate* for a client and seek to secure a change in a system on the client's behalf.

- A social worker can be a *mediator* by helping a client and another individual or system to negotiate with each other so that each may attain their respective goals.

PARTIALIZING TECHNIQUES

During the problem-solving process, a social worker may need to assist a client to break down problems or goals into less overwhelming and more manageable components. This is known as partialization and aims to break complex issues into simpler ones.

Partialization is useful because it may assist a social worker and a client to identify the goals that are easier to achieve first, enabling a client to see results more quickly and gain some success in making harder changes. Partialization can also help individuals to order the problems or goals that need more immediate help from those that can be addressed later. A social worker can use Maslow's hierarchy of needs as one tool to assist in making decisions about more pressing needs. In addition, a client should be asked to prioritize concerns or goals.

ASSERTIVENESS TRAINING

Assertiveness training is when procedures are used to teach clients how to express their positive and negative feelings and to stand up for their rights in ways that will not alienate others.

Assertiveness training typically begins with clients thinking about areas in their life in which they have difficulty asserting themselves. The next stage usually involves role plays designed to help clients practice clearer and more direct forms of communicating with others. Feedback is provided to improve responses, and the role play is repeated. Clients are asked to practice assertive techniques in everyday life.

Assertiveness training promotes the use of "I" statements as a way to help clients express their feelings. "I" statements tell others how their actions may cause clients to be upset, but are in contrast with "you" statements, which are often seen as blaming or aggressive.

Learning specific techniques and perspectives, such as self-observation skills, awareness of personal preferences, and assuming personal responsibility, are important components of the assertiveness training process.

TASK-CENTERED APPROACHES

A task-centered approach aims to quickly engage clients in the problem-solving process and to maximize their responsibility for treatment outcomes. In this modality, the duration of treatment is usually limited due to setting constraints, limitations imposed by third-party payers, or other reasons. Thus, at the outset, the expectation is that interventions from learning theory and behavior modification will be used to promote completion of a well-defined task to produce measurable outcomes. The focus is on the "here and now." This type of practice is often preferred by clients, as they are able to see more immediate results.

The problem is partialized into clearly delineated tasks to be addressed consecutively (assessment leads to goals, which lead to tasks). A client must be able to identify a precise psychosocial problem and a solution confined to a specific change in behavior or a change of circumstances. A client must also be willing to work on the problem. It is essential that a social worker and client establish a strong working relationship quickly. A social worker's therapeutic style must be highly active, empathic, and sometimes directive in this approach.

Assessment focuses on helping a client identify the primary problem and explore the circumstances surrounding the problem. Specific tasks are expected to evolve from this process. Consideration is given to how a client would ideally like to see the problem resolved. Termination, in this modality, begins almost immediately upon the onset of treatment.

PSYCHOEDUCATION METHODS (E.G., ACKNOWLEDGING, SUPPORTING, NORMALIZING)

One of the ways that social workers provide information to clients is through psychoeducation. This model allows a social worker to provide clients with information necessary to make informed decisions that will allow them to reach their respective goals. In addition to focusing on clients' education, it also provides support and coping skills development.

Psychoeducation is delivered in many service settings and with many types of client populations. It is provided to those who are experiencing some sort of issue or problem with the rationale that, with a clear understanding of the problem, as well as self-knowledge of strengths, community resources, and coping skills, clients are better equipped to deal with problems and to contribute to their emotional well-being.

The core psychoeducational principle is that education has a role in emotional and behavioral change. With an improved understanding of the causes and effects of problems, psychoeducation broadens clients' perception and interpretation of them, positively influencing clients' emotions and behavior. In other words, clients feel less helpless about the situation and more in control of themselves.

GROUP WORK TECHNIQUES AND APPROACHES (E.G., DEVELOPING AND MANAGING GROUP PROCESSES AND COHESION)

Group work is a method of working with two or more people for personal growth, the enhancement of social functioning, and/or for the achievement of socially desirable goals.

Social workers use their knowledge of group organization and functioning to affect the performance and adjustment of individuals. Individuals remain the focus of concern and the group is the vehicle of growth and change. *When individual problems arise, group members should be directed to the group for possible solutions as the group is the agent of change. Social workers must remind group members that confidentiality cannot be guaranteed—though seeing an agreement among group members concerning the preserving the confidentiality of information shared should be an initial goal of any group process.*

Contraindications for group: *client* who is *in crisis; suicidal;* compulsively needy for attention; actively psychotic; and/or paranoid

There are different kinds of groups.

Open Versus Closed

Open groups are those in which new members can join at any time. Closed groups are those in which all members begin the group at the same time.

Short-Term Versus Long-Term

Some groups have a very short duration, whereas others meet for a longer duration.

A social worker takes on different roles throughout the group process, which has a beginning, middle, and end.

Beginning

A social worker identifies the purpose of the group and the social worker's role. This stage is characterized as a time to convene, to organize, and to set a plan. Members are likely to remain distant or removed until they have had time to develop relationships.

Middle

Almost all of the group's work will occur during this stage. Relationships are strengthened as a group so that the tasks can be worked on. Group leaders are usually less involved.

End

The group reviews its accomplishments. Feelings associated with the termination of the group are addressed.

FAMILY THERAPY MODELS, INTERVENTIONS, AND APPROACHES

Working with families has always been central to social work practice. Family interventions require treating not just an individual but all those within a family unit, with the focus of assessment and intervention directed at the interaction of family members.

In order to work effectively with families, social workers must:

1. Understand the development of, as well as the historical, conceptual, and contextual issues influencing, family functioning.
2. Have awareness of the impact of diversity in working with families, particularly race, class, culture, ethnicity, gender, sexual preference, aging, and disabilities.
3. Understand the impact of a social worker's family of origin, current family structure, and its influence on a social worker's interventions with families.
4. Be aware of the needs of families experiencing unique family problems (domestic violence, blended families, trauma and loss, adoptive families, etc.).

Social workers use a variety of techniques to work with families. Family therapy treats the family as a unified whole—a system of interacting parts in which change in any part affects the functioning of the overall system. The family is the unit of attention for diagnosis and treatment. Social roles and interpersonal interaction are the focus of treatment. Real behaviors and communication that affect current life situations are addressed. The goal is to interrupt the circular pattern of pathological communication and behaviors and replace it with a new pattern that will sustain itself without the dysfunctional aspects of the original pattern.

Key clinical issues include:

- Establishing a contract with the family
- Examining alliances within the family
- Identifying where power resides
- Determining the relationship of each family member to the problem
- Seeing how the family relates to the outside world
- Assessing influence of family history on current family interactions
- Ascertaining communication patterns
- Identifying family rules that regulate patterns of interaction
- Determining meaning of presenting symptom in maintaining family homeostasis
- Examining flexibility of structure and accessibility of alternative action patterns
- Finding out about sources of external stress and support

The following are some types of family therapy.

Strategic Family Therapy

In strategic family therapy, a social worker initiates what happens during therapy, designs a specific approach for each person's presenting problem, and takes responsibility for directly influencing people.

It has roots in structural family therapy and is built on communication theory.

It is active, brief, directive, and task-centered. Strategic family therapy is more interested in creating change in behavior than change in understanding.

Strategic family therapy is based on the assumption that families are flexible enough to modify solutions that do not work and adjust or develop. There is the assumption that all problems have multiple origins; a presenting problem is viewed as a symptom of and a response to current dysfunction in family interactions.

Therapy focuses on problem resolution by altering the feedback cycle or loop that maintains the symptomatic behavior. The social worker's task is to formulate the problem in solvable, behavioral terms and to design an intervention plan to change the dysfunctional family pattern.

Concepts/Techniques

- Pretend technique—encourage family members to "pretend" and encourage voluntary control of behavior
- First-order changes—superficial behavioral changes within a system that do not change the structure of the system

- Second-order changes—changes to the systematic interaction pattern so the system is reorganized and functions more effectively

- Family homeostasis—families tend to preserve familiar organization and communication patterns; resistant to change

- Relabeling—changing the label attached to a person or problem from negative to positive so the situation can be perceived differently; it is hoped that new responses will evolve

- Paradoxical directive or instruction—prescribe the symptomatic behavior so a client realizes control over it; uses the strength of the resistance to change in order to move a client toward goals

Structural Family Therapy

This approach stresses the importance of family organization for the functioning of the group and the well-being of its members. A social worker "joins" (engages) the family in an effort to restructure it. Family structure is defined as the invisible set of functional demands organizing interaction among family members. Boundaries and rules determining who does what, where, and when are crucial in three ways.

1. Interpersonal boundaries define individual family members and promote their differentiation and autonomous, yet interdependent, functioning. Dysfunctional families tend to be characterized by either a pattern of rigid enmeshment or disengagement.

2. Boundaries with the outside world define the family unit, but boundaries must be permeable enough to maintain a well-functioning open system, allowing contact and reciprocal exchanges with the social world.

3. Hierarchical organization in families of all cultures is maintained by generational boundaries, the rules differentiating parent and child roles, rights, and obligations.

Restructuring is based on observing and manipulating interactions within therapy sessions, often by enactments of situations as a way to understand and diagnose the structure and provide an opportunity for restructuring.

Bowenian Family Therapy

Unlike other models of family therapy, the goal of this approach is not symptom reduction. Rather, a Bowenian-trained social worker is interested in improving the intergenerational transmission process. Thus, the focus within this approach is consistent whether a social worker is working with an individual, a couple, or the entire family. It is assumed that improvement in overall functioning will ultimately reduce a family member's symptomatology. Eight major theoretical constructs are essential to understanding Bowen's approach. These concepts are differentiation, emotional fusion, multigenerational transmission, emotional triangle, nuclear family, family projection process, sibling position, and societal regression. These constructs are interconnected.

Differentiation is the core concept of this approach. The more differentiated, the more a client can be an individual while in emotional contact with the family. This allows a client to think through a situation without being drawn to act by either internal or external emotional pressures.

Emotional fusion is the counterpart of differentiation and refers to the tendency for family members to share an emotional response. This is the result of poor interpersonal boundaries between family members. In a fused family, there is little room for emotional autonomy. If a member makes a move toward autonomy, it is experienced as abandonment by other members of the family.

Multigenerational transmission stresses the connection of current generations to past generations as a natural process. Multigenerational transmission gives the present a context in history. This context can focus a social worker on the differentiation in the system and on the transmission process.

An **emotional triangle** is the network of relationships among three people. Bowen's theory states that a relationship can remain stable until anxiety is introduced. However, when anxiety is introduced into the dyad, a third party is recruited into a triangle to reduce the overall anxiety. It is almost impossible for two people to interact without triangulation.

The **nuclear family** is the most basic unit in society and there is a concern over the degree to which emotional fusion can occur in a family system. Clients forming relationships outside of the nuclear family tend to pick mates with the same level of differentiation.

Family projection process describes the primary way parents transmit their emotional problems to children. The projection process can impair child functioning and increase vulnerability to clinical symptoms.

Sibling position is a factor in determining personality. Where a client is in birth order has an influence on how the client relates to parents and siblings. Birth order determines the triangles that clients grow up in.

Societal regression, in contrast to progression, is manifested by problems such as the depletion of natural resources. Bowen's theory can be used to explain societal anxieties and social problems, because Bowen viewed society as a family—an emotional system complete with its own multigenerational transmission, chronic anxiety, emotional triangles, cutoffs, projection processes, and fusion/differentiation struggles.

COUPLES INTERVENTIONS AND TREATMENT APPROACHES

There are often reasons that couples experience problems including, but not limited to:

- Retriggering emotional trauma and not repairing it
- An inability to bond or reconnect after hurting or doing damage to one another
- Lack of skills or knowledge

Many treatment techniques are used with individuals that can be adapted in work with couples, including:

Behavior modification—Successful couples counseling methods will address and attempt to modify any dysfunctional behavior so that couples can change the way each individual behaves with the other.

Insight-oriented psychotherapy—A good deal of time is spent studying interactions between individuals in order to develop a hypothesis concerning what caused individuals to react to each other in the way they do.

There are also specific couples therapy approaches, including the *Gottman Method*, which is based on the notion that healthy relationships are ones in which individuals know each other's stresses and worries, share fondness and admiration, maintain a sense of positiveness, manage conflicts, trust one another, and are committed to one another.

The Gottman Method focuses on conflicting verbal communication in order to increase intimacy, respect, and affection; removes barriers that create a feeling of stagnancy in conflicting situations; and creates a heightened sense of empathy and understanding within relationships.

With all approaches, there are actions that a social worker can take to facilitate effective couples' treatment.

For example, when developing a collaborative alliance with each person, a social worker should validate the experience of each and explore each person's reservations about engaging in couples therapy. In addition, when developing an alliance with the couple as a unit, a social worker can reframe individual problems in relationship terms and support each person's sense of self as being part of a unit, as well as a separate individual.

THE IMPACT OF OUT-OF-HOME DISPLACEMENT (E.G., NATURAL DISASTER, HOMELESSNESS, IMMIGRATION) ON CLIENTS/CLIENT SYSTEMS

The homes in which clients live are part of their self-definition. They are decorated to reflect likes or dislikes, telling others about their occupants and accommodating interests such as gardening, cooking, and others. Homes are seen as extensions of their residents and distinguish people from each other.

Behavior is also cued by the physical environment. Homes remind inhabitants of experiences which took place in the past, as well as what to do in the future. Homes are familiar and are often viewed as safe havens where clients can behave without being judged.

Thus, involuntary displacement outside the home due to hospitalization, incarceration, needed safety, or long-term care needs can be traumatic for many reasons. First, such movement may be associated with losses such as those due to health issues, financial concerns, or safety problems. These losses alone can cause depression, anxiety, confusion, and/or other emotional reactions, which are compounded from having to move from the communities or homes in which clients live.

In out-of-home placements, clients may have changes in roles, causing them to develop poor self-image. For example, the roles of neighbor, community leader, gardener, and so on, which provided fulfillment and recognition, may be lost and no longer possible. Since there is status attached to these roles, their loss can negatively affect self-image.

There also may be a loss of possessions associated with displacement. Precious items that represent a lifetime of memories may have been destroyed, such as by a natural disaster, or sold/given away as there may be no room to keep them in the new settings—especially if they are shared with others.

There also may be a cost associated with involuntary displacement. For example, long-term care can drain client assets and make clients feel guilty about spending money on themselves or fearful about running out of funds for sustained care and housing.

Out-of-home displacement also often accompanies loss of relationships. Relatives and friends who interfaced with clients in their homes may find it inconvenient or impossible to see them in the new settings. Sometimes the lack of private space in which to visit puts up barriers. Visitors may also be intimidated by the sights and sounds of hospitals, jails, or nursing homes.

Clients frequently do not have the same freedom or control that they had when they were at home. In congregate settings, meals, activities, room cleaning, and bathing may be overseen and scheduled for the sake of organization and efficiency, and there are usually numerous rules, policies, and procedures to follow with less individual autonomy and choice.

PERMANENCY PLANNING

Permanency planning is an approach to child welfare that is based on the belief that children need permanence to thrive. Child protection services should focus on getting children into, and maintaining, permanent homes.

In permanency planning, the first goal is to get children back into their original homes. This can be achieved with a thorough investigation into child protection situations to determine if homes are safe and, if needed, exploring ideas for making them safer or more enriching for children.

Supports can include getting caregivers services for meeting needs or providing education, if needed, to ensure adequate and quality care. If children cannot return to their original homes, steps need to be made so that they can get into permanent living situations as quickly as possible with adults with whom they have continuous and reciprocal relationships, including those made available through adoption.

Family preservation helps keep families together and children out of foster care or other out-of-home placements. Efforts focus on family reunification or adoption if children are removed from homes. Plans for children involved in protection services must be reviewed regularly and "reasonable efforts" must be made to keep families together via prevention and family reunification services. There are often financial subsidies to assist with facilitating the adoption of children with complex needs or disabilities.

MINDFULNESS AND COMPLEMENTARY THERAPEUTIC APPROACHES

Social workers continue to provide the bulk of mental health services. A significant number of persons seek services expecting providers to be aware and knowledgeable about alternatives and complements to Western medical approaches for symptom relief and healing when their medical or behavioral health is disrupted and/or compromised. An ever increasing number of people are seeking complementary and alternative medicine (CAM) or integrated health care (IHC) to address health/behavioral health issues. Not only are clients receptive to the use of complementary approaches, they often request diverse approaches that go beyond medications and psychotherapy to address their overall concerns. Thus, social workers must have knowledge of mindfulness and complementary therapeutic approaches.

Interventions and remedies that some cultures and populations consider conventional others view as alternative, and what some clients assess as successful outcomes, some professionals may not concur.

Mindfulness is the practice of paying close attention to what is being experienced in the present, both inside the body and mind and in the external world. It is a conscious effort to be with whatever is going on right now, without judging or criticizing what we find. In each moment, mindfulness invites being awake, aware, and accepting of ourselves.

The practice of mindfulness is integral to efforts to reduce stress and to increase capacity to cope. Mindfulness can stand alone as a treatment tool or may be incorporated with other treatment modalities. Most settings where social workers practice would be conducive to mindfulness practice.

Social workers and other health/behavioral health providers are increasingly including the practice of mindfulness as a useful tool, not only in building a self-care routine, but also in addressing the needs of their clients.

The multitude of complementary approaches to maintaining health are vast and it is unrealistic for social workers to be informed and knowledgeable about all of them, but it is expected that social workers will be aware of the predominant practices and methods being used among the populations they are serving. Just as important, social workers need to be instilled with a respect for clients' authority in determining the best method to treat their problems when there are no indications of harm to self and/or others. Knowing how to integrate empirically tested and validated medical interventions, along with indigenous approaches preserved for generations, is essential to ensuring culturally competent, holistic treatment.

THE COMPONENTS OF CASE MANAGEMENT

Case management has been defined in many ways. However, all models are based on the belief that clients often need assistance in accessing services in today's complex systems, as well as the need to monitor duplication and gaps in treatment and care.

Although there may be many federal, state, and local programs available, there are often serious service gaps. A client might have a specific need met in one program and many related needs ignored because of the lack of coordination. Systems are highly complex, fragmented, duplicative, and uncoordinated.

Social workers provide case management services to different client populations in both nonprofit and for-profit settings.

The primary goal of social work case management is to optimize client functioning and well-being by providing and coordinating high-quality services, in the most effective and efficient manner possible, to individuals with multiple complex needs.

Five case management activities are (a) assessment, (b) planning, (c) linking, (d) monitoring, and (e) advocacy.

TECHNIQUES USED FOR FOLLOW-UP

The standard of practice is that social workers must involve clients and their families (when appropriate) in making their own decisions about follow-up services or aftercare.

Involvement must include, at a minimum, discussion of client and family preferences (when appropriate).

Follow-up meetings are often important to ensure change maintenance. Many clients continue to progress after termination and follow-up meetings provide opportunities to acknowledge these gains and encourage continuation of such efforts.

Follow-up meetings also provide valuable interactions which can mitigate any unanticipated difficulties. Follow-up meetings provide clients with reassurance that they are not alone as they implement what they have learned. They allow for longitudinal evaluation of practice effectiveness.

It is important that social workers explain to clients that follow-up meetings may be important in the problem-solving process. Social workers must not be intrusive or send messages that clients cannot function on their own. Clients who have difficulty terminating may use follow-up meetings as ways to prolong social worker–client relationships beyond what is needed. Social workers must set clear boundaries and treat follow-up meetings with professionalism—having clearly stated goals for these sessions.

Clients who tell social workers during follow-up about new problems that have arisen should be seen for assessment. Social workers who have already assisted clients resolve issues are often the first ones to which clients disclose new problems which have emerged.

THE ELEMENTS OF A CASE PRESENTATION

When a social worker communicates with others in order to ensure comprehensive and complete care for clients, the social worker completes a case presentation. Case presentations are also used in professional development and learning to provide input into options for treatment and to ensure services are being delivered effectively and efficiently.

There is no universal format for a case presentation in social work practice. However, there are some standard elements, including:

- Identifying data (demographics, cultural considerations)
- History of the presenting problem (family history)
- Significant medical/psychiatric history (diagnoses)
- Significant personal and/or social history (legal issues, academic/work problems, crisis/safety concerns)
- Presenting problem (assessment, mental status, diagnosis)
- Impressions and summary (interview findings)
- Recommendations (treatment plan/intervention strategies, goals, theoretical models used)

Content areas can be added or eliminated based on the reasons for the case presentation and input sought. Information for a case presentation is usually information that a social worker has obtained directly from a client during an interview and/or observation, as well as that collected from collateral contacts, other professionals, and/or case records.

METHODS TO DEVELOP AND EVALUATE MEASURABLE OBJECTIVES FOR CLIENT/CLIENT SYSTEM INTERVENTION, TREATMENT, AND/OR SERVICE PLANS

When social workers are creating intervention or service plans, it is essential that goals are written in observable and measurable terms. In order to achieve this aim, the following should be included in each goal contained in the intervention or service plan.

- *Criteria:* What behavior must be exhibited, how often, over what period of time, and under what conditions to demonstrate achievement of the goal?
- *Method for evaluation:* How will progress be measured?
- *Schedule for evaluation:* When, how often, and on what dates or intervals of time will progress be measured?

There may also be benchmarks or the intermediate knowledge, skills, and/or behaviors that must be learned/achieved in order for a client to reach an ultimate goal.

Objectives break down the goals into discrete components or subparts, which are steps toward the final desired outcome.

TECHNIQUES USED TO EVALUATE A CLIENT'S/CLIENT SYSTEM'S PROGRESS

Evaluating progress is a critical part of the problem-solving process. Examining with a client what has occurred and what still needs to occur involves the client in treatment decisions.

Evaluation methods can be simple or complex. They can rely on quantitative information that shows data on reductions in target behaviors, health care improvements, or psychiatric symptom increases, and/or qualitative information in which a client and/or social worker subjectively report on progress made in various areas.

When evaluating progress, a social worker and client should gather all needed information and identify factors that helped or hindered progress. Goals outlined in the contract/service plan should be modified, if needed, based upon the outcome of the evaluation.

Social workers should assist clients to understand the progress they have made so they can clearly understand and celebrate their accomplishments, as well as identify areas that need attention. This process should ensure that clients understand why progress has happened, as well as include a dialogue about any changes that need to occur in the problem-solving process to facilitate continued growth.

PRIMARY, SECONDARY, AND TERTIARY PREVENTION STRATEGIES

There are three major types of prevention strategies—primary, secondary, and tertiary. Optimally, all three types are needed to create comprehensive strategies of prevention and protection.

Primary Prevention

The goal is to protect people from developing a disease, experiencing an injury, or engaging in a behavior in the first place.

Examples:

- Immunizations against disease
- Education promoting the use of automobile passenger restraints and bicycle helmets
- Screenings for the general public to identify risk factors for illness
- Controlling hazards in the workplace and home
- Regular exercise and good nutrition
- Counseling about the dangers of tobacco and other drugs

Since successful primary prevention helps avoid the disease, injury, or behavior and its associated suffering, cost, and burden, it is typically considered the most cost-effective.

Secondary Prevention

Secondary prevention occurs after a disease, injury, or illness has occurred. It aims to slow the progression or limit the long-term impacts. It is often implemented when asymptomatic, but risk factors are present. Secondary prevention also may focus on preventing reinjury.

Examples:

- Telling those with heart conditions to take daily, low-dose aspirin
- Screenings for those with risk factors for illness
- Modifying work assignments for injured workers

Tertiary Prevention

Tertiary prevention focuses on managing complicated, long-term diseases, injuries, or illnesses. The goal is to prevent further deterioration and maximize quality of life because disease is now established and primary prevention activities have been unsuccessful. However, early detection through secondary prevention may have minimized the impact of the disease.

Examples:

- Pain management groups
- Rehabilitation programs
- Support groups

THE INDICATORS OF CLIENT/CLIENT SYSTEM READINESS FOR TERMINATION

Readiness for termination may be marked when meetings between a social worker and client seem uneventful and the tone becomes one closer to cordiality rather than challenge, as well as when no new ground has been discovered for several sessions in a row.

In termination, a social worker and client (a) evaluate the degree to which a client's goals have been attained, (b) acknowledge and address issues related to the ending of the relationship, and (c) plan for subsequent steps a client may take relevant to the problem that do not involve a social worker (such as seeking out new services, if necessary).

The process of evaluation helps a client determine if goals have been met and if the helping relationship was beneficial. As a result of the evaluation process, a social worker can become a more effective practitioner and provide better services. There must always be a method to evaluate the effectiveness of the services received. Evaluation measures, when compared with those taken at baseline, assist in determining the extent of progress and a client's readiness for termination.

A social worker helps a client cope with the feelings associated with termination. This process may help a client cope with future terminations.

By identifying the changes accomplished and planning how a client is going to cope with challenges in the future, a social worker helps a client maintain these changes.

METHODS, TECHNIQUES, AND INSTRUMENTS USED TO EVALUATE SOCIAL WORK PRACTICE

Social workers have an ethical mandate to ensure that they are providing the most efficient and effective services possible. They also must do no harm and ensure that the intervention provided enhances the well-being of clients.

These goals require the evaluation of practice. Routine practice evaluation by social workers can enhance treatment outcomes and agency decision making, planning, and accountability.

There are two main types of evaluations—formative and summative. Formative evaluations examine the process of delivering services, whereas summative evaluations examine the outcomes.

Formative evaluations are ongoing processes that allow for feedback to be implemented during service delivery. These types of evaluations allow social workers to make changes as needed to help achieve program goals. Needs assessments can be viewed as one type of formative evaluation.

Summative evaluations occur at the end of services and provide an overall description of their effectiveness. Summative evaluation examines outcomes to determine whether objectives were met. Summative evaluations enable decisions to be made regarding future service directions that cannot be made during implementation. Impact evaluations and cost-benefit analyses are types of summative evaluations.

There are ethical standards that must be followed when evaluating practice (*NASW Code of Ethics—Evaluation and Research*). Some of these guidelines include:

1. Obtaining voluntary and written informed consent from clients, when appropriate, without any implied or actual deprivation or penalty for refusal to participate; without undue inducement to participate; and with due regard for participants' well-being, privacy, and dignity

2. Informing clients of their right to withdraw from evaluation and research at any time without penalty

3. Ensuring clients in evaluations have access to appropriate supportive services

4. Avoiding conflicts of interest and dual relationships with those being evaluated

EVIDENCE-BASED PRACTICE

Evidence-based social work practice combines research knowledge, professional/clinical expertise, social work values, and client preferences/circumstances. It is a dynamic and fluid process whereby social workers seek, interpret, use, and evaluate the best available information in an effort to make the best practice decisions.

The promotion of evidence-based research within social work is widespread. Evidence-based research gathers evidence that may be informative for clinical practice or clinical decision making. It also involves the process of gathering and synthesizing scientific evidence from various sources and translating it to be applied to practice.

The use of evidence-based practice places the well-being of clients at the forefront, desiring to discover and use the best practices available. The use of evidence-based practice requires social workers to only use services and techniques that were found effective by rigorous, scientific, empirical studies—that is, outcome research.

Social workers must be willing and able to locate and use evidence-based interventions. In areas in which evidence-based interventions are not available, social workers must still use research to guide practice. Applying knowledge gleaned from research findings will assist social workers in providing services informed by scientific investigation and lead to new interventions that can be evaluated as evidence-based practices.

Decisions are based on the use of many sources, ranging from systematic reviews and meta-analyses to less rigorous research designs.

Social workers often use "evidence-based practice" to refer to programs that have a proven track record. However, it takes a long time for a program or intervention to be "evidence based." Thus, most interventions in social work need more empirically supported research in order to accurately apply the term. "Evidence-informed practice" may be more appropriate.

Some questions guide the selection of intervention modalities:

- How will the recommended modality assist with the achievement of the treatment goal and will it help get the outcomes desired?

- How does the recommended treatment modality promote client strengths, capabilities, and interests?

- What are the risks and benefits associated with the recommended modality?

- Is there research or evidence to support the use of this modality for this target problem?

- Is this modality appropriate and tested on those with the same or similar cultural background as the client?

- What training and experience does a social worker have with the recommended modality?

- Is the recommended modality evidence based or consistent with available research? If not, why?

- Was the recommended modality discussed with and selected by a client?

- Will the use of the recommended modality be assessed periodically? When? How?

- Is the recommended treatment modality covered by insurance? What is the cost? How does it compare to the use of other options?

CASE RECORDING FOR PRACTICE EVALUATION OR SUPERVISION

Case records are often an excellent source of information for evaluating the impacts of services. They are existing sources of data, so there is no additional cost or time associated with their collection. However, there are a few limitations. If looking at records completed by multiple workers, there may be inconsistencies in recording styles or details that may impact on the evaluation. Also, information of interest may not be contained in the records; evaluations would need to be limited to only information that is explicitly stated, which may not reflect all progress that has been made.

In addition, the opinions about how a client views both the process and outcome of service delivery are also critical and may not be fully captured in the record. Ensuring that a client's views are the center of any practice evaluation is critical. Thus, a social worker may want to use the case record as one source of information, but include others as well, to ensure all aspects of a client's care, including satisfaction with services, are included.

Social workers engaged in formal evaluation beyond that used to determine individual client progress should obtain voluntary and written informed consent from clients regarding the use of their records without any penalty for refusal to participate or undue inducement to participate (*NASW Code of Ethics—Evaluation and Research*).

Review of case records by supervisors is also essential. This review will ensure that a social worker is documenting properly and recording information in an unbiased manner. Clients must understand and consent to supervisory review of records.

When reviewing information, supervisors should adhere to the same standards of confidentiality as a social worker. The supervisor should not review the records unless it is for the betterment of a client and only within the supervisory context to ensure the quality of services. If the supervisor is a consultant, a client must consent unless there is a compelling need for such disclosure.

CONSULTATION APPROACHES (E.G., REFERRALS TO SPECIALISTS)

Social workers are often called upon to seek consultation for a problem related to a client, service, organization, and/or policy. Consultation is the utilization of an "expert" in a specific area to assist with developing a solution to the issue. Consultation is usually time limited and the advice of the consultant can be used by a social worker in the problem-solving process. Although a consultant does not have any formal authority over a social worker, a consultant has informal authority as an "expert." However, a social worker is not required to follow the recommendations of a consultant.

Four things are critical in consultation:

1. Defining the purpose of the consultation

2. Specifying the consultant's role

3. Clarifying the nature of the problem

4. Outlining the consultation process

Social workers should seek the advice and counsel of colleagues whenever such consultation is in the best interests of clients, but should only do so from colleagues who have demonstrated knowledge, expertise, and competence related to the subject of the consultation (*NASW Code of Ethics—Consultation*).

When seeking consultation, social workers need to get the permission of clients if any identifying or specific information will be shared. In addition, social workers should only disclose information that is absolutely necessary when interacting with consultants.

Social workers may also provide consultation in-person or remotely. They should have the appropriate knowledge and skill to do so and should follow all ethical standards, including avoiding conflicts of interest and maintaining boundaries (*NASW Code of Ethics—Supervision and Consultation*).

THE PROCESS OF INTERDISCIPLINARY AND INTRADISCIPLINARY TEAM COLLABORATION

Social workers often work together with others from various professions. This is known as an interdisciplinary approach. Some interdisciplinary teams interface daily, whereas others may only meet periodically. Sometimes social workers form interdisciplinary relationships that do not constitute team practice but are nevertheless necessary for effective service. These relationships may be with legal or educational professionals. To practice effectively, social workers must be prepared to work with professionals from all other disciplines that may be needed by a client. In turn, social work knowledge is influenced by, and in turn influences, other disciplines, including family studies, medicine, psychiatry, sociology, education, and psychology.

Interdisciplinary teams are often seen as advantageous to clients because they do not have the burden of navigating multiple service systems and communicating to multiple professionals involved in their care. Interdisciplinary teams can also be cost effective and can increase positive outcomes.

An interdisciplinary approach may also have benefits for social workers as they:

1. Provide peer support, especially when working with stressful problems associated with involuntary service delivery, violence, suicide, and so on.

2. Allow for work to be assigned across multiple professionals.

3. Fulfill professional goals by ensuring all aspects of a client's biopsychosocial–spiritual–cultural care are delivered.

4. Create cross-fertilization of skills between professionals.

5. Facilitate decision making related to all aspects of client care, which can lead to increased job satisfaction.

6. Streamline work practices through sharing of information.

Interdisciplinary collaboration is a rewarding, yet challenging, social work activity. Collaboration, a learned skill that can be improved through practice, is a vehicle for improving services for all clients. It means working with others for the betterment of a client. Collaborative teams are more likely to develop important new and innovative approaches to dealing with problems.

Collaboration goes beyond people sitting around a table. It includes premeeting work (i.e., making telephone calls), how members typically conduct themselves (i.e., being friendly), and how meetings proceed (i.e., choosing to ignore minor irritations in order to get on with the agenda).

Social workers must understand their own styles and focus on their own behavior as part of a group, rather than on how other members should change.

Collaboration involves strong interpersonal communication and group process skills, as well as being able to understand the perspectives of others. It can be discrete (distinct or separate; limited to single occurrence or action) or continuous (ongoing or repetitive).

The following list provides some guidelines that can be helpful when social workers participate in such collaboration.

1. Social workers should clearly articulate their roles on interdisciplinary teams.

2. Social workers should understand the roles of professionals from other disciplines on these teams.

3. Social workers should seek and establish common ground with these professionals, including commonalities in professional goals.

4. Social workers should acknowledge the differences within the field and across other disciplines.

5. Social workers should address conflict within teams so that it does not interfere with the collaborative process and the teams' outcomes.

6. Social workers should establish and maintain collegial relationships.

There are also ethical guidelines that must be followed when social workers are part of interdisciplinary collaboration (*NASW Code of Ethics—Interdisciplinary Collaboration*).

1. Social workers who are members of an interdisciplinary team should participate in and contribute to decisions that affect the well-being of clients by drawing on the perspectives, values, and experiences of the social work profession. Professional and ethical obligations of the interdisciplinary team as a whole and of its individual members should be clearly established.

2. Social workers for whom a team decision raises ethical concerns should attempt to resolve the disagreement through appropriate channels. If the disagreement cannot be resolved, social workers should pursue other avenues to address their concerns consistent with client well-being.

Intradisciplinary teams are composed exclusively of social workers who may have different levels of training and skill within the profession. Intradisciplinary teams are often referred to as unidisciplinary. An interdisciplinary approach differs from a multidisciplinary one due to its holistic nature. Professionals in an interdisciplinary team are charged with working together and a treatment plan is usually developed by the entire group. In service provision, the work of each professional group can and often does overlap. Interdependence throughout the problem-solving process is stressed. Each member contributes to the group's goals. In multidisciplinary teams, the steps are often conducted in isolation and outcomes are later shared with other team members. Intradisciplinary teams in social work practice can be useful in professional development, mentorship, and the provision of supervision. However, working on a team with others in the profession has advantages and disadvantages. Members share the same professional orientation and values, which can facilitate consensus and cohesion within the group, but the ability to generate alternative solutions to problems when viewing problems from multiple professional perspectives can be reduced.

THE BASIC TERMINOLOGY OF PROFESSIONS OTHER THAN SOCIAL WORK (E.G., LEGAL, EDUCATIONAL)

Social workers should maintain access to professional consultation. Often, this consultation may be from qualified professionals in other disciplines. Each discipline has its own set of assumptions, values, and priorities; in order to ensure that the assessment of a client's problems consider all possible root causes (including medical) and all needs of a client are met, the social worker should consult with experts in other fields, as well as refer a client to them when needed.

Social workers often work together with others from various professions. This is known as an interdisciplinary approach. Some interdisciplinary teams interface daily, whereas others may only meet periodically.

Sometimes social workers form interdisciplinary relationships that do not constitute team practice, but are nevertheless necessary for effective service. These relationships may be with legal or educational professionals. To practice effectively, social workers must be prepared to work with professionals from all other disciplines that may be needed by a client.

In turn, social work knowledge is influenced by, and in turn influences, other disciplines, including family studies, medicine, psychiatry, sociology, education, and psychology.

THE PRINCIPLES OF CASE RECORDING, DOCUMENTATION, AND MANAGEMENT OF PRACTICE RECORDS

The proper documentation of client services is paramount to competent practice. Without proper case recording or record keeping, the quality of service may be compromised, the continuity of service may be disrupted, there may be misinterpretation that can cause harm, client confidentiality may be breached, and a client's confidence in the integrity of a social worker may be impacted.

In addition to client harm, a social worker, as well as the social worker's agency, if applicable, may be at risk of liability due to malpractice, negligence, and/or breach of confidentiality.

Some important "rules" about case recording include that it is:

■ A clear, accurate, and unbiased representation of the facts

■ A written record of all decisions

■ Free of value judgments and subjective comments

■ Timely

It should also include only information that is directly relevant to the delivery of services.

The release and storage of case recordings is also critical. Social workers must make sure that records are not released without proper client consent and records are properly stored during and following the termination of services. Records should be maintained for the number of years required by laws, statutes, regulations, and relevant contracts.

Social workers should store records following the termination of services to ensure reasonable future access and maintain them for the number of years required by laws, agency policies, and contracts (*NASW Code of Ethics—Client Records*).

Intervention Processes and Techniques for Use With Larger Systems

METHODS TO ESTABLISH PROGRAM OBJECTIVES AND OUTCOMES

The terms "mission," "goals," "objectives," and "outcomes" are often used interchangeably without being clearly defined.

A *mission statement* is a general, concise statement outlining the purpose guiding the practices of an organization. Outcomes eventually flow from the mission statements of an agency. *Goals* are broad, general statements of what the program intends to accomplish. Goals describe broad outcomes and concepts expressed in general terms (e.g., clear communication, problem-solving skills). Goals should provide a framework for determining the more specific objectives of a program and should be consistent with the mission of the agency. A single goal may have many specific subordinate objectives.

Objectives are brief, clear statements that describe the desired outcomes. They are distinguished from goals by the level of specificity. Goals express intended outcomes in general terms and objectives express them in specific terms.

Outcomes may be knowledge, abilities (skills), and/or attitudes (values, dispositions) that have been obtained. Outcomes are *achieved* results.

METHODS TO ASSESS THE AVAILABILITY OF COMMUNITY RESOURCES

Social workers must respect the rights to self-determination of clients. In order for clients to make informed decisions, it is critical that they understand the range of services available and be informed about any opportunities they have to obtain services from other service providers. Clients should also understand their right to be referred to other professionals for assistance, as well as their right to refuse services and possible consequences of such refusals.

Throughout the problem-solving process, social workers should be assisting clients to access available resources, as well as create new ones if they do not exist or are not appropriate. In order for clients to choose between alternative resources, social workers must review the advantages and disadvantages of using each.

There are important steps, as well as ethical concerns, that must be taken when referring clients for services.

Step 1: Clarifying the Need or Purpose for the Referral

Social workers should refer clients to other professionals when the other professionals' specialized knowledge or expertise is needed to serve clients fully or when social workers believe that they are not being effective or making reasonable progress with clients and that other services are required (*NASW Code of Ethics—Referral for Services*).

Step 2: Researching Resources

When making a referral, it is critical that a social worker refers to a competent provider, someone with expertise in the problem that a client is experiencing. When researching resources, a client's right to self-determination should be paramount. In addition, if a client is already receiving services from an agency, it may be advisable to see if there are available services provided by this agency in order to avoid additional coordination and fragmentation for a client.

Step 3: Discussing and Selecting Options

Social workers are prohibited from giving or receiving payment for a referral when no professional service is provided by the referring social worker (*NASW Code of Ethics— Referral for Services*).

Step 4: Planning for Initial Contact

Social workers may want to work with a client to prepare for the initial meeting. Preparation may include helping a client to understand what to expect or reviewing needs and progress made so that it can be discussed with the new provider.

Step 5: Initial Contact

Social workers who refer clients to other professionals should take appropriate steps to facilitate an orderly transfer of responsibility. Social workers who refer clients to other professionals should disclose, with clients' consent, all pertinent information to the new service providers (*NASW Code of Ethics—Referral for Services*).

Step 6: Follow-Up to See If Need Was Met

Social workers should always follow-up to ensure that there was not a break in service and that the new provider is meeting a client's needs.

METHODS OF SERVICE DELIVERY

The context of social work practice clearly has a profound influence on the quality and standards of professional activities and the ability of social workers to practice ethically and effectively. Social work takes place in a wide variety of settings, including, but not limited to, private practices, public sector organizations (government), schools, hospitals, correctional facilities, and private nonprofit agencies.

To meet the needs of clients, social workers must have work environments that support ethical practice and are committed to standards and good quality services. A positive working environment is created where the values and principles of social workers are reinforced in agency policies and procedures.

To achieve this aim, employers must understand social work practice and provide supervision, workload management, and continuing professional development consistent with best practices.

Policies setting out standards of ethical practice should be written and clear. Social workers should never be required to do anything that would put at risk their ability to uphold ethical standards, including those in the areas of confidentiality, informed consent, and safety/risk management.

The public, including clients, should be regularly informed of agency policies and procedures and provided with information about how to raise concerns or make complaints about them.

Policies that do not tolerate dangerous, discriminatory, and/or exploitative behavior must be in place so that social workers and their clients are safe from harm.

The adoption and implementation of policies and procedures on workload and caseload management contribute greatly to the provision of quality services to clients. In addition, policies and procedures for confidential treatment and storage of records should be established.

Continuing professional development and further training enable social workers to strengthen and develop their skills. Orientation and other relevant training provided to social workers upon hire and when assuming other jobs within the setting are essential.

Good quality, regular social work supervision by professionals who have the necessary experience and qualifications in social work practice is a critical tool to ensure service quality.

Rates of pay for social workers need to be comparable with similar professionals, and the skill and qualifications of social workers must be recognized, while ensuring services are affordable to clients.

THEORIES AND METHODS OF ADVOCACY FOR POLICIES, SERVICES, AND RESOURCES TO MEET CLIENTS'/CLIENT SYSTEMS' NEEDS

Advocacy is one of a social worker's most important tasks. Social workers may advocate when working with an individual client to ensure that the client's needs are met. However, social workers have an ethical mandate to make systemic changes to address the problems experienced by groups of individuals who are vulnerable and/or who are unable to speak for themselves.

A social worker may engage in advocacy by convincing others of the legitimate needs and rights of members of society. Such work can occur on the local, county, state, or national levels. Some social workers are even involved in international human rights and advocacy for those in need in other countries.

Fundamental to social work is advocating to change the factors that create and contribute to problems.

Sometimes advocacy can be achieved by working through the problem-solving process as it relates to a problem, including acknowledging the problem, analyzing and defining the problem, generating possible solutions, evaluating each option, implementing the option of choice, and evaluating the outcomes.

In other instances, social workers may engage in obtaining legislative support or using the media to draw attention to a concern.

In all instances, social workers should be working with clients to have their voices heard and should not be speaking for them. *Often social workers need to help clients to advocate with third-party payers to have their needs met when resources are not adequate.* Social workers must inform clients of appeal processes when services are denied and support them as they advocate to meet their needs. When clients feel that they have not been treated fairly, social workers should empower them by providing education about appeal processes and other methods to change policies, fix services, and/or increase services to meet their needs.

The goal of social work advocacy is to assist clients to strengthen their own skills in this area. Social workers may assist by locating sources of power that can be shared with clients to make changes.

METHODS TO CREATE, IMPLEMENT, AND EVALUATE POLICIES AND PROCEDURES THAT MINIMIZE RISK FOR INDIVIDUALS, FAMILIES, GROUPS, ORGANIZATIONS, AND COMMUNITIES

Social workers should create, implement, and evaluate policies that minimize risk for clients, workers, and practice settings. One critical feature of implementing a comprehensive risk management strategy is conducting a comprehensive ethics audit. An ethics audit entails examining risks through the following steps:

1. Appointing a committee or task force of concerned and informed staff and colleagues

2. Gathering information from agency documents, interviews with staff and clients, accreditation reports, and other sources to assess risks associated with client rights; confidentiality and privacy; informed consent; service delivery; boundary issues; conflicts of interest; documentation; client records; supervision; staff development and training; consultation; client referral; fraud; termination of services; professional impairment; misconduct, or incompetence; and so on

3. Reviewing all collected information

4. Determining whether there is no risk, minimal risk, moderate risk, or high risk in each area

5. Preparing action plans to address each risk, paying particular attention to policies that need to be created to prevent risk in the future and steps needed to mitigate existing risk

6. Monitoring policy implementation and progress made toward reducing existing risk, as well as ensuring that procedures adhere to social work's core ethical principles

Risk management is an ongoing process and must consist of preventive strategies as well as corrective actions that result from audits done routinely or in response to particular concerns or complaints.

CONCEPTS OF SOCIAL POLICY DEVELOPMENT AND ANALYSIS

Policy analysis is a systematic approach to solving problems through policies.

It involves identifying the problem, developing alternatives, assessing the impacts of the alternatives (such as conducting a cost-benefit analysis), selecting the desired option, designing and implementing the policy, and evaluating the outcomes.

Critical to social policy analysis is the identification of alternative policy options and the evaluation of these alternatives. Analyses include developing an understanding of who "wins" and who "loses." Some of the values upon which alternatives are weighed include equity, efficiency, and liberty.

The policy analysis field has become more diversified; thus, it is highly influenced by theories from other fields. Often there are many stakeholders involved, such as federal, state, and local government agencies, stakeholders, community leaders, and clients, all of which will bring in their own set of values. Thus, the chosen approach will be influenced by who participates.

TECHNIQUES TO INFORM AND INFLUENCE ORGANIZATIONAL AND SOCIAL POLICY

Social policy is influenced by many factors, such as the following.

Knowledge/Innovation

Knowledge and innovation create new opportunities to change, as well as information that current practices may need to be reformed. Technological advances are often drivers of changes in policy.

Social, Political, and Economic Conditions/Resources

Good policies are often not adopted because they are proposed without the social, political, or economic resources to move them through the policy process and/or implement them.

Social norms change over time and foster or impede social policy development or revision.

Political and/or economic conditions can also promote or hinder the creation and/or revision of policy, as well as whether policy alternatives are suggested or considered for adoption.

Legal Issues/Laws

Understanding how new policies will influence or interact with existing laws is essential. Policies may not be supported if they are believed to negatively impact on existing policies that are seen as beneficial.

Institutional Influences

The structure of institutions, such as government agencies, private sector organizations, and so on, can also impact the ability to influence and efficiently or effectively implement social policies. Sometimes policies are so complex or integrated into the practices of complex institutional systems that it is difficult to understand them; therefore, change is less likely.

External Influences

The media and other external influences can be very influential. Media can be used to call attention to a problem. More media coverage of one policy alternative may influence its support as it is more familiar. Public opinion is a very salient influence as to whether policies will be proposed and/or adopted.

Social workers who want to promote certain social policies must be aware of these influences and use methods to support policies as they relate to these areas. Contrarily, social workers can decrease the desirability of policies by creating barriers or removing positive influences in these areas.

Problems are also often associated with policy implementation. Policies may not be clearly communicated, leaving implementers and others at a loss as to how to follow them in order to achieve the intended goals. Negative attitudes of service personnel, lack of resources to carry out policies, and/or the conflict with previously established procedures or structures can also be obstacles to implementation.

Cooptation has many meanings, but may be used as a strategy to influence social policy as leaders will try to quiet dissent or disturbances not only by dealing with immediate grievances, but by making efforts to channel the energies and angers of dissenters into more legitimate and less disruptive activities. When coopting, incentives are offered and other efforts are made aimed at complacency.

THE PRINCIPLES AND PROCESSES FOR DEVELOPING FORMAL DOCUMENTS (E.G., PROPOSALS, LETTERS, BROCHURES, PAMPHLETS, REPORTS, EVALUATIONS)

Social workers are expected to communicate effectively and be able to prepare formal documents. Being able to provide quality services is not the only important aspect of social work; all work is undermined by poor recording or documentation.

A good document begins with careful planning—jotting down the report's purpose and some notes about key content to be contained. Many times, drafts need to be made to ensure that the formal document meets its purpose and is written clearly, without punctuation and other mistakes. Editing is usually required before finalizing for dissemination. Typing reports is always preferred for a more professional appearance and to avoid "illegible" handwriting.

From court reports, to grant proposals, to public relations pamphlets, social workers are expected to communicate accurately with others. Poor English skills can affect the quality of reports. Social workers need to be able to write reports that can be taken "seriously" by others.

Quality of content is just as critical as spelling and punctuation. Time must be allotted to be able to do critical analyses, which many formal reports require. It is easy to describe something, but much harder to indicate its significance. Repeating facts may not provide needed professional opinions and observations.

Formal documents will only count if they get to the right people. Social workers must be aware of the purpose of documents to be prepared and to whom they are being written, and then write accordingly. Social workers should avoid irrelevant, inappropriate information; meaningless phrases; and illogical conclusions.

Social workers should expect that their documents may be scrutinized. Thus, they should write just enough to make their points, but not "overdocument" with irrelevant details. Social workers should be specific and avoid characterizations such as "poor outcome," "good result," "moderate compliance," "drunk," "aggressive," and "combative." They should also avoid acronyms and abbreviations and use precise description and specific language (not "it seems," "I suppose," "it appears," "I believe," "I feel," and so on).

Social workers must prepare documents in a timely fashion and consider ethical issues that can be related to their preparation and distribution. Documents should not contain bias wording. Social workers should not alter documents after they are written unless it is appropriate to do so. Social workers must know when communication is "privileged" and should not share information with those without a need to know.

METHODS TO ESTABLISH SERVICE NETWORKS OR COMMUNITY RESOURCES

The need for services to not be duplicative and complement one another is central to meeting client needs. Social workers are often called upon to assist with developing or navigating service networks, as well as creating community resources where they are lacking. Integrating services takes sustained effort and hard work. Though the concept of service integration may seem simple, it is not and usually takes several administrative and operational strategies. Strong leadership and sound management are critical.

In order to effectively meet client needs, organizations are increasingly recognizing collaborations, networks, alliances, and/or partnerships. There are two distinct network forms— mandated network arrangements and self-organizing networks.

Within each of these forms, there may be a lead organization or a model in which all organizations share decision-making power. The former is often associated with a centralized structure, whereas the latter is more indicative of a decentralized one. Networks can also have strong and weak arrangements in which the parameters of integration may or may not be highly regulated.

The willingness and ability of social service organizations to form networks often depends on organizational size, resource dependency, and collaborative experience.

COMMUNITY ORGANIZING AND SOCIAL PLANNING METHODS

Community organizing is focused on harnessing the collective power of communities to tackle issues of shared concern. It challenges government, corporations, and other power-holding institutions in an effort to tip the power balance more in favor of communities.

It is essential for social workers to understand sources of power in order to access them for the betterment of the community. Organizing members to focus these sources of power on the problem(s) and mobilizing resources to assist is critical.

- **Coercive:** power from control of punishment
- **Reward:** power from control of rewards
- **Expert:** power from superior ability or knowledge
- **Referent:** power from having charisma or identification with others who have power
- **Legitimate:** power from having legitimate authority
- **Informational:** power from having information

Community organization enhances participatory skills of local citizens by working with and not for them, thus developing leadership with particular emphasis on the ability to conceptualize and act on problems. It strengthens communities so they can better deal with future problems; community members can develop the capacity to resolve problems.

Social planning is defined as the process by which a group or community decides its goals and strategies relating to societal issues. It is not an activity limited to government, but includes activities of the private sector, social movements, professions, and other organizations focused specifically on social objectives.

Models of social planning in social work practice include those that are based on community participation. Rather than planning "for" communities, social workers as planners engage "with" community members. Social planning does not merely examine sociological problems that exist, but also includes the physical and economic factors that relate to societal issues.

All issues confronting those who are served by social workers are really human or social issues. Social workers can help facilitate the process of planning through all stages: organizing community members; data gathering related to the issue—including identifying economic, political, and social causes; problem identification; weighing of alternatives; policy/program implementation; and evaluation of effectiveness.

METHODS OF NETWORKING

The importance of networking has been stressed heavily in business, but it has received far less attention in social work practice. This void is interesting, because it is critical to the effective delivery of services. Networking involves building relationships with other professionals who share areas of interest. It is about creating a community around common interests and building alliances. It is also about creating opportunities to work with others toward the achievement of mutual goals.

Although networking in business is a way to attract patrons/customers or to get jobs, it has a broader, and more altruistic, focus in social work.

For example, learning about others who do similar or complementary work can result in a sharing of resources and expertise, which could be beneficial to clients by keeping the cost of services contained and/or increasing the skills of practitioners. Learning about the skills of others and establishing professional relationships through networking can also provide resources for clients who may need referrals to other professionals.

Networking helps improve social skills and the ability to relate to others in a variety of settings. It puts social workers "out there" so that others can be aware of the important work that they do. Educating others about social problems is an important part of making systematic changes. Lastly, networking can identify individuals who would be good candidates for jobs. Recruiting qualified individuals into the agencies where social workers are employed results in clients receiving quality care.

TECHNIQUES FOR MOBILIZING COMMUNITY PARTICIPATION

Community participation is critical in social work practice. Community participation informs others about needed changes that must occur. Policies, programs, and services that were effective or appropriate previously have become ineffective or inappropriate.

Community participation also creates relationships and partnerships among diverse groups who can then work together, but may not usually do so.

Community participation puts decision-making power partly or wholly with the community, ensuring that individuals will remain interested and involved over time.

When engaging in community-based decision making, individuals will typically go through various stages.

Orientation stage—Community members meet for the first time and start to get to know each other.

Conflict stage—Disputes, little fights, and arguments may occur. These conflicts are eventually worked out.

Emergence stage—Community members begin to see and agree on a course of action.

Reinforcement stage—Community members finally make a decision and justify why it was correct.

Community members are far more likely to buy into policy that has been created with their participation. Their support over time will lead to permanent change.

Community participation energizes communities to continue to change in positive directions. Once involved in a successful change effort, community members see what they can accomplish collectively and take on new challenges.

Lastly, community members must inform policy-makers and planners of the real needs of the community, so that the most important problems and issues can be addressed. They must also provide information about what has been tried before and worked or not worked.

GOVERNANCE STRUCTURES

Governance concerns those structures, functions, processes, and customs that exist within an organization to ensure it operates in a way that achieves its objectives, and does so in an effective and transparent manner. It is a framework of accountability to clients, stakeholders, and the wider community, within which organizations make decisions and control their functions and resources to achieve their objectives.

Good governance adds value by improving the performance of an organization through more efficient management, more strategic and equitable resource allocation and service provision, and other improvements that lend themselves to improved outcomes and impacts.

Social workers should advocate within and outside their agencies for adequate resources to meet clients' needs and for resource allocation procedures that are open and fair *(NASW Code of Ethics—Administration)*. When not all clients' needs can be met, an allocation procedure should be developed that is nondiscriminatory, appropriate, and consistent. Social workers should take reasonable steps to ensure that adequate agency or organizational resources are available to provide appropriate staff supervision and that the working environment for which they are responsible is consistent with and encourages compliance with the *NASW Code of Ethics*.

THEORIES OF ORGANIZATIONAL DEVELOPMENT AND STRUCTURE

Organizational theory attempts to explain the workings of organizations. Many theories have emerged from varying bodies of knowledge and disciplines. These theories can be useful to social workers in understanding the environments in which they deliver services and the workings of organizations with which clients interact.

Classical Organizational Theories

The *scientific management theory* (Theory X) is based on (a) finding the one "best way" to perform each task; (b) carefully matching each worker to each task; (c) closely supervising workers, using reward and punishment as motivators; and (d) managing and controlling behavior.

Weber's bureaucratic theory emphasized the need for a hierarchical structure of power to ensure stability and uniformity. Weber also put forth the notion that organizational behavior is a network of human interactions, where all behavior could be understood by looking at cause and effect.

Administrative theory emphasized establishing a universal set of management principles that could be applied to all organizations.

The major deficiency with classical organizational theories was that they attempted to explain people's motivation to work strictly as a function of economic reward.

Neoclassical Theories

These theories were based upon the Hawthorne experiments and focused on workers.

The Hawthorne experiments took place at Western Electric's factory at Hawthorne, a suburb of Chicago, in the late 1920s and early 1930s. The original purpose of the experiments was to study the impacts of physical conditions on productivity. The experimenters concluded that it was not the changes in physical conditions that were affecting the workers' productivity. Rather, it was the fact that someone was actually concerned about their workplace, and the opportunities this gave them to discuss changes before they took place.

Human relations theory (Theory Y) evolved as a reaction to the tough, authoritarian structure of classical theory. It displayed genuine concern for human needs in order to produce creativity and emphasized the importance of cohesive work groups, participatory leadership, and open communication.

Modern Organizational Approaches

Systems approach considers the organization as a system composed of a set of interrelated—and thus mutually dependent—subsystems. Thus, the organization consists of components, linking processes and goals.

Sociotechnical approach considers the organization as composed of a social system, technical system, and its environment. These interact with each other, so it is necessary to balance them appropriately for effective functioning of the organization.

Contingency or situational approach recognizes that organizational systems are interrelated with their environment and that different environments require different organizational systems for effectiveness.

THE EFFECTS OF POLICIES, PROCEDURES, REGULATIONS, AND LEGISLATION ON SOCIAL WORK PRACTICE AND SERVICE DELIVERY

Many laws affect social work practice. Although social workers may not be responsible for implementing these pieces of legislation, they provide protections or programs that are critical to those served. Social workers are also expected to keep up-to-date with new public laws and policies.

For example, social workers must be familiar with and fully informed of policies, procedures, regulations, and legislation related to confidentiality, living wills/advance directives, special education services, child abuse and neglect, discrimination, public benefits/welfare, disability rights and accommodations, domestic violence, and other special populations or areas of practice.

Policies, procedures, regulations, and legislation shape practice and service delivery as they exert influence on the social contexts of clients and delivery systems. Policies can optimize or hinder well-being. There are unintended consequences of policies, procedures, regulations, and legislation that are not anticipated and can adversely impact clients and the delivery of social services. Social workers are uniquely positioned to identify policies that promote relationships and improve the well-being of those who may be marginalized or oppressed.

Clients' lives are directly impacted by policies, procedures, regulations, and legislation in systems such as child protection, criminal justice, and/or mental health. Social workers need to be aware of the laws that regulate each system in order to help clients navigate their way through these systems more effectively, and to be able to advocate for reform to improve the goodness of fit between clients and their socio-legal environments.

Policies, procedures, regulations, and legislation govern many relationships of interest to social work clients, including landlord/tenant, employer/employee, physician/patient, spouse/spouse, and parent/child relationships. Thus, knowledge of policies, procedures, regulations, and legislation, as well as their effects, provides social workers with an understanding of their clients' rights and responsibilities in a broad range of social relationships.

Social work is rooted in strong assumptions about rights, fairness, and justice. A focus on poverty and other sources of adversity are essential to eliminating disparities and improving well-being. Social justice is a necessary value for social work practice, research, and pedagogy. Social welfare policies may be an effective means to accomplish this aim.

Policies, procedures, regulations, and legislation are important mechanisms for promoting justice and ultimately health. Advocacy is needed to ensure that the rights of those who may not have power or privilege are respected.

Social workers serve clients in hospitals, schools, correctional facilities, mental health agencies, and other settings. Policies, procedures, regulations, and legislation dictate who is eligible for services, standards for record keeping, confidentiality, and other client rights. Social workers need to understand policies, procedures, regulations, and legislation to ensure that agencies are in compliance with them. Social work must advocate for changes in these settings to promote greater social and economic justice.

Social work practice itself is regulated by policies, procedures, regulations, and legislation. Most states/jurisdictions have licensing or accreditation laws that regulate the practice of social work, including who may practice and what standards of practice are legally enforceable. Social workers must be aware of malpractice laws that identify when they may be legally responsible for causing harm to clients if they perform their professional duties in a manner that falls below a reasonable standard of care.

QUALITY ASSURANCE, INCLUDING PROGRAM REVIEWS AND AUDITS BY EXTERNAL SOURCES

Historically, quality assurance systems have focused on auditing records to monitor and report on the extent of compliance with law and grant requirements. Usually a small number of quality assurance staff within organizations focused on this auditing function, and their reports often had minimal impact on the services delivered by the agency.

Today, many agencies are developing systems that move beyond compliance monitoring. These systems attempt to gather and assess a range of information on quality, and they work to implement needed improvements on an ongoing basis. As a way of differentiating these efforts from traditional compliance monitoring, the new approaches are called continuous quality improvement systems. These systems require that agencies adopt the following steps:

Step 1: Adopting outcomes and standards

Step 2: Incorporating quality assurance standards and processes throughout their work

Step 3: Gathering data and information

Step 4: Analyzing data and information

Step 5: Using analyses and information to make improvements

Funders and accreditors support and encourage the move toward continuous quality improvement processes. This new approach improves upon compliance monitoring in three ways. First, quality improvement programs are broader in scope, assessing practice and outcomes, as well as compliance. Second, they attempt to use data, information, and results to effect positive changes in policy and practice, along with compliance with federal, state, and agency requirements. Third, these programs engage a broad range of internal and external partners in the quality improvement process, including top managers, staff at all levels, clients, and other stakeholders.

THE IMPACT OF THE POLITICAL ENVIRONMENT ON POLICY-MAKING

Social work is unique in its dual focus on assisting clients on an individual level while also working to change the policies that adversely impact them. The personal troubles of clients are linked to the public policies which can help to prevent or address them. Social workers are charged with working with and helping individuals and their families directly, but also working within decision-making bodies to promote these policies.

Social workers must be knowledgeable about the political environment if they are to shape public policy based upon the core values of the profession. As there are always competing interest groups who would like to influence policy-makers in their favor, political advocacy is seen as an important and necessary skill.

Advocacy can be defined as attempting to influence public policy through education, lobbying, or political pressure. Social workers are often called upon to educate the general public as well as public policy-makers about the nature of problems, the legislation needed to address problems, and the funding required to provide services or conduct research.

Social workers should engage in social and political action that seeks to ensure that all people have equal access to the resources, employment, services, and opportunities they require to meet their basic human needs and to develop to their full potential. They should be aware of the impact of the political arena on practice and should advocate for changes in policy and legislation to improve social conditions in order to meet basic human needs and promote social justice *(NASW Code of Ethics—Social and Political Action)*.

LEADERSHIP AND MANAGEMENT TECHNIQUES

There are many different definitions of leadership and management, with little consensus about the differences between the two terms. However, there is agreement that successful organizations need both good leadership and management. Some suggest that leadership can be viewed as a subset of management because a leadership role is inherent in a management position. Leadership is related to being focused on the future, dealing with uncertainty and instability, and prospectively considering the ways in which organizational operations need to change. Leadership also includes initiating, sustaining, and helping to maintain a certain amount of momentum through the change process. Leaders must be attentive to and help to balance stability and change. Management, on the other hand, focuses on efficiency, effectiveness, and planning.

Social work leaders need management skills and social work managers need leadership skills in order to be effective. The skill sets of leaders focus on inspiration, transformation, empowerment, trust, innovation, and creativity whereas managers are concerned with performance, planning, accountability, monitoring, evaluation, cooperation, and teamwork. Managers must govern resources and oversee the tensions between controlling, rationing, and providing needed services.

There is typically little distinction between managers and leaders because leaders are often appointed to management positions. Thus, managers and leaders within organizations are usually the same individuals.

FISCAL MANAGEMENT TECHNIQUES

Human service organizations need to be accountable in the recording and reporting of their financial transactions. Financial management refers to planning for, acquiring, allocating, controlling, and recording/reporting of financial and material resources, as well as the evaluation of methods used to achieve these aims. Financial management involves the following activities/ techniques:

- Planning—the short- and long-term strategies used to ensure fiscal solvency

- Acquisition—the gathering of human, material, and economic resources through such means as fundraising, grant writing, contractual arrangements, fees, purchase of merchandise, and so on

- Allocation—the distribution of resources internally (such as to specific departments) or externally (such as by contracting outside organization or using consultants)

- Internal control—the establishment of standardized policies and procedures relating to all transactions and events involving monetary items (including the use of generally accepted accounting principles and adherence to contractual obligations)

- Recording/reporting—the use of a manual, automated, or computerized system to list and classify all transactions of a fiscal nature in journals and ledgers to generate statements and reports

- Evaluating—the periodic review of financial activities to assess their efficiency and effectiveness at meeting the goal of financial accountability

Social work administrators need to be knowledgeable about financial management techniques because they are responsible for the oversight and operations of their programs. This responsibility includes overseeing fiscal staff and fiscal operations.

EDUCATIONAL COMPONENTS, TECHNIQUES, AND METHODS OF SUPERVISION

There are three components of supervision—administrative, educational, and supportive. *Administrative supervision* aims to ensure that a social worker is accountable to the public as well as to organizational policies. The major responsibility is to make sure that the work is performed in an acceptable manner. *Educational supervision* establishes a learning alliance between a supervisor and a social worker with the aim of teaching new skills or refining existing ones. *Supportive supervision* is focused on increasing performance by decreasing job-related stress that interferes with functioning.

For a social worker to learn job-related material and develop as a skilled professional, the social worker must make appropriate and effective use of educational supervision. The educational component of supervision is concerned with teaching a social worker what the social worker needs to know in order to do the job and helping the social worker through the learning process. In essence, the educational component relates to the transmission of knowledge, skills, attitudes, and values needed by social workers.

In order for learning to occur, a supervisee must be cooperative (willing to work and learn new skills), willing to follow directions (initially doing what is told until able to complete routines without direction), and knowledgeable (about agency procedures). A supervisee also must show initiative (seeking out learning opportunities and applying new knowledge) and accepting of criticism (trying to improve and accepting feedback when it is justified and constructive).

Supervisors also have responsibilities in educational supervision. They must provide education and training (formal and informal opportunities to ensure supervisees have the knowledge and skills needed to do their jobs competently) and feedback (explanations on what is going well and what needs improvement). Identifying the learning needs of supervisees should be done at hire and regularly thereafter. Changes in the field must always be considered. Lastly, supervisors should be aware of supervisees' learning styles and ensure that education is delivered via methods that are most effective. There are three main cognitive learning styles: visual (uses visual objects such as graphs and charts to learn), auditory (retains information through hearing and speaking), and kinesthetic (likes to use hands-on approaches to acquire knowledge).

METHODS TO IDENTIFY LEARNING NEEDS AND DEVELOP LEARNING OBJECTIVES FOR SUPERVISEES

Supervision is an essential way in which social workers acquire knowledge and skills needed for professional practice. It is often the bridge between the classroom and the field. Supervision is necessary to improve client care, develop professionalism, and maintain ethical standards in the field. Supervision has also become the cornerstone of quality improvement and assurance.

Quality supervision is founded on a positive supervisor–supervisee relationship that promotes client welfare and the professional development of the supervisee. A supervisor is a teacher, coach, consultant, mentor, evaluator, and administrator. *Ultimately, effective supervision ensures that clients are competently served.* Supervision ensures that social workers continue to increase their skills, which in turn increases service effectiveness.

Some of the skills that social work supervisors must have in order to effectively teach supervisees include the ability to:

- Identify learning needs and styles.
- Write learning goals and objectives.
- Devise instructional strategies to accommodate needs and learning styles.
- Present material in a didactic manner, using modeling.
- Match learning styles to developmental levels (e.g., provide more instruction to junior supervisees and use guided discovery for those who are senior).
- Explain the rationales for interventions.
- Evaluate supervisees' learning.
- Give constructive feedback to supervisees.

Learning needs of supervisees may result from gaps in knowledge about practice modalities; effective communication strategies; setting, funding, or legal requirements; self-care strategies; and so on. Social work supervisors should be knowledgeable about the skills supervisees acquired from previous professional training and experience, as well as gaps in learning, such as those related to diagnostic assessment and treatment; ethical standards of practice; laws and rules; record keeping; cultural awareness; methods for establishing treatment relationships with clients; methods for including family members in clients' treatment when appropriate; communication with other professionals in developing diagnosis and treatment plans and assuring continuity of care; and so on. Lastly, social work supervisors should solicit input from supervisees about what they view as their greatest learning needs and develop learning objectives to meet these needs in partnership with supervisees. Identifying learning needs and developing learning objectives is a collaborative process between social work supervisors and supervisees.

THE EFFECTS OF PROGRAM EVALUATION FINDINGS ON SERVICES

One of the most significant benefits that a program evaluation communicates is the need to make service improvements. Some examples of improvements that may need to be made include:

- Eliminating services that do not achieve program outcomes
- Adding services that are better designed to achieve outcomes
- Acquiring more adequate resources to support effective services
- Targeting a different group of participants to receive services

Evaluation findings should be viewed and communicated as an opportunity to make programs better. Evaluation results that indicate the need for improvement should not be communicated as an indictment of the failure of a program. Program evaluation findings should be viewed with an excitement about the possibilities of developing an even stronger set of service offerings and improving already successful efforts. An action plan aimed at improvement should be developed, based on evaluation results, and communicated widely to key stakeholders.

METHODS TO EVALUATE AGENCY PROGRAMS (E.G., NEEDS ASSESSMENT, FORMATIVE/SUMMATIVE ASSESSMENT, COST EFFECTIVENESS, COST-BENEFIT ANALYSIS, OUTCOMES ASSESSMENT)

Program evaluation is the systematic assessment of the processes and/or outcomes of a program with the intent of furthering its development and improvement. There are many types of program evaluation including, but not limited to, the following.

- A **cost-benefit analysis** determines the financial costs of operating a program as compared with the fiscal benefits of its outcomes. A *cost-benefit ratio* is generated to determine whether, and the extent to which, the costs exceed the benefits. Program decisions can be made to eliminate or modify the program (by reducing program expenditures) based upon the findings.

- A **cost-effectiveness analysis** is similar to a cost-benefit analysis, but distinct. *It considers the benefits that are not measured in monetary terms*, such as illnesses prevented and/or lives saved. It does not produce a cost-benefit ratio, but may focus on the most financially efficient way to achieve a defined outcome or the cost for producing a specific nonmonetary outcome.

- An **outcomes assessment** is the process of determining whether a program has achieved its intended goal(s). It involves collecting evidence through assessment, analyzing the data, and then *using the findings to make programmatic changes if needed*. It is an iterative process with continual feedback loops.

Content Area III: Practice Questions

The following section has 41 unique practice questions that assess retention of material related to interventions for use across systems and with larger systems. The number of questions reflects the approximate proportion of a typical exam (24%) devoted to this content.

1. Which of the following is **MOST** important for a social worker to remember when helping to increase a client's motivation to change?

   A. Motivation fluctuates from one time to another
   B. Motivation can be increased by working to remove barriers to change
   C. Motivation that is imposed by external forces is more salient than that which is intrinsic

2. Which of the following definitions **BEST** defines evidence-based social work practice?

   A. Interventions that a social worker has gained training and experience in delivering
   B. Treatment that yields the most cost-effective outcomes according to a cost–benefit analysis
   C. Decision making based on research knowledge, clinical expertise, and social work values

3. What are the stages of change in sequential order?

   A. Precontemplation, preparation, contemplation, action, maintenance, and relapse
   B. Preparation, precontemplation, contemplation, action, maintenance, and relapse
   C. Precontemplation, contemplation, preparation, action, maintenance, and relapse

(See answers next page.)

1. **B.** Motivation is a state of readiness or eagerness to change. The role of the social worker is to remove barriers that prevent change and to increase a client's intrinsic motivation. If a client is driven to change internally, it is much more likely that the change effort will be sustained. While motivation can vary over time, knowing this is not as important for a social worker as recognizing the need to remove barriers and instill hope or the belief that life can be different.

Question Assesses

Content Area III—Interventions With Clients/Client Systems; Intervention Processes and Techniques for Use Across Systems (Competency); Methods to Engage and Motivate Clients/Client Systems (KSA)

2. **C.** Evidence-based practice (EBP) combines well-researched interventions with clinical experience and ethics, as well as client preferences and culture, to guide and inform the delivery of treatments and services. Social workers, clients, and others must work together to identify what works, for whom, and under what conditions. This approach ensures that the treatments and services, when used as intended, will have the most effective outcomes as demonstrated by the research.

Question Assesses

Content Area III—Interventions With Clients/Client Systems; Intervention Processes and Techniques for Use Across Systems (Competency); Evidence-Based Practice (KSA)

3. **C.** Precontemplation is denial or ignorance of the problem. It is followed by contemplation in which there is ambivalence about making change. Then comes preparation or experimenting with small changes. Action moves toward achieving a goal, whereas maintenance sustains a new behavior and avoids relapse, which can lead to feelings of frustration and failure.

Question Assesses

Content Area III—Interventions With Clients/Client Systems; Intervention Processes and Techniques for Use Across Systems (Competency); The Phases of Intervention and Treatment (KSA)

4. A social worker is interested in seeing the extent to which current clients are satisfied with a new relapse prevention program. The social worker distributes a client satisfaction survey to those in the program. The social worker then collects the surveys and analyzes the results that are presented to a management team in the agency. Which type of evaluation is the social worker conducting?

   A. Summative
   B. Quasi-experimental
   C. Formative

5. A social worker is facilitating a psychotherapy group for individuals who are in recovery from substance abuse. After group, a client mentions that she has been having problems dealing with job stress without the use of substances. In order to meet this client's needs, the social worker should:

   A. Recommend that the client see the social worker individually in addition to the group therapy because she appears to need some additional support
   B. Suggest that the client bring this topic up in the group next week to see if others are having similar problems
   C. Evaluate whether group therapy is the best treatment modality for the client due to the issue being mentioned to the social worker outside of the group context

6. A family comes into treatment because of their young daughter's behavior. They report, upon intake, that she yells at her parents, doesn't listen, and complains about their behavior. There is little progress during the course of treatment and the girl reports that she has no intention of changing. After the sixth session, a social worker tells the girl that she cannot help with her behavior and she should continue to "do as she wishes." Which strategic family therapy technique is the social worker using in this situation?

   A. Paradoxical intent
   B. Pretend technique
   C. Relabeling paradigm

7. In which of the following circumstances is task-centered treatment recommended?

   A. When the client wants to see immediate results or changes in circumstances
   B. When the client is worried about being part of the change process
   C. When the client is addressing long-standing problems that are causing impairments

(See answers next page.)

4. **C.** Formative evaluations examine the process of delivering services, whereas summative evaluations examine the outcomes. Formative evaluations are ongoing processes that allow for feedback to be implemented during service delivery. These types of evaluations allow social workers to make changes as needed to help achieve program goals. Summative evaluations occur at the end of services and provide an overall description of their effectiveness. Summative evaluation examines outcomes to determine whether objectives were met.

The design described is not quasi-experimental, which does not require randomization, but has more support for causal inferences than does preexperimental designs.

Question Assesses

Content Area III—Interventions With Clients/Client Systems; Intervention Processes and Techniques for Use Across Systems (Competency); Methods, Techniques, and Instruments Used to Evaluate Social Work Practice (KSA)

5. **B.** In group therapy, the group is the major helping agent. Issues should be brought back to the group to address. There is no need for the client to see the social worker for individual therapy.

Question Assesses

Content Area III—Interventions With Clients/Client Systems; Intervention Processes and Techniques for Use Across Systems (Competency); Group Work Techniques and Approaches (e.g., Developing and Managing Group Processes and Cohesion) (KSA)

6. **A.** A paradoxical intent or directive prescribes the symptomatic behavior so the client realizes control over it and uses the strength of resistance to change.

Question Assesses

Content Area III—Interventions With Clients/Client Systems; Intervention Processes and Techniques for Use Across Systems (Competency); Family Therapy Models, Interventions, and Approaches (KSA)

7. **A.** A task-centered approach aims to quickly engage clients in the problem-solving process because it is usually delivered in a time-limited environment. The client is an active part of the change process and the approach is highly structured to attempt to achieve immediate results as goals are broken into defined tasks. Termination begins in the first session. This approach is too brief to address long-standing problems that are complex and is not appropriate for clients who cannot be active participants in the change process.

Question Assesses

Content Area III—Interventions With Clients/Client Systems; Intervention Processes and Techniques for Use Across Systems (Competency); Task-Centered Approaches (KSA)

8. A social worker is working with a client who is anxious about public speaking. The social worker asks the client to close her eyes, visualize herself speaking to a large group, and describe her feelings related to the imaginary situation in detail. Which of the following therapeutic techniques is the the social worker employing?

   A. Covert modeling
   B. Self-modeling
   C. Symbolic modeling

9. A social worker is charged with creating a behavioral objective to assist her client, John, in his educational setting. Which of the following statements is the **BEST** example of this type of objective?

   A. John will make eye contact during conversations in practical arts class at least 75% of the time
   B. John will be motivated to complete his homework daily in order to achieve a grade of a B or better
   C. John will sit in his chair at least 80% of the time

10. Which of the following must be remembered by a social worker before identifying if a client is experiencing a life crisis?

    A. Life crises must be precipitated by major life events
    B. The way crises are addressed significantly impact subsequent functioning
    C. Life crises produce anxiety, tension, and disequilibrium

11. Which of the following is a limitation when using existing case records as the data source for the evaluation of client progress?

    A. There are financial benefits because there are no additional costs associated with data collection
    B. The scope of the evaluation is restricted to that which is explicitly stated in the file
    C. Client consent in writing is needed to use case records for this purpose

(*See answers next page.*)

8. **A.** Covert modeling is when clients are asked to use their imagination, visualize the desired behavior, and describe it in detail.

   Self-modeling is when clients are videotaped demonstrating the desired behavior and this tape is watched and discussed. Symbolic modeling includes watching others who have been videotaped perform the desired behavior.

   Question Assesses

   Content Area III—Interventions With Clients/Client Systems; Intervention Processes and Techniques for Use Across Systems (Competency); Role Modeling Techniques (KSA)

9. **A.** A behavioral objective should be client-oriented and emphasize what a client needs to do. An important element of behavioral objectives is that they are observable. Motivation is not easily observed. The conditions under which the behavior will be performed should also be included. One response choice does not indicate if the expectation regarding sitting is to take place during class or all the time. The correct answer has all the elements—it specifies the target behavior, the conditions under which the behavior will be performed, and the criteria for determining when the acceptable performance of the behavior occurs.

   Question Assesses

   Content Area III—Interventions With Clients/Client Systems; Intervention Processes and Techniques for Use Across Systems (Competency); Methods to Develop and Evaluate Measurable Objectives for Client/Client System Intervention, Treatment, and/or Service Plans (KSA)

10. **C.** Life crises do not have to be a major event. They can be the "last straws" in a series of events that exceed the client's ability to cope. Addressing crises appropriately significantly impacts subsequent client functioning and can assist in the development of healthy coping skills. However, this statement is not related to the identification of a life crisis. Only the correct answer identifies symptoms that a social worker can use to determine if a life crisis may be occurring.

    Question Assesses

    Content Area III—Interventions With Clients/Client Systems; Intervention Processes and Techniques for Use Across Systems (Competency); Crisis Intervention and Treatment Approaches (KSA)

11. **B.** Cost savings is a benefit, not a limitation. There may be gaps in the record or the information that is explicitly stated may not reflect all the progress that has been made which is a limitation. Consent is only required for records that are being used in formal evaluation beyond determining individual client progress and consent does not have to be written.

    Question Assesses

    Content Area III—Interventions With Clients/Client Systems; Intervention Processes and Techniques for Use Across Systems (Competency); Case Recording for Practice Evaluation or Supervision (KSA)

12. During an intake interview, a client uses derogatory language to refer to individuals of a particular ethnic group. This language causes the social worker to become angry. In order to appropriately deal with the anger, the social worker should:

   A. Explain to the client that this language is inappropriate and upsets the social worker
   B. Recognize the anger and discuss it later with the supervisor
   C. Tell the client about the reaction so that a decision can be made about whether the social worker is the best match for the client

13. Which is **MOST** important for a social work administrator to remember when using the services of an agency consultant?

   A. Releases of information are needed when sharing identifiable client information
   B. The agency is mandated to follow a consultant's recommendations
   C. A consultant must have demonstrated knowledge, expertise, and competence

14. Which of the following is the **BEST** definition of empowerment?

   A. Obtaining resources to improve clients' financial and social statuses
   B. Assisting clients in controlling and making changes on their own behalf
   C. Creating alliances or power networks that improve clients' social standing

15. Which client behavior or characteristic is contraindicated for the receipt of group therapy?

   A. Feeling of hopelessness
   B. Compulsive need for attention
   C. Isolation from others

(See answers next page.)

12. **B.** A client must feel understood and valued as a person, though the client's performance may be unsatisfactory. If a client feels judged, the client will not speak freely during a social work interview. Hence, a social worker must be interested, genuinely concerned and encouraging, and at the same time, objective, but neither condemning nor praising. In this scenario, the social worker should use the supervisor to process the feelings that arise as a result of the client's actions. The other response choices involve telling the client about the anger, which could interfere with the helping process. Social workers must be skilled in the principles and techniques of interviewing, as well as appropriately dealing with their emotions in a manner that does not negatively impact the therapeutic process.

Question Assesses

Content Area III—Interventions With Clients/Client Systems; Intervention Processes and Techniques for Use Across Systems (Competency); The Principles and Techniques of Interviewing (e.g., Supporting, Clarifying, Focusing, Confronting, Validating, Feedback, Reflecting, Language Differences, Use of Interpreters, and Redirecting) (KSA)

13. **A.** Although a consultant does not have any formal authority over agency decision making, the consultant has informal authority as an "expert." Releases of information are needed when disclosing client data to a consultant. A consultant should be competent, demonstrating knowledge and expertise, but evaluating the competence is not paramount when "using" a consultant. The skill and competence would be evaluating prior to retaining the consultant. The agency is not required to follow the advice given by a consultant. The final decision rests with the agency administration and board of directors.

Question Assesses

Content Area III—Interventions With Clients/Client Systems; Intervention Processes and Techniques for Use Across Systems (Competency); Consultation Approaches (e.g., Referrals to Specialists) (KSA)

14. **B.** Empowerment aims to ensure a sense of control over well-being and that change is possible. It is not doing something for clients, but assisting them to have skills or resources needed to make desired changes.

Question Assesses

Content Area III—Interventions With Clients/Client Systems; Intervention Processes and Techniques for Use Across Systems (Competency); Strengths-Based and Empowerment Strategies and Interventions (KSA)

15. **B.** Clients who are in crisis, suicidal, actively psychotic, or paranoid are not appropriate for group treatment. In addition, those who have a compulsive need for attention are also not good group participants. Clients who are feeling hopeless and isolated can benefit from the socialization and universality that groups offer.

Question Assesses

Content Area III—Interventions With Clients/Client Systems; Intervention Processes and Techniques for Use Across Systems (Competency); Group Work Techniques and Approaches (e.g., Developing and Managing Group Processes and Cohesion) (KSA)

16. A client enters a social worker's office and is outraged at an interaction that has just taken place with another agency staff member. The client is indignant and demands that the social worker "do something." In this situation, the social worker should **FIRST**:

    A. Explain to the client that the issue is best handled directly with the staff member
    B. Instruct the client to go to the agency director who is in a position to take action
    C. Listen to the client's account of the interaction with the staff member

17. A teenager is having problems initiating conversation with peers. In order to **BEST** assist the teenager, the social worker should:

    A. Ask the teenager to journal thoughts that can be used in later conversations with peers
    B. Explore with the teenager the underlying reasons for the problems with peer relationships
    C. Engage in role play with the teenager to practice needed communication skills

18. When working with an involuntary, court-mandated client, a social worker who is addressing resistance should **FIRST**:

    A. Ask the client to explain the reasons for referral for treatment
    B. Educate the client about information that will be submitted to the court
    C. Acknowledge the client's circumstances and lack of choice in receiving services

19. A mother and teenage child yell at each other almost the entire time of a session. The mother says that she is upset with her daughter's choice in boyfriend, her grades in school, her inappropriate dress, and her lack of help around the house. The daughter says that she is angry as her mother does not listen to her, does not respect her privacy, does not give her any "space," and speaks to the daughter's friends in a demeaning manner. In order to **BEST** assist with helping them resolve their conflicts, the social worker should:

    A. Work with the mother and child to prioritize their concerns
    B. Focus on both the mother's and child's strengths and skills
    C. Acknowledge the level of conflict and discord between the mother and child

20. Which of the following is an incongruent communication?

    A. Smiling at a person who is being annoying
    B. Hugging a person in pain
    C. Yelling at a person who is upsetting

(See answers next page.)

16. **C.** Silence is effective when faced by a client who is experiencing a high degree of emotion. The social worker should not send the client to someone else or take action until the nature of the situation is known. Listening and finding out more is the FIRST step in deciding the appropriate next steps, if any.

Question Assesses

Content Area III—Interventions With Clients/Client Systems; Intervention Processes and Techniques for Use Across Systems (Competency); Verbal and Nonverbal Communication Techniques (KSA)

17. **C.** Role playing is a very effective teaching strategy and provides active learning. None of the other response choices that may be useful provides the teenager with an intervention (as the question is about the best way to assist) that allows the youth to practice communication skills that can be used with peers.

Question Assesses

Content Area III—Interventions With Clients/Client Systems; Intervention Processes and Techniques for Use Across Systems (Competency); The Techniques of Role Play (KSA)

18. **C.** The problem-solving process starts with engagement. Acknowledging the client's circumstances is an action that the social worker can take to show empathy and an understanding of the difficulty of the situation. Some of the other response choices may be useful in working with an involuntary, court-mandated client, but they are not done FIRST.

Question Assesses

Content Area III—Interventions With Clients/Client Systems; Intervention Processes and Techniques for Use Across Systems (Competency); Methods to Engage and Work With Involuntary Clients/Client Systems (KSA)

19. **A.** Given that there is conflict over a number of issues, the social worker should help structure the interactions between the mother and child. Essential is deciding which of the complaints is most salient for the mother and child. Acknowledging the conflict and using the strengths and skills of each party during conflict resolution may be useful, but will not assist in helping with resolution like prioritization, given the number of issues raised.

Question Assesses

Content Area III—Interventions With Clients/Client Systems; Intervention Processes and Techniques for Use Across Systems (Competency); Partializing Techniques (KSA)

20. **A.** Congruence is when the communication of individuals match their feelings. An individual who is being annoyed by someone would not smile. If the facial expression matched the individual's feelings, it would be a frown or grimace.

Question Assesses

Content Area III—Interventions With Clients/Client Systems; Intervention Processes and Techniques for Use Across Systems (Competency); The Concept of Congruence in Communication (KSA)

21. A client who has repeatedly stated that she hates her sister tells a social worker that she has just asked her sister to be the maid of honor in her wedding. The social worker points out that this action appears contradictory to her feelings about her sister. Which of the following therapeutic techniques is the the social worker employing?

    A. Clarification
    B. Paradoxical instruction
    C. Confrontation

22. Which of the following elements of a client crisis will **MOST** directly impact selection of an appropriate intervention approach?

    A. Crises are usually time limited
    B. Crises focus on the "here and now"
    C. Crises are not usually triggered by a major life event

23. A social worker finds that a client has poor interpersonal skills. Which intervention by a social worker will **BEST** address this issue?

    A. Modeling appropriate verbal and nonverbal communication skills
    B. Conducting intensive psychotherapy aimed at addressing the communication deficits
    C. Providing the client with educational instruction on appropriate interpersonal skills

24. Upon coming in for an intake interview, a couple reports that they have not had sexual intercourse for more than a year due to the husband's inability to sustain an erection. He reports that he has had a lot of stress at work and feels overwhelmed by the pressures placed upon him. In order to best diagnose the reasons for the husband's sexual dysfunction, a social worker should **FIRST**:

    A. Ask the husband to provide more information about his job stress
    B. Recommend that the husband see a physician to see if there are any medical problems
    C. Explore whether the couple is having any other problems in the relationship

(*See answers next page.*)

21. **C.** Confrontation is calling attention to something.

   Clarification is reformulating a problem in the client's words to make sure there is a mutual understanding of the issue. A paradoxical instruction is prescribing the opposite of what you want the client to do; it is commonly referred to as "reverse psychology."

   Question Assesses

   Content Area III—Interventions With Clients/Client Systems; Intervention Processes and Techniques for Use Across Systems (Competency); The Principles and Techniques of Interviewing (e.g., Supporting, Clarifying, Focusing, Confronting, Validating, Feedback, Reflecting, Language Differences, Use of Interpreters, and Redirecting) (KSA)

22. **B.** While crises are usually time limited and do not need to be triggered by a major life event, these elements have less impact on selection of an intervention approach. Crisis intervention is focused on the "here and now." The goal is to intervene quickly, using modalities that will provide immediate relief. There is usually a heightened level of activity by the social worker to assist clients in alleviating stress and returning to the previous level of functioning.

   Question Assesses

   Content Area III—Interventions With Clients/Client Systems; Intervention Processes and Techniques for Use Across Systems (Competency); Crisis Intervention and Treatment Approaches (KSA)

23. **A.** Modeling is a very effective method for teaching and should be used whenever possible. Educating a client is empowering but not as effective as demonstrating or showing. The social worker should not assume that the skill deficits are a result of a deeper clinical issue.

   Question Assesses

   Content Area III—Interventions With Clients/Client Systems; Intervention Processes and Techniques for Use Across Systems (Competency); Role Modeling Techniques (KSA)

24. **B.** It is essential to FIRST determine whether the sexual dysfunction is a result of a medical problem that is preventing the husband's ability to sustain his erection. If medical causes are ruled out by a physician, a social worker can examine psychological and/or social factors that are contributing, including work and other pressures. It also may be helpful to determine whether there are other problems in the relationship, but only after medical/ biological etiology has been eliminated.

   Question Assesses

   Content Area III—Interventions With Clients/Client Systems; Intervention Processes and Techniques for Use Across Systems (Competency); Couples Interventions and Treatment Approaches (KSA)

25. During an initial session, a client complains that she feels like a failure because she is getting divorced and could not "save her marriage." She ends by asking whether she is wrong to feel this way. In order to facilitate the therapeutic alliance, the social worker should:

    A. Explore why she thinks that the divorce is causing her to feel this way
    B. Find out more about her past relationships
    C. Explain that such feelings are common in this situation

26. The immediate goal of social work services for a client in crisis is to:

    A. Assist the client to return to the previous level of functioning
    B. Determine whether the stressors have caused the client to be a danger to self or others
    C. Help the client deal with the impacts of the trauma caused by the crisis

27. Which of the following target populations would **BEST** have their needs fulfilled by participation in a psychoeducational group?

    A. Older adults with high blood pressure who need to learn about healthy eating methods
    B. Teens who need support to address issues of addiction
    C. Couples who have experienced loss and are having trouble coping

(*See answers next page.*)

25. **C.** These statements are occurring in the first or initial session. The goal of this session is the building of a therapeutic alliance or engagement. Providing her with assurance that her feelings are not unusual and are shared with others in this situation alleviates anxiety and guilt, making her more open to speak about her difficulties. It also shows the client that the social worker understands what she is experiencing. The other response choices may be done, but are not the best responses given that the answer needed to directly relate to an action that would "facilitate the therapeutic alliance."

Question Assesses

Content Area III—Interventions With Clients/Client Systems; Intervention Processes and Techniques for Use Across Systems (Competency); The Principles and Techniques of Interviewing (e.g., Supporting, Clarifying, Focusing, Confronting, Validating, Feedback, Reflecting, Language Differences, Use of Interpreters, and Redirecting) (KSA)

26. **A.** The goals of crisis intervention are to immediately relieve the stress experienced, return the client to a previous level of functioning or assist with regaining equilibrium, and help develop coping mechanisms.

Question Assesses

Content Area III—Interventions With Clients/Client Systems; Intervention Processes and Techniques for Use Across Systems (Competency); Crisis Intervention and Treatment Approaches (KSA)

27. **A.** The aim of a psychoeducational group is education. With improved education about healthy eating, older adults have information needed to make good food choices. The other target populations could benefit from psychotherapeutic groups as they could benefit from interacting with others who are experiencing the same difficulties. Realizing that they are not alone can help these individuals with shame or isolation. Peer support is usually associated as a benefit from psychotherapeutic groups, not psychoeducational ones.

Question Assesses

Content Area III—Interventions With Clients/Client Systems; Intervention Processes and Techniques for Use Across Systems (Competency); Psychoeducation Methods (e.g., Acknowledging, Supporting, and Normalizing) (KSA)

28. Which of the following observation role poses the **MOST** ethical challenges for a social worker?

    A. Complete participant
    B. Participant as observer
    C. Complete observer

29. The **MOST** important aim of case management is to:

    A. Avoid duplication and gaps in treatment care
    B. Monitor multiple services to ensure efficient and effective service provision
    C. Ameliorate emotional or mental dysfunction in order to maximize well-being

30. A client barges into a social worker's office yelling in a loud and hostile manner. The **MOST** effective method for the social worker to address the situation is to:

    A. Explain to the client that the concerns can be discussed during a scheduled appointment
    B. Listen to the client, providing alternative methods to reach the social worker in the future
    C. Contact agency security immediately to remove the client to address any safety concerns

(*See answers next page.*)

28. **A.** At one end of the continuum, a social worker is a full participant in the activities; at the other end, a social worker is a pure observer, seeking to be as unobtrusive as possible so as not to influence the situation being observed in any way. "Participant as observer" and "observer as participant" fall somewhere along this continuum, since a social worker is either already part of a group or context being researched or seeks to become involved in order to gain access to the information required.

Participation of a social worker raises potential questions of bias and subjectivity that might undermine the reliability and validity of any information gathered. Thus, "complete participant" is the most problematic.

Question Assesses

Content Area III—Interventions With Clients/Client Systems; Intervention Processes and Techniques for Use Across Systems (Competency); The Principles of Active Listening and Observation (KSA)

29. **A.** Case management can be defined in many ways and has numerous aims. Most of them are based on the belief that clients need assistance because the service delivery system is complex, fragmented, duplicative, and uncoordinated. A major case management activity is linking to services to fill treatment gaps. Case management is distinct from psychotherapy. The efficiency and effectiveness of service utilization is not the most important aim as it does not view case management from the client perspective which is more concerned with duplication and gaps.

Question Assesses

Content Area III—Interventions With Clients/Client Systems; Intervention Processes and Techniques for Use Across Systems (Competency); The Components of Case Management (KSA)

30. **B.** The client is clearly exhibiting a lot of emotion. In this state, providing direction or instruction will not be effective and can escalate the situation. Listening or being silent is a good technique to diffuse the hostility, but limit setting may also be needed. The client should be provided with alternate strategies for accessing the social worker if a need arises in the future. There is no immediate safety risk described.

Question Assesses

Content Area III—Interventions With Clients/Client Systems; Intervention Processes and Techniques for Use Across Systems (Competency); Verbal and Nonverbal Communication Techniques (KSA)

31. Which of the following is an appropriate task for a social worker facilitating a group?

    A. Modeling methods for dealing with dilemmas or situations that arise in the group

    B. Explaining the goals of the group during initial sessions

    C. Providing solutions to problems that are raised by the group

32. Which of the following is essential for implementing a strengths-based intervention?

    A. Opportunities must be created for clients to learn or display competencies

    B. Social workers must work to strengthen collaboration and partnership with the client

    C. Current struggles that clients are experiencing must be the primary focus of treatment

33. Federal law requires health care facilities that receive government insurance reimbursement to:

    A. Provide a comprehensive system of medical care to meet clients' needs

    B. Ask clients if they have advance directives and document their responses

    C. Ensure clients have access to all requested medical treatment and services

34. Which of the following is true of networking in both business and social work practice?

    A. Networking creates opportunities for attracting more clients to agencies and organizations

    B. Networking is beneficial for clients as it keeps the costs down through sharing of resources

    C. Networking creates a community and builds alliances around a common interest or goal

(*See answers next page.*)

31. **A.** When working with groups, a social worker should use the group as the major helping agent and not set goals for the group. A social worker should not provide solutions as problem-solving is the responsibility of the group. Social workers are role models and can be helpful in demonstrating ways of dealing with dilemmas or situations.

Question Assesses

Content Area III—Interventions With Clients/Client Systems; Intervention Processes and Techniques for Use Across Systems (Competency); Group Work Techniques and Approaches (e.g., Developing and Managing Group Processes and Cohesion) (KSA)

32. **A.** A strengths-based intervention focuses on client learning and competency. Social workers strengthening collaboration does not focus on viewing client capacities, which is a hallmark of strengths-based intervention. Also, looking at current struggles is not focused on client's as experts in their own lives which needs to be central to the correct answer.

Question Assesses

Content Area III—Interventions With Clients/Client Systems; Intervention Processes and Techniques for Use Across Systems (Competency); Strengths-Based and Empowerment Strategies and Interventions (KSA)

33. **B.** Health care facilities must inform clients of their rights to make decisions concerning their own health care by asking and documenting whether clients have advance directives. Health care providers do not have to deliver all requested services, only those that are medically necessary. Providers are also not responsible for a comprehensive system of care as they may be part of a broader network, with each provider delivering some form of treatment.

Question Assesses

Content Area III—Interventions With Clients/Client Systems; Intervention Processes and Techniques for Use With Larger Systems (Competency); The Effects of Policies, Procedures, Regulations, and Legislation on Social Work Practice and Service Delivery (KSA)

34. **C.** Networking may not attract more clients to social work organizations as agencies may receive clients through court referrals or other means. Networking may also not lower costs as operating costs of social work agencies or services may be fixed. In both business and social work, networking provides opportunities to work with others toward the achievement of common goals and helps in establishing professional relationships or alliances.

Question Assesses

Content Area III—Interventions With Clients/Client Systems; Intervention Processes and Techniques for Use With Larger Systems (Competency); Methods of Networking (KSA)

35. Which of the following is the **MOST** important benefit of community participation in social work practice?

    A. Decision-making power is placed partly or wholly with community members
    B. Community members are informed about the work that needs to be done to make change
    C. Workload demands are divided and distributed among a larger group

36. A client needs to access services from another organization. In order to **BEST** assist this client, a social worker should:

    A. Facilitate a referral to another agency that provides high quality services
    B. Help the client to select an agency that the client thinks will best meet the current need
    C. Contact the client's insurance company to see which agencies are participating providers

37. An agency that employs social workers has detailed job descriptions that delineate the best way to perform functions, closely supervises its employees, and ties employee pay increases to behaviors that promote the goals of the organization. Which of the following approaches is **MOST** likely being used by the agency to manage its workers?

    A. Scientific management
    B. Human relations
    C. Systems

38. The primary objective of social work supervision is to:

    A. Increase the social worker's capacity to work more effectively
    B. Assist the social worker in resolving conflicts or problems
    C. Assure the delivery of the most effective and efficient client services

(*See answers next page.*)

35. **A.** The values and principles of social work practice should be used as the basis for selecting the most important benefit. The correct answer is based on the belief of self-determination or that individuals and groups should take actions that are best for them. The other response choices may be true, but they are not based on this fundamental concept in social work practice.

Question Assesses

Content Area III—Interventions With Clients/Client Systems; Intervention Processes and Techniques for Use With Larger Systems (Competency); Techniques for Mobilizing Community Participation (KSA)

36. **B.** Social workers want to respect a client's right to self-determination and should not select an agency for the client. Working with insurance companies to ensure coverage is a part of the process, but the decision should primarily be based on the client's choice of provider. Just because an agency has a good reputation does not mean that the client will want to use this provider to meet the current need.

Question Assesses

Content Area III—Interventions With Clients/Client Systems; Intervention Processes and Techniques for Use With Larger Systems (Competency); Methods to Assess the Availability of Community Resources

37. **A.** A scientific management approach finds the one "best way" to perform each task; carefully matches each worker to each task; closely supervises workers, using reward and punishment as motivators; and manages and controls behavior.

A systems approach considers the organization as a system composed of interrelated subsystems. A human relations approach emphasizes creativity, cohesive work groups, participatory leadership, and open communication.

Question Assesses

Content Area III—Interventions With Clients/Client Systems; Intervention Processes and Techniques for Use With Larger Systems (Competency); Theories of Organizational Development and Structure (KSA)

38. **C.** Supervision ensures that services are tailored to specific client needs and are delivered in adherence with the professional code of ethics. Supervision is for the benefit of clients, not social workers. Thus, enhancing social workers' capacities or helping social workers make decisions is not the primary intent.

Question Assesses

Content Area III—Interventions With Clients/Client Systems; Intervention Processes and Techniques for Use With Larger Systems (Competency); Methods to Identify Learning Needs and Develop Learning Objectives for Supervisees (KSA)

39. Which of the following is the **BEST** example of client advocacy?

    A. Helping community members draft a letter to legislators about a harmful proposed bill
    B. Writing a press release for a local paper about a growing community problem
    C. Providing community members with education about resources to meet current needs

40. Members of a community are concerned about rising crime rates, drug problems, and high unemployment in their neighborhood. When engaging in community organizing with this group, the social worker should **FIRST**:

    A. Tell community members about strategies that have worked well in other locations
    B. Work with the citizens to prioritize their concerns
    C. Identify a community member who can lead others in taking action

41. As required by law, which of the following are required for students with disabilities to ensure that their learning needs are effectively met?

    A. Wrap around services
    B. Individual education plans
    C. School-based youth services programs

(*See answers next page.*)

39. **A.** Examples of client advocacy activities include helping to modify or influence policies or practices that adversely affect groups or communities; or promote legislation or policies that will result in the provision of requisite resources or services. Writing a press release and educating clients are not directly related to advocacy. Only the correct answer focuses on influencing decision makers to prevent a harmful policy.

Question Assesses

Content Area III—Interventions With Clients/Client Systems; Intervention Processes and Techniques for Use With Larger Systems (Competency); Theories and Methods of Advocacy for Policies, Services, and Resources to Meet Clients'/Client Systems' Needs (KSA)

40. **B.** Community organization aims to develop leadership so that communities can better address their problems. Using the problem-solving process, the social worker should FIRST help the members to figure out which problem they would like to address. The social worker may help the group with other actions, but they are later in the process. The social worker must also not "take charge" because community organizing is about empowering individuals within the community to decide on the problems and take actions to make changes.

Question Assesses

Content Area III—Interventions With Clients/Client Systems; Intervention Processes and Techniques for Use With Larger Systems (Competency); Community Organizing and Social Planning Methods (KSA)

41. **B.** Children with disabilities needing assistance should be provided with individual education plans (IEPs) that are revised at least annually. A team composed of social workers, teachers, administrators, and other relevant school personnel typically create these plans. The parents, and often the children, also participate. The IEPs include a statement of goals, means of attaining goals, and ways of evaluating goal attainment.

Question Assesses

Content Area III—Interventions With Clients/Client Systems; Intervention Processes and Techniques for Use With Larger Systems (Competency); The Effects of Policies, Procedures, Regulations, and Legislation on Social Work Practice and Service Delivery (KSA)

Practice Questions					
Content Area III: Intervention With Clients/Client Systems (24%)					
Competency	**Question Numbers**	**Number of Questions**	**Number Correct**	**Percentage Correct**	**Area Requiring Further Study?**
1. Intervention Processes and Techniques for Use Across Systems	1, 2, 3, 4, 5, 6, 7, 8, 9, 10, 11, 12, 13, 14, 15, 16, 17, 18, 19, 20, 21, 22, 23, 24, 25, 26, 27, 28, 29, 30, 31, 32	32	___/32	___%	
2. Intervention Processes and Techniques for Use With Larger Systems	33, 34, 35, 36, 37, 38, 39, 40, 41	9	___/9	___%	

Content Area IV: Professional Relationships, Values, and Ethics (25%)

9

Professional Values and Ethical Issues

LEGAL AND/OR ETHICAL ISSUES RELATED TO THE PRACTICE OF SOCIAL WORK, INCLUDING RESPONSIBILITY TO CLIENTS/CLIENT SYSTEMS, COLLEAGUES, THE PROFESSION, AND SOCIETY

Social workers frequently encounter ethical and legal issues. In most instances, ethical and legal standards complement each other. However, in some circumstances, ethical and legal standards conflict. The ethical standards for social workers are outlined in the *NASW Code of Ethics*. With regard to legal mandates, social workers must be aware of five distinct sets of requirements: constitutional law, statutory law, regulatory law, court-made/common law, and executive orders.

Ethical and legal issues encountered by social workers fall into four distinct categories:

1. Actions that are compatible with both legal and ethical standards in social work (legal and ethical)

2. Actions that are neither legal nor ethical in social work according to prevailing standards (not legal and not ethical)

3. Actions that are legal, but not ethical according to prevailing standards (legal, but not ethical)

4. Actions that are ethical, but not legal according to standards and laws (ethical, but not legal)

When there are conflicts between ethical and legal standards, a social worker should identify the mandates that conflict. A social worker should also identify the individuals, groups, and organizations that are likely to be affected by the outcome of the conflict. All possible courses of action and the benefits and risks of each alternative should be considered, including the reasons supporting and in opposition to each possibility. Resolution of conflicts should not be done in a vacuum and a social worker should consult with colleagues and appropriate experts. All steps in the decision-making process should be documented. Once a decision is made, the results should be monitored and evaluated.

The *NASW Code of Ethics*—states that all ethical standards are applicable to interactions, relationships, or communications, whether they occur in person or with the use of technology (*NASW Code of Ethics—Purpose of the NASW Code of Ethics*). Technology-assisted social work services include all aspects of practice involving the use of computers, mobile or land-line telephones, online social media, chat rooms, text messaging, email, and emerging digital applications.

Social workers who use technology in the provision of social work services should ensure that they have the knowledge and skills to provide such services competently, including understanding the special communication challenges when using technology and implementing strategies to address these challenges. Additionally, these social workers should comply with the laws governing technology and social work practice in the jurisdictions in which they are regulated and located and, as applicable, in the jurisdictions in which clients are located (*NASW Code of Ethics—Competence*).

PROFESSIONAL VALUES AND PRINCIPLES (E.G., COMPETENCE, SOCIAL JUSTICE, INTEGRITY, AND DIGNITY AND WORTH OF THE PERSON)

The mission of the social work profession is rooted in a set of core values. These core values are the foundation of social work practice:

- Service
- Social justice
- Dignity and worth of the person
- Importance of human relationships
- Integrity
- Competence

Professional ethics are based on these basic values and guide social workers' conduct. These standards are relevant to all social workers, regardless of their professional functions, the settings in which they work, or the populations they serve.

Professional ethics are "rules" based on the core values of the profession that should be adhered to by social workers. They are statements to the general public about what they can expect from a social worker. These standards tell new social workers what is essential for practice based on the profession's core values. Social workers are judged with regard to competency based on these standards.

Professional standards are also helpful in guiding social workers when they are unsure about a course of action or conflicts arise.

The social work profession is based on the belief that every person has dignity and worth. It is essential that social workers respect this value and treat everyone in a caring and respectful fashion. Social workers should also be mindful of individual differences, as well as cultural and ethnic diversity.

Social workers should promote clients' right to self-determination and act as a resource to assist clients to address their own needs. Social workers have a dual responsibility to clients and to the broader society and must resolve any conflicts, in a socially responsible and ethical manner, that arise due to this dual mandate.

TECHNIQUES TO IDENTIFY AND RESOLVE ETHICAL DILEMMAS

An ethical dilemma is a predicament when a social worker must decide between two viable solutions that seem to have similar ethical value. Sometimes two viable ethical solutions can conflict with each other. Social workers should be aware of any conflicts between personal and professional values and deal with them responsibly.

In instances where social workers' ethical obligations conflict with agency policies or relevant laws or regulations, they should make a responsible effort to resolve the conflict in a manner that is consistent with ethical values, principles, and standards.

In order to resolve this conflict, ethical problem solving is needed.

Essential Steps in Ethical Problem Solving

1. Identify ethical standards, as defined by the professional code of ethics, that are being compromised (always go to the *NASW Code of Ethics* first—do not rely on supervisor or coworkers).

2. Determine whether there is an ethical issue or dilemma.

3. Weigh ethical issues in light of key social work values and principles as defined by the *NASW Code of Ethics*.

4. Suggest modifications in light of the prioritized ethical values and principles that are central to the dilemma.

5. Implement modifications in light of prioritized ethical values and principles.

6. Monitor for new ethical issues or dilemmas.

CLIENT/CLIENT SYSTEM COMPETENCE AND SELF-DETERMINATION (E.G., FINANCIAL DECISIONS, TREATMENT DECISIONS, EMANCIPATION, AGE OF CONSENT, PERMANENCY PLANNING)

Self-determination, the concept that clients are qualified to make their own decisions about their lives, is a central concept in the social work profession. It is described in the *NASW Code of Ethics*–as one of a social worker's primary ethical responsibilities. Using a strengths-based perspective, all clients are assumed to be competent to make their own decisions, including those about financial matters and treatment options.

When working with clients, there may be, at times, some concerns about their cognitive or functional abilities to perform life tasks. For example, clients who are not able to complete activities of daily living independently may need services to assist them in these areas. The need to rely on others to assist may limit clients' independence. An assessment which can assist social workers in determining assistance needed in functional life domains is the *World Health Organization Disability Assessment Schedule (WHODAS)*.

When limitations are not physical, but involve mental processes, there may be some unease about clients' abilities to provide consent related to financial, medical, and/or legal treatment. All those over the age of majority (adults) are presumed to be competent to provide consent unless legal proceedings have found otherwise. When clients lack the capacity to provide consent, social workers should protect clients' interests by seeking permission from an appropriate third party and informing clients in a manner consistent with the clients' level of understanding. In such instances, social workers should seek to ensure that the third party acts in a manner consistent with clients' wishes and interests. Social workers should take reasonable steps to enhance such clients' ability to give informed consent (*NASW Code of Ethics—Informed Consent*).

Emancipation and Age of Consent

Treating minors requires social workers to be well versed in state and federal laws related to consent and confidentiality. The age at which minors can obtain services without parental/guardian permission varies by state and the type of service being delivered. Minors also do not have the same legal rights to confidentiality in some instances because parents/guardians may have access to minors' records.

Even when parental/guardian consent is needed for treatment, social workers should provide explanations to minors of all elements required in a consent procedure, using language that can easily be understood. Social workers should also seek the minor's assent or willingness to participate.

During the problem-solving process, social workers treating minors must make clear to them all the limits to their self-determination imposed by legal, financial, and other constraints.

Within our society, minors do not have the same rights as adults. Emancipation is a legal process that ends the rights and responsibilities of parents or guardians over minor children. However, there can be either a partial or complete emancipation. Emancipation involves decision-making authority. Upon achieving emancipation, the minor assumes the rights, privileges, and duties of adulthood before actually reaching the "age of majority" (adulthood). An emancipated minor can enter into a contract, sue others, make health care decisions, and so on. However, the emancipated minor still has to follow other laws and still cannot get a driver's license or drink alcohol prior to the legal age to do so.

All states have laws dealing with the emancipation of minors; that is, laws that specify when and under what conditions children can become independent of their parents or guardians for important legal purposes. Approximately half of the states regulate emancipation by statutes specifically designed for that purpose. These statutes set forth the conditions required or the procedures for seeking emancipation. Statutes vary considerably from state to state, but most states allow for the possibility of court-reviewed emancipation. The age at which minors can apply for or petition for emancipation varies between states.

Under normal circumstances, a minor is presumed to become emancipated from parents/guardians upon reaching the age of majority. In most states, the age of majority is 18.

TECHNIQUES FOR PROTECTING AND ENHANCING CLIENT/CLIENT SYSTEM SELF-DETERMINATION

Social workers respect and promote the right of clients to self-determination and assist clients in their efforts to identify and clarify their goals. Social workers may limit clients' right to self-determination when, in social workers' professional judgment, clients' actions or potential actions pose serious, foreseeable, and imminent risk to themselves or others (*NASW Code of Ethics—Self-Determination*).

THE CLIENT'S/CLIENT SYSTEM'S RIGHT TO REFUSE SERVICES (E.G., MEDICATION, MEDICAL TREATMENT, COUNSELING, PLACEMENT, ETC.)

Social workers should provide services to clients only in the context of a professional relationship based, when appropriate, on valid informed consent. Social workers should use clear and understandable language to inform clients of the purpose of the services, risks related to the services, limits to services because of the requirements of a third-party payer, relevant costs, reasonable alternatives, clients' right to refuse or withdraw consent, and the time frame covered by the consent. Social workers should provide clients with an opportunity to ask questions (*NASW Code of Ethics—Informed Consent*).

In instances when clients are receiving services involuntarily, social workers should provide information about the nature and extent of services and about the extent of clients' right to refuse service (*NASW Code of Ethics—Informed Consent*).

PROFESSIONAL BOUNDARIES IN THE SOCIAL WORKER–CLIENT/CLIENT SYSTEM RELATIONSHIP (E.G., POWER DIFFERENCES, CONFLICTS OF INTEREST, ETC.)

Many standards speak to the professional boundaries that social workers should maintain with clients. These include those related to sexual relationships, physical contact, and sexual harassment.

The standards that govern social work practice address the use of physical contact with clients. Setting clear, appropriate, and sensitive boundaries that govern physical contact are essential for professional practice (*NASW Code of Ethics—Physical Contact*). Social workers should not engage in physical contact with clients when there is a possibility of psychological harm to a client as a result of the contact (such as cradling or caressing clients).

Physical contact or other activities of a sexual nature with clients are clearly not allowed by social workers.

Social workers should under no circumstances engage in sexual activities, inappropriate sexual communications through the use of technology or in person, or sexual contact with current clients, whether such contact is consensual or forced (*NASW Code of Ethics—Sexual Relationships*).

Social workers should not engage in sexual activities or sexual contact with clients' relatives or other individuals with whom clients maintain a close personal relationship when there is a risk of exploitation or potential harm to a client. Sexual activity or sexual contact with clients' relatives or other individuals with whom clients maintain a personal relationship has the potential to be harmful to a client and may make it difficult for a social worker and client to maintain appropriate professional boundaries. Social workers—not their clients, their clients' relatives, or other individuals with whom a client maintains a personal relationship—assume the full burden for setting clear, appropriate, and culturally sensitive boundaries (*NASW Code of Ethics—Sexual Relationships*).

Social workers should not engage in sexual activities or sexual contact with former clients because of the potential for harm to a client. If social workers engage in conduct contrary to this prohibition or claim that an exception to this prohibition is warranted because of extraordinary circumstances, it is social workers—not their clients—who assume the full burden of demonstrating that the former client has not been exploited, coerced, or manipulated, intentionally or unintentionally (*NASW Code of Ethics—Sexual Relationships*).

Social workers should not provide clinical services to individuals with whom they have had a prior sexual relationship. Providing clinical services to a former sexual partner has the potential to be harmful to the individual and is likely to make it difficult for a social worker and individual to maintain appropriate professional boundaries (*NASW Code of Ethics—Sexual Relationships*).

In addition, social workers should not sexually harass supervisees, students, trainees, colleagues, or clients, including sexual advances, sexual solicitation, requests for sexual favors, and other verbal, written, electronic, or physical conduct of a sexual nature (*NASW Code of Ethics—Sexual Harassment*).

Social workers should avoid communication with clients using technology (such as social networking sites, online chat, e-mail, text messages, telephone, and video) for personal or non-work-related purposes and be aware that posting personal information on professional websites or other media might cause boundary confusion, inappropriate dual relationships, or harm to clients. Social workers should avoid accepting requests from or engaging in personal relationships with clients on social networking sites or other electronic media (*NASW Code of Ethics—Conflicts of Interest*).

Clients may discover social workers' posts and interactions on websites, social media, and other forms of technology. Such involvement may affect the ability of social workers to work effectively with some clients (*NASW Code of Ethics—Conflicts of Interest*).

SELF-DISCLOSURE PRINCIPLES AND APPLICATIONS

The decision about whether to disclose personal information by a social worker often arises in practice because the social worker–client relationship involves the discussion of intimate topics. Some self-disclosure by a social worker may be harmless and even therapeutically useful as it can help clients connect during engagement and/or realize that they are not the only ones who have experienced similar problems.

However, some self-disclosure is exploitative, self-serving, and harmful to clients. Many boundary violations begin as a result of social workers discussing personal information with clients. Though not intended to be the start of friendships or more intimate relationships, self-disclosure by social workers, perhaps well meaning, can blur the boundaries between professional and personal relationships.

Sometimes social workers disclose personal information because they have experienced trauma or other problems which have not been adequately addressed and they are looking to connect with others in order to cope with their own challenges. Social workers may also self-disclose about problems because they think that clients can help them in some way, such as giving them legal advice if the clients are lawyers.

Sometimes clients learn personal information about social workers unexpectedly. For example, a social worker may run into a client at a community activity. These situations cannot be anticipated and may provide personal information to a client about a social worker that the social worker would prefer not to have been revealed.

Most therapeutic situations require no self-disclosure by a social worker. In fact, a client having information about a social worker's family, personal interests, and/or relationship status can be an indication of a potential boundary violation.

Prior to disclosing any information about themselves, social workers should engage in consultation or supervision about why such disclosure is being considered and why it is professionally justified in this instance. Only when it will clearly assist clients and there are no other methods for achieving the same outcome should it be contemplated. Better understanding by social workers about their own desire to self-disclose is necessary in order to prevent boundary crossings which are harmful to clients.

LEGAL AND/OR ETHICAL ISSUES REGARDING DOCUMENTATION

In addition to maintaining confidentiality of client records, there are many other obligations related to documentation that social workers must consider in order to follow legal and/or ethical standards.

It is important to document the purpose, goals, plans, services, interventions, and referrals offered and provided to clients. Assessments, evaluations, recommendations, and circumstances of termination should also be documented in the client record. Consultations with supervisors and other professionals and rationale for practice decisions should be documented as well. Client records should include informed consent and release of information documents. All information relevant to client contact should be stated in clear, accurate terms. False, inaccurate, or misleading information in a client record is unethical and may be potentially harmful to clients and pose a liability risk to social workers. It is unethical to alter case notes after the fact. If necessary, social workers should add new notes with current dates indicating that, in review, past entries were found to be inaccurately documented and correction of those inaccuracies should be clearly stated.

In an effort to ensure continuity of service, it is imperative that client contact be documented in a timely, thorough, and accurate manner. Timely documentation is required for optimal service continuity when clients are transferred from one staff member to another in an agency or when clients are referred out of the agency to collaborating agencies. In addition, accurate and timely records are required by insurers, funding agencies, and so on. Lastly, documentation of significant aspects of client contact is also critical to protecting social workers in the event of lawsuits or ethics complaints.

Client contact documentation should include social history, assessment, treatment plans, intervention strategies, dates and times of contacts, methods of evaluation of progress, reasons for termination, documentation of informed consent and release of information signatures, contacts with all third parties, consultation with collaborating professionals, explanation of social worker's reasoning regarding decisions, recommendations, interventions, and referrals and documentation of any critical incidents. Documentation should be completed as soon as possible after contact so as to ensure accuracy and to maintain up-to-date information in the record in the event of an emergency or the social workers' absence or incapacitation that would require another professional to intervene.

Social workers should only include relevant information that is directly related to client issues for the purpose of service provided. Client records should not include subjective or speculative observation, or any extraneous and irrelevant information.

Social workers must be familiar with legal and ethical protections available for clients—including keeping psychotherapy notes in locations which are secure, but separate from clients' files to provide additional confidentiality protections.

LEGAL AND/OR ETHICAL ISSUES REGARDING TERMINATION

Social workers should terminate services to clients and professional relationships with them when such services and relationships are no longer required or no longer serve client needs or interests (*NASW Code of Ethics—Termination of Services*).

Social workers should take reasonable steps to avoid abandoning clients who are still in need of services. Social workers should withdraw services precipitously only under unusual circumstances, giving careful consideration to all factors in the situation and taking care to minimize possible adverse effects. Social workers should assist in making appropriate arrangements for continuation of services when necessary (*NASW Code of Ethics—Termination of Services*).

Social workers in fee-for-service settings may terminate services to clients who are not paying an overdue balance if the financial contractual arrangements have been made clear to a client, if a client does not pose an imminent danger to self or others, and if the clinical and other consequences of the current nonpayment have been addressed and discussed with a client (*NASW Code of Ethics—Termination of Services*).

Social workers should not terminate services to pursue a social, financial, or sexual relationship with a client (*NASW Code of Ethics—Termination of Services*).

Social workers who anticipate the termination or interruption of services to clients should notify clients promptly and seek the transfer, referral, or continuation of services in relation to client needs and preferences (*NASW Code of Ethics—Termination of Services*).

Social workers who are leaving an employment setting should inform clients of appropriate options for the continuation of services and of the benefits and risks of the options (*NASW Code of Ethics—Termination of Services*).

It is unethical to continue to treat clients when services are no longer needed or in their best interests.

Another standard also relevant to termination of services mandates that social workers should make reasonable efforts to ensure continuity of services in the event that services are interrupted by factors such as unavailability, relocation, illness, disability, or death (*NASW Code of Ethics—Interruption of Services*).

LEGAL AND/OR ETHICAL ISSUES RELATED TO DEATH AND DYING

There are many legal and/or ethical issues related to death and dying. Some legal issues involved with dying include, but are not limited to, clients' right to have informed consent to receive or refuse treatment, advance directives, and establishing living wills. Treating professionals, by law, must give clients the opportunity for informed consent. It involves explaining the options for treatment, the possible benefits as well as risks for each treatment, and any recommendations, with rationales, for one treatment over another. Furthermore, clients must know that they have the right to choose whatever treatment they want or to choose to refuse treatment. Particularly when discussing chronic or terminal illness, conditions over which there is little control over the ultimate outcome of care provided, having clients feel as much control over their treatment options as possible is of great importance.

Clients can give written directions, called advance directives, about the type of care they do and do not want to receive when dying. Advance directives are legal written agreements that will be honored in the future when people can no longer communicate their wishes. For example, advance directives can prohibit resuscitation (the act of trying to revive a person whose heart has stopped) or tube feeding, if clients wish.

Advance directives are legal documents which indicate who has the right to make decisions when clients are incapable physically or mentally of making their wants known. The purpose of advance directives is to respond to judicial decisions that have been made indicating that if clients have not made others aware of their wishes, the decision to remove them from life supports or place them on life supports cannot be made. Therefore, it has become increasingly imperative that advance directives be established to memorialize clients' wishes and identify individuals to make these decisions if needed.

Advance directives have been paired with living wills to give clients control over what happens to them in a severe illness or injury. A living will allows individuals to retain some control over what happens at the end of their lives, even if they are then no longer competent to make personal choices for terminal care, by specifying their wishes while they are still healthy and at a time when there is no doubt of their mental competence.

Clients whose death may occur soon should also have Physician Orders for Life-Sustaining Treatment (POLST) documents. These documents are written doctors' orders that reflect preferences for medical care (particularly whether to receive care or not). The documents are kept in clients' medical records and in the home and are used to direct emergency medical personnel in following the clients' preferences. For example, these documents may contain the doctors' orders as to whether people should receive cardiopulmonary resuscitation (CPR), transportation to hospitals, or aggressive treatments (such as blood transfusions or chemotherapy) to relieve symptoms even if death is inevitable.

Although very few people actually take any steps toward causing their own death, many clients who are dying at least consider suicide. Discussing suicide may help sort out the issues and often correct certain problems that prompted consideration of suicide. Pain medicine can be prescribed if clients are uncomfortable and spiritual guidance can help clients find meaning in the remainder of their lives. Making decisions to forgo life-sustaining treatment, forgo food and fluids when near death, or take many drugs or large doses of drugs to relieve symptoms is not considered suicide. Several states have passed laws which allow those who are terminally ill to receive lethal combinations of drugs to take when they decide to die.

RESEARCH ETHICS (E.G., INSTITUTIONAL REVIEW BOARDS, USE OF HUMAN SUBJECTS, INFORMED CONSENT)

Social workers have an ethical mandate to monitor and evaluate policies, the implementation of programs, and practice interventions. They also must promote and facilitate evaluation and research to contribute to the development of knowledge. In addition to doing research themselves, social workers must keep current with emerging knowledge relevant to social work and fully use evaluation and research evidence in their professional practice.

When doing research and evaluation, social workers must consider possible consequences and should follow guidelines developed for the protection of evaluation and research participants. Social workers must protect participants from unwarranted physical or mental distress, harm, danger, or deprivation (*NASW Code of Ethics—Evaluation and Research*). Appropriate institutional review boards should be consulted.

For example, social workers engaged in evaluation or research should obtain voluntary and written informed consent from participants, when appropriate, without any implied or actual deprivation or penalty for refusal to participate or without undue inducement to participate. Informed consent should include information about the nature, extent, and duration of the participation requested and disclosure of the risks and benefits of participation in the research (*NASW Code of Ethics—Evaluation and Research*).

When using electronic technology to facilitate evaluation or research, social workers should ensure that participants provide informed consent for the use of such technology. Social workers should assess whether participants are able to use the technology and, when appropriate, offer reasonable alternatives to participate in the evaluation or research (*NASW Code of Ethics—Evaluation and Research*).

When evaluation or research participants are incapable of giving informed consent, social workers should provide an appropriate explanation to the participants, obtain the participants' assent to the extent they are able, and obtain written consent from an appropriate proxy (*NASW Code of Ethics—Evaluation and Research*).

Social workers should never design or conduct evaluation or research that does not use consent procedures, such as certain forms of naturalistic observation and archival research, unless rigorous and responsible review of the research has found it to be justified because of its prospective scientific, educational, or applied value and unless equally effective alternative procedures that do not involve waiver of consent are not feasible (*NASW Code of Ethics—Evaluation and Research*).

Social workers should inform participants of their right to withdraw from evaluation and research at any time without penalty (*NASW Code of Ethics—Evaluation and Research*).

Social workers should take appropriate steps to ensure that participants in evaluation and research have access to appropriate supportive services (*NASW Code of Ethics—Evaluation and Research*).

Social workers engaged in evaluation or research should ensure the anonymity or confidentiality of participants and of the data obtained from them. Social workers should inform participants of any limits of confidentiality, the measures that will be taken to ensure confidentiality, and when any records containing research data will be destroyed (*NASW Code of Ethics—Evaluation and Research*).

Social workers engaged in evaluation or research should be alert to and avoid conflicts of interest and dual relationships with participants, should inform participants when a real or potential conflict of interest arises, and should take steps to resolve the issue in a manner that makes participants' interests primary (*NASW Code of Ethics—Evaluation and Research*).

MODELS OF SUPERVISION AND CONSULTATION (E.G., INDIVIDUAL, PEER, GROUP)

There are many and varied supervision models, each with its own benefits and limitations. In order for supervision to be effective, it is necessary to take into account both the needs of social workers and the requirements and constraints of organizations when considering the model to be utilized.

Individual supervision has traditionally been the cornerstone of professional skill development. Supervision can be provided in groups, peer-led or facilitated by professional leaders. Group and peer supervision, as well as intensive consultation on a case-by-case basis, are useful and less costly additions to individual supervision, but they may be inadequate as substitutes for one-on-one support.

Individual

Benefits

- Full attention on the skill development, strengths, challenges, and professional enhancement of the individual supervisee
- More time and potentially safer environment in which to explore supervisee's interpersonal dynamics with clients and the impact of the work (e.g., countertransference issues, secondary trauma, compassion fatigue, burnout)
- Less exposure to poor practices of peers, which could be inappropriately modeled or interfere with supervision process

Challenges

- Potential for supervisee to feel intimidated by the supervisor, with no one else present to observe, or break up the intensity of the one-to-one focus
- Costly and time consuming
- No input from others outside the dyad
- No opportunity for supervisee to compare self with others, or gain support from peers

Peer Group

Benefits

- Each group member can offer and receive wisdom, experience, and ideas (i.e., enjoy both "teacher" and "student" roles)
- Shared influence and responsibility regarding how the group is run
- Avoids chance of getting stuck with an unwanted supervisor
- Opportunities for personal growth via group dynamics
- Participants as equals encourages lateral help and peer support

Challenges

- Potential for the unconscious designation of more experienced/skilled members as "de facto" supervisors
- Success is dependent upon how group members exercise their responsibilities

- Mutual trust, openness, and respect are essential
- Usually requires that groups remain closed, at least for a period of time
- Competition, defensiveness, and criticism between peers can occur
- Discussion frequency, depth, and intensity are limited by the time available and the number of members participating in the group

Facilitated Group

Benefits

- Learning occurs from others' practice examples and ways of working
- Self-confirmation occurs through giving feedback
- Opportunities for role play and other action techniques are present
- Less expensive and time consuming than individual supervision
- Opportunities for personal growth via group dynamics

Challenges

- Supervisor must be skilled in working systemically with groups and must be able to facilitate while also supervising (dual tasks).
- Supervisor's anxiety about the supervisor's own competence may pose a barrier, as there is greater exposure of the supervisor's abilities and experience.
- There is less time for each supervisee, as the group must balance the needs of each member.
- Group needs to have a high level of trust in order for supervisees to feel safe.

ETHICAL ISSUES IN SUPERVISION AND MANAGEMENT

Social workers must follow all ethical standards when providing and receiving supervision, as well as engaging in management tasks. These include, but are not limited to, those regarding commitment to clients, self-determination, informed consent, competence, cultural awareness and social diversity, conflicts of interest, privacy and confidentiality, access to records, sexual relationships, physical contact, sexual harassment, derogatory language, payments, clients who lack decision-making capacity, and interruption or termination of services.

Social workers who provide supervision should have the necessary knowledge and skill to supervise or consult appropriately, and they should do so only within their areas of competence. They should also evaluate supervisees' performance in a manner that is fair and respectful (*NASW Code of Ethics—Supervision and Consultation*). Social workers who are in managerial roles should take reasonable steps to ensure that adequate agency resources are available to provide appropriate staff supervision (*NASW Code of Ethics—Administration*).

Social workers who provide supervision are responsible for setting clear, appropriate, and culturally sensitive boundaries. They should not engage in any dual or multiple relationships with supervisees when there is a risk of exploitation of or potential harm to the supervisee, including dual relationships that may arise while using social networking sites or other electronic media (*NASW Code of Ethics—Supervision and Consultation*).

Social workers in managerial roles should advocate within and outside their agencies for adequate resources to meet clients' needs and ensure resource allocation procedures are open, fair, and nondiscriminatory. Social work managers should ensure that working environments are consistent with the *NASW Code of Ethics* and eliminate conditions which are not (*NASW Code of Ethics—Administration*).

Sometimes in practice, ethical issues can arise related to the payment of services. These standards indicate what rules social workers should follow in these situations.

When setting fees, social workers should ensure that the fees are fair, reasonable, and commensurate with the services performed. Consideration should be given to clients' ability to pay (*NASW Code of Ethics—Payment for Services*).

Social workers should avoid accepting goods or services from clients as payment for professional services. Bartering arrangements, particularly involving services, create the potential for conflicts of interest, exploitation, and inappropriate boundaries in social workers' relationships with clients. Social workers should explore and may participate in bartering only in very limited circumstances when it can be demonstrated that such arrangements are an accepted practice among professionals in the local community, considered to be essential for the provision of services, negotiated without coercion, and entered into at a client's initiative and with a client's informed consent. Social workers who accept goods or services from clients as payment for professional services assume the full burden of demonstrating that this arrangement will not be detrimental to a client or the professional relationship (*NASW Code of Ethics—Payment for Services*).

Social workers should not solicit a private fee or other remuneration for providing services to clients who are entitled to such available services through social workers' employers or agencies (*NASW Code of Ethics—Payment for Services*).

Social workers should obtain information on procedures for using insurance coverage when a client wants to use an employee benefit package for behavioral health services.

METHODS TO CREATE, IMPLEMENT, AND EVALUATE POLICIES AND PROCEDURES FOR SOCIAL WORKER SAFETY

Social workers provide services in increasingly complex, dynamic social environments with many client populations. The number and variety of people to whom social workers provide services and the variety of settings in which these services are provided contribute to an increasingly unpredictable, and often unsafe, environment for social work practice. Social workers have been the targets of verbal and physical assaults in agencies, as well as during field visits with clients. Tragically, some social workers have also been permanently injured or have lost their lives.

Most clients and families that social workers serve do not present threats or pose danger. In instances where threats are present, most employers address these issues appropriately. There are, however, social work settings where social workers face increased risks of violence.

Social workers have the right to work in safe environments and to advocate for safe working conditions. Social workers who report concerns regarding their personal safety, or who request assistance in assuring their safety, should not fear retaliation, blame, or questioning of their competency from their supervisors or colleagues. Social workers should routinely practice universal safety precautions in their work. Violence occurs in every economic, social, gender, and racial group. To avoid stereotyping particular groups of people and to promote safety, social workers should practice safety assessment and risk reduction with all clients and in all settings. A thorough understanding of the risk factors associated with elevated risk for violence can inform safety assessments. Social workers should also be aware of the potential that their personal information on the Internet, particularly social networking sites, can be accessed by anyone. Universal safety precautions also include the establishment of safety plans as a matter of routine planning. The adoption of universal safety precautions should not preclude agencies from establishing particular safeguards when social workers are asked to perform dangerous tasks. In those situations, agencies should establish specific policies to reduce the risk of harm.

THE SUPERVISEE'S ROLE IN SUPERVISION (E.G., IDENTIFYING LEARNING NEEDS, SELF-ASSESSMENT, PRIORITIZING, ETC.)

The short-term objectives of supervision are to increase a social worker's capacity to work more effectively, to provide a work context conducive to productivity, and to help a social worker take satisfaction in work. The ultimate objective is to assure the delivery of the most effective and efficient client services.

Social workers who are administrators should take reasonable steps to ensure that adequate agency or organizational resources are available to provide appropriate staff supervision.

Competence is essential for ethical social work practice and social workers must be competent in the services that they are providing (*NASW Code of Ethics—Competence*). In order to be competent, they must keep abreast of new developments in the field and obtain supervision.

Social workers should provide services and represent themselves as competent only within the boundaries of their education, training, license, certification, consultation received, supervised experience, or other relevant professional experience (*NASW Code of Ethics—Competence*).

Social workers should provide services in substantive areas or use intervention techniques or approaches that are new to them only after engaging in appropriate study, training, consultation, and supervision from people who are competent in those interventions or techniques (*NASW Code of Ethics—Competence*).

When generally recognized standards do not exist with respect to an emerging area of practice, social workers should exercise careful judgment and take responsible steps (including appropriate education, research, training, consultation, and supervision) to ensure the competence of their work and to protect clients from harm (*NASW Code of Ethics—Competence*).

If a supervisor needs to talk with a social worker about a problem situation, the supervisor should meet privately with the social worker to discuss the matter.

ACCREDITATION AND/OR LICENSING REQUIREMENTS

Administrative reviews, such as annual reviews from public and private social service organizations, are critical to the fulfillment of the social work mission. They provide accountability to the public about the number of people served, the services delivered, and how funds were allocated. They also may be used by social workers to document unmet needs that should be addressed.

Social workers may be required to engage in grant monitoring, evaluations, program inspections, and accreditation reviews. While each of these reviews serves a different purpose, they all require social workers to use critical thinking/analysis to help clients directly or indirectly.

PROFESSIONAL DEVELOPMENT ACTIVITIES TO IMPROVE PRACTICE AND MAINTAIN CURRENT PROFESSIONAL KNOWLEDGE (E.G., IN-SERVICE TRAINING, LICENSING REQUIREMENTS, REVIEWS OF LITERATURE, WORKSHOPS)

Professions enjoy a high social status, regard, and esteem conferred upon them by society. This high esteem arises primarily from the higher social function of their work, which is regarded as vital to society as a whole and, thus, special and valuable in nature. All professions involve technical, specialized, and highly skilled work, often referred to as "professional expertise." Training for this work involves obtaining degrees and professional qualifications (i.e., licensure) without which entry to the profession is barred. Training also requires regular updating of skills through continuing education.

Professional development refers to skills and knowledge attained for effective service delivery and career advancement. Professional development encompasses all types of learning opportunities, ranging from formal coursework and conferences to informal learning opportunities situated in practice. There are a variety of approaches to professional development, including consultation, coaching, communities of practice, mentoring, reflective supervision, and technical assistance.

Social workers often go through various stages of professional development, including:

1. Orientation and job induction

2. Autonomous worker

3. Member of a service team (independence to interdependence)

4. Development of specialization

5. Preparation to be a mentor or supervisor

10

Confidentiality

THE ELEMENTS OF CLIENT/CLIENT SYSTEM REPORTS

There is no one way to organize information or client files. Some client information and files are obtained and stored in paper format. However, increasingly client records are kept electronically with software to assist professionals in organizing and accessing data.

Whether paper or electronic, client files are usually stored with the following in separate sections or folders:

1. Demographic information and intake materials

2. Assessments, quarterly reviews, and reassessments

3. Service plan(s) with goals

4. Discharge plan

5. Releases of information and referrals

6. Correspondence

Social workers should keep psychotherapy notes in a secure location outside of client files to provide added confidentiality protection.

Often agency policies or requirements imposed by funders dictate the organizational structure for client files. However, regardless of the schema, it is essential that files are secure, up-to-date, and complete, with a format that makes locating information easy and evident.

Social workers are expected to communicate effectively, including in the preparation of written reports for external organizations. Poorly written reports or the inclusion of irrelevant or inappropriate information can have an adverse impact on a client. In the preparation of reports, including those for the courts, social workers are expected to communicate accurately and professionally. Reports generated by social workers must be taken seriously and will not be treated legitimately if there are spelling or grammatical mistakes, or the content is not based on critical thought and analysis.

Social workers also must develop reports as requested or needed, adhering to the standards of confidentiality, as failure to provide professional observations may hinder opportunities for clients. Often, social workers are reluctant to generate reports even when requested by clients and legally allowed to do so.

Critical to developing reports is the knowledge that they must be understandable and useful to recipients with a wide range of educational backgrounds and literacy levels. In addition, social workers must have a keen awareness of the purposes of reports, who they are being written for, and how they should be presented differently depending on the purposes and the audience.

Social workers should avoid irrelevant and inappropriate information, meaningless phrases or slang words, and illogical conclusions in the preparation and writing of reports. Social workers should plan what should and should not be included in the final documents prior to starting to develop them. It is also helpful to prepare drafts for later editing. Having others review draft reports can help catch errors and ensure the clarity of all material.

Social workers' competence and the value of social work services are often judged by the quality of written reports. Thus, it is essential that thought and care be taken in their preparation, and that they adhere to best practices and standards.

Administrative reports, such as annual reports from public and private social service organizations, are critical to the fulfillment of the social work mission. They provide accountability to the public about the number of people served, the services delivered, and how funds were allocated. They also may be used by social workers to document unmet needs which should be addressed.

Social workers may be required to prepare grant reports, evaluations, program proposals, and accreditation reports. While each of these documents serves a different purpose, they all require social workers to use their written communication skills and critical thinking/analysis to help clients directly or indirectly.

For example, a program proposal sets forth a plan of activities needed to begin or modify services in order to (better) meet clients' needs. It includes recommendations to organize or arrange a program in an effective and efficient manner. It describes and recommends procedures and ways to organize services for maximum client benefit. To ensure that it is implemented as intended, it must be clear, accurate, and well-written.

THE PRINCIPLES AND PROCESSES OF OBTAINING INFORMED CONSENT

In instances when clients are not literate or have difficulty understanding the primary language used in the practice setting, social workers should take steps to ensure clients' comprehension. This may include providing clients with a detailed verbal explanation or arranging for a qualified interpreter or translator whenever possible (*NASW Code of Ethics—Informed Consent*).

In instances when clients lack the capacity to provide informed consent, social workers should protect clients' interests by seeking permission from an appropriate third party, informing clients consistent with clients' level of understanding. In such instances, social workers should seek to ensure that the third party acts in a manner consistent with the clients' wishes and interests. Social workers should take reasonable steps to enhance such clients' ability to give informed consent (*NASW Code of Ethics—Informed Consent*).

Social workers who provide services using technology should inform recipients of the limitations and risks associated with such services (*NASW Code of Ethics—Informed Consent*).

Social workers should obtain clients' informed consent before audiotaping or videotaping clients or permitting observation of services to clients by a third party (*NASW Code of Ethics—Informed Consent*).

Social workers should obtain client consent before conducting electronic searches on clients except when needed to protect clients or others from serious, foreseeable, and imminent harm, or for other compelling professional reasons (*NASW Code of Ethics—Informed Consent*).

Social workers should discuss policies with clients concerning the use of technology in the provision of professional services. Social workers who use technology to provide social work services should assess the clients' suitability and capacity for electronic and remote services. Social workers should consider the clients' intellectual, emotional, and physical ability to use technology to receive services and the clients' ability to understand the potential benefits, risks, and limitations of such services. If clients do not wish to use services provided through technology, social workers should help them identify alternate methods of service (*NASW Code of Ethics—Informed Consent*).

Social workers who use technology to provide social work services should obtain informed consent from clients prior to initiating services. Social workers should assess clients' capacity to provide informed consent and, when using technology to communicate, verify the identity and location of clients (*NASW Code of Ethics—Informed Consent*).

When social workers act on behalf of clients who lack the capacity to make informed decisions, social workers should take reasonable steps to safeguard the interests and rights of those clients (*NASW Code of Ethics—Clients Who Lack Decision-Making Capacity*).

In order to obtain informed consent, social workers must use clear and understandable language related to service purpose, risks, limits due to third-party payers, time frame, and right of refusal or withdrawal. If the client lacks capacity or is a minor informed **consent** must be obtained by a responsible third party and **assent** must be obtained from the client.

THE USE OF CLIENT/CLIENT SYSTEM RECORDS

Social workers should provide clients with reasonable access to their records. Social workers who are concerned that clients' access to their records could cause serious misunderstanding or harm to a client should provide assistance in interpreting the records and consultation with a client regarding the records. **Social workers should limit clients' access to their records, or portions of their records, only in exceptional circumstances when there is compelling evidence that such access would cause serious harm to a client**. Both clients' requests and the rationale for withholding some or all of the records should be documented in clients' files (*NASW Code of Ethics—Access to Records*).

Social workers should develop and inform clients about their policies on the use of technology to provide clients with access to their records. These policies must be consistent with prevailing social work ethical standards (*NASW Code of Ethics—Access to Records*).

When providing clients with access to their records, social workers should take steps to protect the confidentiality of other individuals identified or discussed in such records.

The *NASW Code of Ethics* states that a social worker should only solicit information essential for providing services (minimum necessary to achieve purpose). Once private information is shared, standards of confidentiality apply.

LEGAL AND/OR ETHICAL ISSUES REGARDING CONFIDENTIALITY, INCLUDING ELECTRONIC INFORMATION SECURITY

Social workers should respect clients' right to privacy. Social workers should not solicit private information from clients unless it is essential to providing services or conducting social work evaluation or research. Once private information is shared, standards of confidentiality apply (*NASW Code of Ethics—Privacy and Confidentiality*).

Social workers may disclose confidential information when appropriate with valid consent from a client or a person legally authorized to consent on behalf of a client (*NASW Code of Ethics—Privacy and Confidentiality*).

Social workers should protect the confidentiality of all information obtained in the course of professional service, except for compelling professional reasons. The general expectation that social workers will keep information confidential does not apply when disclosure is necessary to prevent serious, foreseeable, and imminent harm to a client or other identifiable person. In all instances, social workers should disclose the least amount of confidential information necessary to achieve the desired purpose; only information that is directly relevant to the purpose for which the disclosure is made should be revealed (*NASW Code of Ethics—Privacy and Confidentiality*).

Social workers should inform clients, to the extent possible, about the disclosure of confidential information and the potential consequences, when feasible, before the disclosure is made. This applies whether social workers disclose confidential information on the basis of a legal requirement or client consent (*NASW Code of Ethics—Privacy and Confidentiality*).

Social workers should discuss with clients and other interested parties the nature of confidentiality and limitations of clients' right to confidentiality. Social workers should review circumstances with clients where confidential information may be requested and where disclosure of confidential information may be legally required. This discussion should occur as soon as possible in a social worker–client relationship and as needed throughout the course of the relationship (*NASW Code of Ethics—Privacy and Confidentiality*).

When social workers provide counseling services to families, couples, or groups, social workers should seek agreement among the parties involved concerning each individual's right to confidentiality and obligation to preserve the confidentiality of information shared by others. This agreement should include consideration of whether confidential information may be exchanged in person or electronically. Social workers should inform participants in family, couples, or group counseling that social workers cannot guarantee that all participants will honor such agreements (*NASW Code of Ethics—Privacy and Confidentiality*).

Social workers should inform clients involved in family, couples, marital, or group counseling of a social worker's, employer's, and agency's policy concerning a social worker's disclosure of confidential information among the parties involved in the counseling (*NASW Code of Ethics—Privacy and Confidentiality*).

Social workers should not disclose confidential information to third-party payers unless clients have authorized such disclosure (*NASW Code of Ethics—Privacy and Confidentiality*).

Social workers should not discuss confidential information in any setting unless privacy can be ensured. Social workers should not discuss confidential information in public or semi-public areas such as hallways, waiting rooms, elevators, and restaurants (*NASW Code of Ethics—Privacy and Confidentiality*).

Social workers should protect the confidentiality of clients during legal proceedings to the extent permitted by law. When a court of law or other legally authorized body orders social workers to disclose confidential or privileged information without a client's consent and such disclosure could cause harm to a client, social workers should request that the court withdraw the order or limit the order as narrowly as possible or maintain the records under seal, unavailable for public inspection (*NASW Code of Ethics—Privacy and Confidentiality*).

A subpoena and court order are not the same. When receiving a subpoena, a social worker should respond and claim privilege, but not turn over records unless the court issues a subsequent order to do so. As stated, when a social worker gets a court order, the social worker should try to limit its scope and/or ask that the records be sealed.

Social workers should protect the confidentiality of clients when responding to requests from members of the media (*NASW Code of Ethics—Privacy and Confidentiality*).

Social workers should protect the confidentiality of clients' written and electronic records and other sensitive information. Social workers should take reasonable steps to ensure that clients' records are stored in a secure location and that clients' records are not available to others who are not authorized to have access (*NASW Code of Ethics—Privacy and Confidentiality*).

Social workers should take reasonable steps to protect the confidentiality of electronic communications, including information provided to clients or third parties. Social workers should use applicable safeguards (such as encryption, firewalls, and passwords) when using electronic communications such as e-mail, online posts, online chat sessions, mobile communication, and text messages. In addition, social workers should develop and disclose policies and procedures for notifying clients of any breach of confidential information in a timely manner. In the event of unauthorized access to client records or information, including any unauthorized access to the social worker's electronic communication or storage systems, social workers should inform clients of such disclosures, consistent with applicable laws and professional standards (*NASW Code of Ethics—Privacy and Confidentiality*).

Social workers should develop and inform clients about their policies on the use of electronic technology to gather information about clients. Social workers should avoid searching or gathering client information electronically unless there are compelling professional reasons, and when appropriate, with the client's informed consent (*NASW Code of Ethics—Privacy and Confidentiality*).

Social workers should avoid posting any identifying or confidential information about clients on professional websites or other forms of social media (*NASW Code of Ethics—Privacy and Confidentiality*).

Social workers should transfer or dispose of clients' records in a manner that protects clients' confidentiality and is consistent with state statutes governing records and social work licensure (*NASW Code of Ethics—Privacy and Confidentiality*).

Social workers should take reasonable precautions to protect client confidentiality in the event of a social worker's termination of practice, incapacitation, or death (*NASW Code of Ethics—Privacy and Confidentiality*).

Social workers should not disclose identifying information when discussing clients for teaching or training purposes unless a client has consented to disclosure of confidential information (*NASW Code of Ethics—Privacy and Confidentiality*).

Social workers should not disclose identifying information when discussing clients with consultants unless a client has consented to disclosure of confidential information or there is a compelling need for such disclosure (*NASW Code of Ethics—Privacy and Confidentiality*).

Social workers should protect the confidentiality of deceased clients consistent with the preceding standards (*NASW Code of Ethics—Privacy and Confidentiality*).

If a client sues a social worker, a social worker has the right to a defense and may need to release client information as part of this defense. A social worker should limit this disclosure only to information required for defense.

Confidentiality of minor records can be challenging, especially if a parent wants access to them and/or consents to their release. Social workers must be knowledgeable about ethical standards and laws that relate to the protection and release of minor records. Parents may have access to these records depending upon the age of the minor and the type of treatment or setting. Social workers treating minors with parents who may have joint or limited custody must also be aware of the rights of all parties to access and/or consent to their release.

LEGAL AND/OR ETHICAL ISSUES REGARDING MANDATORY REPORTING (E.G., ABUSE, THREAT OF HARM, IMPAIRED PROFESSIONALS, ETC.)

Social workers are required to disclose confidential information, sometimes against a client's wishes, to comply with mandatory reporting laws. Laws not only require social workers to report suspected cases of abuse and neglect, but there can be varying levels of civil and criminal liability for failing to do so.

This mandate causes ethical issues for social workers who have a commitment to their clients' interests as well as a responsibility to the larger society.

The majority of all reports of abuse and/or neglect came from professionals including medical personnel, law enforcement agents, educators, lawyers, and social workers.

Social workers who have direct knowledge of a social work colleague's impairment that is due to personal problems, psychosocial distress, substance abuse, or mental health difficulties and that interferes with practice effectiveness should consult with that colleague when feasible and assist the colleague in taking remedial action. Social workers who believe that a social work colleague's impairment interferes with practice effectiveness and that the colleague has not taken adequate steps to address the impairment should take action through appropriate channels established by employers, agencies, NASW, licensing and regulatory bodies, and other professional organizations (*NASW Code of Ethics—Impairment of Colleagues*).

Professional Development and Use of Self

THE COMPONENTS OF THE SOCIAL WORKER–CLIENT/CLIENT SYSTEM RELATIONSHIP

A social worker–client relationship is an emotional or connecting bond. The relationship is the communication bridge whereby messages pass over the bridge with greater or lesser difficulty, depending on the nature of the emotional connection or alliance.

A positive relationship is an important tool of helping. Social workers must create a warm, accepting, trustworthy, and dependable relationship with clients.

In working with a client, a social worker must convey a sense of respect for a client's individuality, as well as the client's right and capacity for self-determination and for being fully involved in the helping process from beginning to end.

The most consistent factor associated with beneficial outcomes of a helping relationship is a positive relationship between a social worker and a client, but other factors, such as a social worker's competence and the motivation and involvement of a client, are also influential.

THE CLIENT'S/CLIENT SYSTEM'S ROLE IN THE PROBLEM-SOLVING PROCESS

Clients often tend to think of themselves and their problems as unique. A client may think that difficulties experienced are so different from those of others that no one else could ever understand them. The client may even enjoy this feeling of uniqueness. It may be a defense against the discomfort of exploring fears of being like others. At this point, a client may not be ready to look at the problem. It is hard to admit difficulties, even to oneself.

There may also be concerns as to whether social workers can really be trusted. Some people, because of unfortunate experiences in their childhoods, grow up with distrust of others. Furthermore, people are generally afraid of what others will think of them.

A client may only be looking for sympathy, support, and/or empathy, rather than searching for a new way to solve difficulties. A client may not see that change must occur. When a social worker points out some of the ways in which a client is contributing to a problem, the client may stop listening. Solving the problem often requires a client to confront issues that have been avoided in the past and the client wants to avoid thinking about in the future.

A client may have struggled to achieve independence. The thought of depending on or receiving help from another individual seems to violate something. A client must constantly defend against a sense of weakness and may have difficulty listening to and using the assistance of another person.

There are also many clients who have strong needs to lean on others. Some spend much of their lives looking for others on whom they can be dependent. In the helping situation, they may constantly and inappropriately seek to repeat this pattern.

THE SOCIAL WORKER'S ROLE IN THE PROBLEM-SOLVING PROCESS

Social worker roles in the problem-solving process include consultant, advocate, case manager, catalyst, broker, mediator, facilitator, instructor, mobilizer, resource allocator, and so on.

Key social work practice roles include the following.

Advocate

In the advocate role, social workers champion the rights of others with the goal of empowering the client system being served. Social workers speak on behalf of clients when others will not listen or when clients are unable to do so. Social workers have a particular responsibility to advocate on behalf of those disempowered by society.

Broker

In the role of broker, social workers are responsible for identifying, locating, and linking client systems to needed resources in a timely fashion. Once client needs are assessed and potential services identified, the broker assists in choosing the most appropriate service option and assists in negotiating the terms of service delivery. Social workers are concerned with the quality, quantity, and accessibility of services.

Change Agent

A change agent participates as part of a group or organization seeking to improve or restructure some aspect of service provision. A change agent, working with others, uses the problem-solving model to identify the problem, solicit input, and plan for change. A change agent acts in a coordinated manner to achieve planned change at multiple levels that helps to shift the focus of institutional resources to meet identified goals.

Counselor

The role of the counselor focuses on improving social functioning. Social workers help client systems articulate their needs, clarify their problems, explore resolution strategies, and apply intervention strategies to develop and expand the capacities of client systems to deal with problems more effectively. A key function of this role is to empower clients by affirming their personal strengths and their capacities to deal with problems more effectively.

Mediator

When dispute resolution is needed in order to accomplish goals, social workers will carry out the role of mediator. Social workers intervene in disputes between parties to help them find compromises, reconcile differences, and reach mutually satisfying agreements. The mediator takes a neutral stance among the involved parties.

The primary role of social workers is to act as a resource—assuming various roles depending upon the nature of client problems.

METHODS TO CLARIFY THE ROLES AND RESPONSIBILITIES OF THE SOCIAL WORKER AND CLIENT/CLIENT SYSTEM IN THE INTERVENTION PROCESS

A social worker can be supportive in these roles, but is not supposed to be the client's support system. Instead, a social worker should assist the client to mobilize or build natural supports. People generally like to give advice. It gives them the feeling of being competent and important. Hence, social workers may easily fall into this inappropriate role without taking into account the abilities, the fears, and the interests of clients and/or their circumstances.

Social workers should also not be insensitive to clients' resistance. When a client does not claim any difficulties, is unable or refuses to talk, explains that it is someone else's fault, and/or denies what has happened, a social worker may try to argue or in other ways exert pressure. This response tends to increase a client's resistance. This approach does nothing for a client.

A social worker may also confuse the situation and hinder clarification of the problem. In an effort to establish a relationship, a social worker may overpraise or fail to confront a client. Clients must look at their own roles in situations and recognize their own limitations.

THE PRINCIPLES AND TECHNIQUES FOR BUILDING AND MAINTAINING A HELPING RELATIONSHIP

Helping is based on acceptance of a client's situation and the ability of the client to make changes only if desired. In a helping relationship, a social worker is trying to constructively assist a client—that is, to have an impact on or to influence thinking and acting. The influence is further presumed to be in the direction of increasing the autonomy, understanding, effectiveness, and skill of a client.

Helping is distinguished from the more common concepts of advice giving, reprimanding, or punishing. These often involve threats and seldom result in more than outward conformity or superficial change. They generally do not increase strength or willingness and ability to carry responsibility.

The core of the helping process is the relationship between a social worker and a client.

The relationship between a social worker and a client is expressed through interaction. This interaction is commonly thought of in terms of verbal communication, which is natural, because the greater part of treatment consists of talking. However, nonverbal behavior is also very important. Body posture, gestures, facial expressions, eye movements, and other reactions often express feelings and attitudes more clearly than do spoken words. It is often for these reasons that a social worker must be aware of personal feelings, attitudes, and responses, as well as those of a client if the social worker is to understand what is taking place and be of assistance.

A social worker cannot be useful in helping others unless the social worker understands and is willing to accept the difficulties that all human beings encounter in trying to meet their needs. A social worker must know that the potential for all the weaknesses and strengths known to humanity exists at some level in every person. Social workers must also understand that human beings become more capable of dealing with their problems as they feel more adequate. Social workers recognize positive, as well as negative, aspects of a client, which will influence efforts to change and successful achievement of goals.

The interaction between a social worker and a client that takes place about a problem involves and is affected by the relationship between the two persons. Human beings act in terms of their feelings, attitudes, and understandings; hence, these must be taken into account and explored if the helping process is to result in change. Both a social worker and a client have objectives; a social worker's perceived objective is to be of assistance. Clarification and definition of these objectives often become important parts of the helping process. Both a social worker and a client have a degree of power (i.e., ability to influence the situation and the results).

Process of Engagement in Social Work Practice

The beginning of the problem-solving process includes activities of a social worker and a client to be helped that are directed at (a) becoming engaged with each other (engagement), (b) assessing a client's situation in order to select appropriate goals and the means of attaining them (assessment), and (c) planning how to employ these means (planning). During engagement, the limits to confidentiality must be explicitly stated at the beginning of this stage. Social workers must also explain their roles and how they can assist clients in addressing their problems.

It is important to consider how a client feels about coming for help and to deal with any negative feelings a client may feel (particularly if a client is involuntarily seeking help). A social worker must be open to discussing these feelings openly, because very little in a client can be changed until negative feelings are addressed. If a social worker is empathic with a client, it may be possible to find a common ground between what a client wishes and what a social worker can legitimately do.

A social worker and a client establish a therapeutic alliance in which they view themselves as allies in the helping process. A working alliance or a willingness by a client to work with a social worker should be established. A working alliance is sometimes referred to as a treatment alliance.

A social worker should express hopefulness that change can occur.

Resistance may occur during this stage. If clients are resistant to engage, social workers should clarify the process or specify what will happen and discuss this ambivalence.

THE CONCEPT OF ACCEPTANCE AND EMPATHY IN THE SOCIAL WORKER–CLIENT/CLIENT SYSTEM RELATIONSHIP

Empathic understanding involves being nonjudgmental, accepting, and genuine.

Empathic Communication

- Establishes rapport with clients—empathic communication is one means of bridging the gap between a social worker and client.
- Starts where a client is and stays attuned to a client throughout the encounter (being perceptive to changes in frame of mind).
- Increases the level at which clients explore themselves and their problems.
- Responds to a client's nonverbal messages (a social worker can observe body language and make explicit a client's feelings).
- Decreases defensiveness and engages a client in processing and testing new information.
- Defuses anger that represents obstacles to progress.

Empathic responding encourages more rational discussion and sets the stage for problem solving. For those clients who have learned to cope with feelings of helplessness and frustration by becoming angry and/or violent, an empathic response may be the first step in engaging in helping relationships.

THE DYNAMICS OF POWER AND TRANSPARENCY IN THE SOCIAL WORKER–CLIENT/CLIENT SYSTEM RELATIONSHIP

Social workers have power and privileges associated with their roles, titles, and education. Being conscious of these privileges is critical because there is a responsibility to challenge hierarchical assumptions and power dynamics inherent in social worker–client relationships. Social workers should use egalitarian and collaborative approaches that give clients choices, decision-making power, and opportunities for honest feedback.

If social workers are transparent and honest about their positions of privilege, they help to undercut the power differentials. Transparency about the process and intent of social work interventions is essential. Role expectations should be discussed and power differences should be acknowledged.

Transparency and power are linked. If clients are not informed about what is going to occur in each stage of the problem-solving process and do not understand the theoretical models which help explain their situations, they cannot be full participants in the change process. Thus, transparency or the provision of all available information is the underpinning of the therapeutic relationship. If social workers deliberately withhold observations or knowledge from clients, they are reinforcing the power differential which inherently exists and disempowering clients. This is not helpful to clients or in accordance with the values of social work practice.

ETHICAL ISSUES RELATED TO DUAL RELATIONSHIPS

Social workers must ensure that they do not engage in dual or multiple relationships that may impact on the treatment of clients. The standards related to this area provide guidelines that can assist social workers if such relationships emerge (*NASW Code of Ethics—Conflicts of Interest*).

Social workers should be alert to and avoid conflicts of interest that interfere with the exercise of professional discretion and impartial judgment. Social workers should inform clients when a real or potential conflict of interest arises and take reasonable steps to resolve the issue in a manner that makes clients' interests primary and protects clients' interests to the greatest extent possible. In some cases, protecting clients' interests may require termination of the professional relationship with proper referral of clients (*NASW Code of Ethics—Conflicts of Interest*).

Social workers should not take unfair advantage of any professional relationship or exploit others to further their personal, religious, political, or business interests (*NASW Code of Ethics—Conflicts of Interest*).

Social workers should not engage in dual or multiple relationships with clients or former clients in which there is a risk of exploitation or potential harm to a client. In instances when dual or multiple relationships are unavoidable, social workers should take steps to protect clients and are responsible for setting clear, appropriate, and culturally sensitive boundaries. Dual or multiple relationships occur when social workers relate to clients in more than one relationship, whether professional, social, or business. Dual or multiple relationships can occur simultaneously or consecutively (*NASW Code of Ethics—Conflicts of Interest*).

When social workers provide services to two or more people who have a relationship with each other (e.g., couples, family members), social workers should clarify with all parties which individuals will be considered clients and the nature of social workers' professional obligations to the various individuals who are receiving services. Social workers who anticipate a conflict of interest among the individuals receiving services or who anticipate having to perform in potentially conflicting roles (e.g., when a social worker is asked to testify in a child custody dispute or divorce proceedings involving clients) should clarify their role with the parties involved and take appropriate action to minimize any conflict of interest (*NASW Code of Ethics—Conflicts of Interest*).

In addition, social workers engaged in evaluation or research should be alert to and avoid conflicts of interest and dual relationships with participants, should inform participants when a real or potential conflict of interest arises, and should take steps to resolve the issue in a manner that makes participants' interests primary (*NASW Code of Ethics—Evaluation and Research*).

THE IMPACT OF TRANSFERENCE AND COUNTERTRANSFERENCE IN THE SOCIAL WORKER–CLIENT/CLIENT SYSTEM RELATIONSHIP

Transference refers to redirection of a client's feelings for a significant person to a social worker. Transference was first described by Sigmund Freud, who acknowledged its importance for a better understanding of a client's feelings.

Transference is often manifested as an erotic attraction toward a social worker, but can be seen in many other forms such as rage, hatred, mistrust, parentification, extreme dependence, or even placing a social worker in an esteemed status.

When Freud initially encountered transference in his therapy with clients, he felt it was an obstacle to treatment success. But what he learned was that the analysis of the transference was actually the work that needed to be done. The focus in psychoanalysis is, in large part, a social worker and a client recognizing the transference relationship and exploring the relationship's meaning.

Since the transference between a client and a social worker happens on an unconscious level, a social worker doing psychoanalysis uses transference to reveal unresolved conflicts a client has with childhood figures.

Countertransference is defined as redirection of a social worker's feelings toward a client, or more generally as a social worker's emotional entanglement with a client. A social worker's recognition of countertransference is nearly as critical as understanding a client's transference. Not only does this help a social worker regulate emotions in the therapeutic relationship, but it also gives a social worker valuable insight into what a client is attempting to elicit.

For example, a social worker who is sexually attracted to a client must understand this as countertransference, and look at how a client may be eliciting this reaction. Once it has been identified, a social worker can ask a client about the client's feelings toward a social worker, and/or explore how they relate to unconscious motivations, desires, or fears.

THE IMPACT OF DOMESTIC, INTIMATE PARTNER, AND OTHER VIOLENCE ON THE HELPING RELATIONSHIP

A type of trauma is that resulting from intimate partner abuse (heterosexual, gay, lesbian, dating, married, cohabitating). The common thread in all abusive relationships is the abuser's need for power and control over another. Domestic violence occurs across all racial, cultural, and socioeconomic groups and can involve physical, sexual, psychological/emotional, and economic/financial abuse.

Signs of abuse are varied.

- Suspicious injury (not consistent with history of injury, unusual locations, various stages of healing, bites, repeated minor injuries, delay in seeking treatment, old scars or new injuries from weapons)
- Somatic complaints without a specific diagnosis (such as chronic pain—head, abdomen, pelvis, back, or neck)
- Behavioral presentation (crying, minimizing, no emotional expression, anxious or angry, defensive, fearful eye contact)
- Controlling/coercive behavior of partner (partner hovers, overly concerned, won't leave client unattended, client defers to partner, fear of speaking in front of partner, or disagreeing with partner)

Cycle of Violence

Phase I:	Tension building
Phase II:	Battering incident—shortest period of the cycle, lasts a brief time
Phase III:	"Loving–contrition" (absence of tension or "honeymoon" phase)—batterer offers profuse apologies; assures attacks will never happen again and declares love and caring

Batterers often learn abusive behavior from their families of origin, peers, and media, as well as from personal experience of being abused as children. Batterers view their victims as "possessions" and treat them like objects. Victims are dehumanized to justify the battering. Batterers are very self-centered and feel entitled to have their needs (physical, emotional, sexual) met "no matter what." Batterers have control over their impulses and give themselves permission to be abusive.

Some of the reasons that clients stay in abusive relationships are:

- Hope that the abuser will change. If the batterer is in a treatment program, the client hopes the behavior will change; leaving represents a loss of the committed relationship

- Isolation and lack of support systems

- Fears that no one will believe the seriousness of abuse experienced

- Abuser puts up barricades so client won't leave the relationship (escalates threats of violence, threatens to kill, withholds support, threatens to seek custody of children, threatens suicide, etc.)

- Dangers of leaving may pose a greater danger than remaining with the batterer

- Client may not have the economic resources to survive independently

Leaving is a process. Over time, the client comes to the conclusion that the abuser will not change; each time the client tries to leave, the client gathers more information that is helpful.

Social exchange theory is based on the idea of totaling potential benefits and losses to determine behavior. People make decisions about relationships based on the amount of rewards they receive from them. A client remains in an abusive relationship because the high cost of leaving lowers the attractiveness (outweighs the benefits) of the best alternative. A client will leave when the best alternative promises a better life (rewards outweigh the costs).

Guidelines for Interventions

- **According to most literature on domestic violence, traditional marital/couples therapy is not appropriate in addressing abuse in the family. It puts victims in greater danger of further abuse.**

- Medical needs and safety are priorities. Note: Consider domestic violence in the context of Maslow's hierarchy of needs.

- In working with a victim of abuse, trust is a major issue in establishing a therapeutic alliance.

THE DYNAMICS OF DIVERSITY IN THE SOCIAL WORKER–CLIENT/ CLIENT SYSTEM RELATIONSHIP

A social worker's self-awareness about personal attitudes, values, and beliefs about cultural differences and a willingness to acknowledge cultural differences are critical factors in working with diverse populations. A social worker is responsible for bringing up and addressing issues of cultural difference with a client and is also ethically responsible for being culturally competent by obtaining the appropriate knowledge, skills, and experience.

Social workers should:

1. Move from being culturally unaware to being aware of their own heritage and the heritage of others.

2. Value and celebrate differences of others rather than maintaining an ethnocentric stance.

3. Have an awareness of personal values and biases and how they may influence relationships with clients.

4. Demonstrate comfort with racial and cultural differences between themselves and clients.

5. Have an awareness of personal and professional limitations.

6. Acknowledge their own racial attitudes, beliefs, and feelings.

THE EFFECT OF THE CLIENT'S DEVELOPMENTAL LEVEL ON THE SOCIAL WORKER–CLIENT RELATIONSHIP

Social workers must be sensitive to the developmental levels of clients. Development levels refer to the functional abilities at which clients find themselves at given moments. The problem-solving process must take these developmental levels into account. Social workers should not rely on chronological age as clients may be functioning at very different developmental levels. Social workers must use engagement and intervention strategies which are appropriate given clients' developmental functioning. Assessments should include determining the psychosocial levels of clients. Clients' development may be delayed or advanced across all domains or inconsistent with some areas more behind than others. Understanding causes for discrepancies between chronological and developmental age also may be important for insight into clients' problems.

SOCIAL WORKER SELF-CARE PRINCIPLES AND TECHNIQUES

Self-care is essential for social workers so that they can practice effectively and honor their professional and personal commitments. Self-care refers to activities and practices that are done on a regular basis to reduce stress and maintain and enhance short- and longer-term health and well-being.

Practicing self-care helps social workers:

- **Identify and manage the general challenges** that hard-working professionals face such as the potential for stress and burnout or interpersonal difficulties.

- **Become aware of personal vulnerabilities** such as the potential for retraumatization (if trauma history exists), vicarious or secondary traumatization (if working with individuals who report their own traumatic experiences), and compassion fatigue (which can be developed from a combination of burnout and vicarious traumatization).

- **Achieve balance in life** by maintaining and enhancing the attention paid to different domains of life in a way that meets personal needs.

Self-care is not simply about limiting or addressing professional stressors. It is also about **enhancing overall well-being**. There are common aims to almost all self-care efforts including:

- Taking care of physical and psychological health
- Managing and reducing stress
- Honoring emotional and spiritual needs
- Fostering and sustaining relationships
- Achieving an equilibrium between meeting personal needs and school/work demands

BURNOUT, SECONDARY TRAUMA, AND COMPASSION FATIGUE

Burnout, secondary trauma, and compassion fatigue have been used interchangeably to express adverse impacts that result from constantly working with those who are experiencing problems or trauma or are in crisis.

Burnout is a state of physical, emotional, psychological, and/or spiritual exhaustion. It can be manifested by cynicism or a lack of satisfaction in working with clients to resolve their problems. Burnout is characterized by emotional fatigue and feeling inadequate due to not being able to change clients' life circumstances. Many factors can contribute to burnout, including client, organizational, and/or contextual variables.

Secondary trauma relates to the behaviors and emotions that result from knowledge about traumatizing events experienced by clients and the stress resulting from helping or wanting to help them. Secondary trauma results from engaging in empathic relationships with clients who have had traumatic experiences and witnessing the effects of those experiences. The symptoms of secondary trauma mirror those experienced by the primary victim of trauma, including, but not limited to, insomnia, chronic irritability or angry outbursts, fatigue, difficulty concentrating, and/or avoidance.

Compassion fatigue is best defined as a syndrome consisting of a combination of the symptoms of secondary trauma and burnout. It usually represents the overall experience of emotional and physical fatigue that social workers can experience due to the prevalent use of empathy when treating clients who are distraught and experiencing emotional pain. Social workers also encounter bureaucratic hurdles that exacerbate agency stress and upset the balance between practice and administrative demands. Much like burnout, compassion fatigue tends to occur cumulatively over time, whereas secondary trauma may have a more immediate onset. Social workers may develop empathy or compassion fatigue as they repeatedly see little or no improvement in client situations. Social workers who treat victims of trauma can find that secondary trauma may contribute to overall compassion fatigue. However, social workers who do not treat those who have experienced trauma may experience compassion fatigue without experiencing secondary trauma.

In order to manage the effects of burnout and secondary trauma, and in an attempt to prevent compassion fatigue, social workers must engage in *self-care* activities which should include, but not be limited to, receiving support from mentors or peers, obtaining therapy, engaging in relaxation and personal endeavors that are nonprofessional activities, and balancing work demands with one's personal life.

THE COMPONENTS OF A SAFE AND POSITIVE WORK ENVIRONMENT

To practice effectively and ethically, social workers need a working environment that upholds ethical practice and is committed to standards and good quality services. A positive working environment is created where the values and principles of employers and social workers are consistent with each other and mutually reinforcing. There is substantial evidence that the most effective social work services are provided in situations where employers understand social work practice, respect their employees, and are committed to implementing professional values.

A framework for supporting good practice needs to take account of ethical principles and ensure effective induction, supervision, workload management, and continuing professional development.

The following are some elements which enable social workers to practice ethically:

- Written policies setting out standards of ethical practice provide clarity and protection for clients, social workers, and agencies. Social workers should never be required to do anything that would put at risk their ability to uphold such ethical standards, including policies on confidentiality, equal opportunities, and risk management.

- Quality social work services draw on research and practice evidence. Policies should be informed by research and practice evidence.

- The public, including clients, should be regularly informed about these standards, policies, and procedures and provided with information about how to raise concerns or make complaints about standards of practice.

- People employed as social workers must be suitable to enter the workforce, hold appropriate recognized qualifications that entitle them to practice as social workers, provide references (including evidence that they are not a risk to clients), and demonstrate that they understand their roles and responsibilities, including their ethical duties.

- Dangerous, discriminatory, or exploitative behavior and practice must be dealt with promptly through the implementation of policies and procedures. Such policies should provide measures to prevent and minimize violence, making it clear to staff, social workers, and clients that violence, threats, or abusive behavior is not acceptable.

- Social workers have a right for their health and occupational safety to be protected. Social workers frequently experience trauma or violence in their work and they are vulnerable to work-related stress and burnout due to the nature of their work.

- The adoption and implementation of policies on workload management make a major contribution to the provision of quality services to clients. Workload practices must consider the basic tenets of social work intervention, including the centrality of human relationships, the need to manage risk and complexity, and the duty to highlight unmet need.

- The physical working environment has an important part to play in the support of effective and ethical practice including, for example, the physical arrangements and procedures required for confidential interviewing and storage of confidential records.

- Continuing professional development and further training enable social workers to strengthen and develop their skills and knowledge and ensure that agencies adapt to the changing needs of clients and changing organizational realities. Orientation and induction training provided to new employees and those changing jobs are essential, including the management of risk, making complex professional judgments, and the fulfillment of statutory obligations such as the protection of minors and vulnerable adults.

- Good quality, regular social work supervision by people who have the necessary experience and qualifications in social work practice is an essential tool to ensure accountable and ethical practice. Research has confirmed that supervision is an important vehicle for supporting the management function in promoting creative and reflective practice, supporting staff resilience and well-being, and continuous professional development.

- Systematic reviews of services and practice, led by social workers who have experience of the field, should be held regularly. These activities identify needed support, training, and action when poor or unethical practice is identified.

- Career development opportunities for social workers wishing to develop advanced practice skills need to be available. These not only meet the individual needs of social workers, but can also constitute an effective tool for retaining valuable practice knowledge and experience and for preventing high staff turnover and difficulties in recruitment that are typical challenges constantly being faced by social work services.

- Rates of pay or fees for social work practice need to be comparable with similar professionals and recognize the skill and qualifications of social workers.

PROFESSIONAL OBJECTIVITY IN THE SOCIAL WORKER–CLIENT/CLIENT SYSTEM RELATIONSHIP

Social worker communication should not be burdened with emotional investment; instead, social workers should be interested, genuinely concerned, and encouraging, while neither condemning nor praising.

The relationship between a social worker and a client must be productive, and must have certain characteristics. There must be mutual acceptance and trust. A client must feel understood and valued as a person, though personal performance may be unsatisfactory. If a client feels judged, the client will not speak freely, and will find ways to defend current and past actions.

A social worker accepts and understands a client's problems, recognizes the demands and the requirements of the situation, and assists a client to examine alternatives and potential consequences. A social worker does not tell a client what to do. Only a client can decide to change because the client acts upon personal feelings and insights, and has a unique view of the problem.

THE INFLUENCE OF THE SOCIAL WORKER'S OWN VALUES AND BELIEFS ON THE SOCIAL WORKER–CLIENT/CLIENT SYSTEM RELATIONSHIP

Social workers must recognize values that may inhibit the therapeutic relationship.

1. **Universalism—There is one acceptable norm or standard for everyone** versus there are other valid standards that have been developed by people that they have determined to be most useful to them.

2. **Dichotomous "either-or" thinking; differences are inferior, wrong, bad** versus differences are just different and coexist.

3. **Heightened ability/value on separating, categorizing, numbering, "left-brain"** versus "right-brain" or "whole picture." Mental activity is highly valued to the exclusion of physical and spiritual experiences. Persons are studied in isolation, not as part of a group or interrelated with their environment.

4. **High value on control, constraint, restraint** versus value on flexibility, emotion/feelings, expressiveness, spirituality. What cannot be controlled and definitively defined is deemed nonexistent, unimportant, unscientific, or deviant/inferior. Reality is defined with the assumption of objectivity; subjective reality is viewed as invalid because it cannot be consistently replicated by many people.

5. **Measure of self comes from outside, and is only in contrast to others** versus value comes from within—you are worthwhile because you were born, and you strive to live a life that is in harmony with others and the environment. Worth is measured by accumulation of wealth or status (outside measures)—therefore, one can only feel good if one is better than someone else, or accumulates more than someone else, or has a higher status.

6. **Power is defined as "power over" others, mastery over environment** versus "power through" or in harmony with others; by sharing power, power can be expanded, and each becomes more powerful.

TIME MANAGEMENT APPROACHES

Time management is planning and consciously controlling the amount of time spent on specific activities, especially to increase effectiveness, efficiency, or productivity. Though time management initially focused on business or work activities, it is now increasingly used to control personal activities as well.

Most time management approaches focus on creating conducive or effective environments, modifying behaviors, setting priorities, and/or reducing time spent on nonpriorities.

The approaches to time management have evolved. Initially, approaches consisted of checklists and notes to recognize the demands on time. These then evolved into calendars and appointment books that focused on looking ahead to anticipate future events. The third approach, often used today, examines efficiency with the focus on prioritizing, planning, controlling, and taking steps toward a goal.

The last approach requires the categorization of daily activities by importance and urgency. Those activities that are urgent and important can be stressful and require immediate action; those who deal with these exclusively will think they are just "putting out fires." Activities that are not urgent or important require little or no attention, and time spent on these activities will result in feelings of disengagement. Activities that are urgent but not important often take up a lot of attention but tend to yield little difference or progress. The last grouping—those things that are important but not urgent—are likely to be put aside yet are critical to personal fulfillment. Time management should include minimizing time spent on activities that are not important and ensuring those that are not urgent but are important, such as building relationships, recreation and leisure, and so on, are also prioritized.

THE IMPACT OF TRANSFERENCE AND COUNTERTRANSFERENCE WITHIN SUPERVISORY RELATIONSHIPS

Transference and countertransference within supervisory relationships can be a parallel process of what is occurring between a social worker and a client. The transference occurs when a social worker recreates, within a supervisory relationship, a presenting problem and emotions occurring in a therapeutic relationship. Countertransference occurs when a supervisor responds to a social worker in the same manner that a social worker responds to a client. Thus, a supervisory interaction replays, or is parallel with, a social worker–client interaction. In essence, the processes at work in the relationship between a social worker and a client are reflected in the relationship between a social worker and the social worker's supervisor.

Parallel process is an unconscious identification with a client and can be used as an important part of the supervisory process. Examining it will assist a social worker and the social worker's supervisor in identifying issues that exist in a therapeutic relationship and allow for techniques to resolve these issues to be identified and discussed.

THE INFLUENCE OF THE SOCIAL WORKER'S OWN VALUES AND BELIEFS ON INTERDISCIPLINARY COLLABORATION

Social workers are increasingly recognized as beneficial members of interdisciplinary teams in addressing the complex needs of clients. A social worker may be on the team because the social worker is a direct service provider (counselor, case manager), an administrator, and/or a consultant.

Interdisciplinary teams can include those from many professions including law, psychology, and education. When working collaboratively, social workers can work "hand-in-hand" or "side-by-side" with others. In the former, social workers and others work together on most issues, whereas in the latter, each discipline works separately to accomplish what needs to be done.

Often when working with others, there can be potential conflicts in both personal and professional values of the team members. In order to mitigate these conflicts, it is important to:

- Outline the parameters that will govern the functioning of the collaborative team, including frequency of contact, other forms of communication, delineation of responsibilities, and leadership positions.

- Understand and define the roles of those who are collaborating.

- Understand and articulate the professional values of each member.

- Agree upon methods of decision making.

- Determine means for resolving disagreements.

The importance of role boundaries, role maintenance, and role clarity are essential in collaborative relationships. These issues should be openly discussed among team members, and obstacles to effective team functioning should be identified and addressed.

In all instances, it is the responsibility of a social worker to understand and reflect upon personal values, ensure that they do not interfere with the collaborative process, and that they are always aligned with ensuring outcomes in the best interest of a client. Areas of sensitivity that require self-reflection include beliefs about differing status among team members, unequal benefits for participation, different levels of personal and time commitments, insecurity about the value of the team approach, and/or lack of administrative support.

Content Area IV: Practice Questions

The following section has 42 unique practice questions that assess retention of material related to professional relationships, values, and ethics. The number of questions reflects the approximate proportion of a typical exam (25%) devoted to this content.

1. Which of the following is **MOST** important for a social worker to remember when engaging in ethical problem solving?

   A. Ethical dilemmas are unavoidable and must be handled with care
   B. Ethical issues should always be resolved in accordance with social work values and principles
   C. Supervision should always be sought when an ethical issue or dilemma emerges

2. A social worker is leaving one agency to work at another. In order to address this situation ethically, the social worker should:

   A. Advise clients to transfer services to the new agency to avoid any interruptions in treatment
   B. Inform clients of appropriate options for the continuation of services
   C. Discontinue services to clients immediately

3. The professional social work code of ethics is primarily used to:

   A. Mitigate liability when malpractice claims are filed
   B. Summarize the values on which service delivery is based
   C. Determine whether social workers have acted unethically

(See answers next page.)

1. **B.** Social worker, not their supervisors, should be able to resolve ethical issues or dilemmas. While ethical challenges do often occur and need careful attention, the most important consideration is that they are addressed consistent with the standards of care identified by the profession.

Question Assesses

Content Area IV—Professional Relationships, Values, and Ethics; Professional Values and Ethical Issues (Competency); Techniques to Identify and Resolve Ethical Dilemmas (KSA)

2. **B.** Social workers who are leaving an employment setting should inform clients of appropriate options for the continuation of services and of the benefits and risks of the options.

Question Assesses

Content Area IV—Professional Relationships, Values, and Ethics; Professional Values and Ethical Issues (Competency); Legal and/or Ethical Issues Regarding Termination (KSA)

3. **B.** The *NASW Code of Ethics* also provides ethical standards to which the general public can hold the profession accountable and social workers can consult if professional obligations conflict. These functions of the *Code* are printed immediately after the preamble. The mitigation of liability by third-party payers is not based on the values of the profession and is not a stated purpose of the *Code*. Additionally, the *Code* cannot determine if an ethical violation has occurred.

Question Assesses

Content Area IV—Professional Relationships, Values, and Ethics; Professional Values and Ethical Issues (Competency); Professional Values and Principles (e.g., Competence, Social Justice, Integrity, and Dignity and Worth of the Person) (KSA)

4. A client has been in therapy for about 4 months and has made substantial progress toward achieving his goals. The social worker and client believe that continued treatment would be beneficial. However, the client recently lost his job and has been informed that his insurance coverage, which has been paying for the services, will end immediately. The client states that he cannot afford to pay the rate paid by the insurance company. In order to facilitate continued progress, the social worker should:

   A. Work with the client to identify services that the client can provide in exchange for treatment
   B. Terminate therapy with the understanding that it will start again once new insurance is obtained
   C. Discuss a feasible amount to be paid by the client while he is uninsured

5. When can a social worker limit a client's right to self-determination?

   A. A client's actions violate policies set forth by the social worker's agency
   B. A social worker does not believe that a client is making appropriate decisions
   C. A client poses a serious and imminent risk to self or others

6. A social worker's ex-husband comes to her agency for therapy services. The ex-husband asks that the social worker provide these services because she is aware of his history and he feels comfortable speaking to her about his problems. They have been divorced for 15 years. The social worker refuses. Based on the professional code of ethics, how should this action by the social worker be assessed?

   A. Unethical because it has been more than 10 years since they were married
   B. Ethical because she had a prior intimate relationship with the client
   C. Unethical because the social worker did not respect the client's wishes with regard to the provision of treatment

7. In order for a social worker to provide services in a new area, the social worker must:

   A. Complete formal coursework or training from a school or university
   B. Seek supervision from a professional competent in the area
   C. Receive training and consultation in the area as needed

8. Which of the following statements **BEST** describes the relationship between ethical and legal actions of social workers?

   A. All illegal behaviors are unethical
   B. Some behaviors are legal, but unethical
   C. A behavior that is illegal can never be ethical

(*See answers next page.*)

4. **C.** A social worker can waive or reduce the fee, but cannot barter in this instance. Both parties agree that continued treatment is needed, so discontinuing until the client has a new insurance plan does not appear appropriate.

Question Assesses

Content Area IV—Professional Relationships, Values, and Ethics; Professional Values and Ethical Issues (Competency); Ethical Issues in Supervision and Management (KSA)

5. **C.** A social worker must respect and promote a client's right to self-determination, even when these decisions may not result in the best outcome in the social worker's opinion or when they violate agency practices. Only in instances that a client poses a serious and imminent risk to self or others can self-determination be limited.

Question Assesses

Content Area IV—Professional Relationships, Values, and Ethics; Professional Values and Ethical Issues (Competency); Client/Client System Competence and Self-Determination (e.g., Financial Decisions, Treatment Decisions, Emancipation, Age of Consent, and Permanency Planning) (KSA)

6. **B.** Social workers should not provide clinical services to individuals with whom they have had prior intimate relationships.

Question Assesses

Content Area IV—Professional Relationships, Values, and Ethics; Professional Values and Ethical Issues (Competency); Professional Boundaries in the Social Worker–Client/Client System Relationship (e.g., Power Differences, Conflicts of Interest, etc.) (KSA)

7. **C.** Social workers should provide services in substantive areas or use intervention techniques or approaches that are new to them only after engaging in appropriate training or consultation. While supervision is also advisable, it is not always feasible as supervision requires formal authority over the actions of the social worker and the social worker may be in private practice. Formal coursework is not required, but can be taken if needed and available.

Question Assesses

Content Area IV—Professional Relationships, Values, and Ethics; Professional Values and Ethical Issues (Competency); The Supervisee's Role in Supervision (e.g., Identifying Learning Needs, Self-Assessment, Prioritizing, etc.) (KSA)

8. **B.** There are some actions that may be legal, like accepting gifts or going to a movie with a client, but are not ethical. In addition, a social worker may engage in public protest, which is not legal in some locations or situations, but this behavior may be ethical.

Question Assesses

Content Area IV—Professional Relationships, Values, and Ethics; Professional Values and Ethical Issues (Competency); Legal and/or Ethical Issues Related to the Practice of Social Work, Including Responsibility to Clients/Client Systems, Colleagues, the Profession, and Society (KSA)

9. A social worker who does not provide adolescent services makes referrals to a very reputable agency in her community when she is contacted for such services. In exchange for each of these referrals, the agency provides a $50 gift card to the social worker. Which **BEST** describes this fee splitting practice by the social worker?

   A. Ethical
   B. Unethical
   C. Illegal

10. A client who has been paying a reduced fee to a social worker in private practice inherits a lot of money from a relative's estate. The client, who was previously poor, is now extremely wealthy and very appreciative of the social worker's services. The client would like to pay the social worker the amount that was discounted for prior services. What **BEST** describes this action by the client?

    A. Ethical as long as the client only pays the amount of the discount
    B. Ethical because the client now has the ability to pay for the prior services
    C. Unethical because the social worker agreed to a reduced fee for services

11. An agency is experiencing financial hardship and social workers are upset because they have not been able to meet with their supervisors in several weeks because the supervisors have had to assist with other agency administrative tasks. In this situation, the social work administrator should:

    A. Terminate services to several clients in order to free up social work staff to provide supervision
    B. Explore the use of peer supervision
    C. Instruct the staff to pay for outside supervision if affordable

12. A private pay client has made substantial progress and achieved all stated treatment goals, but wants to continue to see a social worker "in case something comes up." In this situation, the social worker should:

    A. Continue to see the client at the regular fee in order to respect the client's self-determination
    B. Begin termination with the client
    C. Agree to see the client, but reduce the fee since the treatment goals have been achieved

13. In order for a social worker who is in private practice to terminate services to a client who is not paying an overdue balance, the social worker should:

    A. Conduct a safety assessment to determine if the client is a danger to self or others
    B. Negotiate with the client to reduce the balance to an amount that the client can afford to pay
    C. Locate an alternative service provider who will serve the client at an affordable rate

(See answers next page.)

9. **B.** A social worker should not receive a fee for making a referral because this creates a conflict of interest. This practice is unethical but not illegal broadly as it is accepted practice in some professions.

Question Assesses

Content Area IV—Professional Relationships, Values, and Ethics; Professional Values and Ethical Issues (Competency); Ethical Issues in Supervision and Management (KSA)

10. **C.** A social worker can now charge the client the full amount for services, but cannot charge the client for payments associated with services already rendered.

Question Assesses

Content Area IV—Professional Relationships, Values, and Ethics; Professional Values and Ethical Issues (Competency); Ethical Issues in Supervision and Management (KSA)

11. **B.** Social workers who are administrators should take reasonable steps to ensure that adequate agency or organizational resources are available to provide appropriate staff supervision. Peer supervision may be a feasible method for receiving feedback and input into treatment decisions that do not result in hardships to either clients or workers.

Question Assesses

Content Area IV—Professional Relationships, Values, and Ethics; Professional Values and Ethical Issues (Competency); Models of Supervision and Consultation (e.g., Individual, Peer, and Group) (KSA)

12. **B.** It is unethical to continue to treat when services are no longer needed or serve the client's interests. The fee charged is not relevant to this standard.

Question Assesses

Content Area IV—Professional Relationships, Values, and Ethics; Professional Values and Ethical Issues (Competency); Legal and/or Ethical Issues Related to Termination (KSA)

13. **A.** Social workers in fee-for-service settings may terminate services to clients who are not paying overdue balances if the financial contractual arrangements have been made clear to the clients, *if clients do not pose an imminent danger to themselves or others*, and if the clinical and other consequences of the current nonpayment have been addressed and discussed.

Question Assesses

Content Area IV—Professional Relationships, Values, and Ethics; Professional Values and Ethical Issues (Competency); Legal and/or Ethical Issues Related to Termination (KSA)

14. A social worker who is in a private mental health practice recently earned a doctorate from an accredited university in an unrelated field. She adds "Dr." to her name on her social work private practice business card. How should this action by the social worker be assessed?

A. Unethical since it is not related to social work treatment
B. Ethical since she earned a doctorate
C. Unethical unless she explains that the degree is in another field

15. Which of the following is one of social work's core values as stated in the professional code of ethics?

A. Service
B. Loyalty
C. Resiliency

16. A social worker receives a court order to provide records of a former client. In addition to submitting the records, the social worker should:

A. Attempt to contact the client to provide information about the disclosure
B. Provide the court with the client's current contact information to assist with notification
C. Seek consultation and supervision

17. A social worker cannot release confidential information when a client:

A. Poses a serious risk to self and others
B. Abuses a child emotionally or psychologically
C. Commits a violent criminal offense

18. A social worker receives a subpoena from the courts in the mail for a former client's records. In this situation, a social worker should:

A. Send a copy of the records to the courts
B. Prepare a summary of the records to send
C. Claim privilege and attempt to contact the client

(See answers next page.)

14. **A.** Social workers should represent themselves as competent only within the boundaries of their education, training, license, certification, consultation received, supervised experience, or other relevant professional experience. Listing herself as a "Dr." on a card for mental health treatment can be misleading to clients who would believe that the degree is related to the services advertised on the card.

Question Assesses

Content Area IV—Professional Relationships, Values, and Ethics; Professional Values and Ethical Issues (Competency); The Supervisee's Role in Supervision (e.g., Identifying Learning Needs, Self-Assessment, Prioritizing, etc.) (KSA)

15. **A.** The core values include service, social justice, dignity and worth of the person, importance of human relationships, integrity, and competence.

Question Assesses

Content Area IV—Professional Relationships, Values, and Ethics; Professional Values and Ethical Issues (Competency); Professional Values and Principles (e.g., Competence, Social Justice, Integrity, and Dignity and Worth of the Person) (KSA)

16. **A.** Social workers should inform clients, to the extent possible, about the disclosure of confidential information and the potential consequences, when feasible, before any disclosure is made. This applies whether social workers disclose confidential information on the basis of a legal requirement or client consent.

Question Assesses

Content Area IV—Professional Relationships, Values, and Ethics; Confidentiality (Competency); Legal and/or Ethical Issues Regarding Confidentiality, Including Electronic Information Security (KSA)

17. **C.** Social workers are mandatory reporters of child abuse and can breach confidentiality if there is a danger to self or others. Committing a violent crime does not mean that the client poses an imminent danger and is not an exception to maintaining confidentiality.

Question Assesses

Content Area IV—Professional Relationships, Values, and Ethics; Confidentiality (Competency); Legal and/or Ethical Issues Regarding Confidentiality, Including Electronic Information Security (KSA)

18. **C.** A subpoena is not a court order and no documents should be sent unless ordered by the court. However, a social worker does have to respond and should not send the records or a summary when receiving a subpoena unless the client has provided a written release. Attempting to contact the client is advisable so the client is aware of the request for records.

Question Assesses

Content Area IV—Professional Relationships, Values, and Ethics; Confidentiality (Competency); Legal and/or Ethical Issues Regarding Confidentiality, Including Electronic Information Security (KSA)

19. A client abruptly stops coming to therapy after the sixth session. She shows up at the office several weeks later demanding a copy of her records. The social worker does not believe that the information in the record could cause harm to the client, but denies access because the client did not provide any reason for the abrupt termination or reason for wanting the copies. How should these actions by the social worker be assessed?

    A. Unethical because the client should have access to the record
    B. Ethical because the reason for the release must be disclosed
    C. Ethical because the client terminated services without notice

20. A social worker in private practice designs a standard intake form that includes questions about the client's demographic information including age, gender, marital status, sexual orientation, education, and drug/alcohol use. Which **BEST** describes the use of this form?

    A. Ethical as some of the information might be needed to work with the client effectively
    B. Ethical since all of this information will be kept confidential
    C. Unethical since this information may not be needed for treatment

21. A social worker sees that a colleague is distracted when interacting with clients and is showing up for appointments late. The social worker learns that this behavior began several weeks earlier, after the death of the colleague's husband. In this instance, the social worker should:

    A. Monitor the colleague's actions to see if the behavior subsides over time
    B. Speak to a supervisor to see if the colleague's workload could be reduced
    C. Speak to the colleague directly about the observations

22. A client's insurance company threatens to discontinue to pay for services immediately if it does not receive the current treatment goals of the client. The social worker sends these goals without written consent from the client. How should this action by the social worker be assessed?

    A. Ethical since the client would not be able to continue services without the insurance payments
    B. Unethical because such a release requires written consent
    C. Ethical since treatment goals can be sent to an insurance company without written consent

23. A social worker is running a group with adolescents. One of the group members calls the social worker because she is very upset that something that she said in group was disclosed to others in her school by another group member. The **BEST** action by the social worker to address this situation is to:

    A. Contact the group member who disclosed the information to discuss the concern
    B. Terminate the group member who disclosed the information
    C. Suggest that the issue be raised during the next group session

(See answers next page.)

19. **A.** A social worker who is concerned that client access to records could cause serious harm to the client can limit access to the record or portion of the record when the rationale for the request is documented in the file. This scenario clearly states that the social worker is not concerned that releasing the record to the client would be harmful, so it must be released and to not do so is unethical.

Question Assesses

Content Area IV—Professional Relationships, Values, and Ethics; Confidentiality (Competency); The Use of Client/Client System Records (KSA)

20. **C.** Social workers should respect clients' right to privacy. Social workers should not solicit private information from clients unless it is essential to providing services or conducting social work evaluation or research. Information about the client's sexual orientation and/or drug or alcohol use may not be relevant to the presenting problem or treatment.

Question Assesses

Content Area IV—Professional Relationships, Values, and Ethics; Confidentiality (Competency); The Use of Client/Client System Records (KSA)

21. **C.** A social worker with direct knowledge of a colleague's impairment due to personal problems, psychological stress, and so on, that interferes with practice effectiveness should consult with the colleague when feasible and assist the colleague in taking remedial action.

Question Assesses

Content Area IV—Professional Relationships, Values, and Ethics; Confidentiality (Competency); Legal and/or Ethical Issues Regarding Mandatory Reporting (e.g., Abuse, Threat of Harm, Impaired Professionals, etc.) (KSA)

22. **B.** Social workers should not disclose confidential information to third-party payers unless clients have authorized such disclosure.

Question Assesses

Content Area IV—Professional Relationships, Values, and Ethics; Confidentiality (Competency); Legal and/or Ethical Issues Regarding Confidentiality, Including Electronic Information Security (KSA)

23. **C.** There is no legal mandate for group members to safeguard information disclosed in groups. However, this disclosure may be a violation of the rules that the group established for itself. It is appropriate for the group to discuss and decide what actions, if any, should take place. Such disclosures may threaten the psychotherapeutic goals of the group, but any confrontation should be done in the group context.

Question Assesses

Content Area IV—Professional Relationships, Values, and Ethics; Confidentiality (Competency); Legal and/or Ethical Issues Regarding Confidentiality, Including Electronic Information Security (KSA)

24. With regard to confidentiality, a deceased client has:

    A. All the same rights to confidentiality as a living client
    B. Some of the same rights to confidentiality as a living client
    C. None of the same rights to confidentiality as a living client

25. Which of the following statements is true with regard to client consent?

    A. Consent and assent have the same legal meaning
    B. When treating those who lack capacity to provide informed consent, consent should be obtained by the responsible third party and assent should be obtained by the client
    C. Client consent should be obtained before the onset of treatment

26. A social worker providing psychotherapy in a mental health agency is concerned about protecting the confidentiality of client records. In order to provide the greatest protection for clients while adhering to best clinical practices, the social worker should:

    A. Keep all psychotherapy notes in client files in a secure and locked location
    B. Store the psychotherapy notes in a secure and locked location separate from client files
    C. Not keep any documentation, including psychotherapy notes

27. In instances in which clients are not literate and are having difficulty understanding the primary language used in the practice setting, which is the **MOST** acceptable practice by a social worker?

    A. Asking a client's family member to translate information
    B. Providing verbal explanations to written policies when a client asks for further information
    C. Employing a qualified interpreter to translate information

(See answers next page.)

24. **A.** Social workers should protect the confidentiality of deceased clients consistent with the same ethical standards that apply to those who are living.

    Question Assesses

    Content Area IV—Professional Relationships, Values, and Ethics; Confidentiality (Competency); Legal and/or Ethical Issues Regarding Confidentiality, Including Electronic Information Security (KSA)

25. **B.** Consent is a legal term that means a client is willing to, and has the legal authority to, give permission to receive treatment. Assent is a willingness to participate, but does not have the same legal meaning because it may be granted by clients who are not their own guardians. Consent is not obtained *before* the provision of treatment as consent is obtained always. There may be times when consent is needed *during* treatment to release information. Specific consent should be obtained when taping clients as they must be informed about the storage and release of audiotapes or videotapes.

    Question Assesses

    Content Area IV—Professional Relationships, Values, and Ethics; Confidentiality (Competency); The Principles and Processes of Obtaining Informed Consent (KSA)

26. **B.** A social worker may not disclose psychotherapy notes for any purpose unless a client's authorization is obtained.

    In order to take advantage of extra protection afforded to psychotherapy notes, notes must be kept "physically separate" from the rest of a client's record. The term "physically separate" is not defined so there is some discretion as to whether they are kept in a separate file, a separate file cabinet, or simply in a separate part of the same file as the rest of the record. It is safer to at least keep the information in a separate file folder or physical/electronic location.

    Question Assesses

    Content Area IV—Professional Relationships, Values, and Ethics; Confidentiality (Competency); The Elements of Client/Client System Reports (KSA)

27. **C.** In instances when clients are not literate or have difficulty understanding the primary language used in the practice setting, social workers should take steps to ensure clients' comprehension including arranging for qualified interpreters or translators. Using family members is not acceptable due to confidentiality concerns, as well as possibilities that interpretations or impressions of family members will be included in the translation. Providing verbal explanations when a client asks for them is not adequate.

    Question Assesses

    Content Area IV—Professional Relationships, Values, and Ethics; Confidentiality (Competency); The Principles and Processes of Obtaining Informed Consent (KSA)

28. A woman who is deaf and uses American Sign Language (ASL) to communicate comes to a community-based agency to see a social worker who is also deaf and proficient in ASL. The woman is in need of mental health services that are not provided at this agency. In this situation, the social worker should:

A. Provide the mental services as it is unlikely that she will be able to find an appropriate clinician

B. Contact a mental health agency with the woman to see what accommodations are available

C. Offer whatever services are available in the agency so the woman gets some help

29. An agency hires a consultant to assist a social worker to become more competent in addressing substance use issues. The social worker shows the consultant a few client assessment documents and case notes to provide needed background on the kinds of substance use problems that the social worker is facing in practice. How should these actions by the social worker be assessed?

A. Unethical because the clients need to consent to disclosure of this information

B. Ethical as the consultant can see this information without client consent

C. Ethical because this information is available to all agency personnel

30. A social work administrator is having trouble finding a group home manager for a new program scheduled to open in 2 weeks. Further delays in locating staff will delay clients from moving into the program. The administrator temporarily hires her niece, who just graduated with a social work degree, for this position. How should this action by the social work administrator be assessed?

A. Unethical as the hiring results a conflict of interest

B. Ethical as the position is temporary and ensures clients get the services needed

C. Unethical as clients will experience staff turnover when a new manager is hired

31. Which of the following inhibits the establishment of a therapeutic relationship?

A. A universalism approach or the acceptance of a standard set of norms or standards

B. Viewing client problems as resulting from role ambiguity rather than individual deficits

C. Flexible treatment approaches that consider the subjective realities of clients

32. A client who was in a battering relationship is reluctant to disclose information to a social worker. The social worker encourages the client to examine the benefits of sharing against the risks. Which of the following theoretical approaches is being used by the social worker to assist with strengthening the helping relationship?

A. Social exchange

B. Functional

C. Psychoeducational

(*See answers next page.*)

28. **B.** Providing mental health services calls for the social worker to work outside the social worker's designated scope of practice. Offering available services does not meet the woman's need. The social worker should help her get connected with a mental health organization.

Question Assesses

Content Area IV—Professional Relationships, Values, and Ethics; Confidentiality (Competency); The Principles and Processes of Obtaining Informed Consent (KSA)

29. **A.** Social workers should not disclose identifying information unless the client has consented to disclosure of confidential information. In addition, social workers should not disclose identifying information when discussing clients with consultants unless the client has consented to disclosure of confidential information or there is a compelling need for such disclosure. A consultant is not agency personnel as the consultant is not an employee of the organization.

Question Assesses

Content Area IV—Professional Relationships, Values, and Ethics; Confidentiality (Competency); Legal and/or Ethical Issues Regarding Confidentiality, Including Electronic Information Security (KSA)

30. **A.** Social workers should avoid situations interfering with impartial judgment. Hiring a family member creates a dual relationship and should be avoided.

Question Assesses

Content Area IV—Professional Relationships, Values, and Ethics; Professional Development and Use of Self (Competency); Ethical Issues Related to Dual Relationships (KSA)

31. **A.** Universalism is based on one acceptable norm or standard for everyone versus many valid standards that have been developed by clients that they have determined to be most useful to them.

Question Assesses

Content Area IV—Professional Relationships, Values, and Ethics; Professional Development and Use of Self (Competency); The Influence of the Social Worker's Own Values and Beliefs on the Social Worker–Client/Client System Relationship (KSA)

32. **A.** Social exchange theory is based on the idea of totaling potential benefits and losses to determine behavior. A client will take action when the alternatives are seen as better than the current risks (rewards outweigh costs).

Question Assesses

Content Area IV—Professional Relationships, Values, and Ethics; Professional Development and Use of Self (Competency); The Impact of Domestic, Intimate Partner, and Other Violence on the Helping Relationship (KSA)

33. Upon admission, a client reports that he has always feared disapproval and rejection from others in his life. Several weeks later, the client appears anxious and worried. When asked about his behavior, he states that he feels judged by the social worker and that the social worker is being critical of him when he sees her. Which of the following term **BEST** describes the client's feelings?

    A. Countertransference
    B. Paranoia
    C. Transference

34. A client expresses an attraction to the social worker during a therapy session. In order to address this issue ethically, the social worker should:

    A. Explore the feelings as a therapeutic issue and document the disclosure in the client file
    B. Ignore the overture as it is not relevant to treatment
    C. Terminate services immediately as the client's actions are inappropriate

35. Which of following actions by a social worker will be **MOST** effective in demonstrating empathetic communication to a client?

    A. Providing detailed explanations to client questions
    B. Listening attentively when the client explains feelings and concerns
    C. Approaching all issues with unconditional positive regard

36. A woman who is in a relationship that is physically abusive would like to begin couples counseling because she believes that helping her boyfriend to see her point of view may assist in decreasing the violence. In order to appropriately address this request, the social worker should:

    A. Suggest that she and her boyfriend begin therapy to address these issues
    B. Explain that couples counseling should not take place at this time given the physical abuse
    C. Inform the woman that these issues will be discussed after an individual assessment is completed

(*See answers next page.*)

33. **C.** Transference refers to redirection of a client's feelings for a significant person to a social worker. Transference is often manifested as an erotic attraction toward a social worker, but can be seen in many other forms such as rage, hatred, mistrust, parentification, extreme dependence, or even placing a social worker in an esteemed status.

Question Assesses

Content Area IV—Professional Relationships, Values, and Ethics; Professional Development and Use of Self (Competency); The Impact of Transference and Countertransference in the Social Worker–Client/Client System Relationship (KSA)

34. **A.** A social worker must address this expression within an appropriate therapeutic context. Ignoring or terminating is not appropriate and ignoring it does not assist the client in understanding why these feelings are occurring. The social worker should never act on these feelings and engage in a relationship with a client.

Question Assesses

Content Area IV—Professional Relationships, Values, and Ethics; Professional Development and Use of Self (Competency); The Impact of Transference and Countertransference in the Social Worker–Client/Client System Relationship (KSA)

35. **C.** Listening and providing detailed explanations are helpful but do not demonstrate empathy in the same way as unconditional positive regard. Being nonjudgmental is the best method for strengthening the therapeutic relationship and shows clients that acceptance will be the basis of helping.

Question Assesses

Content Area IV—Professional Relationships, Values, and Ethics; Professional Development and Use of Self (Competency); The Concept of Acceptance and Empathy in the Social Worker–Client/Client System Relationship (KSA)

36. **B.** Traditional marital and couples therapy are not appropriate in battering relationships. It puts victims in greater danger of further abuse. The woman needs to be informed of such a risk. It would be inappropriate for the social worker to start a helping relationship with the woman without discussing her service request. Seeing both the woman and her boyfriend would be inappropriate.

Question Assesses

Content Area IV—Professional Relationships, Values, and Ethics; Professional Development and Use of Self (Competency); The Impact of Domestic, Intimate Partner, and Other Violence on the Helping Relationship (KSA)

37. A client is starting a new business and really needs a partner to assist with start-up activities. Without this help, the client will experience extreme financial hardship because she will not be able to bring in needed income to her household. The social worker has a lot of business expertise that would be valuable to the client. In this situation, the social worker should:

   A. Continue to serve the client, providing only emotional support during this crisis
   B. Terminate services to assist with the business so that the client does not experience financial loss
   C. Stop billing the client for a short period while assisting the client with the business start-up

38. Upon intake, a woman tells a social worker that she was brutally beaten by her boyfriend 6 months ago, but it was an isolated incident and there have been no further acts of violence. Since that time, he has been remorseful and attentive. In this situation, the social worker should **FIRST**:

   A. Document the incident in the assessment
   B. Explore the impact of the incident on her relationship with her boyfriend
   C. Evaluate the need for medical and protective services

39. Which of the following is a dual relationship between a social worker and client?

   A. A social worker continuing to provide therapy to someone dating his adult son
   B. A social worker providing clinical consultation for a former employer
   C. A social worker choosing a clinical supervisor who is a faculty member at her university

40. At the beginning of the initial session, a client states, "I am so glad that I am here because I really need you to tell me how to solve my problems." The social worker should:

   A. Clarify the social worker's role in the problem-solving process
   B. Praise the client for her willingness to be open to feedback
   C. Explore which problems are considered a priority at this time

(*See answers next page.*)

37. **A.** Social workers should not terminate services to pursue social, financial, or sexual relationships with clients. Social workers should also not engage in dual relationships with clients. Stopping the billing of the client does not permit the social worker to become involved in the business.

Question Assesses

Content Area IV—Professional Relationships, Values, and Ethics; Professional Development and Use of Self (Competency); Ethical Issues Related to Dual Relationships (KSA)

38. **C.** The cycle of abuse indicates that this may be the "honeymoon" phase that happens after a battering incident. Just because there has not been any violence in the last 6 months does not mean that the battering will not occur in the future. The "honeymoon" phase leads to "tension building" and then violence in the future. The social worker must address the medical needs and safety issues of the client FIRST according to Maslow's hierarchy of needs.

Question Assesses

Content Area IV—Professional Relationships, Values, and Ethics; Professional Development and Use of Self (Competency); The Impact of Domestic, Intimate Partner, and Other Violence on the Helping Relationship (KSA)

39. **A.** Social workers should not provide services to or supervise friends or relatives, including the romantic partner of a child. There may be ethical considerations with the incorrect response choices, but they do not involve clients.

Question Assesses

Content Area IV—Professional Relationships, Values, and Ethics; Professional Development and Use of Self (Competency); Ethical Issues Related to Dual Relationships (KSA)

40. **A.** As part of engagement, the roles of the social worker and client in the problem-solving process should be discussed and clarified, if needed.

Question Assesses

Content Area IV—Professional Relationships, Values, and Ethics; Professional Development and Use of Self (Competency); The Principles and Techniques for Building and Maintaining a Helping Relationship (KSA)

41. Which of the following is the **MOST** important social work role?

    A. Providing a client with a support system

    B. Establishing rapport with a client

    C. Helping a client to develop coping and problem solving skills

42. Which of the following is the **MOST** critical factor for the delivery of effective culturally competent services?

    A. The social worker and client must be from the same cultural group

    B. The social worker must have self-awareness about cultural differences with the client

    C. The social worker must have discuss cultural practices and norms with a supervisor

(*See answers next page.*)

41. C. Social workers can have many roles including, but not limited to, consultant, advocate, case manager, catalyst, enabler, broker, mediator, facilitator, and instructor. A social worker can be supportive in these roles, but is not supposed to be the client's support system. Instead, a social worker should assist clients to mobilize or build their own natural supports. Establishing rapport is also not a social work role, but instead a part of the helping process. Social workers want clients to become self-sufficient and solve their own problems so helping clients develop coping skills is critical.

Question Assesses

Content Area IV—Professional Relationships, Values, and Ethics; Professional Development and Use of Self (Competency); Methods to Clarify the Roles and Responsibilities of the Social Worker and Client/Client System in the Intervention Process (KSA)

42. B. Social workers' self-awareness about their own attitudes, values, and beliefs about cultural differences and a willingness to acknowledge racial and cultural differences are critical factors for effectively working with diverse populations.

Question Assesses

Content Area IV—Professional Relationships, Values, and Ethics; Professional Development and Use of Self (Competency); The Dynamics of Diversity in the Social Worker–Client/Client System Relationship (KSA)

Practice Questions Content Area IV: Professional Relationships, Values, and Ethics (25%)					
Competency	**Question Numbers**	**Number of Questions**	**Number Correct**	**Percentage Correct**	**Area Requiring Further Study?**
1. Professional Values and Ethical Issues	1, 2, 3, 4, 5, 6, 7, 8, 9, 10, 11, 12, 13, 14, 15	15	___/15	___%	
2. Confidentiality	16, 17, 18, 19, 20, 21, 22, 23, 24, 25, 26, 27, 28, 29	14	___/14	___%	
3. Professional Development and Use of Self	30, 31, 32, 33, 34, 35, 36, 37, 38, 39, 40, 41, 42	13	___/13	___%	

Full Length Practice Test

170-Question Practice Test

This practice test contains 170 questions but remember that your score on the actual examination will be based on 150 questions because 20 items are being piloted. As you won't know which items will be scored and determine whether or not you pass, you will need to complete all 170 questions. Thus, this test has 170 questions so that you can gauge the length of time that it takes you to complete an equivalent number of questions. The questions in each domain or area are in random order on this practice test, as they are on the actual examination, and there is a similar distribution of questions from each section as will appear on your actual examination.

Human Development, Diversity, and Behavior
in the Environment

46 Questions

Assessment and Intervention Planning

41 Questions

Interventions With Clients/Client Systems

41 Questions

Professional Relationships, Values, and Ethics

42 Questions

The best way to use this practice test is as a mock examination, which means:

a. Take it **AFTER** you have completed your studying—do not memorize answers to these questions.

b. Do not apply the answers to these questions to the actual examination or you may miss subtle differences in each question that can distinguish the correct from the incorrect response choices.

c. Take it in its entirety during a 4-hour block of time to show yourself that you can finish in the allotted time period for the examination.

d. Do not look up the correct answers until you are completely finished with the entire practice test, and do not worry if you get questions incorrect. Remember, this examination is not one in which you can expect to get all of the answers correct. **The number of questions that you will need to answer correctly generally varies from 93 to 106 correct of the 150 scored items**.

1. During the fifth meeting with a social worker, a client tells the social worker about the recent engagement of her daughter with whom she was previously estranged. The client asks the social worker to attend the wedding which will occur in the next few months. To best assist the client, the social worker should:

   A. Tell the client that the professional *Code of Ethics* prohibits the social worker from attending
   B. Discuss with the client the reason(s) for the request
   C. Ask to speak to the daughter to gather her thoughts about the social worker attending

2. A social worker is working with an elderly woman whose husband just died suddenly. The woman is lethargic, reports feeling depressed, and is hesitant to speak about future plans. In this situation, the social worker should **FIRST**:

   A. Assess the client for suicide risk
   B. Recommend a medical evaluation to identify any medical etiology
   C. Help the client to identify activities of interest with others which will enhance socialization

3. A school social worker is seeing a family who recently immigrated from another country. During the initial interview, the 12-year-old son cries about the physical discipline that he receives when he gets bad grades. The parents state that punishment is needed, citing that his grades have improved since its onset in recent weeks. In order to help the family, the social worker should **FIRST**:

   A. Ask the parents about their academic expectations for their son
   B. Report the situation to the child welfare agency for screening and assistance
   C. Determine the nature and severity of the punishment techniques used

4. A social worker is seeing a single mother of three small children. The client is temporarily staying with a friend after leaving her home due to intimate partner violence. The client tells the social worker that she plans to return home in a week where the perpetrator is still living. In this situation, the social worker should:

   A. Discuss with the client the impact of violence on the development and well-being of children
   B. Make a report of the situation to the child abuse hotline
   C. Recognize that the client is not ready to leave her abuser

5. A client who is gender non-conforming comes to see a social worker due to reports of depression, sadness, and feelings of isolation. During the initial meeting, the client tells the social worker that they never really felt connected to others, citing a lack of friendships and intimate relationships as a reason for current unhappiness. Recently, the client has questioned their sexual orientation and interest in sexual relationships generally. In order to assist the client, the social worker should **FIRST**:

   A. Refer the client for a medication evaluation for depression
   B. Complete a sexual history on the client to identify past experience and encounters
   C. Explore with the client past and current emotional connections

6. A 30-year-old man comes to a social worker due to problems with his current girlfriend. The girlfriend is overly controlling and demanding, requiring him to call her repeatedly throughout the day. She recently discovered that he had gone out to lunch with a female coworker which resulted in her screaming at him in a rage. The client is nervous about speaking to her about his concerns for fear of her reaction. In order to best assist the client, the social worker should:

   A. Help the client alleviate his apprehension by role playing the meeting with the girlfriend
   B. Suggest that the social worker see the client and his girlfriend together to establish clear and appropriate boundaries
   C. Educate the client about the characteristics of healthy intimate relationships so that he can better understand his girlfriend's behavior

7. A social worker who has been working with clients in crisis notices that she is feeling lethargic, depressed, and apathetic toward her work. She has had few days off since starting the job due to client demands. After discussing the situation with her supervisor, she realizes that these thoughts have been getting progressively more pronounced and interfering with her ability to provide effective care. To **BEST** address this problem, the social worker should:

   A. Ask for assistance in covering job duties while taking a needed vacation
   B. Implement workload adjustments while receiving supervision and consultation
   C. Evaluate the need for self-care strategies and coping skills to deal with vicarious trauma

8. A school social worker is informed that a student plans to transition to the opposite gender during the next year. The student previously identified as male and met with the social worker many times in the past about issues that were not related to gender identity. The student arrives for the next meeting with the social worker dressed in male clothing with no change in appearance. The social worker should:

   A. Identify the student by the name and gender pronouns used in the past
   B. Ask the student to identify the name and gender pronouns that should be used
   C. Explore with the student why gender identity was not discussed during their meetings in the past

9. A social worker is contacted by a former client who is engaged in a child custody fight with her abusive ex-husband. The court has asked the client to provide a copy of the treatment records which were previously agreed upon by the social worker and client. The client asks the social worker to delete her diagnoses as they will likely be used against her in the court proceedings. The social worker agrees to do so as she has concerns about the ex-husband's ability to parent. Which **BEST** describes the social worker's actions?

   A. Unethical as the social worker should not alter a record after it has been created
   B. Unethical as social worker has not been appointed as an examiner of the court
   C. Ethical as the diagnoses are not relevant to the court proceedings so they should remain privileged

10. A couple seek treatment with a social worker after unsuccessful infertility treatment. Most recently, the couple has decided to discontinue in-vitro fertilization as it has not been successful. The couple report that they feel isolated as their friends have children and many of the group activities are focused on children's activities. They question why they have had difficulty conceiving and feel shame that they will not have biological children. In order to **BEST** assist the couple, the social worker should:

    A. Help the couple explore methods to adopt so that they can feel that their family is complete

    B. Work with couple to construct their own life story with the goal of realizing it is possible to live a rewarding life without biological children

    C. Refer the couple to a mutual aid group with others who have encountered similar struggles so that they realize that they are not alone

11. A social worker serves clients in a rural community so the social worker is diligent in discussing appropriate boundaries with them upon intake. The social worker, a well-known member of a community choral group, is approached by a client who would like to join as it would be greatly beneficial to her future plans to perform professionally. The client asks for a referral to another social worker so that she can join the group. In order to address the situation appropriately, the social worker should:

    A. Inform the client that it is inappropriate for her to join the group as she has already been seeing the worker

    B. Identify other opportunities for the client to develop her singing skills besides joining the group

    C. Help the client to identify another social worker who can meet her need

12. A school social worker receives a referral from a teacher of a 11-year-old child with disabilities due to the child's behavior. The child's hygiene is poor and the child appears unkept. Additionally, the child has difficulty leaving the teacher's side and tantrums when her parents come to pick her up at the end of the day. The social worker should **FIRST**:

    A. Conduct a child welfare assessment

    B. Meet with the parents to determine whether the child is having behavioral problems at home

    C. Assess the appropriateness of the current school supports in place to help the child with hygiene and behavior management

13. An adult client with significant developmental disabilities has recently moved into a group home after his aging parents found it difficult to continue to care for him. During the first month, he spends a lot of his time in his room and has made few friends in the house. The family reports that he was very talkative at home and loves to participate in family activities. What is **MOST** likely the cause of the client's behavior?

    A. Concern over the declining health of his parents due to aging

    B. Deficits in socialization that result from his developmental disability

    C. Expected adjustment to new living conditions

14. A social worker at an after-school program learns that a 7-year-old child, whose sibling was tragically killed last year, is struggling academically. The child has stopped participating in extracurricular activities that were done in the past. The social worker should **FIRST**:

    A. Explore with the child how the loss of the sibling may be impacting on current functioning and well-being
    B. Contact the parents of the child to determine what struggles may be occurring within the home
    C. Arrange for socialization and academic supports to assist the child and family during this emotional crisis

15. A client who is being treated for a history of depression reports to a social worker that his longtime girlfriend just ended the relationship. The client is shocked and distraught as the girlfriend had just moved in with him a month ago, indicating to him that the relationship was going to continue. After comforting the client who was crying, the social worker should **NEXT**:

    A. Help the client to identify what had changed in the relationship that may be the cause of the breakup
    B. Complete a suicide risk assessment
    C. Suggest to the client that he may need additional support during this time

16. A social worker gets a referral from a concerned relative for a woman who has recently been fired from her job. During the initial interview, the client tells the social worker that she has a chronic physical illness, has assumed responsibilities for an aging parent, and is involved in an unhappy marriage which has been abusive in the past. In order to assist the client, the social worker should **FIRST**:

    A. Refer her to a physician to identify any current medical issues which may interfere with functioning
    B. Determine the impacts of the marital abuse on the other aspects of her functioning
    C. Help her to identify the desired outcomes for service receipt

17. A family seeks treatment after their 16-year-old daughter was diagnosed with cancer. The child has been undergoing painful treatment which have left her weak and tired. During the initial interview, the parents argue about the severity of the illness, blame one another for recent problems, and speak to the child like she is a baby. The daughter reports anger at being sick and has trouble speaking to her parents at all given the tension in the household. She states that she "can't stand it anymore." When establishing treatment goals, it is **MOST** appropriate to:

    A. Ensure that the parents understand how their behavior is impacting on the emotional well-being of their daughter
    B. Focus on how the illness has impacted the interaction and communication patterns within the family
    C. Assist the family to get all needed concrete services so that they can focus on the daughter's medical prognosis

18. A social worker agrees to meet with a father and his 14-year-old son due to the boy's recent suspension from school due to fighting. The father states that the boy has no problems with fighting at home or in the neighborhood. When asked about the incident, the son provides little information about the cause or nature of the school conflict. Which action will likely be **MOST** helpful in identifying the problem?

    A. Speaking candidly with the son alone
    B. Obtaining the son's developmental history from the father
    C. Gathering information on the son from the school counselor

19. A child welfare social worker is meeting with a family due to allegations of abuse. During the intake, the social worker observes a bruise on one of the child's legs. The mother admits that she spanked the child on the leg in frustration as she had to bring the child to work with her due to not being able to afford camp during the summer. The account is confirmed by others and no other signs of maltreatment are observed. In this situation, is it **MOST** appropriate for the social worker to:

    A. Identify other living arrangements for the child until the incident can be investigated more fully
    B. Suggest that the mother attend parenting classes aimed at strengthening the bond with the child
    C. Arrange for the child to attend a subsidized camp program during the summer

20. A social worker receives a referral for a family that has been served by the agency in the past. During the assessment, the social worker learns that the children are often tardy from school, the family has been repeatedly homeless in prior years, and there is poor communication within the household. Family members often interrupt each other, each identifying different concerns that they feel need to be addressed. To assist this family, the social worker should **NEXT**:

    A. Help the family to identify their specific service needs
    B. Complete a biopsychosocial assessment on each family member
    C. Review the prior service records to determine what has been done in the past

21. A school social worker is seeing a 16-year-old girl due to increasing conflicts with her mother after her father's death two years ago. The girl reports that her mother is dating men who are not appropriate and spending her money on them foolishly. The relationship with the mother has become increasingly strained. It is **MOST** appropriate for the social worker to:

    A. Arrange a session with the mother to determine her thoughts about her relationship with the girl
    B. Help the girl better understand role complementarity in the family unit
    C. Explore whether the girl has any unresolved grief due to the father's death

22. A social worker is working with a client who is experiencing ego-dystonic homosexuality. Upon entering the office, the client whispers to the social worker that the receptionist appears uncomfortable as she "thinks that I am gay." Which defense mechanism is the client **MOST** likely exhibiting?

   A. Projection
   B. Reaction formation
   C. Displacement

23. A social worker finds that a 17-year-old student with poor academic achievement is spending increasing amounts of time developing his artistic ability. He has become an accomplished painter, winning many recent awards for his work. Which defense mechanism is the student **MOST** likely exhibiting?

   A. Conversion
   B. Sublimation
   C. Compensation

24. Which defense mechanism's primary function is to keep anxiety-provoking thoughts or situations out of conscious awareness?

   A. Repression
   B. Introjection
   C. Denial

25. A client is seeing a social worker due to a long-term opioid addiction which resulted from prescribed painkillers after back surgery. His addiction has caused many problems in his life including unemployment and a marital breakup. He feels helpless and cannot imagine a life without the painkillers. Which of the following will **MOST** likely be needed by the client?

   A. Individual therapy
   B. Medication-assisted treatment
   C. Mutual aid or peer support

26. Which of the following **BEST** defines cultural relativism?

   A. People have ethnocentric views about the importance of culture on their own behaviors
   B. Actions or beliefs must be viewed within the cultural contexts of those doing or having them, respectively
   C. Some cultural groups are more valued by society based on institutional discrimination

27. Which **BEST** describes the difference between assimilation and acculturation in diverse societies?

   A. In assimilation, a minority group is absorbed into the majority by assuming its customs, beliefs, and/or practices while the two groups remain distinct in acculturation with changes occurring in both
   B. In acculturation, a minority group is absorbed into the majority by assuming its customs, beliefs, and/or practices while the two groups remain distinct in assimilation with changes occurring in both
   C. Assimilation is the successful coexistence of a minority group within a culture dominated by a majority group whereas acculturation is indicative of cultural rifts which prevent pluralism

28. A social worker is doing a home visit with a 2-year-old boy. When looking out of the window, the boy points at a cat run across the street, exclaiming, "dog, dog, dog!" The mother mentions that the child has never seen a cat in real life, causing the boy to mistake it for a small dog like the one that they own. Which **BEST** describes the child's mental processing?

    A. Intellectualization
    B. Accommodation
    C. Assimilation

29. A social worker learns about a new therapeutic technique that is an evidence-based practice for major depressive disorder. The social worker believes that it would be good for all his clients, including those with other diagnoses. What is the **MOST** significant concern about implementing the therapeutic technique universally?

    A. Randomization
    B. Reliability
    C. External validity

30. A social worker is planning to employ an experimental design to evaluate the effectiveness of an intervention. Which of the following will **MOST** likely be the focus of ethical issues associated with the methodology?

    A. Instrumentation
    B. Confidentiality
    C. Randomization

31. A social worker is employed in an agency that work with clients who have co-occurring substance use and mental health disorders. The social worker feels that a larger proportion of women are dropping out of the program than men. In order for the social worker to evaluate the reason for this problem, it is important to **FIRST**:

    A. Identify the possible factors correlated with program drop out
    B. Speak to the program participants to see if modifications to the program are needed
    C. Understand the history of service utilization in other agencies

32. A social worker is instructed to ask all new clients who have immigrated from other countries about their documentation status. Those who do not have legal status will be denied services and will be referred to other agencies. Which of the following is **MOST** likely the basis of the concerns by a social worker who strongly objects to this process?

    A. Client confidentiality
    B. Service continuity
    C. Social justice

33. Which of the following methods is **MOST** effective for screening a client for psychosis?

    A. Asking the client open-ended questions that require elaboration
    B. Speaking to the client's family about recent levels of functioning
    C. Observing the client during his daily routine

34. A social worker begins a session with a client by summarizing what was discussed during the last meeting. This interviewing technique by the social worker is **MOST** effective in achieving which of the following aims?

   A. Focusing the client's session to ensure continuity and avoid duplication of treatment
   B. Validating the client's feelings by demonstrating that the social worker was listening
   C. Assisting the client to acknowledge progress made since the onset of treatment

35. A social worker received a referral from an employee assistance program for a man who has been accused of several incidents of harassment in the workplace. The client acknowledges that his behavior has been inappropriate and wants to work with the social worker. In order to effectively work with the client, the social worker should **NEXT**:

   A. Review the nature of the allegations with the client to hear his account of the incidents
   B. Ask the client about his work history in other settings
   C. Identify mutually agreed upon goals for the sessions

36. A hospital social worker gets a referral from a nurse as an elderly woman appears very agitated when her family visits her. The woman spends most of her time in bed, transported occasionally in a wheelchair if needed. She is nonverbal and has severe dementia. When the family enters the room, the woman flails her arms and legs wildly, requiring medical staff to calm her. In order to assist in this situation, the social worker should **FIRST**:

   A. Speak to the family about the impact of their visits on the woman's well-being
   B. Explore whether elder abuse may have occurred in the home
   C. Determine the possible reasons for the woman's behavior

37. A social work supervisor needs to create a professional development plan for an employee. Which of the following will be **MOST** important for the supervisor to review?

   A. Evidence-based practices in the employee's professional discipline
   B. Employee's personnel file which includes past performance appraisals
   C. Knowledge and skills needed to fulfill current professional responsibilities

38. A social worker receives a referral for a woman who has had multiple treatment failures in the past. During the intake, the client reports skepticism that any progress will be made this time. The client reports that treatment will likely be "more of the same," but commits to coming weekly. During the initial meetings, it will be **MOST** important for the social worker to:

   A. Address the resistance that the client has about seeking treatment again
   B. Identify the factors which hindered client progress in the past
   C. Determine client's expectations about the services to be provided

39. A social worker who is running a parenting group is concerned about a comment made during a session by one of the members. The parent reports regularly "beating some sense" into a child when the child does something wrong. The parent then laughs at the comment, discounting the punishment as "not that harsh." The **BEST** course of action for the social worker is to:

A. Provide instruction about proper child discipline techniques to all group members

B. Ask group members during the session to react to the parent's comment and reaction

C. Speak to the parent after the group to get more information about the physical punishment

40. A social worker is seeing a polyamorous couple who have recently been having marital troubles. Each of them has been involved in many romantic relationships throughout the years with the consent of the other. In the last year, the couple report constant fighting due to many issues including poor communication, lack of sexual interest, and disrespect for the other's viewpoint. The social worker should **FIRST**:

A. Determine if feelings for other romantic partners are interfering with marriage

B. Identify the goals for their relationship with one another

C. Meet with each person separately to gather information that may be relevant to the problem

41. Which of the following symptoms are **BEST** treated by fluphenazine (Prolixin)?

A. Hallucinations

B. Depression

C. Mania

42. A social worker is working with a 19-year-old girl who has diabetes. The client, who lives with her parents, reports that they have many marital problems and that the stress caused by their fighting results in problems managing her health condition. She has urged them to stop, but there has been little change. To **BEST** assist the client, the social worker should:

A. Ask to meet with the parents to explain the impact of their behavior on their daughter's health

B. Help the client to find another living arrangement that is more suitable

C. Assist the client to develop coping skills aimed at stress reduction

43. Which of the following policies by a social work administrator is the **BEST** example of ethnocentrism?

A. Holding mandatory staff trainings only on Saturdays

B. Requiring direct care staff to receive vaccinations for hepatitis B

C. Asking staff to provide information on their ethnicity on new employee paperwork

44. A social worker is meeting with parents who are distressed as their 5-year-old son recently began bedwetting after being toilet trained for more than a year. The parents report that the behavior started right after their daughter was born. They are worried as the son has also been acting out in school and at home. Based on this report, the son's behavior is **MOST** likely going improve if the parents:

A. Increase the attention and praise given to the son during individual and family activities

B. Implement a behavior modification program which punishes negative behaviors

C. Provide more structured activities in his routine both at home and school

45. Which of the following **BEST** defines the purpose of an amicus brief?

    A. Summarizes a client's progress in treatment for consideration when sentencing in criminal matters
    B. Assists to declare a client not competent to stand trial due to reasons of mental incompetence
    C. Provides an appellate court relevant information or arguments to consider before making a ruling

46. Which type of disorder is disruptive mood dysregulation disorder (DMDD) according to the *DSM*?

    A. Depressive disorder
    B. Neurodevelopmental disorder
    C. Disruptive, impulse-control, and conduct disorder

47. Reflective listening is primarily used by a social worker to:

    A. Ensure that the social worker understands the client's communication
    B. Demonstrate a commitment to helping the client solve existing problems
    C. Provide structure to the interactions between the social worker and client

48. A social worker is meeting with an 8-year-old child and her grandmother who is her primary caregiver. During the session, the social worker observes the child tantrum after she is told that she cannot have candy that is in the grandmother's purse. Eventually the grandmother gives her the candy to calm her down. The grandmother reports that the child's tantrums are becoming more frequent. Which of the following **BEST** explains the increase in the child's maladaptive behavior?

    A. Negative reinforcement
    B. Positive reinforcement
    C. Negative punishment

49. Which of the following is the **BEST** reason for using client self-monitoring in the problem-solving process?

    A. Client self-monitoring provides greater validity during assessment to ensure that effective treatment planning occurs
    B. Client self-monitoring enhances the involvement of clients in understanding problems and tracking progress
    C. Client self-monitoring extends the evaluation period to ensure treatment effectiveness and sustainable change

50. A social worker receives a referral for a client from a different cultural group. In order to **BEST** prepare for the initial meeting with the client, the social worker should:

    A. Reflect on how cultural differences between the client and social worker may impact the process
    B. Consult with a supervisor or colleague who has treated a client from this cultural group in the past
    C. Review professional skills that will be helpful to working with the client based on what is known

51. Which of the following interventions is based on unconditional positive regard?

    A. Psychoanalysis
    B. Group treatment
    C. Client-centered therapy

52. A school social worker receives a referral for a student who is afraid to ride the school bus. The social worker designs a behavior management program which incrementally rewards the child for walking up to the bus; getting on, but not riding it; sitting in the bus while the engine is on; and eventually riding the bus for the short ride to the school. Which of the following techniques is being used by the social worker?

    A. Shaping
    B. Chaining
    C. In-vivo desensitization

53. A hospital social worker learns that a 6-year-old boy will be cared for by his 22-year-old brother after the parents were killed in an automobile accident. The adult brother works full-time and lives in a studio apartment. The young child has learning difficulties that require extra help with homework and some activities of daily living. Which of the following interventions will **BEST** assist these brothers?

    A. Grief counseling to help address the recent loss of their parents
    B. Case management to identify and coordinate needed resources
    C. Educational supports to provide extra homework assistance

54. A social worker is meeting with a 30-year-old woman for an assessment. The client states that she often dates a lot of people who are not good for her while rejecting many potential partners who are loving and caring. The client recently renewed contact with an ex-boyfriend with whom she ended the relationship to "show him what he is missing." She is fearful of commitment, but states that she has feelings for someone who has told her that he just wants to be friends. Based on this report, the client **MOST** likely has which of the following attachment styles?

    A. Dismissive-avoidant
    B. Anxious-preoccupied
    C. Disorganized

55. A nursing home social worker is working with a long-time client who recently has rapid onset of significant cognitive impairment and appears confused. Her symptoms vary significantly throughout the day, but her attention does not appear impacted. She was recently diagnosed with a severe urinary tract infection which requires high doses of antibiotics. Which of the following **MOST** likely is the cause of the client's mental state?

    A. Depression
    B. Dementia
    C. Delirium

56. Which of the following statements **BEST** describes social workers' ethical duty with regard to physical contact with clients?

   A. Social workers should never have physical contact with clients in order to set appropriate boundaries and avoid psychological harm
   B. Social workers can have physical contact with clients as long as there is no possibility of psychological harm
   C. Social workers must follow agency policy regarding cradling and/or caressing clients

57. A social worker observes unethical conduct by a colleague in the agency setting. What should the social worker do **FIRST** to ethically address the situation?

   A. Contact the regulatory body or licensing board for the state or jurisdiction
   B. Report the behavior to a supervisor to ensure that it is address according to agency policy
   C. Discuss the concern with the colleague when feasible

58. Which of the following is a systemic barrier for treating pregnant women with a substance use disorder?

   A. Lack of evidence-based practices which are effective with this population
   B. Stigma resulting from the belief that substance use is chosen over concern for the babies' health
   C. Increased access to treatment due to eligibility guidelines that prioritize those who are pregnant or don't allow residential options for other minor children

59. A social worker is seeing a 14-year-old client whose parents consented to treatment. During the third visit with the social worker, the client tells the social worker about physical abuse by the parents which result in a mandatory report to the child welfare agency. The parents contact the social worker wanting a copy of the record, but the social worker is concerned that there may be information in the record that could cause the child harm. The social worker should:

   A. Contact the child welfare agency to determine whether the file can be released to the parents
   B. Send the record to the parents as the child is under the age of consent
   C. Refuse to release the record after documenting the request and reason for the denial in the record

60. A social worker is meeting with the parents of an adult son due to their extreme worry about his current whereabouts and mental health. They report that he had been hospitalized in the past for suicidal gestures and was on psychotropic medication but stopped taking it a few months ago. The parents are unsure of his diagnosis but stated that that he abruptly left the home after weeks of not sleeping. He had recently been arrested for roof jumping between apartment buildings and had abruptly spent all his savings on comic books. Which is the **BEST** diagnosis based on the parent's report?

   A. Bipolar II disorder
   B. Bipolar I disorder
   C. Cyclothymic disorder

61. Which of the following is **MOST** characteristic of schizoid personality disorder?

    A. Lack of desire for close relationships with others
    B. Disordered thinking or reasoning
    C. Delusions or hallucinations

62. A social worker has been working with a 35-year-old woman who has had long-standing problems in her personal relationships and with non-suicidal self-injury. During a session, she reports being madly in love with her partner who she calls repeatedly throughout the day and for whom she buys lavish gifts. A week later, the client states that she "can't stand" the partner, hoping to never see him again, though she is extremely worried about being alone. This "love-hate" pattern reoccurs with the client also reporting unprotected sexual behavior with multiple others, including some who she met at the time of the encounters. Which of the following is the **BEST** diagnosis based on these behaviors?

    A. Borderline personality disorder
    B. Narcissistic personality disorder
    C. Schizotypal personality disorder

63. Which of the following is **MOST** advantageous of clients taking long-acting injectable antipsychotic medications?

    A. Reduced risk of accidental overdoses or missed doses
    B. Greater interaction between clients and medical personnel
    C. Less perceived stigma associated with mental health

64. Which of the following **BEST** describes the main aim of community capacity building?

    A. Community capacity building involves a short-term process to assist communities to develop and implement their own solutions
    B. Community capacity building maintains social structures to ensure widespread applicability and serve broad interests
    C. Community capacity building focuses on local leadership development to enhance the future ability of members to problem solve

65. Social capital is **BEST** defined as a(n):

    A. Interconnected network of relationships between individuals and groups that can be used for collective and individual benefit
    B. Government safety net that assists recipients to raise their socio-economic standing so that they increase their influence
    C. Central source of human manpower that controls the economic and political conditions with a societal community

66. A social worker receives a call from a man who needs transportation to doctor's appointments as he has recently stopped driving. During the conversation, the social worker learns that the man lives in another county that is not served by the agency and is very upset about his declining health. He states that he really needs to speak to someone regularly as he is becoming lonely since he is no longer driving. In to **BEST** assist, the social worker should:

    A. Ask the agency director to serve him even though he is outside the catchment area

    B. Help him connect with a social service agency that can meet or coordinate his needs

    C. Contact his insurance provider as he may be eligible for medical transportation and counseling

67. A social worker is upset about the long wait time for processing applications for Temporary Assistance for Needy Families (TANF). Which of the following actions will likely be **MOST** effective in helping address the problem?

    A. Calling the offices of federal legislators

    B. Meeting with state officials from the executive branch

    C. Collecting data on the time period between application and service receipt

68. Which of the following benefit distribution systems maximizes client self-determination?

    A. Cash

    B. Voucher

    C. In-kind

69. A social worker learns that a cash assistance program to assist clients with purchasing food has not raised its benefit amounts in the last decade. Based on this information, which of the following is **MOST** likely impacting the current effectiveness of this program?

    A. Distribution method

    B. Inflation

    C. Birth rate

70. A social worker has been hired to assist with an inner-city revitalization effort. The community members meet with the social worker to express their excitement about the effort. After acknowledging the group's enthusiasm, the social worker should **NEXT**:

    A. Assist with establishing long- and short-term goals

    B. Investigate past revitalization efforts in the area

    C. Engage in asset mapping

71. A social worker has been hired by a hospital to assist those with breast cancer who are undergoing chemotherapy. The social worker assists clients with managing medical appointments, eating health, and augmenting their medical treatment with complementary therapies, such as yoga and acupuncture. Which of following **BEST** describes the focus of the social worker?

    A. Secondary prevention

    B. Tertiary prevention

    C. Primary prevention

72. A social worker is asked by a client, who is starting a new business after bankruptcy, to follow the social media account of the new company. The client states that getting a lot of followers is important to attract potential investors. The client has struggled financially in the past and the social worker is very supportive of the client's new venture. In order to handle this situation ethically, the social worker should:

A. Discuss with the client potential conflicts that can arise before declining the invitation

B. Inform the client that following the business would be unethical, but agree to promote the business without disclosing the professional relationship to others

C. Agree to follow the client's business social media account with the understanding that the social worker will not comment on posts

73. A social worker receives a referral for a man whose spouse recently passed away. The man has mental health insurance through his employer and would like to use this benefit for any services received. During the first meeting, the social worker and client complete a detailed assessment and the social worker identifies goals for treatment. The client reports that he would also like to use complementary therapies to help relax. When the social worker discusses the first meeting with a supervisor, the supervisor expresses concerns. What is **MOST** likely the cause of the supervisor's unease?

   A. The social worker did not advise the client that complementary therapies are not usually covered by insurance

   B. The social worker should have told the client about the need to formalize a psychiatric diagnosis to justify treatment

   C. The social worker independently identified the goals for treatment without involving the client

74. Which of the following statements **BEST** describes those with obsessive-compulsive disorder (OCD) as compared to those with obsessive-compulsive personality disorder (OCPD)?

   A. People with OCD feel distressed by their behaviors or thoughts while those with OCPD typically believe that their actions have an aim and purpose

   B. The aberrant behaviors or thoughts of people with OCD tend to be pervasive and stable over time while those associated with OCPD fluctuate in response to anxiety

   C. People with OCPD are more likely to seek treatment for their maladaptive behaviors or thoughts than those with OCD

75. A social worker is seeing a 75-year-old man who has a long history of abusive behavior. While he is still married, his adult children do not speak to him due to years of abuse. The client often yells at the social worker and is rude. The social worker realizes that she strongly dislikes the man as he reminds her of her own father. These feelings are negatively impacting the helping process. In order to appropriately address this situation, the social worker should:

   A. Refer the client immediately to another social worker

   B. Speak to the client candidly about the impact of his actions

   C. Seek supervision to process feelings about the client

76. A social worker learns that a new client is prescribed clozapine to treat schizophrenia. Which of the following will be **MOST** critical when taking this medication?

   A. Bloodwork

   B. Mental status testing

   C. Food restrictions

77. A client of a social worker received a prescription for Zoloft as a result of a medication evaluation at the agency. For which concern is this drug **MOST** likely prescribed?

    A. Psychosis
    B. Depression
    C. Substance use

78. A social worker works at a grassroots organization and is planning a community baby shower. The primary purpose of this event is to:

    A. Gain corporate sponsors to fund programs for parents and their children
    B. Increase community awareness about infant mortality and childhood illnesses
    C. Provide essential items and education needed by new parents

79. Which of the following is the **BEST** definition of mindfulness?

    A. Cognizant of the feelings and emotions of others
    B. Aware of the present moment and focusing attention on the here and now
    C. Sensitive to the impact of one's behavior on other's actions

80. At what age do **MOST** children begin to understand the irreversibility of death?

    A. Age 10
    B. Age 5
    C. Age 3

81. A social worker is using behavioral therapy to work with a client who has not been promoted in her job. The client is very angry as the person who was selected for the supervisory job has not been at the company as long as the client and had less favorable job appraisals. While the client has enjoyed her current position, she wants to quit her job even though is not financially secure. Using the principle of radical acceptance, the social worker should help the client to:

    A. Make an inner commitment to accept the situation as it is currently
    B. Determine the reasons that she was not accepted for the position
    C. Focus on resolving the anger which is fueling her negative emotions

82. Which of the following ethical principles **MOST** directly relates to the mandate to engage in evidence-based practice?

    A. Social justice
    B. Integrity
    C. Competence

83. A social worker is hired to work with a Hmong community even though the social worker is not a member of this ethnic group and has little knowledge about its practices. Which of the following actions will **BEST** provide an understanding about behavior and attitudes of this ethnic group overall?

A. Speaking with social workers who have Hmong clients

B. Learning about the values and traditions of Hmong people

C. Observing the daily routines of several Hmong community members

84. A social worker has been appointed by the court to work with a client. The client has consistently shown up late, provided very little information in the initial sessions, and made little eye contact with the social worker. What is likely to be **MOST** effective in helping to engage the client?

A. Reassuring the client that the social worker is there to help

B. Asking the client open-ended questions about experiences and interests

C. Exploring with the client what led to his recent arrest

85. During an initial session with a client who has a long history of abuse, the client begins to speak about incidents of emotional maltreatment during childhood. The **BEST** course of action for the social worker is to:

A. Ask questions of the client to demonstrate that the social worker is listening

B. Listen to the narrative provided by the client without interruption as a way of building rapport

C. Provide the client with interpretations throughout the narrative to increasing understanding

86. A social worker is supervising an employee who has not passed a job promotion examination several times due to test anxiety. The employee is worried about an upcoming test date, proclaiming that she "will likely fail." The employee states that she wants to reschedule the test date until she is "sure that she will pass." The social worker tells her to take the test on the original date even if she knows that she will fail. Which of the following intervention techniques is being used by the social worker?

A. Reaction formation

B. Double bind

C. Paradoxical directive

87. A social worker is meeting with a supervisor and mentions receiving a referral for an elderly gentleman from the protective service agency. In describing the client, the social worker repeatedly refers to this new "case" that she has received. The social work supervisor is **MOST** likely going to view the social worker's communication as:

A. Positive since the social worker is refraining from using identifying information about the client

B. Negative since the social worker is referring to the client in a dehumanizing manner

C. Negative since the social worker is vague when referring to the client which can lead to confusion

88. Forensic interviewing in social work is **MOST** often associated with which of the following social problems?

A. Child abuse
B. Mental health
C. Gun violence

89. A client has been consistently late for the first five sessions with a social worker. The social worker asks the client generally if everything is alright each week when the client enters late. The client reports that "everything is fine." To address the issue, what would be the social worker's **BEST** response to the client's lateness in the future?

A. "It is really important that you come on time as it inconveniences others"
B. "We really need to discuss underlying resistance which may result in you showing up late"
C. "Would it be more convenient to make our meetings at another time as you are having trouble arriving on time?"

90. Which is best practice with regard to obtaining releases of information from clients?

A. Having clients sign release of information forms upon intake that allow social workers to release all documents for a predefined time period
B. Asking clients' permission throughout the problem-solving process each time a document is requested by a third-party
C. Having clients sign release of information forms upon intake that allow social workers to release certain documents for a predefined time period

91. Which of the following statements **BEST** reflects the impact of social workers' beliefs and identity during the treatment process?

A. Social workers' race, culture, and background impact the therapeutic relationship, so introspection by clients is essential
B. Social workers' race, culture, and background have little to no impact on the therapeutic relationship as social workers are trained to be accepting of difference
C. Social workers' race, culture, and background impact the therapeutic relationship, so introspection by social workers is essential

92. Which of the following is foundation of pathology according to psychodynamic theory?

A. Intrapsychic conflicts
B. Dysfunctional beliefs
C. Physically stored memories

93. What is **MOST** important for a social worker, who is part of an interdisciplinary team. to inform a client when gaining informed consent?

A. Clients will be asked whether they want information to be shared among team members each time such sharing is relevant
B. All information provided to social workers is not shared among team members unless it involves danger to self or others
C. Relevant information provided to social workers is shared among team members

94. A social worker has decided to form a treatment group and is advertising for members. What will be **MOST** important to include in the solicitations?

    A. Target problem to be addressed
    B. Cost of each session
    C. Outcomes to be achieved

95. A client who is married to someone of the opposite gender reveals that having a homosexual affair for the last year has resulted in questioning of the client's current sexual orientation. The client is nervous about speaking to the spouse about the situation as the client thinks that the spouse will leave the relationship despite them having two small children. The **BEST** action by the social worker is to:

    A. Help the client to understand the legal implications of ending the marriage
    B. Assist the client to speak to the spouse about current sexual desires and interests
    C. Educate the client about the importance of being truthful with the spouse about the affair

96. When working with clients who have comorbid substance use and mental health disorders, it is important to:

    A. Treat the substance use before addressing the mental health concerns
    B. Stabilize the mental health issues before providing substance use intervention
    C. Address the substance use and mental health problems simultaneously

97. A social worker has an adult client with significant trust issues. The client is consistently worried about being exploited and views others as dishonest. Which of the following ethical principles will be **MOST** important for the social worker to stress in client interactions?

    A. Integrity
    B. Competence
    C. Importance of human relationships

98. When doing rapid rehousing, where are social workers focused on moving clients who are homeless?

    A. Transitional housing
    B. Shelters
    C. Permanent housing

99. Which of the following is the **MOST** significant ethical issue when getting a "friend request" from a client on social media?

    A. Consent
    B. Confidentiality
    C. Boundaries

100. A social worker is seeing a mother who seeks to strengthen her relationship with her child. The mother reports that the child always wants to help with cooking and cleaning. The social worker recommends asking the child to help out more. What is the social worker encouraging?

   A. Words of affirmation
   B. Acts of service
   C. Gift giving

101. A social worker receives a referral for a 11-year-old boy who is severely malnourished and dirty but performs well in school. He has few friends and is withdrawn, often making eye contact with others. The boy has not been able to participate in physical education for the past few weeks as he has not worn sneakers to school. What is **MOST** likely the cause of the client's behavior?

   A. Child neglect
   B. Physical abuse
   C. Emotional abuse

102. A social worker has just completed an assessment on an adult client. The social worker feels strongly that the client, who lived with both parents, was abused as a child though it was not explicitly stated. Which one of the following factors is the most salient predictor of this abuse?

   A. The client's mother has short-term mental health issues
   B. The client has a long history of legal involvement
   C. Both of the clients' parents have long-term substance use disorders

103. A social worker has agreed to see a client for a sliding scale fee as the client is in the process of obtaining insurance. All legal consents and intake forms completed with clients have the standard fees listed. In order to handle this situation ethically, the social worker should:

   A. Modify all legal forms to reflect the fees agreed upon
   B. Ask the client to refrain from signing the legal forms until the full fee can be paid
   C. Require the client to sign the legal forms with the standard fees, but only pay what was agreed upon

104. Which of the following represents the **MOST** significant barrier to innovations in interviewing children who are alleged victims of abuse?

   A. Consent of children
   B. Fear of false positive findings
   C. Training of professional interviewers

105. A nursing home social worker is working with a client who has been deemed competent but is confused and disoriented during the interview. The client is resisting going to a medical appointment that is essential given a recent medical diagnosis. The client's

husband wants her to go to the appointment, but the client believes that there is no value. In order to handle this situation ethically, the social worker should:

A. Respect the client's right to refuse to go to the required medical appointment
B. Arrange for the client to go to the appointment while educating her about its importance
C. Explain the ethical dilemma to a supervisor to obtain guidance about an appropriate course of action

106. Which of the following **BEST** defines emotional disturbances using the ecological perspective?

A. Dysfunctional environments that cause reduced opportunities for individuals to grow
B. Pattern of maladaptive transactions between individuals and their environments
C. Systematic social inequities that result from trauma and exploitation of others

107. A social worker is treating a pregnant 28-year-old woman who admits to using cocaine and methamphetamine throughout the pregnancy. The client promises to stop using, citing the upcoming birth of the baby as a "wake-up call" and the impetus for changing her behavior. In this situation, the social worker should:

A. Develop a plan to assist the client to abstain from using illicit drugs
B. Report the client's drug use to the child protection agency
C. Ask the client if her physician can be informed to assist with the impacts to prenatal care

108. A social worker is conducting an intake with a new client. During the meeting, the social worker asks a lot of open-ended questions aimed at learning more about feelings and experiences. Which of the following interviewing techniques is being used by the social worker?

A. Exploration
B. Interpretation
C. Explanation

109. In which situation would it be **MOST** appropriate for a social worker to use a topical shift during social work interviewing?

A. When the client raises a sensitive topic that is causing a high degree of emotion
B. When the client makes an offensive topic that causes the social worker to be uncomfortable
C. When the client has exhausted a subject and the discussion is becoming unproductive

110. A client would like to end his marriage after many years but is worried about the implications. The social worker asks the clients to imagine what would happen and to weigh the risks and benefits. Which of the following techniques is being used by the social worker?

A. Psychoeducation
B. Logical reasoning
C. Encouragement

111. A client feels extreme guilt about not being able to care for her young child and placing it up for adoption. The client says, "many people in your situation would have made the same decision." Which of the following **BEST** describes the statement by the social worker?

    A. Interpretation
    B. Universalization
    C. Clarification

112. Reflection of feelings is appropriately used by a social worker with a client to:

    A. Explore the reasons for client's underlying problems
    B. Analyze the client's reactions
    C. Validate the client's emotional response

113. A social worker receives a doctorate in literature (PhD) after receiving her social work degree. On her social work business cards, she lists her social work degree and license, as well as uses the title "Dr." in front of her name. According to the ethical standards of the social work profession, the social worker's actions are considered to be:

    A. Unethical as clients are likely to assume that her doctorate is in social work
    B. Unethical as a social worker should never list degrees in other disciplines
    C. Ethical as she has earned all of the degrees listed on her business card

114. According to critical race theory, which of the following **BEST** describes the root cause of racism?

    A. Lack of socialization with others from different racial groups
    B. Unfair policies that systematically disadvantage some racial groups
    C. Lack of legal enforcement of existing discrimination laws

115. Which of the following can **BEST** assist social workers to develop the critical consciousness necessary for practicing competently?

    A. Recognizing the power differential between social workers and clients
    B. Having clients participate in peer-facilitated interactions to solve problems
    C. Engaging client communities in making needed changes

116. Which of the following is a distinguishing difference between schizoid personality disorder and schizotypal personality disorder in the *DSM*?

    A. Social and interpersonal deficits
    B. Social isolation from others
    C. Distorted and strange thinking patterns

117. Which **BEST** describes the difference between hypomania and mania?

    A. Hypomania, unlike mania, can cause hospitalization as it results in elevated mood for longer periods of time
    B. Elevated mood in hypomania, unlike mania, is not enough to significantly impact school, work, and/or home life

C. Mania, unlike hypomania, may be triggered by substance use, such as recreational drugs or alcohol

118. A social worker is using a standard intake form for all clients seeking treatment from an agency. Which of the following is **MOST** likely a concern of this assessment approach?

   A. Clients prefer personal interaction when providing information about their problems
   B. Clients have different reasons for seeking services or treatment
   C. Some clients are illiterate and have difficulty with reading

119. Sociopathy and psychopathy are associated with which of the following personality disorders?

   A. Schizoid
   B. Schizotypal
   C. Antisocial

120. A social worker is meeting with a supervisee who is discouraged about the lack of opportunities provided to her at the agency. The supervisee is a person of color and comments that she sees a lack of ethnic diversity in the upper administration. The social worker tells the supervisee that "everyone can succeed in this agency if they just work hard enough." Which of the following reflects the message given to the supervisee by the social worker?

   A. There will be lots of opportunities for you to help diversify the agency if you keep working hard
   B. People of color have not worked hard enough to deserve promotions
   C. There is a commitment to work together to ensure that everyone, regardless of race, succeeds

121. In the *DSM*, encopresis is classified as which of the following types of disorders?

   A. Sleep-wake
   B. Neurocognitive
   C. Elimination

122. During an initial meeting, a social worker realizes that the person completing paperwork is the spouse of an existing client who has reported violence in the relationship. The social worker believes that it would be a conflict of interest to accept the spouse as a new client. In order to address the situation ethically, the social worker should:

   A. Contact the spouse after the intake meeting stating that the social worker is not accepting new clients
   B. Discuss the situation with the current client to see if the client agrees that there is an existing conflict
   C. Tell the spouse that the social worker will not be able to provide services, but can offer referrals if needed

123. A social worker overhears a colleague talking about using marijuana recreationally in the evenings after work hours. While the use of marijuana is legal in the jurisdiction,

it is strictly prohibited by the agency. The colleague's supervisor also overhead the conversation. In this situation, the social worker should **FIRST**:

A. Ask the supervisor about whether action will be taken against the colleague
B. Speak to the colleague directly about the violation of agency policy
C. Report the incident to an administrator to ensure follow up with the colleague and supervisor

124. When a social worker is interviewing a client, which is **MOST** critical to establish at the onset of the meeting?

A. Length of time that will take place for questioning
B. Purpose of the social work interview
C. Whether rapport is present between social worker and client

125. When interacting with client, social workers should generally avoid the use of social work jargon, terminology, and acronyms as their use:

A. Stresses the power differential between social workers and clients
B. Decreases understanding of clients about their problems and interventions
C. Inhibits rapport building between social workers and clients

126. When is asking for verification of client information **MOST** appropriate?

A. There are inconsistencies between client reports and observed data collected
B. Documentation is needed by third parties for benefit eligibility of needed resources
C. There is a need for more detailed information than the client can provide

127. Which of the following differentiates sociopathy from psychopathy?

A. Disregard for rules
B. Lack of remorse
C. Etiology

128. A social worker is seeing a client as she has been worried about her 14-year-old daughter's behavior in recent weeks. The daughter is an excellent student and has a group of good friends. The mother was worried as the daughter has recently been dressing differently and has dyed her hair green. She has asked to get a tattoo as well as several piercings. In order to best address the mother's fears, the social worker should:

A. Assure the mother that all teenagers act in a similar manner
B. Ask to meet with the daughter alone to gain insight into her behavior
C. Explain to the mother about the psychosocial stage related to identity formation

129. A married couple who are seeing a social worker admit to a history of domestic abuse. They have been faithfully receiving services and making progress toward meeting their goals. Prior to a meeting, one spouse tells the social worker that the other made life threating comments the day before, causing fear and concern. In order to handle the situation, the social worker should **FIRST**:

    A. Complete a safety assessment that includes advising the concerned spouse about available resources

    B. Confront the spouse who made the comments during the meeting so it can be openly discussed

    C. Evaluate the efficacy of the treatment intervention given these recent events

130. A social worker is responding to a disaster in a community of indigenous people, a group to which the social worker does not belong. Which of the following will be **MOST** important for the social worker to consider in order to develop an effective intervention plan?

    A. Acknowledgement that all communities are unique, with highly individual cultures and belief systems

    B. Engagement of traditional leaders can assist with mobilization and provide essential feedback

    C. Emphasis must be placed on values and beliefs of clients during all aspects of the helping process

131. Which of the following **BEST** describes historical trauma found in many indigenous communities?

    A. People in indigenous communities often lack good social skills resulting in increased violence between members

    B. Most indigenous communities have been exposed to generations of violent colonization, assimilation policies, and general loss

    C. Many indigenous communities ceased to exist due to traumatic events in the environment such as floods and fires

132. Which is **MOST** critical to viewing addiction as a disease?

    A. Addiction is chronic and progressive if untreated

    B. Addiction results in death or other negative biological impacts

    C. Addiction is so powerful that it cannot be controlled

133. A social worker is employed in a substance abuse agency that employs an abstinence-only policy with clients. The policy dictates that clients who are found using any substances are automatically discharged from all services. The social worker is increasingly more uncomfortable with this policy. Which of the following is **MOST** likely the basis of the social worker's ethical struggle?

    A. Self-determination

    B. Confidentiality

    C. Consent

134. A social worker is meeting with a client whose husband passed away suddenly. The client is having difficulty coping and cries throughout the session. The meeting is scheduled for 50 minutes, as is typical with all clients, but lasts 2.5 hours. Which of the following **BEST** describes this situation?

A. Dual relationship

B. Boundary crossing

C. Ethical violation

135. A social worker is working with an adult client who has a chronic medical condition that has been successfully managed for many years. During a recent visit, the client appears despondent and withdrawn. The social worker is worried about the client's current emotional state. Which of the following will be **MOST** helpful in identifying a plan to address these concerns?

    A. Speaking to the doctor, with the client's consent, to identify changes in medical status

    B. Completing a suicide risk assessment to determine dangerousness to self

    C. Determining current changes in life circumstances and stressors

136. A client enters the third meeting with the social worker yelling in a loud and menacing voice. In order to **BEST** handle the situation, the social work should:

    A. Reschedule the session until the client is calm

    B. Assure the client that there will be time to speak about the concerns

    C. Assess the client for danger to self or others

137. A couple contact the social worker due to the recent and unexpected death of their child. The couple arrive for the initial meeting looking distraught and clearly upset by their loss. The social worker should **FIRST**:

    A. Ask the parents what they hope to accomplish in the session

    B. Find out more about the circumstances of the child's death

    C. Acknowledge the apparent emotional state of the parents

138. A geriatric social worker is charged with assisting an elderly client with acclimating to a nursing home after it was determined that she was unsafe to live alone. During the meeting, the client does not acknowledge that she has recently moved, focusing discussions instead on her life years ago. In order to meet this woman's needs, the social worker should:

    A. Redirect discussion to the reasons for the relocation

    B. Determine if she is experiencing early stages of dementia

    C. Encourage discussion about her experiences in the past

139. A couple seek counseling from a social worker after the husband's cancer diagnosis. The husband underwent chemotherapy and radiation and is now in remission. The husband reports that the wife has been distant, refusing to be intimate since the onset of his illness. The wife confirms that she feels disconnected from her husband which has impacted her desires for intimacy. In this situation, the social worker should **FIRST**:

    A. Recommend seeing the wife separately for individual therapy

    B. Explore the couple's feelings about the husband's diagnosis and illness

    C. Complete a sexual history on the couple

140. A school social worker is told by a student that she recently visited a family planning clinic without parental permission which was needed due to her young age. When asked about how consent was obtained, the client confesses that she forged a parent's signature. The client feels guilty about her actions and not being honest with her parents. She is very upset by her deception and is experiencing sleeplessness and worry. The social worker should **FIRST**:

    A. Explore the girl's current and past relationship with her parents
    B. Inform the girl that this incident needs to be reported to the clinic given her age
    C. Encourage the girl to speak with her parents to explain the nature of her actions

141. When appointed as an expert by the court, which of the following tasks or skills will be **MOST** critical in fulfilling this role competently?

    A. Forming an opinion based on speculative facts or data which are available to all parties
    B. Preparing analytical reports, exhibits and demonstrations as needed and requested
    C. Remaining impartial regardless of whether working for one of the parties or the court

142. A family comes to a social worker due to their 11-year-old's behavior. The child has been suspended from school and involved in several fights. During the assessment, the parents engage in a destructive pattern of fighting and admit to marital problems. After speaking to all parties, the social worker is convinced the child's behavior is a result of marital conflicts. The social worker should **NEXT**:

    A. Refer the parents for marital therapy
    B. Suggest treating the parents and child separately as their problems are different
    C. Discuss the impact of the marital issues on the child

143. Children of parents who are narcissistic are **MOST** likely to:

    A. Prioritize the needs of themselves above others
    B. Enjoy praise and compliments from colleagues and peers
    C. Refrain for asking for help from others

144. Which of the following is the **MOST** important reason for diagnosing a client is to:

    A. Ensure reimbursement from third-party payers
    B. Inform a plan of care for client treatment
    C. Project prognosis for improvement of client symptomology

145. A social worker is working with a 54-year-old client who has a long history of substance use but has not used substances in many years. The client reports that he has fallen recently for no apparent reason and is having trouble with his vision. He fears that he will lose his assembly job as he is no longer able to perform the required tasks. Based on the client self-report, the social worker should rule out which of the following?

    A. Substance use relapse
    B. Early onset dementia
    C. Neurological conditions

146. A social worker in an agency setting is evaluating client outcomes as part of the problem-solving process. The **MOST** important use of data generated during this process is to:

   A. Guide the direction of planned change efforts
   B. Determine the ability of the agency to effectively serve clients
   C. Identify training and professional development needs of agency staff

147. A social worker is opening a private practice and contacts prior clients who have been helped by the social worker in the past. The social worker is careful only to reach out to those who, because of their particular circumstances, are not vulnerable to undue influence. The social worker asks for testimonial endorsement for the website, agreeing to use pseudonyms for all clients. The social worker's actions are:

   A. Unethical because social workers should never solicit clients or former clients for testimonials
   B. Ethical as only clients who were not vulnerable were solicited for testimonials
   C. Ethical as clients were only identified by pseudonyms instead of their actual names

148. Which of the following is **MOST** critical when empowering a community?

   A. Identification of and addressing direct and indirect power blocks
   B. Education about mobilization and development techniques that have been found effective
   C. Engagement of community leaders in change efforts

149. A social work supervisor is meeting with an employee who is having difficulty engaging with clients. The employee states that the clients are often uncooperative and the employee "does not know what to do" when addressing client resistance. The employee feels frustrated and is thinking of moving to another job in the agency. The **BEST** response by the social worker is to:

   A. Support the employee by validating the frustration felt when working with a difficult population
   B. Help the employee increase knowledge about and skills for addressing resistance
   C. Assess whether burnout is interfering with the employee's ability to engage with clients

150. A social worker is engaged in the preplanning process to develop a community program. Which of the following questions is **MOST** essential in determining whether more formal steps should follow?

   A. "Does the community identify the proposed need as important?"
   B. "What factors will impede addressing the need?"
   C. "What has been done before to address this need?"

151. A social worker is providing teletherapy to a client who needs to return to her native country due to the death of her mother. The client will be in a time zone that is 12 hours earlier than the social worker and asks the social worker to see her for an appointment at 10 p.m. so that it does not conflict with the mourning rituals of the client's family. The social worker typically does not see clients past 7 p.m. so tells the client that the request cannot be honored as it does not comply with the established policy. What is the **MOST** critical ethical concern related to the social worker's decision?

A. There is no flexibility given the mourning practices and culture of the client

B. The social worker has not adjusted for time differences that occur in international service provision

C. The client will likely feel abandoned during her time of need

152. When developing a program, the primary purpose of planning is to:

A. Involve community leaders in the initial phase of planning

B. Identify the driving and restraining forces for creating the service

C. Gather demographic data on potential service users

153. A social worker is hired to do community planning and would like to examine demographic data on the population living locally. Which of the following would be the **BEST** method for obtaining this information?

A. Sending paper-and-pencil and online surveys to community residents

B. Examining tax and school records of the municipalities and districts locally

C. Obtaining census and health data available via governmental sources

154. Which of the following is the **BEST** method for soliciting "buy-in" and generating interest from community members about new program development?

A. Social media posts

B. Town hall meetings

C. Focus or neighborhood group gatherings

155. A social worker finds that a client has poor impulse control, often acting on urges with little forethought. Which of the following is **MOST** likely responsible for the client's behavior?

A. Superego

B. Id

C. Ego

156. A social work supervisor has an employee who needs to take an extended leave due to a medical issue. What is the **BEST** practice when gathering the medical information needed?

A. Inform human resource personnel so that they can work with the employee directly

B. Suggest that the employee put all the needed documentation in writing to the social worker

C. Refer to the agency handbook regarding policies on the handling of employment information

157. A community finds that Chinese immigrants are specifically targeted for acts of violence. Which of the following is **MOST** likely responsible for this behavior?

    A. Xenophobia

    B. Individual discrimination

    C. Systematic discrimination

158. A school social worker is providing an educational workshop for teachers in the school. One of the teachers expresses frustration as students often challenge rules, questioning "what is in it for them." They seem to respond well to rewards for good behavior but fail to recognize that good behavior is needed to have a productive learning environment. In order to speak to the teacher about students' current level of moral development, which of the following levels should be discussed?

    A. Postconventional

    B. Conventional

    C. Preconventional

159. Which of the following parenting styles is the **BEST** predictor of positive outcomes for children?

    A. Permissive

    B. Authoritative

    C. Authoritarian

160. Which of the following statements **BEST** describes social work involvement in political action?

    A. All social workers should engage in political action to ensure equal access to resources and opportunities

    B. There is no ethical duty for social workers to engage in political action, but it is helpful for making needed systemic changes

    C. Social workers should ensure that political action is not part of their professional practice as it alienates clients with differing political views

161. What is the **BEST** method for determining the proper pronouns to use with new clients?

    A. Directly inquiring after rapport has been established

    B. Discussing during the first meeting

    C. Asking on an intake form completed prior to the first session

162. A couple come to see a social worker because of their 6-year-old child's behavior. The child had been sleeping soundly in her room for months, but now only wants to sleep on the couch closer to the parent's bedroom. The child also complains of frequent stomachaches, requiring attention by the parents. The child also reports having nightmares. What is **MOST** likely the cause of these behaviors?

    A. Generalized anxiety disorder

    B. Separation anxiety

    C. Panic disorder

163. A social worker is working with a wife who is having difficulty progressing through the stages of loss and grief after the death of her husband. She reports feeling numb and states that the loss "just hit her," even though her husband died two years ago. The client is **MOST** likely experiencing which type of grief response?

   A. Anticipatory
   B. Ambiguous
   C. Complicated

164. A social worker and client identify that there is a need for individual supportive grief therapy. Which will **MOST** likely be a goal given the effects of separation?

   A. Reducing isolation
   B. Acknowledging loss and grief
   C. Strengthening family bonds

165. A social worker learns that there is a potential conflict of interest with a current client after 5 months of treatment. In order to resolve it ethically, the social worker should:

   A. Inform the client and attempt to resolve the situation in the client's best interest
   B. Seek supervision or consultation to brainstorm alternative courses of action
   C. Monitor the situation to determine if an actual conflict of interest results

166. A social worker is forming a group for clients who are living with serious mental illness to help them manage their disorders. Which of the following factors will be **MOST** important to consider when identifying members?

   A. Length of time since initial diagnosis
   B. Gender and racial composition of the group
   C. Insight about their problems and disorders

167. A social worker is working with a couple who is in the process of a high conflict divorce. When intervening with the couple, the social worker will **MOST** likely be engaged in which of the following roles?

   A. Broker
   B. Resource allocator
   C. Mediator

168. A social worker in a community housing agency is working with a client who has an ongoing dispute with a landlord. The dispute focuses on the client's responsibility to pay the rent during extensive renovations to the apartment building. The client and landlord agree to have the matter handled by an appointee of the court who will make a binding determination. Which **BEST** describes this court process?

   A. Mediation
   B. Arbitration
   C. Due process

169. A client is considering doing genetic testing to identify relatives using a popular online company. The client is worried about the use of his medical information and struggling with the decision. In assisting the client to make the decision, the social worker should:

    A. Explore the concerns that the client has about the information to be revealed
    B. Review the procedures for obtaining the genetic sample and how the matching works
    C. Discuss the uses of the genetic information collected and limits to consent for use of the data

170. Which of the following **BEST** describes the ethical standards relating to internet searching for client information?

    A. Internet searching should only be done with clients' informed consent unless there are compelling reasons for conducting such searches
    B. Internet searching should never be done as it invades clients' personal privacy
    C. Internet searching should only be done if there are reasons to do so for health or safety

Full Length Practice Test Answers

1. **B.** The client's request may indicate the need for support at this event. There is nothing in the professional *Code of Ethics* that prohibits attendance if linked to the service goals of the client. A social worker should avoid a dual relationship or socializing with a client on a personal level. However, there is nothing in this question that indicates that the client's request is inappropriate. The question indicates that the client was previously estranged from her daughter. She may feel nervous about attending, which will only be revealed through discussion about the request. The question focuses on choosing the response choice that will best assist the client. Discussion will help understand the client's request.

   Question Assesses

   Professional Relationships, Values, and Ethics

2. **A.** The client has experienced a sudden loss. The symptoms that she is experiencing may subside over time as she is able to cope with the death. The question asks what the social worker should do FIRST. While many of the response choices may be helpful, there are only two that deal with health and safety which must be addressed initially. There is no indication that the client has any medical problems so recommending a physical evaluation is not supported by question wording. The feelings and behaviors presented may be associated with suicidality which needs to be ruled out before other actions are taken.

   Question Assesses

   Assessment and Intervention Planning

3. **C.** There are two response choices, ask the parents about their academic expectations and determine the nature and severity of the punishment, that focus on assessment of the situation, which is needed before acting. There is not enough information to know whether a child abuse report is warranted. The social worker should FIRST determine the nature and severity of the punishment to determine whether there are safety concerns. If there is a danger, the social worker will need to refer to the child welfare organization.

   Question Assesses

   Assessment and Intervention Planning

4. **A.** The question identifies from the onset that the client has children. There is no indication of how long that she can stay with the friend, but the sentence right before the stem focuses on her "plans" to return home. The decision needs to be the focus of the intervention. It is not appropriate to assume that she is not ready to leave. Perhaps she sees no other option. Often survivors of intimate partner violence have poor self-esteem because their self-worth has been eroded. Understanding the impact of the violence on her children may be the impetus that she needs to decide not to return. There is no qualifying word (FIRST, etc.) in the question so the order is not the focus of the question.

Question Assesses

Human Development, Diversity, and Behavior in the Environment

5. **C.** The reasons for seeking help from the social worker are rooted in the client's concern about the lack of personal relationships in their life. The answer should focus on this presenting problem. The scope of the issue is not isolated to sexual relationships. It is necessary to focus on the emotional connections that the client currently has with others, as well as those which have existed in the past.

Question Assesses

Assessment and Intervention Planning

6. **A.** The client's main concern is his nervousness in speaking with her about his concerns. The correct answer provides the client with the opportunity to practice his responses. It helps him to anticipate her reaction and formulate alternatives before actually speaking to her. The client is the man so working with the couple together should not occur. There is no indication in the question that the client does not understand the girlfriend's behavior—just that he is fearful about her reaction when hearing his concerns. The correct answer directly addresses the source of his nervousness.

Question Assesses

Interventions with Clients/Client Systems

7. **B.** The question requires the social worker to address this problem. The question indicates professional impairment as the social worker is not able to "provide effective care." While a vacation may be helpful, it is not a long-term solution. The correct answer ensures that the social worker is adjusting her schedule while getting ongoing support through supervision and consultation. The need for self-care and coping skills has already been established.

Question Assesses

Professional Relationships, Values, and Ethics

8. **B.** The process by which an individual begins to live as a member of another gender—can be complex. It may involve many steps for some and fewer for others. These steps might include changes to legal documents, gender confirmation surgery, alterations to physical appearance, name and pronoun changes, and hormone replacement therapy. Some individuals may not pursue certain aspects of transition, whether through personal choice, lack of resources, or lack of access. There is no single "right" way to transition. A person's gender identity does not depend on appearance.

Use of the prior name and pronouns does not acknowledge the student's decision and may send the message that the social worker is unaccepting. Additionally, the student does not have to discuss gender identity with the social worker as the interactions may have been focused on other aspects of the student's life.

Question Assesses

Human Development, Diversity, and Behavior in the Environment

9. **A.** Despite the concern, it is unethical for the social worker to alter the record even by simply omitting information. If the record contains diagnoses, they must be included in the record release. A court order or signed release of information by the client for the entire record must contain all information. Additionally, the scenario gives no indication that the social worker has ever met with or had the ex-husband as a client. The social worker should not be evaluating the ex-husband's fitness to parent simply based on information gathered from the client.

Question Assesses

Professional Relationships, Values, and Ethics

10. **B.** Although there is a large body of research addressing the emotional impact of infertility while couples are actively undergoing treatment, the aftermath of infertility is almost never addressed. In this scenario, the focus of the couple's presenting problem is their feeling of isolation and that not having a biological child will impact their identity. Couples can feel marginalized or stigmatized and there may be guilt. Social workers have the opportunity to focus on normalizing, validating, and educating. They need to recognize that couples who make the decision to stop treatment continue to identify their infertility as the primary component of their "self" for quite some time. It is fundamental in helping to integrate the loss into one's life story.

Helping the couple explore methods to adopt is not a good response choice as nothing in the question has indicated that the couple are interested in adopting. Mutual aid can be helpful, but the question states that the social worker is supposed to assist the client—not have a group help them.

Question Assesses

Interventions with Clients/Client Systems

11. **C.** The client has expressed the desire to join the group given her professional goals. The client would like to see another worker to avoid a potential conflict of interest. The first sentence of the question indicates that discussions routinely occur with clients about boundaries. Thus, the client is likely making an informed choice.

It is the social worker's responsibility to refer the client appropriately. It is not appropriate for a social worker to terminate services in order to have a social or intimate relationship with a client. The client joining the singing group is not an indicator of a social or intimate relationship. The client has appropriately expressed the need to avoid a dual relationship with the social worker. Helping the client to find another social worker, which is her request, is the most appropriate action in this situation.

Question Assesses

Professional Relationships, Values, and Ethics

12. **A.** The qualifying word in the question, FIRST, is critical. The question describes the child clinging to the teacher and upset when she has to go home. While abuse is not the only reason for these behaviors, abuse can be one cause, especially given her poor hygiene and apparent care. There are some good response choices listed, but the social worker should initially rule out any abuse or neglect and there are some signs which may indicate that child welfare is an issue. Once it has been eliminated, the social worker can explore other etiologies and supports for the child.

Question Assesses

Human Development, Diversity, and Behavior in the Environment

13. **C.** The question indicates that the client is an adult, and his parents are aging. Given this background, it is likely that he has lived with his parents for a long time, perhaps in the same house. The client has only been in the group home for a month and the question does not say that he has had any difficulty besides staying in his room. It also does not state that he has made no friends, just a "few." The change in behavior is likely due to adjustment to his new living arrangement. Information provided states that he is talkative and loves activities so no deficits in socialization are indicated. There is also no evidence that his behavior is linked to his parents' aging.

Question Assesses

Human Development, Diversity, and Behavior in the Environment

14. **B.** The first sentence in the question states that the child is struggling academically, but it is not known whether school performance was a problem before the sibling's death. However, the child is no longer participating in activities that were done in the past. It is essential that the social worker initially identify the cause of the issue, as FIRST is a qualifying word. The first response choice assumes that the loss of the sibling is the reason for the change.

The child mentioned in the question is only 7 years old so well-being will be greatly impacted by the support given and the dynamic in the home. Contacting the parents to determine whether the child's problem is isolated, or part of a larger family issue is essential given the principles of systems theory and the impact of disability and death on family systems.

Question Assesses

Human Development, Diversity, and Behavior in the Environment

15. **B.** The first sentence indicates that the client has a history of depression. Not all clients who are depressed are at risk of suicide, but it is background information in the question that must be considered. The presenting and immediate problem is the client's shock and emotional reaction to the breakup. Appropriately, the social worker acknowledged the emotion being expressed by the client but should immediately assess for self-harm. The use of the qualifying word NEXT indicates that the question is concerned with the order of actions. Safety is an basic concern based on Maslow's hierarchy of need. After safety is addressed,

the social worker can help the client better understand the reasons for the breakup and identify additional supports that may be needed during this difficult time.

Question Assesses

Human Development, Diversity, and Behavior in the Environment

16. **C.** The question does not identify what problems that the client sees as a problem or what services she is seeking. She has identified many issues, but these may be long-standing and not a priority for the client. In the engagement process, a social worker needs to determine why a client is seeking assistance and what should be accomplished.

There is no indication that her long-term physical problems are currently interfering with her functioning or that the impact of the past abuse is the reason for her other problems. Incorrect response choices may be important but should not be done FIRST. The qualifying word is critical as the social worker needs "to start where the client is" in problem identification.

Question Assesses

Assessment and Intervention Planning

17. **B.** The client in the question is the family so treatment goals must focus on the family—not the parents. The presenting problem in the question focuses on the feelings and communication related to the illness. While concrete services are important, they are not mentioned as an issue in the scenario.

Question Assesses

Assessment and Intervention Planning

18. **C.** The reason for the meeting is the boy's behavior in school. The fighting appears to be isolated to the school setting with the boy providing little information about the reasons why the altercation occurred. The only answer which directly mentions the school is the correct one. The social worker needs to obtain additional information in order to determine the cause of the issue. The incorrect response choices will provide data, but perhaps not that which directly relates to the difficulty experienced in school. The school counselor will likely be able to provide more detail about the incident.

Question Assesses

Assessment and Intervention Planning

19. **C.** The question indicates that the source of the mother's frustration is having to take the child to work due to lack of resources to pay for camp. The correct answer addresses the underlying problem. There are no other signs of maltreatment so further investigation is not needed. While striking the child is not appropriate, parenting classes will not alleviate the stress associated with lack of day care for her child. Additionally, the problem presented is not the psychological well-being of the child, but rather the lack of resources of the family. The correct answer always needs to address the problem presented in the question.

Question Assesses

Human Development, Diversity, and Behavior in the Environment

20. **A.** The assessment identified many needs, with family members not agreeing on the priorities. In the problem-solving process, planning occurs after assessment. The qualifying word NEXT indicates the need for goal setting since assessment has occurred. Completing biopsychosocial assessments and reviewing prior service records are both assessment tasks that will not help the family reach a consensus about the service needs, a requirement for proper effective intervention.

Question Assesses

Assessment and Intervention Planning

21. **B.** The client is the girl, so it is not appropriate to meet with the mother to conduct an assessment. The presenting problem focuses on the girl's views about her mother's dating. There is no mention of grief associated with the father's death. The judgment about the mother's behavior is focused on her dating and relationships with men. The death of the father changed the composition of the family unit, and the girl may have different expectations regarding the mother's recent behavior. Role complementarity focuses on acting in an expected manner. Clearly the mother's behavior does not meet the daughter's expectations, which need to be better understood.

Question Assesses

Human Development, Diversity, and Behavior in the Environment

22. **A.** The client is likely projecting his own discomfort about his sexuality onto the receptionist. The background provided about the client is that his homosexuality is ego-dystonic, meaning that it is at odds with his idealized self-image. Therefore, it causes anxiety and makes him uncomfortable with his sexual orientation. He is attributing his discomfort to the receptionist which is projection. Reaction formation is acting in a manner opposite of one's unconscious belief which is not described in the scenario. Displacement is shifting emotion or blame caused by an external situation or person to a less threatening target. The discomfort comes from his own feelings which makes projection the best choice.

Question Assesses

Human Development, Diversity, and Behavior in the Environment

23. **C.** The first sentence in the question speaks about how the student struggles academically. His focus on art appears to be compensation as he developed skills in one area to make up for deficits in another. Conversion requires a physical manifestation to repressed anxiety which is not mentioned in the question. Sublimation is when socially unacceptable impulses or idealizations are transformed into socially acceptable actions or behavior. No such impulses or idealizations are present in the question.

Question Assesses

Human Development, Diversity, and Behavior in the Environment

24. **A.** Repression pushes painful thoughts, impulses, and/or memories from awareness. It is a primary ego defense. Introjection occurs when the values or qualities of others are incor-

porated into one's ego structure. Denial has a conscious component as a person may lie or minimize actions, though aware of them.

Question Assesses

Human Development, Diversity, and Behavior in the Environment

25. **B.** While therapy and peer support may be helpful, these interventions will likely be ancillary to medication assisted treatment. Buprenorphine, methadone, and naltrexone are used to treat opioid use disorders to short-acting opioids such as heroin, morphine, and codeine, as well as semi-synthetic opioids like oxycodone and hydrocodone. These medications are safe to use for months, years, or even a lifetime. Buprenorphine suppresses and reduces cravings for opioids. Methadone reduces opioid cravings and withdrawal and blunts or blocks the effects of opioids. Naltrexone blocks the euphoric and sedative effects of opioids and prevents feelings of euphoria.

Research shows that those who receive medication-assisted treatment are much less likely to relapse. It is an evidence-based practice for opioid addiction which can be used with the other interventions listed. However, medication-assisted is essential while the others can be used in conjunction with one another or individually as appropriate. Medication-assisted treatment assists with the physical withdrawal and cravings which must be addressed immediately for the psychological aspects of addiction to be treated over time.

Question Assesses

Interventions with Clients/Client Systems

26. **B.** This question requires knowledge about principles of diversity and difference. Cultural relativism is the principle of regarding the beliefs, values, and practices of a culture from the viewpoint of that culture itself. It is used to avoid cultural bias, as well as to avoid judging another culture by the standards of one's own culture. For this reason, cultural relativism has been considered an attempt to avoid ethnocentrism.

Question Assesses

Human Development, Diversity, and Behavior in the Environment

27. **A.** Cultural assimilation (often just referred to as assimilation) is a process of integration whereby members of an ethno-cultural community are "absorbed" into another, generally larger, community. Assimilation implies the loss of the characteristics of the absorbed group, such as language, customs, ethnicity, and self-identity. Assimilation may be spontaneous or forced.

Whereas acculturation is the exchange of cultural features that results when groups come into continuous firsthand contact; the original cultural patterns of either or both groups may be altered, but the groups remain distinct.

Question Assesses

Human Development, Diversity, and Behavior in the Environment

28. **B.** Piaget said that children develop schemas to help them understand the world. Schemas are concepts (mental models) that are used to help categorize and interpret information. When children learn new information, they adjust their schemas through two processes: assimilation and accommodation. First, they assimilate new information or experiences in terms of their current schemas. Assimilation is incorporating new experiences into existing schemas. It is the blending of previous information with new information. Accommodation describes when schemas are changed based on new information. Intellectualization and repression are defense mechanisms.

Question Assesses

Human Development, Diversity, and Behavior in the Environment

29. **C.** External validity is the extent to which findings can be generalized to other situations, people, settings, and measures. Just because the therapeutic technique has demonstrated effectiveness for one disorder does not mean that it will be useful with another.

Question Assesses

Assessment and Intervention Planning

30. **C.** Random assignment is a key element of experimental design. Random assignment places participants into treatment and control groups with one group getting the treatment and another not. It ensures that these groups are comparable with any differences between them due to random factors. The main issue with experimental designs is the unequal access of participants in the two groups. For this reason, experimental designs are often not used in practice. Social workers are reluctant to deny treatment if there is even a chance of it helping. If the treatment is found effective, those in the control group will not have had the opportunity to receive it for the duration of the evaluation. There are no differences in instrumentation or confidentiality procedures used between the two groups, so they are not ethical concerns.

Question Assesses

Assessment and Intervention Planning

31. **A.** The question indicates that the correct answer should focus on evaluating "the reason for this problem." There is also a qualifying word, FIRST, that indicates the order in which the response choices occur is critical. Identification of the correlates is a crucial first step. Speaking to participants about modifications will occur later after the root cause of the problem is known. The history of service utilization in other agencies is irrelevant to evaluating the potential problem in this agency.

Question Assesses

Interventions with Clients/Client Systems

32. **C.** Social workers play a critical role in redefining policies surrounding historically marginalized populations, including immigrants. The creation of the concept of the "undocumented immigrant" reflects an embedded discriminatory aspect of immigration policy

and becomes reinforced in policies that actively dehumanize undocumented immigrants, inhibiting their social integration.

The ethical code provides an ideal foundation for social workers to pursue roles as social justice activists. The policy that those who are documented will receive services and those who are undocumented will not is based on inequity. Thus, the social worker is concerned with the ethical value of social justice.

Question Assesses

Professional Relationships, Values, and Ethics

33. **A.** Only asking open-ended questions and observing the client's routine involve obtaining data directly from the client. Speaking with the family will not indicate whether the client is actively delusional or hallucinating. Psychosis is best assessed through understanding client's thought and cognitive processes. Observing daily routine will not yield this information but asking the client to speak freely will likely provide insight into symptoms associated with psychosis. Clients can have distorted thinking, but still function appropriately throughout the day.

Question Assesses

Assessment and Intervention Planning

34. **A.** Summarization enables the social worker to pull together key ideas and themes regarding the most important aspects of the client's problems, and also provides focus and continuity to the interview. In this question, it is occurring at the beginning of the meeting to help focus the interactions. Validation is not the goal and the summarization process in the question only focuses on the last meeting so there is no review of overall treatment success.

Question Assesses

Interventions with Clients/Client Systems

35. **C.** The social worker is employed in an employee assistance program (EAP) designed to assist employees in resolving personal problems that may adversely affect performance. There is likely a zero-tolerance policy for harassment in the workplace so both the client and employer will have goals for eradicating the behavior. As the social worker has received "buy in" from the client, it is now appropriate to identify what he would like to accomplish. This information is broadly collected during engagement and is then the focus of planning—both critical stages of the problem-solving process. His work history is not related to the problem at hand. Reviewing the allegations will likely inhibit progress and the question emphasizes effectively working with the client which is based on mutual agreement.

Question Assesses

Assessment and Intervention Planning

36. **C.** As the woman is nonverbal, her behavior may result from significant excitement at seeing her family. There is no indication in the question that elder abuse is a possible issue. There may be a need to structure family visits or even prescribe additional medication,

but the cause of the behavior needs to be determined. The qualifying word, FIRST, makes determining the reason for the behavior correct. Assessment always comes before intervention, such as speaking to the family about the woman's behavior.

Question Assesses

Assessment and Intervention Planning

37. **C.** Professional development refers to continuing education and training to help develop skills. A professional development plan is unique for each employee based on job responsibilities and existing competency. Evidence-based professional practices are not directly relevant as they may not be germane to the employee's job responsibilities. The personnel file may contain confidential information that should not be seen by the supervisor. Also, past appraisals may be for different positions within the organization and may not reflect current competency. The question has a qualifying word—MOST. Understanding the knowledge and skills needed for an employee's current job will provide a benchmark for determining strengths and areas of growth in order to excel in the workplace. Specific development goals can then be tailored to the employee's growth needs.

Question Assesses

Professional Relationships, Values, and Ethics

38. **B.** The client has committed coming weekly which demonstrates motivation, not resistance. The question focuses on the inability of the woman to achieve treatment goals and make progress. It is not surprising that she is skeptical and wondering what will be different this time. In order for the outcome to be different, the social worker should work with the client to identify the barriers or factors that have prevented progress. Determining the client's expectations will not ensure that the current treatment plan addresses the issues which have historically prevented success.

Question Assesses

Assessment and Intervention Planning

39. **C.** As this disclosure may involve physical abuse, it is BEST handled individually and not in the group session. There is no need to educate all group members about child discipline as there is no indication that it is a chosen focus of the sessions. Until the social worker better understands the nature of the "beatings," encouraging discussion of them in the group is not advised. The parent needs to be asked specific questions by the social worker to determine if a child abuse report is needed. The collection of more information is critical to handling the situation appropriately.

Question Assesses

Human Development, Diversity, and Behavior in the Environment

40. **B.** While the couple is polyamorous, the question gives no indication that the problems involve this aspect of their relationship. Polyamorous relationships involve the practice of engaging in multiple romantic (and typically sexual) relationships, with the consent of all the people involved. The presenting problem appears to be focused on the communica-

tion and connection between the married couple. The couple is the client so assessment, planning, and intervention should involve them both. Meeting with them separately may be necessary at some point in the process, but FIRST the couple must agree on treatment goals. These goals should be mutually discussed and decided given that the couple is the focus of the intervention.

Question Assesses

Assessment and Intervention Planning

41. **A.** Prolixin (fluphenazine) is an antipsychotic medication that treats schizophrenia and other psychotic disorders. Symptoms of schizophrenia include hallucinations, delusions, disorganized thinking, trouble speaking clearly, and so forth.

Question Assesses

Assessment and Intervention Planning

42. **C.** The client is the daughter, who is an adult, so the intervention must be focused on her. Intervening with the parents is not correct. The parents may continue to fight if the daughter moves out, perhaps continuing to cause her stress. There is no indication that the fighting only happens in the home or that the stress is worse because she lives with them. Thus, helping the client to find alternate housing is not correct. The correct answer is the only one that attempts to reduce stress. Enhanced coping skills can help the client manage other stressful situations which could negatively impact her well-being in the future.

Question Assesses

Interventions with Clients/Client Systems

43. **A.** Ethnocentrism views cultures according to preconceptions originating in the standards and customs of one's own culture. Having all staff training on Saturdays is an example of ethnocentrism as some religious groups reserve Saturdays for worship. Staff who adhere to these religious practices are precluded from attending based on their religious beliefs. The social work administrator should be sensitive to scheduling all training courses on this day and making them mandatory. The social work administrator may attend religious services on Sunday or may not participate in any formal religious practices at all. In either instance, the administrator is expecting the customs to be based on the social worker's own routine or practices. Administrators can require vaccines and disclosure of ethnicity as it may be required for health/safety and required by legal, respectively.

Question Assesses

Human Development, Diversity, and Behavior in the Environment

44. **A.** The child appears to be engaging in the defense mechanism of regression which was prompted by the birth of his sibling. The bedwetting and acting out are likely attention seeking. Focusing on the negative behaviors would not be useful and, based on his age, he may not fully understand the reason for his behavior. There is no indication that lack of structure is a problem so providing more is not warranted. Ensuring that the boy feels that he is still an important part of the family unit will likely reduce the regression over time.

Question Assesses

Interventions with Clients/Client Systems

45. **C.** An amicus curia is a person who is not a party to a legal case. This person can assist an appellate court by offering additional, relevant information or arguments the court may want to consider before making its ruling. The phrase, amicus curiae, is Latin for "friend of the court." Amicus briefs—shorthand for the formal term "amicus curiae briefs," are legal briefs filed in appellate courts by amicus curiae. Their goal is to show the court that its final decision will impact people other than the parties. Amicus briefs can be filed by any attorney but are usually filed by advocacy groups or organizations. NASW has filed many amicus briefs on subjects of importance to the social work profession and those served.

Question Assesses

Professional Relationships, Values, and Ethics

46. **A.** Disruptive mood dysregulation disorder (DMDD) is a type of depressive disorder. Children diagnosed with DMDD struggle to regulate their moods and emotions in an age-appropriate way. As a result, children with DMDD exhibit frequent temper outbursts in response to frustration, either verbally or behaviorally. DMDD symptoms typically begin before the age of 10, but the diagnosis is not given to children under 6 or adolescents over 18. A child with DMDD experiences irritable or angry mood most of the day, nearly every day; severe temper outbursts (verbal or behavioral) at an average of three or more times per week that are out of keeping with the situation and the child's developmental level; and trouble functioning due to irritability in more than one place (e.g., home, school, with peers). Symptoms must be present for 12 or more months.

Question Assesses

Assessment and Intervention Planning

47. **A.** Reflective listening focuses on the client, helping to ensure that a social worker understands what is being communicated by the client. It is essential in rapport building as it encourages having the client comfortably communicate. The social worker seeks cues about what is important, sorts these cues, and expresses the essence of the communication back to the client. Reflective listening attends to both the thoughts and feelings expressed by the client. It does not aim to provide structure in interactions between the social worker and client or demonstrate a commitment to help a client solve problems.

Question Assesses

Interventions with Clients/Client Systems

48. **B.** In operant conditioning, positive and negative do not mean good and bad. Instead, positive means adding something, and negative means taking something away. Reinforcement can be positive or negative, and punishment can also be positive or negative. All reinforcers (positive or negative) increase the likelihood of a behavioral response. All punishers (positive or negative) decrease the likelihood of a behavioral response. In this scenario, the grandmother is giving the child what she wants (positive) after her behavioral outburst, causing the maladaptive behavior to be reinforced and more likely to occur in the future.

Question Assesses

Human Development, Diversity, and Behavior in the Environment

49. **B.** Self-monitoring is a form of data-gathering in which clients are asked to systematically observe and record their own thoughts, emotions, feelings, and behaviors. One aim is to help people to understand how what they think and do affects the way they feel. The process of self-monitoring can help clients better appreciate the links between situations, thoughts, emotions, body sensations, and their responses. It is often used as part of cognitive behavioral therapy. Its greatest strength is client involvement in the problem-solving process. Social workers want to ensure that clients are responsible for the change process and developing insight/enhancing client skills should be the focus of all therapeutic work.

Question Assesses

Interventions with Clients/Client Systems

50. **A.** The focus of the question is that the social worker and client are from different cultures. It is critical for the social worker to be self-aware about how this difference may impact all aspects of the problem-solving process. Consulting with another professional who has worked with someone from this cultural group is not helpful as we know that there are many intracultural differences. The degree to which this client adheres to cultural norms is not yet known. Additionally, the social worker does not yet know what professional skills or competencies will be helpful.

Question Assesses

Human Development, Diversity, and Behavior in the Environment

51. **C.** This is a recall question which requires knowing about unconditional positive regard, as well as the treatment modalities listed. Unconditional positive regard is the attitude of complete acceptance. It does not mean approval of all others' actions, but instead acceptance at a level deeper than surface behavior. The purpose is to build a positive, trusting relationship between the social worker and client. It is a defining feature of client-centered therapy, in which clients are accepted and supported by social workers no matter what they say or do.

Question Assesses

Interventions with Clients/Client Systems

52. **B.** The social worker is using forward chaining. Riding the school bus is a series or chain of behaviors. Practically any complex behavior is part of a chain or a multitude of chains: eating, getting dressed, using the computer, brushing teeth, riding a bike, walking to school and so on. Chaining is the reinforcement of successive elements of a behavior chain. Forward chaining begins with reinforcing the first element in the chain and progresses to the last element. Shaping is a way of adding a specific behavior to a client's repertoire. In shaping, what is reinforced is some approximation of a single target behavior. Approximation means any behavior that resembles the desired behavior or takes the person closer to the desired behavior. In this instance, the child was able to do the individual behaviors, but

needed to be reinforced as part of an overall series or chain. In-vivo desensitization is used to reduce or eliminate phobias, in which the client is exposed to stimuli that induce anxiety.

Question Assesses

Human Development, Diversity, and Behavior in the Environment

53. **B.** Multiple challenges are identified in the question including the work schedule of the adult brother given the needs of the younger sibling. Additionally, the adult brother lives in a studio apartment. While the incorrect response choices may be helpful, identifying and coordinating the concrete service needs are essential to sustaining this caregiving relationship. There is no evidence of unresolved grief in the question. The challenges are not confined to the school setting so educational supports will not be sufficient.

Question Assesses

Interventions with Clients/Client Systems

54. **C.** This adult attachment style is disorganized (a.k.a., fearful-avoidant). The client appears confused and essentially has both the dismissive and the anxious styles combined—both wanting emotional closeness and also pushing it away. Those with this style are often fearful of fully trusting others and yet need approval or validation. They often deny their feelings or are reluctant to express them.

Those with a dismissive-avoidant attachment style do not recognize that intimacy and emotions are important, focusing instead on being self-reliant. They become loners, preferring to be alone rather than take the chance of having a relationship.

Those with an anxious-preoccupied attachment style constantly worry about making their partners love and keep loving them. They tend to be jealous, clingy, needy, full of anxiety, and fearful that if they make one tiny mistake or if the other person meets someone better, then the relationship will be over.

Question Assesses

Human Development, Diversity, and Behavior in the Environment

55. **C.** Delirium and dementia are the most common causes of cognitive impairment, although affective disorders (such as depression) can also disrupt cognition. Delirium and dementia are separate disorders but are sometimes difficult to distinguish. In both, cognition is disordered; but delirium affects mainly attention while dementia affects mainly memory. Delirium is typically caused by acute illness or drug toxicity and is often reversible. Dementia is typically caused by anatomic changes in the brain, has slower onset, and is generally irreversible. The rapid onset described in the first sentence of the sentence eliminates dementia while no described signs of depression are mentioned in the question, resulting in its elimination as well.

Question Assesses

Assessment and Intervention Planning

56. **B.** The ethical duty of social workers with regard to physical contact is outlined in the *Code of Ethics*. Social workers should not engage in physical contact if there is a possibility of psychological harm to client as a result of this contact. Cradling and caressing are not allowed even if it permissible in the agency policy.

Question Assesses

Professional Relationships, Values, and Ethics

57. **C.** The ethical duty of social workers with regard to colleague incompetence is outlined in the *Code of Ethics*. Social workers who believe that colleagues have acted unethically should discuss concerns with these colleagues when feasible. Only if the discussions are not likely to be productive or the acts are dangerous should social workers skip this important step. This question has a qualifying word, FIRST, and does not indicate a lack of feasibility or danger, making going directly to the colleague a critical initial step.

Question Assesses

Professional Relationships, Values, and Ethics

58. **B.** When pregnant women are given access to comprehensive, compassionate treatment, positive outcomes are likely. Substance use disorder requires appropriate medications and behavioral change. No one protocol can ensure every client does well every time. Medication assisted treatment, trauma-informed care, therapy, and prenatal care and that emphasize patient autonomy are associated with treatment success. Increased access is not a deterrent to treatment. Stigma associated with inappropriate beliefs that pregnant women are willfully choosing substances over their babies' health remains a significant barrier.

Question Assesses

Human Development, Diversity, and Behavior in the Environment

59. **C.** The first sentence states that that the parents consented to treatment, indicating that the child is under the age of consent in this state. The age of consent varies between states and within states depending on the nature of treatment. Typically, in this scenario, the parents would have access to the minor's records as they are the legally responsible party, but the question states that the social worker is concerned that there may be information that could cause the client harm. Ethical provisions in the *Code of Ethics* allows a social worker to limit access to records when "only in exceptional circumstances when there is compelling evidence that such access would cause serious hard to the client." The rationale for withholding the file must be documented in the client's file.

Question Assesses

Professional Relationships, Values, and Ethics

60. **B.** Bipolar disorder is a brain disorder that causes changes in mood, energy, and ability to function. These mood episodes are categorized as manic/hypomanic (abnormally happy or irritable mood) or depressive (sad mood). Bipolar disorder is a category that includes three different diagnoses: bipolar I disorder, bipolar II disorder, and cyclothymic disorder. Bipolar I disorder is diagnosed when a person experiences a manic episode which is clearly

described in this question. A diagnosis of bipolar II disorder requires at least one major depressive episode and at least one hypomanic episode. Cyclothymic disorder is a milder form of bipolar disorder involving many "mood swings," with hypomania and depressive symptoms that occur frequently.

Question Assesses

Assessment and Intervention Planning

61. **A.** Schizoid personality disorder is characterized by a pervasive pattern of detachment from and general disinterest in social relationships and by expression of few emotions in relationships. Those with schizoid personality disorder seem to have no interest in close relationships with others and prefer to be by themselves. They strongly prefer solitary activities but may have hobbies which can be engaged in alone (such as video gaming, stamp collecting, etc.).

Question Assesses

Assessment and Intervention Planning

62. **A.** Borderline personality disorder is a mental health disorder that includes self-image issues, difficulty managing emotions and behavior, and a pattern of unstable relationships. With borderline personality disorder, there is an intense fear of abandonment or instability. Inappropriate anger, impulsiveness and frequent mood swings may push others away, even though there is a desire for loving and lasting relationships. Some of the other characteristics described in the question that are consistent with borderline personality disorder include risky behaviors and self-injury.

Question Assesses

Assessment and Intervention Planning

63. **A.** Long-acting injectable antipsychotics have many advantages for clients with schizophrenia or other psychotic disorders, especially those with risk factors for medication non-adherence. Additionally, injectable medication can be useful for clients with comorbid substance use, cognitive impairment, ambivalence or negative attitudes towards medications, and poor insight. As the injections are given at mental health or other medical facilities, there is reduced risk for overdoses and missed doses as clients are not responsible for administering the medications themselves.

Question Assesses

Assessment and Intervention Planning

64. **C.** Community capacity building is about promoting the capacity of local communities to develop, implement and sustain their own solutions to problems. They are heavily rooted in social justice and use a bottom-up approach. Community capacity building is a continuous process that allows communities, through their members, to take responsibility for their own development.

Community capacity building initiatives are not undertaken to help to maintain the status quo rather they challenge government or corporate interests and act as a catalyst for change. Community capacity building is also not a short-term process.

Question Assesses

Interventions with Clients/Client Systems

65. **A.** This recall question requires knowledge about social capital. Social capital is a network of relationships among people who live and/or work together, enabling effective functioning. It focuses on trust and shared identity, norms, values, and mutual relationships.

Question Assesses

Human Development, Diversity, and Behavior in the Environment

66. **B.** The man in the question should be served by an agency in his own county. The man is not a client and requires someone who can assist with his concrete service and emotional needs. The social worker's agency does not regularly work with individuals within his county so serving him is ill advised. The man is better served by an agency that has established working relationships with other providers. The social worker should not contact his insurance provider as he is not a client. It would be confusing for the man and insurance provider for the social worker to become involved. The company can be contacted by a representative of the agency that ultimately serves him.

Question Assesses

Interventions with Clients/Client Systems

67. **B.** Temporary Assistance for Needy Families (TANF) is a federal benefit in the United States but is administered by each state. Calling federal legislators will not help as they have no legitimate power in making needed state-level changes. In each state, the executive branch is headed by a governor who works with state officials to ensure fulfillment of governmental functions. Meeting with a commissioner or representative from the state agency charged with TANF implementation will likely help with raising awareness about the problem and brainstorming solutions. Social workers must be knowledgeable about which public programs are under state versus federal control.

Question Assesses

Interventions with Clients/Client Systems

68. **A.** Cash assistance allows clients the ability to spend distributed funding or money for their individual needs, allowing maximum decision-making power. Cash assistance is also the least stigmatized form of benefit distribution as no one knows the source of cash. A voucher is a coupon that is redeemable for a set service or product. Clients may have a choice of providers but have to use certificates for designated purposes. In-kind is when services or goods are supplied directly to intended beneficiaries and these delivery systems have the least client autonomy.

Question Assesses

Interventions with Clients/Client Systems

69. **B.** The question states that clients are receiving cash assistance. There has been no change in the distribution method. The presenting problem relates to the inability to raise the benefit amounts in the last 10 years. Cash assistance provides more client autonomy than vouchers or in-kind support. Cash assistance programs are also dependent on the size of household. The overall birth rate would have no bearing on program effectiveness. It is likely that the cost of food has risen over the years so clients can purchase less food now than they could a decade ago. Inflation greatly impacts cash assistance programs, which often are not increased to account for higher costs of living over time.

Question Assesses

Interventions with Clients/Client Systems

70. **C.** While the social worker is working with a community rather than an individual or family, the process is still driven by the planned change or generalist intervention model—engage, assess, plan, intervene, evaluate, and terminate. The question indicates that the social work has acknowledged the group's enthusiasm which is an engagement task. NEXT is used as a qualifying word so response choices that involve assessment should be considered. Establishing goals is planning, thereby warranting its exclusion. Investigating past efforts may not directly be beneficial to the current initiative.

Asset mapping provides information about the strengths and resources of a community and can help uncover solutions. Once community strengths and resources are inventoried, it is easier to set goals to address community needs and improve health. Thus, asset mapping is the assessment method that should be used in this situation.

Question Assesses

Interventions with Clients/Client Systems

71. **B.** This question requires knowledge about the types of prevention. Primary prevention aims to improve the overall health of the population by universally screening or treating all. Secondary prevention works with those at risk to identify diseases in the earliest stages before the onset of signs and symptoms. Tertiary prevention manages disease after diagnosis to slow or stop disease progression.

Question Assesses

Interventions with Clients/Client Systems

72. **A.** Social workers should avoid accepting requests from or engaging with clients on social networking sites or other electronic media to prevent boundary confusion or inappropriate dual relationships. The social worker has no affiliation with the client's business and would be following it on social media due to knowledge gleaned as part of a therapeutic relationship. It is best for the social worker to avoid promoting the client's business or helping with financing as it is outside the scope of social work practice.

Question Assesses

Professional Relationships, Values, and Ethics

73. **C.** The question specifies that the social worker identified the goals for treatment. Intervention planning must be done collaboratively with the social worker and client. Some insurance companies cover complementary therapies as part of their wellness program. The social worker should not be discussing insurance coverage with the client and never be diagnosing to "justify treatment."

Question Assesses

Assessment and Intervention Planning

74. **A.** People with obsessive-compulsive disorder (OCD) often feel distressed by the nature of their behaviors or thoughts, even if they are unable to control them. People with obsessive-compulsive personality disorder (OCPD), however, typically believe that their actions have an aim and purpose. Symptoms of OCD tend to fluctuate in association with the underlying level of anxiety. Because OCPD is a personality disorder that's defined by inflexibility, the behaviors tend to be persistent and unchanging over the long term. Those with OCPD may also avoid seeking professional help. In some situations, the traits of OCPD can even translate to success—someone who is overly dedicated to their job and conscientious of every detail might see benefits at work, even if struggling in other life areas.

Question Assesses

Assessment and Intervention Planning

75. **C.** Countertransference occurs during the therapeutic process and understanding it can be helpful to social workers' professional development. The client does not need to be referred to another social worker. The problem stems from the social worker's feelings so referring the client would be detrimental to him for no reason. As the client is not responsible for the social worker's reaction, it is inappropriate to speak to him about the social worker's feelings, even if they result from his actions. Processing feelings toward clients is a great use of supervision and can help social workers gain better insight into emotional triggers.

Question Assesses

Professional Relationships, Values, and Ethics

76. **A.** Clozapine (sold under the brand name Clozaril among others) is an antipsychotic medication used mainly with those who have schizophrenia. It is used by mouth or injectable. Clozapine is associated with a relatively high risk of low white blood cells (agranulocytosis), a condition of suppressed immunity which may result in death. To decrease this risk, it is recommended that the white blood cell count be regularly monitored via bloodwork.

Question Assesses

Assessment and Intervention Planning

77. **B.** Zoloft (generic name: sertraline) is an antidepressant belonging to a group of drugs called selective serotonin reuptake inhibitors (SSRIs). Sertraline affects chemicals in the brain that may be unbalanced in people with depression, panic, anxiety, or obsessive-compulsive symptoms.

Question Assesses

Assessment and Intervention Planning

78. **C.** Community baby showers help low-income pregnant and new parents prepare for the arrival of their new babies by providing them with essential items needed. Often these events also include maternal and early childhood education and resources. They can also include financial assistance to lessen the burden associated with parenting.

Question Assesses

Interventions with Clients/Client Systems

79. **B.** Answering this question correctly requires knowledge about mindfulness, which is a critical complementary treatment to social work practice. Mindfulness is the basic human ability to be fully present, aware of surroundings and activities, and not overly reactive or overwhelmed by happenings.

Question Assesses

Interventions with Clients/Client Systems

80. **B.** Death's irreversibility (that once the body is dead, it cannot ever be alive again) is not understood until ages 4–5. The other two aspects of death—nonfunctionality and universality—are learned a bit later. Nonfunctionality is the idea that a dead body can no longer do things that a living body can do. Before this concept is understood, children will affirmatively answer questions like, "Can a dead person feel?" Universality is the notion that every living thing dies. Before children understand universality, many believe that there are certain groups of people who are protected from death, like teachers, parents, and themselves.

Question Assesses

Human Development, Diversity, and Behavior in the Environment

81. **A.** Radical acceptance allows clients to move on rather than getting stuck. In this situation, the client has little power over changing administrators' minds about selecting another candidate for the position. She also needs the job due to her financial situation and the situation is unfair, frustrating, and upsetting. Accepting radically does not mean approving of the situation; it can still be viewed as unfair. However, it does mean that fully accepting that this the way things are right now, rather than getting stuck in a vision of what "should be." The questions states that the correct answer should be consistent with the principles of acceptance.

Question Assesses

Interventions with Clients/Client Systems

82. **C.** Evidence-based practice (EBP) is a process in which social workers combine well-researched interventions with experience to guide and inform the delivery of treatments and services. This approach ensures that the treatments and services will have the most effective outcomes as demonstrated by the research. While all ethical principles inform EBP, its use ensures the delivery of competent (i.e., efficient, and effective) services. EBP is less focused on social justice (i.e., equal treatment and opportunities) or integrity (i.e., trustworthiness and honesty).

Question Assesses

Professional Relationships, Values, and Ethics

83. **B.** Values and traditions drive attitudes and behavior. If a social worker wants to understand behavior overall, it would be BEST to understand the potential root causes. The correct response choice does not indicate how this learning will take place. It would be useful to speak with those in the community directly as well as use reliable sources for reading and studying. Speaking with social workers who have Hmong clients will only provide information based on limited experience with some individuals and/or families. Additionally, observing daily routines of community members will not "provide an understanding" which is asked for in the question.

Question Assesses

Human Development, Diversity, and Behavior in the Environment

84. **B.** The question is asking the MOST effective method to address resistance. Reassuring the client that the social worker would like to assist is not effective as the client has no evidence to support the assertion. The client may be reluctant to speak about legal matters for fear that the information will be reported to the court. Asking about topics which the client is used to discussing will assist with getting the client to speak more openly, reducing resistance.

Question Assesses

Interventions with Clients/Client Systems

85. **B.** The question is asking about the initial session with a client. Asking the client questions should happen during assessment once engagement has occurred. If the client is speaking to the social worker about emotional events, the social worker should not interrupt. It is too early to interpret the client's narratives as it is the first session.

Question Assesses

Professional Relationships, Values, and Ethics

86. **C.** Paradoxical interventions or directives involve advocating for the continuation or even the worsening of problems rather than their elimination. It is commonly referred to as "reverse psychology." Paradoxical directives help individuals see that they have control over the symptoms of their problems and are not powerless.

Question Assesses

Interventions with Clients/Client Systems

87. **B.** Social workers should use person-first terminology and not refer to people by their social problems. For example, it is not appropriate to refer to people who lack housing as "the homeless." Additionally, referring to people as "cases" is dehumanizing as it does not recognize any of their individual characteristics and calls them by a generic, derogatory term. Clients are not "cases" that need to be fixed. Use of respectful language is critical to viewing clients as partners in the planned change process. Each has unique attributes that should be recognized and should not be grouped with others as "cases."

Question Assesses

Professional Relationships, Values, and Ethics

88. **A.** Forensic interviewing is a first step in most child protective services (CPS) investigations, one in which social workers interview children to find out if they have been maltreated. In addition to yielding the information needed to determine whether abuse or neglect has occurred, this approach produces evidence that will stand up in court if the investigation leads to criminal prosecution. Properly conducted forensic interviews are legally sound in part because they ensure social workers' objectivity, employ non-leading techniques, and emphasize careful documentation.

Question Assesses

Human Development, Diversity, and Behavior in the Environment

89. **C.** There is no indication that the lateness inconveniences others or results from resistance. There is no information about why the client is late, so it is important for the social worker to assess for the underlying reason. Asking about the convenience of the time will raise the issue of lateness in a non-threatening manner.

Question Assesses

Interventions with Clients/Client Systems

90. **B.** Social workers should maximize the decision-making and autonomy of clients so requiring their consent for each requested document provides them the opportunity to decide which are acceptable for release and which are not. Having clients sign releases of information at intake for all or certain documents is not best practice as clients are not aware of the content of the documents as they have not yet been created. Also, social workers should not be making decisions within the specified time periods about document releases—clients should do so. Lastly, consent does not have to be written. Verbal consent is equally valid and should contain all the elements covered on written forms. If verbal consent is obtained, it should be documented in the client's file.

Question Assesses

Professional Relationships, Values, and Ethics

91. **C.** Social workers' beliefs, background, sexual orientation, prejudices, and racial and/or cultural identity impact the problem-solving process, especially when working clients with backgrounds different from their own. Social workers' ability to be introspective and understand the potential impact of their personal beliefs and attributes on the therapeutic process is essential for achieving sensitive, unbiased treatment. Included in this understanding is social workers' examination of their degree of privilege and the potential for abuse of power.

Question Assesses

Professional Relationships, Values, and Ethics

92. **A.** This question requires recall of information about psychodynamic theory. Treatments are based on theoretical underpinnings. Psychodynamic theory states that childhood events have a great influence on adult lives, shaping personality. Events that occur in childhood can remain in the unconscious, and cause problems as adults. These problems result from struggles or conflicts between the id, ego, and superego.

Question Assesses

Human Development, Diversity, and Behavior in the Environment

93. **C.** Interdisciplinary collaboration can be one of the most rewarding, yet challenging, aspects of social work practice. In order for it to be effective, services are provided by those from varying disciplines who make decisions as a group. If clients choose this treatment approach, keeping information from other team members is not possible so having clients make decisions each time sharing is needed is not possible. Social workers should not lead clients to believe that all of their information will not be used for group treatment recommendations. The strength of interdisciplinary collaboration is that each professional decision is informed by the expertise of all team members, making information sharing among team members essential.

Question Assesses

Professional Relationships, Values, and Ethics

94. **A.** Many groups are designed to target a specific problem, such as depression, obesity, panic disorder, social anxiety, chronic pain, or substance abuse. Other groups focus more generally on improving social skills, helping people deal with a range of issues such as anger, shyness, loneliness, and low self-esteem. It is important for potential members to understand the focus of the group. The cost is important, but not relevant if the group is not appropriate to address clients' identified problem. There is no way to predict the outcomes as the group sets its specific goals so they cannot be established until the group is formed.

Question Assesses

Human Development, Diversity, and Behavior in the Environment

95. **B.** There is no indication that the marriage will end as the client's thoughts about the spouse's reaction may not be accurate. The social worker is also not a lawyer so helping the client to understand the legal implications is not advisable. The sexual orientation of the client transcends the affair and will impact the ongoing relationship with the spouse. Working with the client to address the nervousness anticipated by the conversation with the spouse is the BEST action. Educating the client about being truthful will not assist the client in addressing the presenting problem.

Question Assesses

Interventions with Clients/Client Systems

96. **C.** Research shows that an integrated approach to treating co-occurring disorders, now an evidence-based practice, results in the best possible outcomes. The integrated treatment

model addresses the problem of access by ensuring that one visit, in one setting, is sufficient to receive treatment for both disorders.

When both mental health and substance use services are provided by the same person or team, the client has one treatment plan, one set of goals, and one relapse plan.

Question Assesses

Assessment and Intervention Planning

97. **A.** Social workers are bound by all of the ethical principles at all times. However, the question specifically mentions that the client is concerned about the social worker's honesty and trustworthiness. The ethical principle of integrity is directly related to behaving in a trustworthy manner. It mandates that social workers act honestly and responsibly to promote ethical practices.

Question Assesses

Professional Relationships, Values, and Ethics

98. **C.** This question requires recall knowledge about evidence-based housing solutions. Rapid rehousing is an intervention, informed by a housing first approach, that connects individuals and families experiencing homelessness to permanent housing through the use of financial assistance and targeted supportive services.

Question Assesses

Interventions with Clients/Client Systems

99. **C.** The *Code of Ethics* dictates that social workers should avoid accepting requests from or engaging in personal relationships with clients on social networking sites or other electronic media to prevent boundary confusion, inappropriate dual relationships, or harm to clients. While situations which arise on social media may also relate to the other response choices, boundary confusion is the MOST pressing issue when "friending" clients.

Question Assesses

Professional Relationships, Values, and Ethics

100. **B.** People express and experience love in different ways—often called "love languages." While originally developed to describe romantic relationships, these languages are also applicable for use with children. Critical is understanding what others value. People tend to naturally give love in the way that they prefer to receive love, and better relationships result when one demonstrates caring in this manner. The "languages" are acts of service, gift giving, physical touch, quality time, and words of affirmation.

As described in the question, the child is using acts of service to express love. When that child asks to cook or clean, the child wants emotional love. Words of affirmation are praise or encouragement which is also not specified. Lastly, gift giving is also a way to express and give love, but it is not described either.

Question Assesses

Interventions with Clients/Client Systems

101. A. Child neglect is supported by the wording in the question. The child is malnourished, dirty, and has not been able to bring the needed clothing item to school. His emotional reaction may result from shame or a lack of acceptance by his peers due to his situation. No marks are described in the question, causing physical abuse to be eliminated. There may be emotional neglect, but much of the question focuses on appearance and lack of resources.

Question Assesses

Human Development, Diversity, and Behavior in the Environment

102. C. The strongest predictor is impairment of both parents due to substance use. Legal involvement can be caused by many factors, independent of parental caregiving. Short-term mental health issues of one parent will not have the same deleterious impacts as long-term impairment of both parents.

Question Assesses

Human Development, Diversity, and Behavior in the Environment

103. A. Social workers should never ask clients to sign forms that do not accurately reflect the terms of service. The forms serve to outline the parameters of the working relationship, in addition to the fees, so delaying the signing of them is not advisable.

Question Assesses

Professional Relationships, Values, and Ethics

104. B. Interviewing of children who have allegedly been abused, often referred to as forensic interviewing, focuses on investigating possible maltreatment. There are numerous barriers to policy change in forensic interviewing with one being increased false positives. The admission that a technique is prone to false positive findings may call prior legal decisions into question. The reliability and validity of forensic interviewing techniques are critical as they will lead to prosecution of perpetrators and potential removal of children from their current living situations. False positives (i.e., concluding abuse occurred when it did not occur) need to be minimized.

Question Assesses

Human Development, Diversity, and Behavior in the Environment

105. B. Self-determination is a vital ethical principle in social work practice and consent of the client is required when making decisions. The first sentence of the question provides critical background information. The client is legally competent but is confused and disoriented. The *Code of Ethics* states that a social worker should protect clients' interests by seeking permission from an appropriate third party, while informing clients consistent with their level of understanding, in instances when clients lack capacity to provide informed consent. In such a situation, the social worker needs to ensure that the third party acts in a manner with the clients' interests. Explaining the ethical dilemma to a supervisor is not required as there is no indication that the supervisor is a social worker or will have any additional information to inform the social worker's actions. The incoherence of the client may be temporary, perhaps due to the medical condition mentioned. Respecting the client's decision is correct when the consent is informed. The client appears to lack the ability to make an informed choice at this time. Thus, the husband's opinion needs to be considered as does the reason for the client's refusal—that the appointment has "no value." The correct answer of arranging for her to go to the appointment while educating her about its importance helps to enhance her ability to give informed consent in the future while still acting in her best interest.

Question Assesses

Professional Relationships, Values, and Ethics

106. **B.** This question requires recall of the ecological perspective, an approach to social work practice that addresses the complex transactions between people and their environment. Using this perspective, emotional disturbances result from a pattern of maladaptive transactions between individuals and their environments. Environmental activity shapes individuals and individuals' social functioning influences environments.

Question Assesses

Human Development, Diversity, and Behavior in the Environment

107. **B.** Each state has its own guidelines for mandatory reporting, so it is important for social workers to be aware of state guidelines. However, the licensure exam will not be state specific. Mothers who use drugs or alcohol while pregnant may give birth to infants who show signs of that exposure. Federal legislation requires states to have systems that address the needs of these infants. Whether required by state law or not, social workers should make a report when substance abuse is suspected or confirmed so that support can be provided. Criminalization of the behavior is not appropriate, but the mother's drug use can have negative effects on the unborn child. The child welfare system will provide needed resources.

Question Assesses

Human Development, Diversity, and Behavior in the Environment

108. **A.** Exploration through questioning is useful when social workers are collecting relevant data for diagnostic purposes and may lead clients to think about various unexplored areas of problems. Interpretation focuses on drawing new meanings about provided information and explanation helps educate clients when there is a gap in knowledge or skill development is needed.

Question Assesses

Interventions with Clients/Client Systems

109. **C.** A topical shift is when the social worker purposely changes the subject of discussion perhaps because the topic under discussion is unproductive. Topical shifts may be used when the emotions expressed are not ones that the client can handle at present, but expressing high degrees of emotion, especially when the client raised the topic can be therapeutic. Just because the topic changes does not mean that it will not be raised again. Social workers should never change subjects because they are uncomfortable.

Question Assesses

Interventions with Clients/Client Systems

110. **B.** When using logical reasoning, social workers involve clients in a systematic and rational analysis of a situation that requires a decision. Social workers encourage clients to weigh alternative responses and to predict the possible consequences of each of the responses. Psychoeducation involves giving clients information. Encouragement is done through expressing confidence in clients' abilities, recognizing achievements and expressing pleasure in successes.

Question Assesses

Interventions with Clients/Client Systems

111. **B.** Universalization is used to minimize guilt or anxiety feelings by generalizing the nature of events or reactions. It is also referred to as normalization or generalization. Interpretation enables social workers and clients to go beyond stated problems and begin to delve more deeply. Interpretation can provide clients with an alternative way of viewing the problem. Clarification seeks specificity on what clients are thinking, feeling, and experiencing.

Question Assesses

Interventions with Clients/Client Systems

112. **C.** When reflecting feeling, social workers restate and explore clients' affective (feeling) messages. The emphasis of the question is on feelings, eliminating the answer focused on exploring the reasons for the problem. Reflection is not focused on analysis but rather the strengthening of rapport or validation.

Question Assesses

Interventions with Clients/Client Systems

113. **A.** The question indicates that the business card is for social work services. A social worker needs to clearly represent credentials, education, and qualifications to clients. The literature degree is not directly relevant to the provision of social work services. By just using the title "Dr.," clients are likely to inappropriately assume that the doctorate is in social work, making the action unethical. A social worker can list her PhD, such as on her resume, but must make it known that it is in literature. Just using "Dr." on a social work business card may lead to confusion by clients.

Question Assesses

Professional Relationships, Values, and Ethics

114. **B.** Critical race theory (CRT) posits that racism is systematic within policies and procedures and counters discussions that situates discrimination and disparities within the realm of individual behaviors or psychological deficits. Lack of equal opportunities are seen for people of color in all aspects of life—housing, education, employment, wealth, health, safety, and justice. CRT speaks to the universal way that racism immobilizes minoritized people—thereby providing an almost unwavering advantage to some people.

Question Assesses

Human Development, Diversity, and Behavior in the Environment

115. **A.** Employing critical consciousness—personal reflection about one's lived experiences, worldviews, and biases—can reduce the chances of social workers imposing their beliefs onto clients. Social workers must collaborate with clients, remaining cognizant of power imbalances. Having clients participate in peer-facilitated interactions does not assist social workers to develop critical consciousness. While engaging client communities is important and social workers must be aware of the contexts in which clients reside, critical consciousness about power differentials transcends empowerment and is essential for all competent practice.

Question Assesses

Professional Relationships, Values, and Ethics

116. **C.** There are many similarities between schizotypal and schizoid personality disorder including social and interpersonal deficits and social isolation. A distinct difference is that schizoid personality disorder does not have any paranoid ideation or suspiciousness. This means that people with a schizoid personality disorder will not be overly worried about other people's motivations or worried that people are out to get them. However, people with schizotypal personality disorder will have these kinds of beliefs.

Question Assesses

Assessment and Intervention Planning

117. **B.** Mania and hypomania make people feel elated, very active, and full of energy. Hypomania is a milder form of mania. Mania and hypomania both involve periods when people feel excited or experience energized mood. Mania may result in hospitalizations whereas hypomania does not. A hypomanic episode can be caused by highly stimulating situation or environment (e.g., lots of noise, bright lights, and large crowds), a major life change (e.g., divorce, marriage, and job loss), lack of sleep, and substance use, such as recreational drugs or alcohol. A distinguishing difference between hypomania and mania is the elevated mood in hypomania is not enough to cause impairment or impact in life areas.

Question Assesses

Assessment and Intervention Planning

118. **B.** The question specifically identifies the use of a standard intake form. Standard means that all clients are asked the same questions. This approach is "cookie cutter" by not allowing questions asked to be tailored to the reasons for services or treatment. Intake forms can be read to the client so literacy and reading are not the MOST (qualifying word) important concerns. It is fine to have clients complete written assessments, even if they prefer personal interactions. However, the questions should be tailored to their needs—not standard.

Question Assesses

Assessment and Intervention Planning

119. C. This question requires recall knowledge about the personality disorders which are often asked about on the licensure test. Antisocial personality disorder is characterized by an ingrained pattern of behavior in which individuals consistently disregard and violate the rights of others around them.

The symptoms of antisocial personality disorder can vary in severity. The more egregious, harmful, or dangerous behavior patterns are referred to as sociopathic or psychopathic.

Question Assesses

Assessment and Intervention Planning

120. B. The comment by the social worker reflects a microaggression and fails to acknowledge that race plays a role in opportunities and successes. Critical race theory posits that racism is not merely the product of individual bias or prejudice, but also something embedded in systems and policies. The social worker's comment ignores that racism, not skill level, has caused unequal promotion.

Question Assesses

Professional Relationships, Values, and Ethics

121. C. Elimination disorders involve the elimination of feces (encopresis) or urine (enuresis). There are many predisposing factors, including genetics, psychological factors, and psychosocial stress. Encopresis can be voluntary or involuntary.

Question Assesses

Assessment and Intervention Planning

122. C. The question clearly states that the social worker believes that there is a conflict of interest in this situation. The *Code of Ethics* mandates that conflicts of interest should be avoided. The social worker should not complete the intake with the spouse or lie about not accepting clients. It is also not appropriate to speak to the current client as it is the social worker's ethical duty to identify the conflict, not the client's responsibility. Additionally, the current client may not know that the spouse is seeking treatment. The most appropriate way to address the situation ethically is that the social worker should immediately inform the spouse that the social worker cannot provide services but is happy to provide referrals.

Question Assesses

Professional Relationships, Values, and Ethics

123. B. While the reported behavior is legal, it is against agency policy, perhaps for good reason. Thus, the behavior cannot be ignored despite being legal and occurring after work hours. The question has a qualifying word—FIRST, indicating that the order of the response choices is critical. The remaining response choices all address the issue in different ways. The *Code of Ethics* states that social workers should speak to colleagues initially when there is a problem with their actions. Thus, asking the supervisor about the actions and reporting the incident to an administrator might occur sequentially after the correct answer, depending upon the situation and the colleague's subsequent actions.

Question Assesses

Professional Relationships, Values, and Ethics

124. B. Interviewing occurs during all phases of the social work process—engagement, assessment, planning, intervening, evaluating, and terminating. The length of time will be dictated by the purpose of the interaction. Rapport building is ongoing as is not "established" at any one point. The social worker would not be focused on determining whether rapport is present as it develops over time.

Question Assesses

Interventions with Clients/Client Systems

125. B. It is important that clients are partners in the planned change process and are able to easily communicate with social workers. Social work jargon, terminology, and acronyms are learned in coursework that has only been taken by the social worker. It will be easy for a client to not understand or misunderstand what is being communicated if words and concepts with which the client is not familiar are being used.

Question Assesses

Interventions with Clients/Client Systems

126. A. The question asks about a valid reason for requesting "proof" or verification of client information. Verification is evidence used to establish the accuracy of client information. This means that social workers need to gather documentation from third parties to show that reported client information is correct. While documentation may be needed for benefit eligibility and there may be a need for additional information, these are not for verification or checking purposes.

Question Assesses

Assessment and Intervention Planning

127. C. Sociopathy and psychopathy share many characteristics such as disregard for rules and lack of remorse. The etiology or cause of psychopathy is different from that of sociopathy. Psychopathy is the result of "nature" (genetics), while sociopathy is the result of "nurture" (environment). Psychopathy is related to a physiological defect that results in the underdevelopment of the part of the brain responsible for impulse control and emotions. Sociopathy is more likely the product of childhood trauma and physical or emotional abuse.

Question Assesses

Assessment and Intervention Planning

128. C. Given the age of the daughter, she is likely in Erikson's stage of psychosocial development which focuses on identity. During this stage, adolescents explore their independence and develop a sense of self. The question indicates that the answer must "address the mother's fears" so meeting with the daughter alone is not correct. The daughter is also not the client. Assuring the mother is not as effective as educating her so she understands the daughter's behavior in light of typical psychosocial development. Education will allow her to anticipate future behaviors and stages.

Question Assesses

Interventions with Clients/Client Systems

129. **A.** The question has a qualifying word—FIRST—which means that the order of the social worker's actions is important. Completing a safety assessment must always be first. Confrontation may agitate the situation. After resources have been accessed to ensure safety, there may be a need to assess the efficacy of treatment. However, the question does not indicate that the couple are receiving services aimed at reducing abuse. They may be receiving services aimed at other problems that are unrelated to domestic abuse.

Question Assesses

Assessment and Intervention Planning

130. **C.** All of the response choices are accurate and helpful in social work practice. When responding to a traumatic event in an indigenous community, it is important to tailor the response efforts to the experiences of the community. Remember that because of the survivors' past experiences of violence and cultural degradation, there is likely increased fear and mistrust of responders outside of the community. Showing respect for the culture increase credibility while identifying and engaging traditional leaders is also important. However, acknowledging differences in communities and engaging leaders are not the most important considerations. Emphasis of traditional values, beliefs, and expressions of culture will be essential. Social workers must be respectful of culture and values for interventions to be effective.

Question Assesses

Assessment and Intervention Planning

131. **B.** This question requires knowledge about indigenous communities. Historical trauma is the cumulative, multigenerational, collective experience of emotional and psychological injury in communities and in descendants due to exploitation by others. The effects of historical trauma may include overall poor physical and emotional health, depression, substance abuse, and high rates of suicide.

Question Assesses

Human Development, Diversity, and Behavior in the Environment

132. **A.** Addiction is progressive and chronic. Addiction can be fatal if left untreated but has negative impacts besides those affecting physical health. Addiction can be controlled and managed. This question requires knowledge of addiction theories and concepts. Understanding the chronic and progressive nature of addiction is essential for designing effective and comprehensive treatment services.

Question Assesses

Human Development, Diversity, and Behavior in the Environment

133. A. Abstinence-only policies of some agencies are in opposition to some values as codified in the *Code of Ethics*, particularly the emphasis on client self-determination. In abstinence-only programs, the expected standard is complete refrain from the substance or activity. Penalizing clients by expelling them from treatment interferes with access to treatment. There are no unique issues related to confidentiality or consent. The main dilemma focuses on punishing decisions made by clients and ignoring that relapse is part of the disease model of addiction.

Question Assesses

Professional Relationships, Values, and Ethics

134. B. It is not an ethical violation to meet with a client longer than scheduled. Unlike a boundary violation, a boundary crossing is not necessarily harmful and can be engaged in intentionally and therapeutically. Extending the length of the session appears warranted given the information provided in the question. There is no stated dual relationship between the social worker and client.

Question Assesses

Professional Relationships, Values, and Ethics

135. C. The question asks for the response choice that will be "MOST helpful in identifying a plan." Planning is driven by information obtained by assessment. There are no indicators of suicide risk. Many people who are despondent and withdrawn are not suicidal. Additionally, the question does not ask what should be done first, which often focuses on medical issues and safety. A suicide risk assessment does not drive planning. There is no indication that the emotional changes are due to her chronic medical condition which rules out speaking to the doctor. The most helpful will be to determine what changes in the client's life may be responsible for the current emotional state.

Question Assesses

Assessment and Intervention Planning

136. B. There is no evidence in the question that the client is a danger to self or others, so assessment is not needed. Yelling in a loud and menacing voice could result from a bad experience while driving to the meeting—it does not indicate dangerousness. The social worker would never reschedule the session as to do so is not addressing the issue or problem presented by the client. The client must be engaged in order to respond to a request and assuring is an engaging task. Competently being able to intervene with an angry client is an important social work skill.

Question Assesses

Interventions with Clients/Client Systems

137. C. The question is asking for the response that should occur FIRST (qualifying word) in the initial meeting. Finding out more about the child's death is an assessment task which would only be appropriate after establishing rapport. Asking about what they hope to accomplish is also premature. Acknowledging their feelings is engaging. The social worker should acknowledge the emotional state and focus on the here and now. The circumstances of the death are not known and raising the topic is not advisable until later in the problem-solving process.

Question Assesses

Interventions with Clients/Client Systems

138. **C.** The social worker should engage with the client and only the correct answer encourages her to speak to the social worker openly. Redirecting her does not address the problem. An assumption should not be made that the woman is experiencing dementia. Speaking about past events may be comforting to the woman, easing her anxiety. Additionally, recounting these recollections may be a way of bonding with the social worker, which can assist with acclimation and adjustment to the new environment.

Question Assesses

Professional Relationships, Values, and Ethics

139. **B.** The client is the couple so the correct answer will focus on both the husband and wife. It is important to identify the client in each question on the licensure exam to assist with selection of the correct answer. Seeing the wife for individual therapy is not correct since the couple is the client. There is no indication in the question that the couple had any sexual problems before the husband's illness so completing a sexual history is also not correct. The issues with intimacy are based on feelings and emotions so understanding them more will assist with identifying the problem. The use of FIRST as a qualifying word in the question indicates that the other actions in the other response choices may eventually be done, but not until the nature of the problem is understood.

Question Assesses

Assessment and Intervention Planning

140. **A.** The unauthorized visit to the family planning clinic has caused guilt and remorse in the client. The problem is the client's feelings about her actions. There is a qualifying word in the question—FIRST. No action should be taken to report the action to the clinic or even encourage her to speak to her parents until there is a better understanding of her relationship with them.

Question Assesses

Professional Relationships, Values, and Ethics

141. **C.** An expert should ensure that testimony is based upon sufficient facts or data, and the product of reliable data collection methods. Speculation (forming of a theory or conjecture without firm evidence) should never be done. Court-appointed experts often prepare reports and other related documents but remaining impartial is more important to ensuring that information provided is not biased or based on insufficient data collection or analytic methods.

Question Assesses

Professional Relationships, Values, and Ethics

142. **C.** The family is the client in the question so the social worker should be addressing the problem from a family system's perspective. The qualifying word indicates that the correct answer is the one that comes immediately after identification of the problem. While the incorrect response choices may be helpful at some point in the problem-solving process, it is necessary for the family to understand the problem in order to plan (the next step in the planned change model). Once the problem is fully understood by all, a solution can be identified.

Question Assesses

Assessment and Intervention Planning

143. **C.** Children of narcissistic parents often do their best to avoid the limelight. Qualities include refraining from asking for help. Children of narcissistic parents do not focus on their own needs. They do not like compliments as they do not know what to do with them.

Question Assesses

Human Development, Diversity, and Behavior in the Environment

144. **B.** Diagnosis is part of the assessment phase of the problem-solving process. The purpose of assessment is to inform planning and ultimately intervention. Social workers should not be diagnosing to justify treatment and not all clients with diagnoses have services reimbursed by insurance companies or other third-party payers. There is also much variability between clients with the same diagnosis, so prognosis is not known until response to treatment is evaluated.

Question Assesses

Assessment and Intervention Planning

145. **C.** While the client has a substance use history, he has not used substances in many years and there are no signs of relapse reported. His cognitive functioning appears intact, so dementia is unlikely. While he is having difficulties with his vision, the type of trouble is not specified. Vision and balance are often the result of neurological problems which need to be considered. He also may be having problems with motor control as he is not able to do his assembly job. Motor impairment may also be a sign of an underlying neurological condition.

Question Assesses

Assessment and Intervention Planning

146. **A.** Data and information should be used for decision making and determining whether discharge should occur, or reassessment is needed to modify the existing service plan. The assessment of a single client does not determine agency effectiveness. Data would need to be analyzed in the aggregate. Identifying the training needs of staff is important, but evaluation should focus on client well-being. The question has a qualifying word— MOST—which means that the correct answer must be discerned from other, less critical, functions of evaluation.

Question Assesses

Interventions with Clients/Client Systems

147. **B.** The *Code of Ethics* states that social workers should not engage in solicitation of testimonial endorsement from current clients or those who are vulnerable to undue influence. The social worker did not reach out to current clients or those who were vulnerable, making the action ethical. Clients' actual names can be used with their consent. The use of pseudonyms further protects their privacy but is not required.

Question Assesses

Professional Relationships, Values, and Ethics

148. **A.** Empowerment is focused on helping those who have been marginalized take control of their lives. Based on empowerment theory, social work explores direct and indirect power blocks. Direct power blocks are the structures that stop people from achieving goals such as better employment, advanced education, or safe housing. Examples include inequitable access to well-funded and high-quality schools, discriminatory lending practices in housing, or sexist attitudes in corporate culture. Indirect power blocks refer to internalized oppression. Groups with histories of mistreatment often absorb the negative messaging of the abuse they receive. They develop stories about their limited options and ability to achieve and then pass those ideas down across generations. However challenging, these deeply ingrained thoughts need to be resolved. None of the incorrect response choices address factors that oppress people, which need to be removed for empowerment to occur.

Question Assesses

Human Development, Diversity, and Behavior in the Environment

149. **B.** There are three functions of supervision—administrative, supportive, and educational. The question clearly states that the employee does not know how to work with resistance. Providing the employee with new knowledge and skills BEST (qualifying word) addresses the root cause of the problem. Support is important to avoid burnout, but only enhancing the competency of the worker (educational function) will address the problem. Professional development is essential for ethical, competent practice.

Question Assesses

Professional Relationships, Values, and Ethics

150. **A.** During preplanning, social workers evaluate the feasibility of an idea. Considering whether the need is important to the community is paramount. Understanding the barriers is also critical but can be done later in the process. It is premature to do a thorough and complete review of all that has been done prior to determining with there is support for program development broadly.

Question Assesses

Interventions with Clients/Client Systems

151. **A.** The request by the client is not unreasonable given the circumstances. Applying the same policy to all clients is not always appropriate and does not consider cultural and situational differences. While it may be critical for the client to speak to the social worker, there is no information about why the client is in therapy or that the meeting would be

focused on the client's recent loss, so the social worker is not necessarily abandoning the client. There is also no indication that the social worker sees clients internationally on a regular or routine basis so creating a policy for international service provision is not the most critical concern.

Question Assesses

Professional Relationships, Values, and Ethics

152. **B.** Planning should inform decisions about the viability of program development. Identifying the factors that promote and hinder development are the most important functions. Gaining support of community leaders is essential but will occur later when the decision to implement the program has been made. Gathering demographic data may be helpful but does not specifically focus on assessing the feasibility for program development which is the aim of planning.

Question Assesses

Interventions with Clients/Client Systems

153. **C.** The integrity of demographic data depends on it being collected systematically, with care to its reliability and validity. It is far too large a task for the social worker to do individually so sending surveys to residents is not advisable. Tax and school records will only provide data on segments of the population—namely, homeowners and families with children. Many others will be excluded. There are many government organizations charged with collecting and reporting population data. Using information from one or more of them will ensure that the information is collected in a comprehensive and uniform manner. Since these entities do data collection routinely, it also allows for comparisons over time.

Question Assesses

Assessment and Intervention Planning

154. **C.** Getting the support of community members is critical when developing new services or programs. While multiple outreach efforts are always helpful, smaller neighborhood or focus groups allow for an exchange of ideas which is BEST (qualifying word). These gatherings bring small groups of community members together which can help with coalition building. Town hall meetings are too big for effective discussion and interaction. Social media posts do not facilitate "buy-in" which results from in-depth conversation and dialogue. This type of communication occurs most effectively in synchronous interaction.

Question Assesses

Interventions with Clients/Client Systems

155. **B.** According to Freud psychoanalytic theory, the id is the primitive and instinctual part of the mind that contains drives that are likely the cause of the client's urges. The superego operates as a moral conscience which is not mentioned in the question, and the ego is the realistic part that mediates between the desires of the id and the superego. The question contains MOST as a qualifying word, indicating that the likely cause of the behaviors is

being sought. The urges are likely unconscious, not subconscious as the client is probably not aware of their presence.

Question Assesses

Human Development, Diversity, and Behavior in the Environment

156. **A.** When employees need to provide sensitive information for legitimate employment purposes, it is best that the information is "handled" by the fewest number of people possible. Having an employee provide the information to the social worker is an extra step that is not needed as the documents will eventually be sent to human resources. It is unlikely that policies in a handbook will have the specificity needed to address all issues and questions that may arise. Human resource personnel are trained in the standards related to family and medical leave. Having employees work with them directly is optimal.

Question Assesses

Professional Relationships, Values, and Ethics

157. **A.** The question states that Chinese immigrants are specifically targeted. Xenophobia is dislike of or prejudice against those from other countries. Violent acts are not a form of individual discrimination which requires differential treatment by an individual. Additionally, the differential treatment is not codified in a policy or practice, excluding systematic discrimination.

Question Assesses

Human Development, Diversity, and Behavior in the Environment

158. **C.** Kohlberg reviewed people's responses and placed them in different stages of moral reasoning. According to Kohlberg, an individual progresses from the capacity for preconventional morality (before age 9) to the capacity for conventional morality (early adolescence), and toward attaining postconventional morality (once Piaget's idea of formal operational thought is attained), which only a few fully achieve. Each level of morality contains two stages, which provide the basis for moral development in various contexts. The age of the children is not provided, but they are at the preconventional level based on their actions. Throughout the conventional level, morality is tied to personal and societal relationships. In the postconventional level, morality is defined in terms of more abstract principles and values. People now believe that some laws are unjust and should be changed or eliminated.

Question Assesses

Human Development, Diversity, and Behavior in the Environment

159. **B.** This question requires recall knowledge about parenting styles. The authoritative parenting style has been identified as the best approach to parenting with children raised using this style being more capable, happy, and successful. Authoritative parents act as role models and exhibit the same behaviors they expect from their children. Consistent rules and discipline also allow children to know what to expect. These parents tend to exhibit good emotional understanding and control. Their children also learn to manage

their emotions and learn to understand others. Authoritative parents also allow children to act independently. This freedom teaches kids that they are capable of accomplishing things on their own, helping to foster strong self-esteem and self-confidence. Permissive parenting fails to set firm limits, to monitor children's activities closely or to require appropriately mature behavior of their children. Authoritarian parenting is characterized by high demandingness and low responsiveness, with strict rules enforced with little consideration of children's feelings or social-emotional and behavioral needs.

Question Assesses

Human Development, Diversity, and Behavior in the Environment

160. **A.** The *Code of Ethics* states that social workers should engage in political action to ensure equal access to resources, employment, services, and opportunities. Ethical standards apply to all social workers, and they cannot choose to ignore them. While social workers should not impose their own political beliefs on clients, they are called upon to engage in political action to advocate for just policies and systems and must include such activities in their practice.

Question Assesses

Professional Relationships, Values, and Ethics

161. **B.** Social workers need to be mindful about using the proper pronouns when working with clients. Establishing rapport is not possible if the social worker is not respectful of a client's gender identity so determining the correct pronouns must happen before rapport is established. While intake forms may ask about pronoun usage, it is BEST (qualifying word) to discuss during the first meeting. Clients may be apprehensive about disclosing their pronouns on an intake form, especially if they do not match the gender that they were assigned at birth. The last response choice indicates that the intake form is completed prior to the first session. The client may not feel comfortable being truthful as there is no context about why this question is asked. A discussion will provide this needed context.

Question Assesses

Human Development, Diversity, and Behavior in the Environment

162. **B.** While the child is exhibiting anxiety and panic, it is focused on being close to and requiring attention by the parents. Given the child's age, separation anxiety is the best choice. The behavior appears developmental given the child's age. The incorrect response choices are mental disorders that should not be diagnosed as the full criteria are not exhibited and the child is very young.

Question Assesses

Human Development, Diversity, and Behavior in the Environment

163. **C.** Grief support consists of assisting clients and families with progression through the stages, phases, or tasks of grief and with adjustment to life following a loss. Grief can be categorized as anticipatory when it occurs before the actual loss or death. Complicated grief occurs when a client has difficulty progressing through the stages of loss and grief.

Question Assesses

Human Development, Diversity, and Behavior in the Environment

164. B. All of the response choices may be related to the provision of grief therapy. However, the question asks for "a goal" of this intervention. Acknowledging and expressing grief are the primary aims of this treatment type. Not all individuals who experience loss and grief are isolated or have family bonds that need to be strengthened. Understanding the dynamics and effects of loss, separation, and grief is important for competent social work practice.

Question Assesses

Human Development, Diversity, and Behavior in the Environment

165. A. The *Code of Ethics* indicates that social workers should inform clients when real or potential conflicts of interest arise and take reasonable steps to resolve issues in a manner that makes clients' interests primary and protects clients' interest to the greatest extent possible. Seeking supervision is always a good idea in practice, but this response choice does not inform the client and protect the client's interests which are required ethically. Monitoring the situation does not describe action which is required when potential conflicts arise.

Question Assesses

Professional Relationships, Values, and Ethics

166. C. When forming a group, there are many factors to consider. Since the group is for those living with serious mental illness, the correct answer will be related to the presenting problem, eliminating gender and racial composition which are not critical factors to managing disorders. The length of time since initial diagnosis is not the MOST (qualifying word) important consideration. Group cohesion and effectiveness will be contingent on the insight of members so self-reflection need to be carefully considered when identifying members. Benefitting from a group requires members to have insight into their problems.

Question Assesses

Human Development, Diversity, and Behavior in the Environment

167. C. When a social worker acts as a mediator, a problem-solving intervention is used to assist and guide others toward resolution. The mediator does not decide the outcome, but helps clients understand and focus on the important issues needed to reach a resolution. In a high conflict divorce, intervention will be directed at compromise to address important issues related to both person and property. The broker role involves the process of making referrals to link others to needed resources. When doing resource allocation, social workers are establishing or implementing rules that allows fair allocation of resources or funding to be made to those who need extra support.

Question Assesses

Professional Relationships, Values, and Ethics

168. B. Arbitration, a form of alternative dispute resolution, is a process in which disputing parties agree that one or several individuals can decide about the dispute after receiving evidence and hearing arguments. Arbitration is different from mediation because the neutral arbitrator has the authority to decide about the dispute. Due process is the guarantee that an individual will be able to exercise legal rights, which can include receiving a fair and impartial trial. Social workers must be aware of legal terms related to practice with individuals, families, organizations, and communities.

Question Assesses

Professional Relationships, Values, and Ethics

169. C. The presenting problem is that the client is "worried about the use of his medical information." Thus, understanding uses of genetic information and limitations associated with consent are the most relevant and should be discussed. If the client is not comfortable with these terms, there is no need to review the procedures for obtaining the genetic sample. Exploring the concerns is an assessment task that occurs after the client understands consent and confidentiality issues.

Question Assesses

Professional Relationships, Values, and Ethics

170. A. The *Code of Ethics* states that social workers should avoid searching or gathering client information electronically unless there are compelling professional reasons, and when appropriate, with the client's informed consent. Thus, social workers may do internet searches without consent for health or safety reasons. Internet searching is allowed and may be appropriate (with client consent) for gathering important electronic information.

Question Assesses

Professional Relationships, Values, and Ethics

Evaluation of Results

Content Area	Question Numbers	Number of Questions	Number Correct	Percentage Correct
Human Development, Diversity, and Behavior in the Environment (27%)	4, 8, 12, 13, 14, 15, 19, 21, 22, 23, 24, 26, 27, 28, 39, 43, 48, 50, 52, 54, 58, 65, 80, 83, 88, 92, 94, 101, 102, 104, 106, 107, 114, 131, 132, 143, 148, 155, 157, 158, 159, 161, 162, 163, 164, 166	46	___/46	___%
Assessment and Intervention Planning (24%)	2, 3, 5, 16, 17, 18, 20, 29, 30, 33, 35, 36, 38, 40, 41, 46, 55, 60, 61, 62, 63, 73, 74, 76, 77, 96, 116, 117, 118, 119, 121, 126, 127, 129, 130, 135, 139, 142, 144, 145, 153	41	___/41	___%
Interventions With Clients/Client Systems (24%)	6, 10, 25, 31, 34, 42, 44, 47, 49, 51, 53, 64, 66, 67, 68, 69, 70, 71, 78,79, 81, 84, 86, 89, 95, 98, 100, 108, 109, 110, 111, 112, 124, 125, 128, 136, 137, 146, 150, 152, 154	41	___/41	___%
Professional Relationships, Values, and Ethics (25%)	1, 7, 9, 11, 32, 37, 45, 56, 57, 59, 72, 75, 82, 85, 87, 90, 91, 93, 97, 99, 103 105, 113, 115, 120, 122, 123, 133, 134, 138, 140, 141, 147, 149, 151, 156, 160, 165, 167, 168, 169, 170	42	___/42	___%
Overall Masters Examination Knowledge	–	170	___/170	___%

Index